"Let us consider that we are all partially insane. It will explain us to each other; it will unriddle many riddles; it will make clear and simple many things which are involved in haunting and harassing difficulties and obscurities now."

— **Mark Twain**

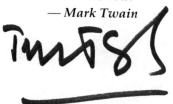

Other Cabinet of Curiosities Books by Troy Taylor

Cabinet of Curiosities 1
The History of the Supernatural in 20 Objects

Cabinet of Curiosities 2
America's Unexplained in 20 Objects

CABINET OF CURIOSITIES

3

The Haunted History of America's Prisons
Hospitals & Asylums in 20 Objects

TROY TAYLOR

with stories from April Slaughter & Rene Kruse

AMERICAN HAUNTINGS INK & WHITECHAPEL PRESS

Original Cover Artwork Designed by
© Copyright 2015 by April Slaughter & Troy Taylor

This Book is Published By:
Whitechapel Press
American Hauntings Ink
Jacksonville, Illinois / 1-888-GHOSTLY
Visit us on the internet at http://www.whitechapelpress.com

First Edition – March 2015
ISBN: 1-892523-93-0

Printed in the United States of America

TABLE OF CONTENTS

INTRODUCTION

I was sitting alone in the former library of the old Ohio State Reformatory in Mansfield. I was tired, my feet hurt, and I was covered with a film of dust that I had picked up after several hours of wandering in and out of cellblocks, climbing stairs, and exploring every dark corner, nook, and cranny that I could find in the massive stone structure. I needed a short rest. I found a shadowy corner, away from the ghost hunters who were roaming the building and sat down.

I was only in the room for a few minutes when I heard the unmistakable sound of someone's footsteps walking across the floor of the library. It was covered with debris and it was impossible to step silently as you walked. I peered into the darkness, but I couldn't see anyone. Worse, I knew that if I could not see them, they certainly couldn't see me and I was just about to give someone the fright of their life. Before they noticed me there, lurking in the dark, I decided to announce my presence. I cleared my throat and said loudly that I was in the room and didn't want to frighten anyone.

There was no response, but the footsteps abruptly stopped. Apparently, I had scared them after all. I switched on my flashlight to signal where I was sitting, but I didn't see anyone. I waved the light around the room, pointing it in the direction that I heard the sound coming from, but there was no one there. The wide, open room was completely and utterly empty.

And that night became one of my first experiences with ghosts at the Mansfield Reformatory. It would not be my last and I have long maintained that the former prison is one of the most haunted American places that I have ever visited. There are spirits that linger at the reformatory. If you haven't been there, you'll have to take my word for it. If you have, then you likely know what I mean.

This installment in the ongoing "Cabinet of Curiosities" series manages to combine two things that have long been passions of mine – hauntings and abandoned places. Anyone reading this book who has picked up a past title of mine is well aware that ghosts have been a part of my life for many years, but abandoned places have been a big part of my world for just as long. When I was a child, traveling around the country, it was rare when a road trip didn't include several stops at ghost towns, old broken-down stories and abandoned structures that have given up their life on the side of a dusty road in the far corner of a distant state. When I was older, and living in Utah for a while, a favorite hobby was to take off on the weekends and search for ghost towns and lost mines. I never struck it rich at any of those places, stumbling across some forgotten mine that was still filled with gold or silver, but the memories that remain are something I'll always treasure.

I'm not sure how this fascination began, but suspect that it has something to do with an incident that occurred one summer when I was about 13. I stumbled across an old, abandoned house in the woods. Such unusual finds were not uncommon for me. I grew up on a farm in a rural part of Illinois and during the summer months, I would often explore the back roads, cemeteries, and stretches of forest near my parent's home. This particular house turned out to be a little more unusual than most, though.

It was situated pretty far back in the woods and it didn't look as though anyone had lived there for a long time. Whatever path or driveway that had once led to it was long overgrown and covered with decades of fallen leaves. In spite of the passing years, the house was in decent shape. The porch was sagging and the front door leaned a little, but I was able to open it and go inside.

Strangely, all of the furniture in the house had been left behind, even to the point that there were still photographs on the walls and coats left hanging in the closet. The years had not been kind to the place, but overall, it was eerily preserved – and remarkably unsettling. I found the kitchen to be the strangest. It was there that I found the last real vestiges of human occupation in the house. There were still plates and silverware resting on the table and pots and pans still sitting on the cold, metal stove. It was as if the family that had once lived here had suddenly just gotten up and walked away one day never to return. What could have happened that this family had just walked away from their home one day, leaving everything that they owned behind?

I'll never know the answer to that. The house was later destroyed and I never found out who owned it, or what happened to them. But as time has passed, I have never forgotten the empty house in the woods and the mystery of what became of those who lived there. I have since come to realize that this puzzle will never be solved. I also realize, though, that this is where my obsession with abandoned places first began. After that, I was always on the lookout for empty crumbling buildings, decaying structures, and more. There is nothing that will make me turn off the highway faster than the sight of a long forgotten farm, abandoned church, or desolate farm house.

Sadly, though, places like this have become harder to find as the years have passed. In far too many cases, modern "progress" and urban renewal have wiped out historic spots across the country. This means that otherwise ordinary buildings and homes that lay scattered across the American landscape don't stand a chance. Too often, demolition sites include the abandoned prisons, hospitals, and asylums that lie within the pages of this book. History is often lost while so many of us are too busy to see that it's happening.

And it's not just the physical sites and the history that will be lost – it's the supernatural history as well. On more than one occasion, my search for the places left behind by the people of yesterday also led to encounters with ghosts. That has happened in all sorts of places, from abandoned homes to hospitals, prisons, asylums, and more. The places that are featured in this book go behind merely abandoned places, though. They are the places from which nightmares are born. They are the worst possible places that we can imagine, locked up, confined, and broken, behind bars of steel and within walls of stone. Is it any wonder that inmates of such places leave a bit of themselves behind?

Once again, I have chosen to tell the haunting tales of these places through a collection of objects. They have been ensconced in a Cabinet of Curiosities of sorts, although it's the kind that can be found within the pages of a book. During the Renaissance era, Cabinets of Curiosities were collections of marvels and unusual objects that were dedicated to things that, in those days, were not yet defined. Modern man would categorize the books, writings and artifacts found in these cases as pieces of natural history, geology, archaeology, religious or historic relics, art, and sometimes outright bits of humbug like petrified mermaid carcasses and fish with fur. But no matter what the cabinets contained, they were collections of the unexplained. Even in those days, everyone loved a mystery. Man has always loved to question, to wonder, and to be baffled by things that he cannot understand. Cabinets of Curiosities were all the rage among those who could afford them and were eventually considered to be a precursor of the modern museum.

My own cabinet is a different sort. There are no fossils in it, no badly preserved bodies of mysterious animals – no, my cabinet is different, although it's just as puzzling as those of history. My cabinet contains records and remnants of the supernatural – a curious collection of objects (both literal and figurative ones) that tell the story of the occult in our modern world. In this case, they tell the story of the prisons, hospitals, and asylums that once dominated both the small towns and big cities of America – and how so many left a haunting presence in their wake.

In the pages ahead, I'll be presenting a collection of 20 objects from 20 unique locations. Through the stories of these objects, the reader will enter the lives of the men and women who lived, died, and suffered because of these objects, or at least came into contact with them. I'll also reveal the secrets of the ghosts attached to each place and the bizarre events that made the objects famous. Some items will be easily recognized for their importance: a surgical tool that performed the first lobotomies; the straitjacket that restrained the incurably insane; chains worn by prisoners who dared to escape; a papier-mâché that fooled guards at America's greatest escape-proof prison; a piece of wood carved into the shape of a pistol; an electric chair that sent scores of men to their death. Others will be largely unknown and might not even constitute material that most historians would call important: a cloth hood; a hospital gurney; a collection of pins and buttons; a key; a scalpel.

But each of them tells a story and in this book, the 20 objects that I have chosen will offer a chilling look at how the locations from which they came have affected the history of crime, medicine, mental illness, and the supernatural in America. Every one of them represents one of the darkest places in the country – each of them tragic, horrific, and terrifying in their own right.

Troy Taylor
Winter 2015

THE PRISON IN AMERICA

When compiling a list of some of the most haunted places in America, prisons and jails fall high on the list. The amount of trauma, pain and terror experienced by men who are incarcerated often leaves a lasting impression behind. The horrible events carried out by such men, which led to them being locked away from society – along with the horrible events that occur behind prison walls – often cause the spirits of the men who lived and died behind bars to linger behind.

America's prisons, jails and reformatories can be terrifying places – for those in this world and the next.

One of the first institutions brought to the New World by the early settlers was the jail, a place where lawbreakers could be held while they awaited trial and subsequent punishment. There were more than 150 offenses in those days for which the punishment was death, and for the rest, there was whipping, branding, beatings or public humiliation. There was little tolerance for the criminal, even in a place founded in freedom and settled by many who had left their homelands only one step ahead of the law. At that time, the jail was not a place where criminals were kept for punishment. In fact, the idea of a penitentiary was a purely American institution that would have a profound effect on both this country and around the world.

The idea of a place of confinement for criminals awaiting punishment dates back to the Ancient Romans. The first known system was the vast Mamertine Prison, which was essentially a series of dungeons built under the sewers of Rome. Prisoners were kept in cages at first and, later on, in stone quarries and other places originally created for other purposes.

The Christian custom of "sanctuary," or asylum, dates back to the fourth-century reign of Constantine. Wrongdoers were placed in seclusion, which was considered conducive to penitence. More formal places of punishment were developed during the Middle Ages with the walls of monasteries and abbeys as a substitute for sentences of death. Prisons built to lock up heretics during the Inquisition of the fourteenth and fifteenth centuries were similar in concept, if not in operation, to prisons later built in America. These early prisons, with their concept of reformation by isolation and prayer, had some influence on the later penitentiaries to come.

The construction of *gaols* (jails) in England was authorized in 1166 by the Assize of Clarendon. Called by Henry II, this step in the evolution of forms of imprisonment has a grim history. Sheriffs often extorted huge fines by holding people in pre-trial confinement until they gave in and paid. If the fine was not paid, they died in jail. No attempt was made to separate the prisoners by age, sex, or crime. Sheriffs typically sold food at exorbitant prices, forcing the inmates with no money to go hungry.

An institution that was related to the gaols was "Bridewell," a workhouse built in 1557 for the employment and housing of London's criminals. Bridewell was such a success that Parliament ordered each county in England to construct their own version of it. It started with good intentions. The proliferation of Bridewell houses was originally a humanitarian effort intended to cope with the unsettling social conditions caused by the destruction of the feudal system and the increasing numbers of people who flocked to the large cities. They were not meant to be extensions of poorhouses, but were to serve as penal institutions for minor criminals – ranging from pickpockets to prostitutes – who were compelled to work under strict discipline.

The workhouses followed closely behind. Although workhouses were intended to be used for the training and care of the poor, not as penal institutions, they soon became indistinguishable from the Bridewells. Conditions and practices in both types of institutions steadily deteriorated and by the turn of the eighteenth century, they were no more humane than the gaols.

Banishment became a popular punishment for serious offenders. Each nation's leaders had a favorite place of exile for convicted prisoners: Russia's political prisoners were sent to Siberia; Spain and Portugal's went to Africa; England's prisoners were sent to the American colonies and later, after America achieved independence, to Australia. France emptied its prisons to New Orleans and to its penal colonies in French Guiana and New Caledonia. The horrors of French Guiana's infamous Devil's Island, once the world's most dreaded penal colony, did not end until it closed shortly after World War II.

Even though banishment removed thousands of prisoners to other continents, European prisons continued to be overcrowded and filled with violence and disease. The inmate death rate was staggering. In the seventeenth and eighteenth centuries, overcrowding forced most European cities to convert some buildings into prisons. Women, children, criminals, and the insane were all held together in group cells.

Another method of dealing with overcrowding was the convict hulks. First used in the late eighteenth century, the hulks, sometimes called "hell holes" or "floating hells," were broken-down war ships and abandoned freight vessels. Stripped and anchored in bays and rivers throughout the British Isles, they were unsanitary, vermin-infested, unventilated, and run by keepers who flogged the inmates and forced them into degrading labor. The conditions were even worse than in the gaols, houses of correction, and workhouses of the time. Disease ran rampant in the hulks, often wiping out entire prisoner populations, and sometimes the crew and neighboring villages and settlements as well. This "temporary solution" to overcrowding lasted at least 80 years, with the last hulk being maintained as late as 1875.

The American colonists brought the methods of punishment they were familiar with from England. Public punishment and degradation – including whippings, beatings, and humiliation in the stocks -- were commonly given out for minor offenses. Hanging, burning at the stake, and breaking on the rack were among the ways of carrying out capital punishment for more serious offenses.

The settlers built the first jails soon after their arrival. They were used to detain those who awaited corporal and capital punishment. Often unsanitary and understaffed, they became a dumping place for men and women of all ages convicted for all types of crimes. The jails soon became overcrowded "hell holes" of disease, filth, vermin, and vice.

The beginning of prison reform in the colonies can be traced to the arrival of William Penn in 1682 with a sizable land charter from Charles II. Penn established a penal code that retained a death penalty only in cases of murder, and allowed the substitution of imprisonment at hard labor for former bloody punishments. Penn's code, aimed at deterring crime, had a number of significant provisions: All prisoners were to be eligible for bail; those wrongfully imprisoned could recover damages; prisons were to provide free food and lodging; the lands and goods of felons could be sold to provide restitution to injured parties; and all counties were to provide houses of detention to replace the pillory, stocks, and whipping posts.

The principles underlying Penn's attempts to reform penal practice were not supported by Queen Anne, who succeeded Charles II. The laws were repealed by the queen, only to be re-enacted by the Province of Pennsylvania, where they continued in force until Penn's death in 1718. The old laws were restored in 1718 and remained in effect until the American Revolution. A number of offenses were judged to be capital crimes under these laws, including treason, murder, burglary, rape, sodomy, buggery, malicious maiming, manslaughter by stabbing, witchcraft by conjuration, and arson.

One of the earliest efforts to operate a state prison for felons was the notorious Newgate, which was established in an abandoned copper mine in Simsbury, Connecticut in 1773. It was an underground pit, where prisoners were chained together and forced into hard labor. Many of the first prisoners were British sympathizers during the American Revolution, but they were joined by hardened criminals of every sort. It was overcrowded and dank. The prisoners were secured with iron fetters around the ankles. While they were at work, a chain fastened to a block was locked to the fetters. The sentences served by the men were unforgiving: "burglary, robbery and counterfeiting were punished for the first offense with imprisonment not exceeding ten years; second offense for life." In 1776, the first prison riot occurred there as a result of "violence, poor management, escapes, assaults, orgies, and demoralization." The riot occurred after a man who attempted to escape set fire to a wooden door leading to the outside. The resulting blaze caused smoke to fill the abandoned mine, choking a number of the prisoners to death and quelling any rebellion in the rest.

Newgate became the first "hell hole" of American prisons, but it would not be the last. Almost immediately, social reformers appeared to govern and criticize the inhumane treatment of lawbreakers. In many cases, though, it has been questioned whether their efforts helped or harmed the prisoners they were trying to protect. The first prison reform was attempted in 1790 at Philadelphia's Walnut Street Jail. It was renovated by the Quakers because the jail had been described as being a scene of "universal riot and debauchery... with no separation of those accused but yet untried... from convicts sentenced for the foulest crimes." The jail was remodeled in 1790 and for the first time, men and women were housed separately in large, clean rooms. Debtors were placed in another part of the jail from those being held for serious offenses and children were removed from the jail entirely. Hardened

13

offenders were placed in solitary confinement in a "penitentiary house" and prisoners were given work and religious instruction. This method of discipline, developed through the ideas and efforts of such reformers as Dr. Benjamin Rush, became known as the "Pennsylvania System."

Rush, who lived from 1745 to 1813, was a prominent physician, political leader, member of both Continental Congresses, and a signer of the Declaration of Independence. He believed that prisoners should be housed in a large prison building, equipped with individual cells for dangerous inmates, and apartments for the remainder of the population. He also believed that prison systems should include gardens so prisoners could obtain both food and exercise. Rush also insisted that prison industries should provide products that could be sold to the outside world so that the money could help support the prison system. The purpose of the punishment of the prisoners, Rush believed, was to reform the inmate, prevent the further perpetration of crimes, and to remove those persons from society who have manifested, by their criminal nature, that they are unfit to live in that society.

Many of Rush's ideas were incorporated into the Walnut Street Jail's "Pennsylvania" system of discipline. The system called for solitary confinement without work. It was assumed that offenders would be more quickly repentant and reformed if they could reflect on their crimes all day. As the negative physical and psychological effects of this isolation became apparent, work was introduced, along with moral and religious instruction.

Despite the promise of its beginnings, poor planning led to the breakdown and ultimate failure of the Pennsylvania System. Regardless, the Walnut Street Jail had a permanent influence on the development of the correctional institutions that followed in its wake.

As the eighteenth century came to a close, the move for prison reform gained in importance. The decade after the Walnut Street Jail opened was full of hope for the concepts established there, however imperfectly. In the handful of years that followed, two parallel correctional philosophies emerged. These systems, the already mentioned "Pennsylvania" and the "Auburn," were based on the belief that regimens of silence and penitence would prevent the spread of disease and also encourage behavior improvement in prisoners.

The first to open has largely been forgotten today. The Western State Penitentiary was built in Pittsburgh in 1826. Its design was based on the multiple-cell isolation wing of the Walnut Street Jail. This proposed octagonal monstrosity provided for solitary confinement and no labor. The legislature amended the program three years later, adding a provision that inmates perform labor in their cells. In 1833, the small, dark cells were torn down and larger outside cells were built. These efforts influenced the development of the Eastern State Penitentiary in Philadelphia.

Eastern State was designed by John Haviland and was completed in 1829. It became the model for the entire Pennsylvania "separate" system. The prison had seven original cell blocks, radiating out from a hub-like center. A corridor ran down the center of each block with cells on each side. It was meant to further the Quaker idea of prisoner isolation as a form of punishment. Prisoners were confined in windowless rooms with running water and toilets. Each prisoner also had his own exercise yard surrounded by a high brick wall. The walls between the cells were thick and soundproof so prisoners never heard and, in the early years, never saw each other. The cells were intended to contain only one prisoner. Soon after the penitentiary was opened, however, separate confinement with no contact between prisoners became obviously impractical. The prisoners developed various methods of communication, such as tapping codes on water pipes. Doubling up the prisoners became necessary after the prison's population quickly surpassed legislative appropriations for construction.

Meanwhile, in New York in 1816, a rival system was founded when construction began on a prison in the town of Auburn. The prison had been built, for reasons of economy, with cells back to back in tiers within a hollow building. The doors of the cells opened out on galleries that were eight to ten feet from the outer wall. This was the first interior cell block in America and it soon became one of the unique characteristics of prisons in this country.

Auburn was patterned after other early American prisons with a few isolation cells to conform to the idea of solitary confinement being used for punishment and larger night cells to accommodate most prisoners. In 1821, officials at Auburn tested the efficiency of the Pennsylvania System by confining a group of inmates to their cells without labor. Many of the inmates became sick and insane. The experiment was abandoned as a failure in 1823, and most of the inmates involved were pardoned.

As they tried to figure out what went wrong, prison officials became convinced that the Pennsylvania system would fail because the prisoners spent too much time in isolation and could not "pay for their keep" through convict labor. At Auburn, the prisoners began working together all day fulfilling labor contracts and then were isolated at night. Even though they worked together, inmates were forbidden to talk to one another and were forced to march from place to place in the prison with their eyes always directed downward. They worked and ate together in communal settings, but in complete silence. If a prisoner was caught speaking, he would be severely punished. This plan of confinement at night, usually in interior cell blocks,

15

with silent labor in workshops by day, became known as the "Auburn System." This system became the pattern for over 30 state prisons in the next half-century, including Sing Sing at Ossining, New York in 1825.

Auburn's warden, Elam Lynds, believed the purpose of the system was to break the spirit of the prisoners. He personally whipped the men and urged the guards to treat the prisoners with brutality and contempt. One standard punishment consisted of fastening a prisoner's neck with an iron yoke and then pouring an ice-cold stream of water onto his head. At other times, a man would be chained to a wall and then the water would be turned on him with a high-pressure hose. While the pain was unbearable, it left no marks.

The Auburn system began to be adopted throughout America because it was much cheaper to operate than the Pennsylvania system. The cells were much smaller and money could be made from the inmate labor. In 1829, Massachusetts opened a cell block for the separate confinement of 304 prisoners, and Maryland built a wing with 320 exterior cells, formally adopting the Auburn System. Vermont, New Hampshire, Illinois, and Ohio followed with new cell blocks patterned after Auburn. In the 1840s, Georgia and Kentucky also converted to the Auburn System. Thus, all early American prisons, except those in Pennsylvania, adopted the Auburn plan. Subsequently, from 1825 to 1870, 23 new state prisons were built after the Auburn plan across America.

As the system spread across the country, the treatment of the prisoners became even more cruelly imaginative. The striped uniform was first introduced at Sing Sing and floggings, the sweatbox, the straitjacket, the iron yoke, the thumbscrews, and the stretcher became widely used.

The "stretcher" had a number of variations. A man might be handcuffed to the top of the bars of his cell so that his feet barely touched the floor, then left that way all day. Or his feet might be chained to the floor and his wrists tied to a pulley on the ceiling. When the rope was pulled, the prisoner was stretched taut. Sweatboxes were metal chambers that were so small that the prisoner literally had to crawl inside. They might be left in such confinement all day and, in some cases, the boxes were moved close to a furnace so that the heat inside them would be intensified.

The Auburn system was based on cruelty and repression, with the idea that such treatment would reform prisoners and make them change their ways. Instead, it was a failure and led to riots, death and the closure of many of the institutions. Architecture, programs, and often rules, regulations, and punishments were substantially the same in all of the prisons that adopted the plan. Each had multi-tiered interiors, dimly-lit cells, daily labor, Sunday religious services, prisoner uniforms, a meager and monotonous diet, ever-changing politically-appointed personnel, petty rules, and brutal punishments.

In far too many cases, the death penalty would have been preferable to the years that many men spent inside the hell-hole prisons of the nineteenth century. Few of them survived long if they managed to be released. Their bodies, health and minds were broken behind the high stone walls.

American Reformatories

In the years that followed the devastating accounts of prisoner abuses during the Civil War, new ideas began to be experimented with. In 1870, the American Prison Association was formed and the reformatory system was introduced. The system was characterized by a program of education and trade training, grades and marks, unusual sentencing guidelines, and parole. It was meant to reform criminals rather than merely punish them.

The first institution of this new type was the Elmira Reformatory, which opened in New York in 1876. Its superintendent was Zebulon Brockway, a member of the American Prison Association, who decided to concentrate his attentions on creating an institution for young offenders where they could receive individual attention and be released when they appeared ready to return to society. Although the reformatory plan was originally intended for all ages, prisoners at Elmira were limited to men between 16 and 30, all of whom were serving their first prison sentence. When a prisoner entered Elmira, he was automatically placed in the second of three grades. When he showed improvement, he was moved to the first grade and, upon continued effort, was eventually paroled. If he turned out to be a troublemaker, he was sent down to the third grade and had to work his way back up. Many of the prisoners were even sentenced to indeterminate terms so that they could be released when they proved worthy. With great emphasis on reforming the young men incarcerated there, they were given extensive training in trade work and offered academic education.

Over the next 25 years, reformatories opened in 17 states, but there were scores of problems and by 1910, the plan was largely considered dead. Most guards and wardens were incapable of administering the grading program and fell back on favoritism rather than reformation. Because of this, many of the men who were paroled, and were allegedly "reformed," went right back out and committed new crimes. When work contracts were outlawed, it appeared that there would be no training programs. Military drills and organized athletics were introduced as substitutes and they became regular features of the reformatory system, although it was not what the founders had in mind.

17

The reformatory was meant to prevent future crime. The movement came at a time when public education was rapidly developing as the social reformers' answer to many problems. It's not surprising that education also became a deterrent to crime. The education program that Zebulon Brockway established at Elmira was a valuable contribution to the American penal system. Aside from the religious services that were mandatory in many early prisons, it was the first attempt to organize a program of positive reformation on a scale that would include all inmates of a correctional institution. The glaring problem, however, was that this type of educational program required a high quality of leadership and staff to maintain it. The need for specialists to work with socially maladjusted young men soon became evident to everyone but the officials who hired the instructors and held the program's purse-strings disagreed. The same type of personnel who had always worked in prisons were hired in the reformatories, along with a few underpaid and overworked instructors who were in way over their heads.

Reformatories soon became nothing more than "junior prisons," where education and trade training was available for some of the inmates. The majority of them, though, were merely serving their time. With too many strikes against them with the grading system to take part in the educational classes, they carried on with the usual institutional routine and learned other, less desirable skills from their peers.

Chain Gangs and Prison Camps

Outside of the reformatories, the familiar American prison system continued on. By 1869, "good time" laws, which automatically reduced prison sentences for good work and good behavior, were passed in 23 states. During the period between 1870 and 1900, all of the prisons built were of the Auburn type with the only improvements being the introduction of ventilating systems and steel cells with plumbing and running water in each. Still, 77 prisons used the "bucket system" of waste disposal as late as the 1930s. Most of these prisons had some kind of rudimentary education program, including a prison library. Official chaplains regularly conducted religious services on Sunday. Except where things changed, like abandoning the rules of silence, the old system of discipline and hard labor remained the same.

The early part of the twentieth century became known as the "industrial period" in American prison history. Factory prisons, producing a broad range of finished products for the military, public, and state governments (the always popular license plates) flourished across the nation. Silence was no longer enforced and there was less emphasis on education and religious instruction. Greater emphasis was placed on using parole as an incentive for good behavior rather than relying solely on corporal punishments, solitary confinement, and the loss of privileges.

Many states also began opening prison farms, which used inmate labor to work land, tend crops, care for livestock, and harvest the fields. The underlying motive for establishing the large farms was, of course, profit for the state. Most of the large prison farms could be found in the southern states. While prisoners in the north were growing pale and anemic from prolonged confinement in huge, institutional buildings, the situation was different in the south since many of the prisoners worked outside and faced problems of other kinds.

Not only did states open prison farms, but the practice of "leasing" convicted offenders to private contractors to perform different types of hard labor continued into the 1920s in several states. They have become the stuff of legend, story, and song – chain gangs. Offenders were chained together to work in gangs, while dogs and mounted armed guards watched over them. Since the guards were fined or fired when men escaped, scores of fugitives were shot every year.

Other types of prison facilities appeared in the 1920s, when inmates were used to build state and county projects like roads, levees, and railroads. Prison camps began to be established to relieve overcrowding in the penitentiaries and to provide profitable outdoor work that was said to "aid in rehabilitation." More likely, it was merely to make more money for the state. Residents in the camps were usually men who had earned the positions, though. It was much better to serve out time in the outdoors than in a dank, damp, overcrowded, and dangerous prison. The men were on their honor to abide by camp regulations and were rarely guarded or locked up. In most facilities, the penalty for escaping from one of the camps was an additional five-year sentence in a much less appealing institution.

More Criminals, More Prisons

Between the years of 1890 and 1925, the American prison population more than doubled. The growth was relatively slow at the start of the twentieth century, but after 1920, crime began wreaking havoc on the prison system – and things didn't slow down until the outbreak of World War II.

One of the greatest contributors to a growing crime rate in the early 1920s was an increase in unemployment after World War I. However, Prohibition just made things worse. When the sale and manufacture of alcohol became a federal crime, bootlegging became the answer for many of the men who had been left without jobs.

In 1919, the National Motor Vehicle Theft Act was passed and made the interstate transportation of stolen vehicles a federal offense and provided for the arrest, prosecution, and incarceration of car thieves. This crime, once seen as rather innocuous since there weren't that many cars in the country, caused an overflow of the courts and criminal system. The Act began to be rigorously enforced by the Federal Bureau of Investigation (FBI), which used it to justify its existence in 1924. The new national police force recruited agents in every state and enforced new federal laws against kidnapping, bank robbery, and taking stolen vehicles across state lines.

The rising populations forced more prisons to be constructed. Between 1900 and 1925, 31 major prisons and seven reformatories were built in the United States and all but two of them are still in use today. In general, the prisons were large, fortress-like structures that held over 1,000 and, in some cases, 2,000 inmates. Most of them were of the Auburn style with multiple tiers of small, steel, interior cells designed for a single inmate. The cells were furnished with open plumbing and running water. Most were built, in the words of a prison official, "as cold and hard and abnormal as the prisoners whom they were intended to persuade toward better things."

The seven reformatories built during this period were the last gasp of the dying movement that had started in 1870. By 1919, there were 29 reformatories in America, 18 for men and 11 for women. A number of prisons that started off as reformatories still bear that designation today, but it's in name only. All of them have since been turned into state prisons.

But overcrowding was not the only problem to emerge in this era. Many of the problems, like disease, poor medical care, lack of proper food, and violence, hearkened back to the prison conditions of the early nineteenth century. Many of the problems stemmed from state legislatures that were reluctant to provide the funds needed to accommodate the ever-increasing numbers of prisoners. In many cases, two, three, and four inmates were crowded into cells designed for one person. In addition to psychological and social difficulties, this situation created dire medical problems, especially during a time when tuberculosis was sweeping the country. Many inmates were paroled, only to find themselves confined to sanatoriums due to the illnesses they contracted in prison.

Most prisons lacked proper medical facilities. There was no way to quarantine sick patients from the rest of the inmate population. In most cases, inmates who were mentally ill were kept in solitary confinement because there was no place else to put them. Epidemics swept through prison after prison, including mumps, measles, typhoid fever, and tuberculosis. Many illnesses were caused by improper sanitation. Lacking indoor plumbing, waste buckets, often called "honey pots," were kept in the cells and had to be emptied into the sewer trough each day.

Public scrutiny of prison policy and conditions in any part of the United States was, as always, minimal. Most prisons were located in rural areas and far from the cities that provided most of the inmates. The "out of sight, out of mind" policy was common. Facing overcrowded facilities with insufficient resources and staff and crumbling buildings, prison officials emphasized control and conformity rather than modifying the prisoner's behavior.

Administrators were judged by their ability to produce goods for sale and keep prisoners in. The reformation of the inmates became an unplanned by-product of prison industry. Prison work, whether it was agricultural or industrial, was primarily seen as supporting control by keeping prisoners busy and providing income for the state. Teaching useful skills was purely coincidental.

American prison policy between 1900 and 1925 can be summed up in three words: custodial, punitive, and productive. It relied on total control, punishment, and hard labor. Aside from a greater emphasis on production and profit and less emphasis on education and moral instruction, correctional practices in American prisons in the early twentieth century was almost identical to what it had been 100 years before.

Women Behind Bars

American women first became involved in correctional reform in the nineteenth century, when the status and role of women were changing rapidly. Both upper- and middle-class women, as well as educated women entering the male world of employment, supported reforms for "fallen women." Foremost was the belief that female criminals could be rehabilitated only if they were isolated from the corrupting influence of men, by keeping them in prisons for women only, with female staff. Before that time, female offenders had been considered beyond reform. In straying from the "proper" womanly role, they were committing acts considered only within the capability of evil men. Thus, women were confined in wings, rooms, and attics of men's penitentiaries, separated from male inmates but supervised by male correctional officers.

Women – regardless of their crimes, age, background, health, or maternal status – lived together in one area. To be a woman in prison was "worse than death," said Chaplain B.C. Smith of Auburn Penitentiary in 1832. Only a few individuals, with religious motives, came forward to help female prisoners at first, but others were eventually established. One, the House of Refuge, founded in New York, was for juvenile offenders, but it later served women too. Many other private and religious societies appeared to help female offenders. Among the most notable were the Women's Prison Association and the Hopper Home, both in New York. These

21

societies established homes that were forerunners to modern halfway houses. Christian, moral women provided female offenders with a place to live, religious and vocational instruction, and medical care. However, such societies and homes in which women supervised women were exceptions to the rule of male supervision for female inmates. In response, reformers began to demand more female corrections officers to become a permanent part of American prisons and jails.

One of the few matrons for women between 1825 and 1873 was Eliza W.B. Farnham, a feminist, reformer, wife of an attorney, and friend of members of the Brook Farm intellectual circle in Massachusetts. As head matron of the women's section of Sing Sing from 1844 to 1848, she separated the women from the men entirely, even hiring female officers to supervise the prisoners. She also tried to make the prison environment like a home in which the staff and inmates behaved like family. Believing that environmental conditions caused criminal behavior, she believed her changes would alter the mental state of the inmates. She ended the silence rule, provided educational instead of religious training, and invited women from the outside to speak to the inmates. Farnham's innovative programs and radical, secular approach met with harsh criticism. After she was dismissed in 1848, her improvements were eliminated and conditions deteriorated.

Despite the setbacks and the narrow-minded thinking of prison officials, women's groups were able to eventually convince legislators to separate women's prisons and to hire full-time female superintendents and matrons. The first prison for women was the Indiana Reformatory Institution for Women and Girls, which opened in 1873 with Sarah Smith as superintendent. Later reformatories were opened in Framingham, Massachusetts (1877), Bedford Hills, New York (1901), and Clinton, New Jersey (1913).

A major assumption – and an incorrect one – underlying the development of women's prisons was that women were "naturally passive" and, therefore, not as dangerous as male offenders. This gave the administrators of women's institutions more latitude in programming. In addition, it's a little-known fact that many of the first female superintendents from 1884 to 1932, most of whom were well-educated and experienced in social work and reform, developed many correctional innovations. Such innovations included educational classes, libraries, art and music programs, work release, recreation, vocational programs, and classification based on behavioral criteria. Other "firsts" included community service volunteer groups, venereal disease clinics, and centers for studying the causes of female criminal behavior.

Early superintendents were faced with problems that still persist today, like inadequate funding and difficulty in attraction quality female professionals to work in the institutions. In spite of such obstacles, early female officials pioneered many important aspects of the correctional system that are still in use today.

Prisons During the War Era

The period between World War I and the years after World War II (1926-1950) saw profound and fundamental changes in the purpose and nature of American prisons. The gradual disappearance of the striped uniform and the lockstep march from cell to yard were early signs of change. Most significantly, though, was the subtle shift in the conception of the criminal as sinner to the idea of a criminal as sick, needing specialized diagnosis and treatment. During this period, the prison became the correctional center, in name if not in fact.

The single more powerful factor affecting correctional systems during this period was overcrowding resulting from changes in social order and the nation's economy during the Depression, World War II and post-war period.

The marked decline in foreign immigration after World War I resulted in the need for America's larger industries to look to the southern states to fill the constant demand for unskilled labor. A new migration of African-Americans to the north brought a rapid increase in their numbers in prison populations.

At the same time, mounting crime rates in the 1920s – most significantly caused by Prohibition – dramatically increased the number of state and federal offenders. Responding to this situation, the Herbert Hoover administration created the U.S. Bureau of Prisons, which from its early years, was influential in shaping the development of American prisons.

The economic hardships of the Depression led 33 states to pass laws in the 1930s prohibiting the sale of convict-made products on the open market. However, Eleanor Roosevelt interceded to secure the president's backing in creating the U.S. Bureau of Prison's prison industries as an independent corporation, making sure that it survived as a source of prisoner training and government-use production program. The National Recovery Act became a catalyst for state programs to implement measures to relieve the pressures of overcrowding and inmate idleness.

During this period, a fear of rising crime rates and increasing pressure for standardized sentencing guidelines were reflected in the increasing number of prisoners in the United States. But at the same time, the idea of social causes of crime gained acceptance over the traditional definition of the criminal as a "sinner." Imprisonment as a justifiable express of public moral indignation declined, at least in the ranks of influential correctional professionals.

A number of extremely serious prison riots occurred during this period, as well as the horrible tragedy of the Ohio Penitentiary fire, which caused 322 deaths, and this resulted in dramatic efforts to find new ways to house inmates. New designs for prisons emerged and once again, state prisons turned to the development of honor farms, road crews, forestry camps, prison farms, and more expedient systems for traditional parole release programs to ease overcrowding.

Overall, though, there was little advance in prison reform. Although advances were made by reform wardens like Thomas Mott Osborne and Lewis E. Lawes, much of the outright cruelty and squalor of the earlier prisons had been considerably reduced, however, many of the extreme punitive concepts persisted. The 1930s saw the introduction of Alcatraz, a place meant to be a place of punishment, not rehabilitation. The prison, called by some the "American Devil's Island," was the worst of the federal prisons and was said to be escape-proof. According to some estimates, almost 60 percent of the inmates went stir crazy there. Alcatraz left an extreme mark on the prisoners and on the guards and staff members, as well. It soon lost its original purpose as a place of confinement for escape artists and troublemakers and became a place to put inmates who it was deemed deserved harsher treatment, like mobster Al Capone. By 1963, Alcatraz was shut down, having proven to be a failure.

During World War II, the product of prison labor earned a new respect, thanks to the war effort. The old adage that "prison made means poorly made" was disproved when vast quantities of products made in prison met the rigid inspection requirements of all branches of the armed forces. Carloads of items poured from prisons to meet the urgent needs of government agencies during the war years. Prisons made shoes, uniforms, mattresses, model planes for pilot training, worked on aircraft engines, assembled assault boats, assembled ration books, and donated hundreds of thousands of gallons of blood to the American Red Cross.

By 1950, the corrections field had expanded into an acceptable area of study and social service. It would never again be the isolated realm of the authoritarian warden and convict code. In addition, prison conditions had now become newsworthy. The end of the war marked the end of massive prison war industry and training programs, but the needs of inmate programs in these and related areas were finally firmly established.

Locked Up in America

There is an old adage that states, "The more things change, the more they stay the same." Many of the same problems that plagued American prisons in the nineteenth century are still problems today – overcrowding, violence, sanitary conditions, and a lack of adequate medical care and mental health treatment. In many ways, the American prison system can be considered a failure. Many critics have charged that prisons have failed to reform criminals or even to act as a deterrent to crime. Eventually, prisoners are simply released, mostly due to lack of space, and they go right back out and commit new crimes. In numerous cases, the brutal conditions of the prisons have led to permanent injury, insanity, trauma, and death.

Beginning in the 1950s, riots and other major disturbances began rocking American prisons. Between 1950 and 1966, there were more than 100 riots across the country. The eruption of major prison violence during this time heightened public awareness of the conditions behind the walls of the prison system and paved the way for legal changes that began in the 1970s.

But before that could happen, far too much blood was shed. Investigations into the riots found that they stemmed from lack of money in prison funding; guards who were nearly as brutal as the inmates; forced idleness; inadequate food; and, of course, overcrowding.

All of this caused the prisons to turn into battlegrounds. A long series of riots occurred. The two worst of the period were at Attica State Prison and at New Mexico State Penitentiary. Attica, New York, exploded in September 1971, ending with a death toll of 43, while the riot in New Mexico in February 1980, left 36 dead. But they were not the only tragedies to occur.

In April 1959, violence broke out at the Montana State Prison in Deer Lodge. It was instigated by veteran convict Jerry Myles and his 19-year-old lover, Lee Smart. George Alton, a fellow inmate who worked in the prison garage, had access to gasoline, so the trio doused a guard with gas and made torches from mop handles and rags. They threatened to light the guard on fire, and he surrendered his rifle and keys to them. The trio released the other inmates from their cells, and the mob took all the guards hostage. The inmates made their way to the office of Deputy Warden Ted Rothe. Smart killed him with a shotgun blast to the chest. Warden Floyd Powell contacted the governor, who called in the Montana National Guard, launching a 36-hour armed standoff. During that time, Myles spoke to the media, claiming that he'd incited the riot to improve conditions at the prison. In actuality, Myles was buying time for an escape tunnel that was being dug under the wall near the northeast guard tower. During the early morning of hours of April 18, the National Guard stormed the prison. Most of the inmates surrendered peacefully, and the hostages were rescued unharmed. But Myles and Smart continued to exchange fire with the guards, until Myles finally shot his lover and then turned the gun on himself.

In July 1973, the Oklahoma State Prison at McAlester erupted into a terrible riot. Crowded conditions that led to the riot had been in place almost since the facility's construction in 1911. Housing capacity for 1,100 inmates was surpassed in 1920, and by 1973, the prison population exceeded nearly double that number. Governor David Hall's refusal to sign parole recommendations for drug offenders and individuals convicted of violent crimes had contributed to prison overcrowding. Ill-qualified and too few correctional officers, violence perpetrated by the "convict bosses," and other factors also led to prisoners' discontent.

On Friday, July 27, 1973, the prison exploded into violence. That afternoon, inmates in the mess hall stabbed Captain C. C. Smith and Lt. Thomas Payne, who were later treated at a hospital. Prison official Jack Hall and Deputy Warden Sam Johnston both attempted to help but were attacked by 11 or 12 inmates and became the first of at least 21 hostages that were taken. Three inmates were killed. That evening, the inmates seized control of the hospital and set the prison on fire. Among the demands the inmates made for the release of hostages were total amnesty for the ringleaders of the riot, media coverage, and access to U.S. Justice Department and American Civil Liberties Union attorneys. On July 28, at 12:30 p.m., inmates released the hostages but retained control of the prison until August 4.

The riot caused more than $20 million in damage to 24 buildings, and the state considered closing the prison. A special committee was formed to investigate the riot and came to the conclusion that McAlester should function only as a maximum security prison for no more than 300 to 500 prisoners and that personnel should be improved by in-service training and higher salaries. Unfortunately, these provisions were never fully implemented and, thus, did little to solve the problems. In March 1974, inmate Bobby Battle, won a law suit against Warden Park J. Anderson and the Oklahoma Department of Corrections for alleged cruelty and discrimination. U.S. District Court Judge Luther Bohanon ruled in favor of Battle and subsequently handed down a written opinion listing 43 orders to corrections officials concerning minimum standards for the prisoners' medical care, housing, and safety. Despite changes in prison conditions, another riot occurred at the Oklahoma State Prison in December 1985.

The aforementioned Attica riot remains perhaps the most infamous in American history. This was another case of an overcrowded prison suffering from high tensions, but the final impetus for the riot came from a series of misunderstandings. On September 8, a guard mistakenly thought that two inmates were fighting and took them away for punishment. False rumors spread that the inmates were being tortured. The following morning, prisoners scuffled with guards until things finally reached a breaking point. Approximately 1,000 inmates took over a large section of the prison, causing extensive damage and taking 42 staff members hostage. A large percentage of the inmates at Attica were minorities and believed the racist warden and his guards inflicted needless brutality on them. They demanded that the federal government take control of the prison and improve conditions.

The standoff lasted four days as negotiations went back and forth. However, New York Governor Nelson Rockefeller refused to visit the prison to speak with the inmates and also refused their demand to receive amnesty for the riot. Finally, on the morning of September 13, Rockefeller ordered the state police and the National Guard to take back the prison. After tear gas was dropped into the yard, the authorities stormed in. When the siege ended, 10 hostages and 33 inmates had lost their lives. It was later determined that all of the hostages were killed by friendly fire. The decision to storm the prison was highly controversial and would tie up the courts for decades. The families of the victims eventually collected substantial financial settlements for the civil rights violations committed during the re-taking of Attica.

The series of riots was followed by a landslide of litigation in the 1970s. A prisoner's rights movement that began in the mid-1960s gained dramatic momentum in the wake of the many violent incidents and brought judicial intervention into the prisons.

In the 1970s, the federal courts found nine correctional systems to be unconstitutional in their operations. In January 1982, 42 state systems were under court order for overcrowding and conditions of confinement. Almost every aspect of correctional operations was challenged and scrutinized – housing, health care, recreation, mail privileges, and food, just to name a few.

Until the late 1960s, federal courts had operated under a "hands-off" policy that allowed correctional administrators to determine, basically without legal interference, policies and procedures outlining inmate rights. With the abandonment of this policy, case after case began being brought to court.

Many believed the answer to reform was to simply end overcrowding. The best way to do this, it was believed, was to build more prisons. But new prison construction could not keep up with the expanding inmate population and as public dollars became scarcer in recent years, many prisons – both new and old – were shut down by cutbacks and staff reductions. Widespread overcrowding continues to this day, along with the violence, horror, trauma, and death that have all wreaked havoc behind the walls of American prisons for centuries.

Is it any wonder that prisons and jails have become known as such haunted places?

1. A BURLAP HOOD
EASTERN STATE PENITENTIARY

After the changes at the Walnut Street Jail in 1790, the Quakers of Philadelphia began to search for a new method of incarceration for criminals in which "penitence" would become essential in the punishment of the lawbreaker. The Quakers' concept of such incarceration would involve solitary confinement, a method already popular in Europe with members of monastic orders. It was believed that if monks could achieve peace through solitary confinement and silence, then criminals could eventually be reformed using the same methods. From their efforts, the word "penitentiary," and the system itself, would be born.

After years of overcrowding at the Walnut Street jail, a new prison was proposed within the city limits of Philadelphia. Before it could be constructed, though, Western State Penitentiary was opened in Pittsburgh in 1926. Philadelphia architect William Strickland was hired to design and oversee the construction of the eight-sided prison wall, with individual cells arrayed around the wall and a great courtyard in the center. It opened with great fanfare, but it quickly became apparent that Strickland's design was defective. The cells were poorly placed, making it possible for the inmates to remain in constant communication with one another, plus the placement of the cells around the wall created a "double frontage" that made surveillance impossible. This also made labor impossible, and prisoners were left in their cells with nothing to occupy them. It was a situation that one visitor called "too horrible and unjust to be thought of."

Plans were proposed for the new penitentiary in Philadelphia. It would be designed to hold 250 prisoners in total solitary confinement and was slated to open in 1829. An architect named John Haviland was hired, and he set to work creating an institution in the popular "hub and spoke" design. This layout had been used in prisons throughout Europe and was highly effective, allowing for a constant surveillance of the prison from a central rotunda. The original design called for seven cell blocks to radiate outward from the center house and guard post.

However, controversy surrounded the initial construction. William Strickland refused to be held responsible for the work, as it was not his design. This led to his dismissal by the board, which replaced him with Haviland. Construction began on the prison in May 1822. The site selected for it was an elevated area that had once been a cherry orchard. Because of this, the prison later acquired the nickname of "Cherry Hill." As construction began, changes forced John Haviland to create new designs so that the prison could hold an additional 200 prisoners. At that time, the prison was the most expensive single structure ever built, but Haviland's design would become so popular that it would be copied for nearly 300 institutions around the world.

The plan for the penitentiary was simple in its complexity. Prisoners were confined in windowless rooms that were small, but were equipped with both running water and toilets. This was an amazing innovation for the time as very few public or private buildings were equipped with indoor facilities. In those days, even the White House did not have indoor plumbing. Of course, the reason for this was not for the comfort of the prisoner but to keep him out of contact with other people. The walls were thick and soundproof, so prisoners never saw or heard one another. Each prisoner was given his own exercise yard, surrounded by a brick wall, furthering the sense of extreme isolation. They would see no other inmate from the time they entered the prison until the time they were released.

Although the prison would not be completed until 1836, it began accepting prisoners in 1829. The first inmate was Charles Williams, who was sentenced to two years for burglary. Like all of the other prisoners who would be incarcerated behind the high stone walls, Williams was stripped of his clothing, measured, weighed, and given a physical examination. He was also given a number and was not referred to by his name until the day he was released. A record was made of his height, weight, age, place of birth, age, complexion, color of hair and eyes, length of feet, and, if he was able to write, the prisoner signed his name on the record. After the prisoner was examined, he was given a pair of wool trousers, a jacket with a number sewn on it, two handkerchiefs, two pairs of socks and a pair of shoes. Then, a mask that resembled a burlap bag was pulled over his head so that he would be unable to see the prison as he was taken to his cell. It was believed that if an inmate was unable to see in which direction to go, it would be harder for him to escape. The masks were eventually discontinued in 1903. As the prisoner entered his cell, he would be forced to stoop down (as a penitent would) because the doorways were shortened to remind the prisoners of humility. Above him would be the only lighting in the cell: a narrow window in the ceiling that was called the "Eye of God." It was a constant reminder that someone was watching him.

Life at Eastern State was rigorous. Prisoners woke between 4:30 and 5:00 a.m. and were allowed one hour of exercise in their private yards – weather permitting – except on Sunday. Meals were served at 7:00 a.m., noon and 6:00 p.m. and bedtime was between 9:00 and 10:00 p.m. Prisoners ate reasonably well for this era: coffee for breakfast, about a half-pound of meat (beef or pork), potatoes and a pint of soup for lunch, and a type of corn mush for supper. They also received a pound of bread each day. Two cells in cellblock seven served as Eastern State's kitchen during the late 1830s, providing meals for all of the inmates at that time.

The penitentiary had eight basic rules that were posted in each cell:

1. Keep all cells and utensils clean.
2. Obey all directions from officials and guards.
3. All uneaten food was to be returned to the overseer.
4. Apply themselves to work tasks and education offered by books.
5. Complaints about guards should be made to the warden, while complaints about the warden should be made directly to the prison inspector.
6. All penitentiary officials should be treated with respect.
7. The Sabbath should be respected. It read, "Though you are separated from the world, the day is no less holy.
8. All prisoners must remain silent and refrain from speaking with other inmates at all times.

The rule of silence became the most difficult for the prisoners to follow. Silence was to be maintained at Eastern State at all times. The guards even wore socks over their shoes while they made their rounds. By doing this, they moved in secret around the prison, and while the inmates could not hear them, the officers could hear any sounds coming from inside the cells. The prisoners could not communicate with anyone in any way. If they were caught whistling, singing or talking (even to themselves), they were deprived of dinner or were taken to one of the punishment cells. Any prisoner who repeatedly broke the rules was placed in a punishment cell and restricted to a half-ration of bread and water.

Even though communication was forbidden, most of the prisoners attempted it anyway. The easiest way to do this was to attach a note to a small rock and toss it over the wall into the next exercise yard. It was probably the quietest form of communication and the most popular. Other forms of contact ranged from coded tapping on the walls to soft whistles and whispers. Since there were vents for heat in every cell, a limited amount of contact could be made through the ducts. Prisoners could also tap on the vents and be heard by several listeners at one time. However, if they were caught, they knew with certainty that they would be punished.

At first, punishment at Eastern State was mild compared to other institutions. Most prisons used the lash, a leather strap that was administered to the back, but officials at Eastern State believed that solitary confinement was punishment enough. However, as the prisoners began to repeatedly break the rules, the punishments became more intense. The first disciplinary tactic was to take away the inmate's access to work, books, and writing materials, all of which had been given to him as a "favor." If the inmate still acted out, the warden had him placed in a darkened cell, with no outside light. In extreme cases, more severe punishments were brutally applied. They included the shower bath, straitjacket, the mad chair, and the iron gag.

The shower bath usually took place outdoors and under frigid conditions. Prisoners were stripped naked and hoisted up on their own exercise yard wall. A guard then climbed a ladder and dumped a dozen buckets of water over the man's head. In the winter months, the cold water would freeze on the inmate's body and icicles formed in his hair. This punishment, along with those described next, belied Eastern State's claims of humanitarisim and, in at least one case, led to a prisoner's death.

The straitjacket was commonly used by mental institutions to restrain crazed patients and to keep them from hurting themselves or others. At Eastern State, the jacket was used in a different way. Inmates would be bound into the jacket so tight that their face, hands and neck would become numb. Eventually, they would turn black from a lack of blood flow and the inmate would usually pass out. The use of the straitjacket was finally discontinued around 1850.

The mad chair was another form of punishment, or restraint, adapted from mental asylums. Here, the prisoner would be tied to the chair by chains and leather straps and held so firmly that he was unable to move at all. After long periods of time, his limbs would become very painful and swollen. Prisoners who spent any length of time in the chair would find themselves unable to walk for hours (or even days) afterward.

The iron gag was the most commonly used punishment. It was a device that was placed over the prisoner's tongue while his hands were crossed and tied behind his neck. His arms were then pulled taut and the hands secured just behind the man's neck. The gag was then attached to his tongue and his hands and locked in place. Any movement of the hands would tear at the gag and cause intense pain. The inmate's mouth would be bloody and sore by the time he was released from his bonds.

While punishments and seclusion were undoubtedly hard on the health of the prisoners, the diseases within the prison were even worse. During the first few years of the prison, poor planning caused the odor of human waste to constantly invade every part of the building. This was caused by the design of the vents and by the plumbing and heating methods that were used. Water was supplied to every cell for the toilets and for running water. Since the prisoners were only permitted to bathe every three weeks, they were forced to wash themselves in the basins inside of their cells. To heat the water and the rest of the prison, coal stoves were placed in tunnels underneath the floors. Since the sewer pipes from the toilets ran alongside the pipes for the fresh water, the coal stoves also heated the waste pipes. Because of this, the prison always smelled like human waste. The problem was finally corrected in later years because of the frequency of illnesses among the prisoners and the guards.

More damaging to the inmates than torture and disease was the toll that the place took on their mental health. The inmates at Eastern State often went slowly insane because of the intense and utter isolation. Others were already mentally unbalanced when they arrived, a fact that went unnoticed due to the primitive treatments for insanity at the time. Once placed in solitary confinement, these prisoners often lost control. For instance, in January 1840, a prisoner named Isaac Thomas tried to castrate himself with his own shoe-making knife. Another man cut his own throat in the courtroom after being sentenced to two years at Eastern State. Eventually, there were so many cases of insanity reported that the penitentiary doctors had to invent other reasons for outbreaks of mental illness. It was believed at that time that excessive masturbation could cause insanity. Because of this, the doctor's log book of the period listed many cases of insanity, always with masturbation as the cause. It was also noted that many of the men went insane because of their genes and these two diagnoses remained popular throughout the 1800s. It was never documented that the total isolation caused any of the men's breakdowns.

Without question, though, being imprisoned at Eastern was mind-numbing. The prisoner was required to remain in his cell all day and all night in solitary confinement, thinking of nothing but his crimes. The system was brutal on the inmates, but hard for the warden and guards, as well. The first warden at Eastern was Samuel Wood, and it was up to him to ensure that the punishment of total solitary confinement was carried out. He and his family were required to reside on the premises and were not allowed to leave for periods of more than 18 hours without permission from the prison commission.

One of the biggest problems in the early days at Eastern was keeping the guards sober. It was so boring making the rounds and maintaining total silence that the guards often drank to combat the monotony. At one point, the guards were even given a ration of alcohol during the workday so that they would not drink too much. However, so few of them remained sober that the prison commission eventually passed a rule that threatened anyone found drunk on the job with immediate termination.

Eastern State Penitentiary became the most notorious prison in America and tourists came from all over the country to see it. Some sightseers traveled from even farther abroad. Perhaps the most famous Eastern State tourist was the author Charles Dickens. He came to the prison during his five-month tour of America in 1842, and named it as one of his essential destinations, right after Niagara Falls. Although he came to the prison with the best of intentions, he really did not believe the officials knew what damage the isolation was doing to the minds of the prisoners. He later wrote about his trip to the prison in 1845 and stated, "The system here is rigid, strict, and hopeless. Solitary confinement, I believe it, in its effects, to be cruel and wrong." He went on to write about the inhumane treatment of the inmates and after speaking to many of them, came to believe that the solitary conditions were a "torturing of the mind that is much worse that any physical punishment that can be administered."

The prisoners often rebelled in a variety of different ways. For instance, an inmate named G. Brewer was denied dinner for refusing to work on November 12, 1835. This was a mild form of resistance, and occasionally prisoners opted for something a little more dramatic. On April 20, 1856, inmate number 3333 committed suicide by cutting his own throat with a shoemaker's knife. In August 1857, number 3387 tried unsuccessfully to hang himself in his cell, and two months later, he opened a vein in his arm with scissors. The following year, number 3572 tried a similar trick, losing half a gallon of blood before the penitentiary staff could stop the bleeding. John Baird committed suicide by using a handkerchief to hang himself a few months after receiving a sentence of two years for receiving stolen goods. Sometimes the inmates directed their aggressions outward, like in May 1860, when number 4261 flooded his cell during a fit of "mental alienation." Another prisoner was reprimanded by the warden for drawing obscene pictures in the penitentiary's books, while prisoners 3300 and 3323 were punished for talking to other prisoners.

Of course, the ultimate misbehavior was escape, and though Eastern State was designed to be an escape-proof prison, inmates still found a way out. The easiest way to get out was to scale the wall of the exercise yard and then make it to the high wall or the front gate. This had to be done without attracting the attention of the guards.

The first escape came in 1832. Prisoner number 94, a prison baker named William Hamilton, was serving dinner in the warden's apartment. The warden stepped out of the room for a moment and Hamilton managed to tie several sheets together and lower himself out the window. He was not caught until 1837, but after he was recaptured, he was locked back into his former cell.

Others planned escapes using the tools that they had been given to labor in their cells. In 1834, an inmate named Samuel Brewster managed to escape because he was allowed to leave his cell to sharpen his carpentry tools. Little by little, he managed to beat solitary confinement and learn the layout of the prison. Using some small planks, he fixed the locks on his cell door so that the metal bolt could not be inserted all the way, which allowed him to leave the cell once the guards had retired for the night. Climbing over the wall of his exercise yard, he scaled the main wall using a ladder that he had secretly been building in his shop. Built in pieces, he hid the separate parts with the scrap lumber, and no one noticed. Using screws for silence, he scaled the wall. Unfortunately for Brewster, while the grade was level inside the prison, outside, the walls on the south end are ten feet higher than the walls on the north to compensate for the fact that Eastern State was built on a hill. Brewster swung his ladder over the wall and lowered it, but when he realized that it was too short, he dropped it. Stuck on the wall and realizing that he would be punished if he was caught, he decided to take a chance and jump. He injured his leg when he landed, but managed to limp about five miles to Kensington. He was soon recaptured, hiding in a pile of wood in a relative's cellar.

In 1852, an inmate named William E. Crissey didn't bother to come up with an elaborate plan – he simply walked out the front door. Crissey had been ordered to press some clothes for an inmate whose sentence had run out and was being released. Instead, Crissey put on the civilian clothes and walked out the front gate, telling the guard on duty that he had been visiting an incarcerated relative and was going home. Crissey was later recaptured living in Montgomery County under an assumed name.

Nine years later, inmate George Race, who had (unbelievably) been trained as a locksmith while in the penitentiary, used the prison's tools to fashion duplicate keys to all of the locks. While the guards were distracted, he opened the front gate and strolled out to the street. While he was eventually recaptured, it was evidence that perhaps some of the labor forced onto the inmates was not in the best interests of penitentiary officials.

More often, prisoners merely waited for convenient opportunities to escape. For instance, in 1847, prisoner 2120 asked one of the guards to come into his cell and read. Once the man was inside, 2120 darted out of the open door and slammed it shut behind him, locking the rather clueless guard inside. Inmate 2120 managed to free another prisoner, but his "escape" was short-lived. He was captured before he could leave the penitentiary and placed in a dark cell as punishment.

Despite the many incidents of escape and near-escape, prison officials continued to maintain in 1871 that Eastern State Penitentiary "presents such a secure appearance that it would seem impossible for anyone to attempt an escape." However, there are numerous examples from this period of prisoners doing just that. In fact, in that same year, three inmates managed to escape through the sewer system that ironically had been designed to allow the penitentiary to keep prisoners in their cells. John and William Thomas and Thomas Dare, who were all trusted prison inmates and who were allowed unusual privileges because of this, pulled up a grate in one of the cellblocks and lowered themselves into the tunnels under the penitentiary. They were discovered missing, but since no one had seen them go over a wall or through the gate, officials were not entirely sure the three men had escaped. Later that evening, they climbed out of a sewer grate on Corinthian Avenue – the street that bordered the penitentiary on the east – in full view of a crowd. No one stopped them and the prisoners, who were still wearing their convict uniforms, walked away. Whether or not these men were ever recaptured remains a mystery, but the prison staff did install bars across the sewer tunnels so that no further access would be allowed to the outside.

On August 26, 1908, John Edwards and John Berger climbed over the penitentiary's southern wall using ladders and a rope that they had fashioned in the prison by weaving together 200 scraps of old rope. Berger was a "trusty," which allowed him to wear a special blue uniform and not prison stripes, and a greater freedom to move around the grounds. When they escaped, Berger made it to the ground with no problems, but while Edwards was climbing down, the rope snapped and he fell, breaking his leg. Edwards screamed for Berger to run, then sat on the ground for a while. He was soon approached by a police officer named McClanahan, who asked what he was doing. Edwards had a hammer with him and he began tapping on the wall, telling the officer that he was repairing a crack. Eventually, McClanahan got Edwards to admit that he had escaped, and the officer dragged the prisoner back into the penitentiary. Edwards shrugged off the escape. "There are other days coming" he said.

Edwards and Berger were not the only inmates who tried going over the wall. In 1913, a pair of inmates named Homer Wiggins and Charles Taylor made a similar escape. In late August, they filed the lock off their cell door and replaced it with a phony one made from wood. They snuck out of the cell and went down to the penitentiary's carpentry shop, where the two men worked. Using tools, they had built a collapsible ladder and then carefully hid it until they needed it. Slipping out of the shop, they crossed the yard – getting past five guards and six bulldogs – and climbed to the top of the wall. Once they got over the top, they slid down 48-foot of vine growing on the outer wall of the penitentiary and disappeared into the night.

The numerous – and increasingly elaborate escapes – were only one of the negative effects of the overcrowding in the prison. Another was violence, which increased markedly in the late nineteenth and early twentieth centuries. In 1873, a counterfeiter named Gregar smashed his cellmate's head into a wall over and over again, causing nearly fatal injuries. In June 1900, Cornelius Bush killed his cellmate, James Pratt. A guard had stopped at their cell to give the men their breakfast and after opening the wooden door, the guard asked Bush where his cellmate was. Bush reportedly responded, "He won't bother you anymore." Looking down, the guard saw a bundle on the floor. Calling for another guard, the two officials entered the cell to find that the "bundle" was Pratt's body – minus his head. Pratt's head was found wrapped in a shirt and sitting on a table in the cell. The two men had quarreled over religion and Bush had ended the argument by smashing Pratt's skull with a stool and cut off his head.

On most occasions, the prisoners directed their violence at themselves. On March 27, 1881, inmate Charles Decker hanged himself using a linen shirt. Apparently, the prison issued clothing irritated his skin, so he was allowed to have some shirts from home. Late one night, he tied the shirt to a bracket in the ceiling and leaned forward, slowly and painfully choking himself to death. Eight years later, John Pfeiffer strangled his cellmate, John McBride, and then committed suicide. A year later, Rheinhard Buch slashed his own throat with a razor, dying almost immediately.

Inmates were not the only victims of violence; often the guards were targeted too. In April 1873, a guard was slashed in the throat while transferring an inmate from one cell to another. Later that same year, another guard heard strange noises coming from a cell. He walked to the cell door, but was met by the inmate, demanding to know what right the guard had to enter his cell. The inmate them seized a "spiked club" (apparently a tool used in whatever form of labor he had been assigned) and swung it at the guard. Luckily for the officer, it missed and hit the wall. If it had struck him in the head, it surely would have killed him. Fortunately, another guard, alerted by the noise, appeared at the cell door and used his revolver to subdue the inmate. In 1881, newspaper stories noted that a notorious inmate, dubbed "Barney," had been threatening the lives of the warden and various officers.

By the latter part of the nineteenth century, misbehaving prisoners were no longer placed in the iron gag or the straitjacket. Eastern State had an underground cell where inmates were sent for punishment. In 1897, the warden denied such cells existed, but there was no question that the stories were true. Men were locked in total darkness and put on a diet of bread and water.

Some of the ongoing problems at the prison were undoubtedly due to the fact that Eastern State still continued to house some of Pennsylvania's mentally ill. According to newspaper articles in the 1880s, there were at least ten insane inmates at the penitentiary, not counting those who were mentally handicapped. The stress of dealing with insane convicts often proved more than Eastern's guards could handle, resulting in violence against inmates. Insane convicts (and those feigning insanity) were usually chronic rule breakers, and the guards sometimes reported to clubbing them as punishment. Whether this is what happened to inmate Archibald White – or if he slipped in the shower as guards claimed – but it is known that his injuries were the catalyst for a major investigation of Eastern State's facilities and administration in the spring of 1897.

Philadelphia Judge Gay Gordon was visited in November 1896 by the aunt of Archibald White, who she stated was sick and dying and that his nose had been broken by a guard because White was not able to work. She begged the judge to have her nephew moved to an asylum, where he could get the treatment he needed. Gordon decided to investigate and visited the prison, where he later testified that he found an emaciated White, naked and chained to the floor of his cell. Gordon immediately summoned the warden, who told the judge that White was not insane; he was malingering so that he would not have to work. The warden also assured the judge that White's sentence was due to expire in February, so he would not be there much longer. Gordon immediately requested that White be moved to a mental hospital and to Gordon's outrage, he had to wait five days for the warden's response – a resounding "no."

The warden and Eastern State's resident physician claimed that White was only pretending to be insane. Gordon responded by returning to the penitentiary with a commission of local philanthropists and doctors, who ruled that White was, in fact, insane. Based on their findings, Gordon had the legal authority to have White removed to an asylum, which he did immediately. However, this was not the end of the controversy because Gordon decided to investigate how many other "malingerers" were locked up at Eastern State.

In December 1896, the *Philadelphia Inquirer* published the story of Gordon's investigation under the headline "Prison Walls Echo Maniac's Shrieks." Gordon charged that Eastern's cells were filthy, the food was inedible, and the guards routinely abused the inmates. His most explosive claim was that an inmate had died of injuries sustained at Eastern State after being transferred to Norristown State Hospital. The penitentiary's inspectors vigorously denied Gordon's accusations, but administrators managed to perjure themselves during the hearings, denying that there were insane prisoners at the facility, even though they kept a list of them on file. The hearings went on for months and eventually resulted in few changes. The guard that was deemed responsible for the injuries inflicted on the inmate who died at the Norristown hospital was later tried, but acquitted for murder. The committee refused Gordon's request that inmates and employees who testified against the warden be given immunity, and they also refused to allow the judge to interrogate his own witnesses.

Public opinion, however, was on Gordon's side. Numerous newspaper articles were written on his behalf and the 1897 investigation added support to calls for a state hospital for the insane, which finally opened in 1912.

The method of total solitary confinement was finally abandoned in the 1870s. It was largely considered a failure in that it was too expensive to manage and had showed little in the way of results. It was decided that Eastern State would become a regular prison. From this point on, being sent to solitary confinement was a punishment and not a normal part of the penitentiary's operations. The prisoners were no longer confined strictly to their cells, and a dining hall and athletic field were built. Since the prisoners no longer needed the individual exercise yards, the areas were converted into cells to help with the overcrowding that affected the prison. Between 1900 and 1908, many of the original cells were also renovated, and what had once been a small chamber for one man, became close quarters for as many as five. Along with these changes came new cell blocks, a wood shop, a new boiler room and other buildings where the prisoners could labor.

By this era, Eastern State's wardens were declaring that the early rehabilitation plans of the prison were a failure. It was a place of punishment, not rehabilitation. Eastern State had become a holding pen for some of Pennsylvania's worst offenders. It was a place of violence, riots, escapes, and even a plot to blow up the penitentiary.

One of the penitentiary's most controversial wardens was Robert J. McKenty, who took over in 1909. He came at a time of massive transformation for the penitentiary and believed that inmates could be rehabilitated. He once stated, "I have dealt with some criminals in my time and I have sent some to the gallows, but even those who went to the gallows went there without any ill feeling in their hearts for me. I have always done my duty, but I have never found it necessary to do so viciously."

McKenty's administration was immediately criticized as "idealistic," but he embraced new innovations, like inmate self-government. Called the "Honor and Friendship Club," it was designed to help inmates and newly discharged prisoners, as well as give the prisoners a voice in the penitentiary's administration. The idea was making its rounds at other prisons, like Sing Sing in New York, and seemed to have positive results – on the surface anyway. Not everyone was convinced that McKenty had the best interests of the inmates in mind. His tenure was wracked by riots and protests against the conditions at Eastern State.

In 1919, there was a "virtual riot" in Eastern's courtyard during a visit by a grand jury to the penitentiary, which was an attempt to get better food and medical attention. According to the inmates, the warden had been notified beforehand that the grand jury would visit and therefore, had prepared "an extra fine meal" that day, but in general, the food was poor and insufficient. While this was going on, McKenty smiled as the inmates poured out their complaints, then denied the charges when he had them alone in his office. As a result, the grand jury omitted any reference to the inmate's complaints in its report to Judge Joseph P. McCullen.

McKenty got his revenge just two hours after the grand jury visit, when he deposed every officer and member of the Honor and Friendship Club. The inmates retaliated by demanding that the warden do something about the random acts of brutality committed against the inmates by the guards and about the general quality of the food. If he didn't, they promised, they would send a letter to the governor demanding an investigation. McKenty apparently agreed to their demands, rather than risk another investigation, but the conditions barely improved.

Regardless, investigations into McKenty's administration continued. He was eventually exonerated, but conditions at Eastern State had continued to deteriorate and the administration could not truly claim to be in control of the institution. One obvious sign of its lack of control was the rising amount of narcotics entering the penitentiary, which became a huge scandal in the 1920s. Narcotics in the prison became front-page news in 1922, when Dr. E.E. Dudding, president of the Prisoner's Relief Society of Washington, claimed that Eastern State was rife with drugs, which guards were supplying to the inmates. Warden McKenty called Dudding a "confounded liar."

Unfortunately, Dudding's charges turned out to be partially true. In the spring of 1923, a grand jury investigation revealed numerous breakdowns in prison security and confirmed that narcotics were widely available at Eastern State. According to a newspaper report, the grand jury discovered a liquor still in one of the cells, and a member of the grand jury even bought some heroin from one of the inmates. Eventually, six former guards and seven inmates were indicted on charges of smuggling and selling drugs. Naturally, McKenty claimed that the still and the drugs were planted by his political opponents to "discredit his record as warden."

These revelations brought to light a penitentiary-wide drug-smuggling ring led by a group of inmates known as the "Four Horsemen," who claimed to function as "the self-appointed administrators of the big prison." They were a sort-of "self-government committee," which created its own system within the system. They even printed passes, labeled "peacemaker," which allowed inmates bearing the cards unfettered access to any cellblocks at any time. Even the guards respected the peacemaker cards because running afoul of the Four Horsemen meant a confrontation with a gang "strong-arm squad" who beat up guards and punished prisoners who ran afoul of the leaders.

The situation came to a head that spring, when rioting broke out at Eastern State that lasted, on and off, for an unbelievable five weeks. The violence was blamed on poor food, corrupt and low-paid guards, lack of sufficient work, overcrowding, and filthy living conditions. Prisoners carried out guerilla warfare against not only the guards, but each other. Basically, the population had broken into rival gangs: the Four Horsemen, who had some sort of official status, and their rivals, the Prisoner's Mutual Welfare Association. The gangs made up about twenty percent of the prison's population, which left the remaining eighty percent frantically petitioning the board of inspectors for permission to be locked in their cells day and night in order to escape the violence. The riots were eventually quelled, but a search that followed yielded more than 400 knives, several hundred "other types of weapons," and a large amount of narcotics.

In the aftermath, Warden McKenty was forced to tender his resignation on April 22, 1923, and 33 inmates, including the Four Horsemen, were transferred to Western

State Penitentiary in the hope that, with the troublemakers gone, prison officials could restore order.

However, this did not staunch the problem of drugs at Eastern State. By 1924, there were enough addicts that they were segregated and held in the gallery of cellblock five, which became known as "Doper's Row." Officials even tried putting guards undercover in the cells to see how drugs were getting into the penitentiary, but with only minor success. Several men were arrested for narcotics smuggling, including the prison's cook and a guard named Sergeant Pike A. Harper. But each time one smuggling avenue was closed, another one opened.

After McKenty's resignation, the new warden, John C. Groome, tried to reassert control over the penitentiary. After founding and organizing Pennsylvania's State Troopers in 1905, and serving as their first commander, Groome joined the U.S. Army and served as the acting provost marshal general in charge of the military police during World War I. After the war ended, Groome was twice offered the position of warden at Eastern State, and he refused both time. But when the riots broke out in 1923, he accepted. Unlike McKenty, who believed that inmates could be rehabilitated and should be treated like citizens, Groome abolished all forms of self-government for the inmates and began programs that would deal harshly with every type of infraction. This was a direct repudiation of Eastern State's philosophy, which had (at least in theory) emphasized rehabilitation and penitence over retribution and punishment. Groome's tenure as warden began a new era in the penitentiary's history.

The new warden launched an investigation into reports that inmates were bribing guards and discovered that at least one, Hugh Drum, smuggled letters into the prison for at least one inmate. Groome also fired 14 guards, some for their age and others for neglect of duties. He transferred 26 others to Western State. It turned out to be an ill-concealed attempt to cleanse the administration of McKenty supporters. In addition, Groome armed the penitentiary guards, a practice that his predecessor had discontinued. In just a few short months, Groome made it clear that he intended to run a very different penitentiary than McKenty had.

He tightened regulations and cracked down on the prisoners, which, naturally, caused a great deal of resentment against him. Groome ordered the construction of enclosed guard boxes on each of the penitentiary's corner turrets, where the guards would be armed with Krag repeating rifles and Thompson submachine guns. In addition, he moved the warden's office from the corridor between cellblocks eight and nine (where it had been for decades) back into the gatehouse at the front of the prison. Finally, Groome discontinued the practice of allowing inmates to meet with visitors in specially designed cells on each cellblock, creating instead a special area in the east side of the gatehouse, where inmates and visitors were separated by a barrier to prevent smuggling.

Needless to say, the new regulations were not popular. Eighteen inmates jammed their mattresses against their cell doors and set them on fire in protest. Groome quickly crushed this minor rebellion and punished the inmates involved. For prisoners who got out of line, the likely punishment was a trip to "Klondike," a series of darkened cells on the gallery of cellblock four. Inmates sent to the punishment cells were stripped naked and given only food and water. It was similar to the same punishments doled out by earlier administrations, but public scrutiny of the prison had increased to the point that information about places like "Klondike" did not stay behind the penitentiary's walls. Newspaper reporters seized on the fact that isolation, which had once been used to rehabilitate inmates, was now being used savagely to punish the worst offenders. It was a shocking reversal of the penitentiary's founding philosophy. Inmates made numerous complaints against Groome for brutality, but he was eventually cleared of all charges.

The charges were not the only thing to damage Groome's reputation. There were also a number of escapes and escape attempts that demonstrated how challenging administering Eastern State had become. This point was driven home by the discovery, in May 1923, of a plot to blow up the prison. Officials found a "large quantity of high powered explosive" in a cell facing Eastern State's back wall. Apparently, the plan had been to blow a hole in the wall so that all of the inmates could escape. It was a far-fetched idea, but it would not be the last attempt over the next few years.

On July 15, 1923, six inmates escaped by climbing over the penitentiary's eastern wall and hijacking a truck. The inmates had been detailed to clean up the prison's southeastern yard and while working, they rushed two guards, bound them, and locked them in the sentry box. They scaled the wall using an ingeniously constructed ladder that broke down into a number of parts that were designed to look like penitentiary-issued furniture. Using a hook and rope, they lowered themselves to the ground – while a group of local residents stood by and watched. The fugitives hijacked the truck using revolvers – which had obviously been smuggled into the prison – and sped away. Six blocks from the penitentiary, they ditched the truck for a sedan driven by Thomas McAlister, who was on his way to a Sunday School picnic. The convicts eventually drove to Elkton, Maryland, where McAlister escaped. Warden Groome offered a $250 reward for each inmate, and while they were later reported in Pocomoke City, Maryland, and Atlantic City, New Jersey, they were never recaptured. Rumor had it that the escapees had paid the guards $30,000 to "look the other way," a stinging blow to Groome's administration, which was based on rooting out corruption.

In November 1923, three more inmates escaped, killing a guard in the process. Groome had ordered the warden's living quarters converted into office space, mostly to distance himself further from McKenty. A number of inmates were detailed to do the work and to paint the deputy warden's quarters. While working on the renovations, four inmates came down the stairs and into the guardhouse, where one of them black-jacked one of the duty guards. The other inmates shot at the second guard and fled through the penitentiary's front door. They unsuccessfully attempted to commandeer a taxi cab and then fled east down Fairmount Avenue. One of the inmates was recaptured a short time later by the police and a second was recaptured in Los Angeles in 1926. The most interesting was Francis Joseph Flynn, who had himself arrested and placed in the Berks County Jail for vagrancy. He was sure the authorities would never look for him in jail, and it was only dumb luck that the Berks County warden recognized Flynn from his picture in the newspaper.

Another memorable escape attempt occurred in 1926. Eight prisoners took turns tunneling under cells 24 and 25. They went down about eight feet and then started digging toward the outer wall. The tunnel had been extended nearly 35 feet before they were caught. A similar tunnel actually succeeded in making it out of the prison in April 1945. A group of prisoners, using wood from the prison shop for reinforcement, managed to dig a shaft under the prison and beyond the wall. After it was completed, the men went out at slightly different times to avoid being noticed. By the time they all reached the tunnel's exit, the guards had realized they were missing and the last two were caught climbing out of the tunnel. The others were apprehended a few blocks away.

One of the worst escapes during Groome's tenure occurred in 1927, when two inmates threw a guard off the wall as they climbed over. Late in the evening of September 4, William Lynch and William Peter Bishie walked to the northeast tower with a lead pipe wrapped in a towel and a rope made of twine for making boats in the prison's model shops. The two men worked as electricians inside the penitentiary and so they were taken out of their cells that night to repair a broken telephone line. They climbed the ladder to the guard box, where a single guard, Floyd Reynolds, was waiting for them. One of the inmates hit the guard with the pipe and, in the struggle that followed, the guard fired off his rifle, alerting the guards in the other three towers. One of them immediately reached for the cord that sounded the signal alarm – but nothing happened. The two inmates had already cut the wires, so no alarm could be raised. Lynch and Bishie pushed Reynolds over the wall and the guard fell 35 feet to the ground. After tying their makeshift rope to an iron rail, they slid down, dropping the last several feet because the rope was too short. Leaving the badly injured guard behind, they hurried off into the darkness.

Warden Groome retired after five years and was replaced by his deputy warden, Herbert "Hardboiled" Smith. Many of Groome's initiatives continued under Smith. Like Groome, he was dubious about rehabilitating Eastern's inmates, calling the idea a "joke." Smith was rumored to be a heavy drinker (bank robber Willie Sutton's memoirs recalled one inebriated evening when Smith charged into the cellblock and drunkenly fired off a revolver) and had a reputation for blunt aggressiveness. Sutton alleged that, when he arrived at the penitentiary, that Smith threatened the famed jail-breaker that if he tried to escape, the guards had been ordered to "blow your fuckin' head off." In spite of this, though, nearly everyone still managed to describe Smith with one word: fair.

Smith's tenure as warden was also marred by a series of well-publicized riots and escapes. In August 1933, prisoners staged a hunger strike, in March 1942, they rioted over war rationing, and tried to blow up the penitentiary with dynamite in December 1944.

And then there were the riots over the stiff sentences received for inmates who broke out during the infamous "Willie Sutton Tunnel" escape in April 1945. Tunnels had long been a problem for prison officials. Many prisoners had gone over the wall, but others tried to go under it. There were numerous attempts to tunnel under Eastern State's massive walls, which extend 10 feet under the ground.

On February 13, 1940, Warden Smith discovered a tunnel leading from cell 50 on cellblock nine toward Fairmont Avenue. An informant had apparently given up the secret of the 25-foot long tunnel to Smith, and the six inmates involved were immediately placed in solitary. One of them, James Wilson, committed suicide at the prospect of more time being added on to his sentence. The following day, another tunnel was discovered, this time in cell 29 in cellblock ten. In both cases, inmates had cut holes near their toilets and then covered the holes with precast slabs that perfectly covered the openings. Tunnel building became something of a pastime for Eastern State inmates. Most were serving long sentences and figured they had nothing to lose and everything to gain.

But there is no escape story better known than the "Willie Sutton Tunnel." There has been some contradiction as to how great of a role that Sutton – a prolific bank robber who allegedly stole over $2 million in his 40-year criminal career and escaped from prison three times, becoming known for the adage that he robbed banks "because that's where the money is" – played in the escape. In Sutton's version, he was the tunnel's mastermind, but others say he was a latecomer to the plan and was only reluctantly accepted by the other plotters.

Regardless, one of the main characters in the drama was inmate Clarence Klinedinst, a mason by trade who was sent to Eastern State on forgery and burglary charges. He was a quiet, unassuming man, plodding, patient, introverted, and physically unremarkable, but a hard worker and a good mechanic – in other words, the perfect man to build an escape tunnel.

In March 1944, Klinedinst managed to get himself transferred to cellblock seven and immediately began work on his tunnel. For the first three days that he was in his cell, Klinedinst was either allowed or ordered to keep a wet blanket over his cell door, which blocked the guard's view inside. Klinedinst was supposed to be working on the cell and the blanket was supposed to keep the plaster dust inside. In reality, the blanket was used to keep the guards from seeing as he broke through the wall of the cell. Klinedinst then covered the tunnel entrance with a board that was painted to match the cell walls and which he fastened using small hooks on the inside of the tunnel. Around the seams, he used a mixture of Vaseline and dirt to give the impression that it was just a part of the wall. As a final touch, he hung a metal wastebasket over the panel. A few days later, during an inspection, the deputy warden congratulated Klinedinst on the nice job that he had done renovating the cell.

Given the conditions that he was working under, Klinedinst's tunnel was very sophisticated. Using secreted materials, he made a seven-foot ladder that extended from his cell down to the tunnel. He used boards to shore up the tunnel walls and installed a string of electric lights that he plugged into an outlet in his cell. It is believed that he also had a fan in the tunnel so that he didn't overheat while digging. The tunnel varied in widths from three feet to just over one foot, and it was estimated that it must have taken 850 trips to move the quantity of dirt that he moved with a ten-quart pail. No one is sure how the inmates managed to get rid of that much dirt, but the most likely explanations are that they flushed it down the toilets, dumped it into an underground creek that was discovered during the excavation, or stuffed their pockets and emptied it out as they walked about the penitentiary's yard.

To gather all of the items he needed – and to remove the dirt – Klinedinst had to have help. Forced to tell other inmates what he was working on, he enlisted the help of James Van Sant and Frederick Tenuto. Both men were assigned to the penitentiary's trash detail, which was used to get rid of the large rocks that were found in the tunnel. With the prison being overcrowded, Klinedinst knew that he would eventually be assigned a cellmate, which could be fatal to the plan. However,

Van Sant and Tenuto turned to a friend, William Russell, and convinced him to put in a request to become Klinedinst's cellmate. He soon became part of the plan, as did Willie Sutton, who was said to have figured out what was going on and insinuated himself into the conspiracy. An inmate named Bob McKnight, who worked in the prison's dental office, stole some plaster so that Klinedinst could make a bust to leave in his bed at night while he worked in the tunnel. How many other inmates were involved in building the tunnel, as opposed to those who saw an opportunity to escape and took it, is impossible to say. Obviously, a lot of people knew what was going on, which presented a constant danger to the plan.

Another danger, which grew more extreme with each passing day, was the possibility of a tunnel collapse. In the summer of 1944, a portion of the roof caved in. No one was injured, but it took a month and a half to repair the damage. Then, in August 1944, a guard was killed at the penitentiary. The tunnel builders heard about the murder through the prison communication system and immediately closed down the digging operation for three weeks while the state police investigated the murder. That December, a passerby threw three sticks of dynamite over the penitentiary wall, which caused a lockdown while prison officials searched for evidence of any other explosives on the premises. Klinedinst and the other men were sure they would be discovered and tensions ran high for a time. The sense of crisis eventually abated, and work continued on the tunnel.

At 7:00 a.m. on Tuesday, April 3, 1945, 12 inmates managed to squeeze through the tunnel, crawl 100 feet under Eastern State's massive walls, and emerge in the flower beds that lined the penitentiary's front façade. Klinedinst and the crew had broken through the night before, but decided to wait until morning to escape – a disastrously bad decision. As the men scurried through the tunnel, they emerged onto a busy street in front of scores of startled onlookers. Tenuto, Van Sant, and Klinedinst were the first three to emerge from the tunnel, and Sutton was the last. Unfortunately for the notorious bank robber, Sutton popped out of the ground just as two Philadelphia police officers rounded the corner onto Fairmount Avenue. Sutton was immediately recaptured and, by the end of the day, five additional escapees were brought back to the penitentiary.

William Russell was tracked down a week later, when he visited an old girlfriend dressed as a sailor. He was carried back to the prison – when he walked into the girlfriend's apartment, he was met by a squad of Philadelphia police officers, who shot him seven times. Tenuto and Van Sant were caught a few weeks later in New York, planning a robbery. One of the escapees actually returned to the penitentiary on his own. Eight days after the robbery, guards were stunned when they heard a knock at the massive front door at just after 5:00 a.m. They answered the door to find escapee James Grace, asking to be let back in. Grace, who wasn't a native of Philadelphia, hid under a bridge in nearby Fairmount Park for a week and then tired, hungry, and with nowhere else to go, went back to Eastern State. He was fed and then placed in solitary with the rest of the men who had been part of the tunnel plot.

There was a reason that so many inmates wanted to escape the confines of Eastern State Penitentiary. By the late 1920s, it had become an increasingly dangerous and violent place. It had been designated a maximum-security facility for "chronic recidivists and others for whom rehabilitation was not deemed likely." These inmates were often serving life sentences and were well aware that they would never get out of prison. They had little to lose in trying to escape or injure, maim, or kill guards or fellow inmates. Historians called the prison "brutal" in those days and many anecdotes exist to say that this was an apt description. In September 1922, Ambrusio Silva bashed in his cellmate's skull, which resulted in his death two days later. The reason for the dispute? An argument over the proper pronunciation of a word. An inmate named Peter Marone killed his cellmate, Frank Saris, after arguing about the price of phonograph records. Ignazio Crino was stabbed to death by a fellow inmate, Joseph Kelly, who refused to say why he did it. In June 1948, Robert McGrogan and William Palmer stabbed inmate Richard J. Rafer with knives made from sharpened kitchen spoons. Three years later, Marshall Pepperissa smuggled a baseball bat into the cellblock after a game in the yard and beat William Van Arsdale to death. It was a dangerous and unpredictable place.

Guards were not immune to the violence and were always sensitive to possible threats. In March 1936, an inmate was making noise by throwing furniture about in his cell. When the guard entered the cell, the inmate hit him with a bar of soap. The other inmates on the block cheered on the inmate and cursed the guards, who responded by throwing gas grenades into the cellblock. The fear of organized violence was one of the reasons why, shortly after he arrived in 1923, Warden Groome ordered the construction of "head gates," or barred doors that could quarantine individual cellblocks and prevent riots from spreading throughout the penitentiary. This created a heightened sense of tension that could occasionally lead to embarrassing overreactions, such as in August 1947, when Philadelphia police were called after a report that someone was trying to tunnel into the penitentiary late one evening. The would-be "escape artist" turned out to be a young man digging for worms for an upcoming fishing trip.

One man might have been digging for worms, but the tension that guards faced at Eastern State was very real and, occasionally, it boiled over and led to violence against the inmates. In November 1923, a grand jury investigation delved into injuries received by inmate James Fraley. When Fraley was asked how his arm and jaw had gotten broken, he refused to answer, but other inmates confided that Fraley had been "unmercifully beaten by the guards" for assisting four inmates during an escape earlier in the year. Acting warden Herbert Smith said that Fraley had been injured in a fall and resisted a court order that demanded Fraley appear before the grand jury and admit what had happened. The warden said he was too ill to travel. Fraley did eventually testify, though, asserting that he had been beaten in his cell by none other than Smith and Deputy Warden Charles Santee. Smith was eventually exonerated of these charges, but Santee was indicted and convicted of beating Fraley.

Violence continued, riots took place over overcrowding and poor food, and after laws were passed that officially ended the penitentiary's original ideas of rehabilitation, it had lost everything that had once made the place unique. Inmates were no longer separated from one another, and the penitentiary's architectural plan, which was designed to allow guards to survey all of the cellblocks, had been transformed into a disjointed series of buildings disconnected from one another. As the twentieth century dragged on, administrators were less convinced that inmates could be rehabilitated.

But there were exceptions, like Henry G. Brock, who, after he was released from Eastern State in 1923, was appointed by Governor Pinchot as a trustee of the penitentiary. Brock, from a wealthy Pennsylvania family, was convicted of manslaughter after he killed three people in a car while driving drunk. There were also inmates like Abe Buzzard, who, after spending 42 years in prison, devoted himself to becoming a minister and worked with prison populations.

However, skeptical prison officials were more apt to point to men like Lew Edwards, who was known as the "toughest guy" who ever served time at Eastern State. After he was released, he publicly went straight but was, in reality, leading a gang of ex-convicts who robbed businesses all over Philadelphia. Understandably, guards and administrators became skeptical about the possibility of reform. More than one guard told newly paroled inmates: "See you soon."

In the 1950s, Eastern State underwent sweeping reforms, but despite the renovations that followed, it remained a dangerous and depressing place. Even though the population had finally started to decline, violence and suicide remained ongoing problems. During Eastern State's last years as a state penitentiary, the prison was rocked by the suicide of an inmate named Norman Maisenhelder. He was a lifer, sentenced in 1953 for murdering his wife, and he had spent some time in a mental institution during the late 1950s because he exhibited obsessive-compulsive and aggressive tendencies. During his time at Eastern State, the administration created a number of mental "supports" to help Maisenhelder cope with incarceration. He was assigned to the kitchen, where he worked alone, and was a regularly scheduled patient at the penitentiary's counseling department. He was passionately devoted to his daughter, who was placed with another family following her mother's murder and her father's conviction. Maisenhelder kept in regular touch with his daughter through letters from her foster family, but it was ultimately these letters that drove him to suicide.

In August 1969, Maisenhelder received a letter from his daughter's caregiver that disturbed him. Apparently, the glowing reports that they had been sending him about his daughter's condition were largely untrue. The young woman was, in reality, taking drugs and was close to failing school. Maisenhelder snapped. He took two knives from the kitchen and climbed atop the intake and parole building between cellblocks eight and nine at lunchtime. To get the administration's attention, he slit open one of his wrists, causing cries to go up from the men who were watching. The spectacle on top of the building had quickly drawn a crowd. Officials worked quickly to set up a telephone line so that Maisenhelder could speak to his daughter. Someone attached an extension wire to a phone, which was passed out of a window and up onto a roof via a ladder. Unfortunately, the call didn't go through and Maisenhelder responded by throwing the telephone from the roof and shouting, "That's it!" His arm swung wide and he plunged one of the knives into his chest. It skidded off his ribcage, doing only minor damage, and so he tried again. The second knife plunged into his heart and he collapsed. The wound proved fatal, and Maisenhelder died a short time later in the penitentiary hospital.

Violence – and what the guards often referred to as "skirmishes" – broke out frequently. In November 1953, Robert Robinson, one of Eastern State's barbers, fatally stabbed Emmanuel L. Porter with an eight-and-a-half-inch table knife. Five years later, Charles A. Barr stabbed Edward Huber in the penitentiary's reception area while the two men were left unguarded. Apparently, they had gotten into a fistfight earlier in the day, but it had been broken up by the guards. Barr accosted Huber later in the day, renewed the fight, and stabbed Huber with a makeshift knife. In 1967, William Jennings Mundy died at Eastern State after being found unconscious in his cell. He had been slashed in the arm with a razor, but since no razor was found in the cell, it didn't appear to have been a suicide attempt. In another incident, Robert Lee Jackson injured three guards during a "skirmish" that started when Jackson refused to obey an order. It took six guards to subdue the man and he was later charged with multiple counts of assault. In March 1967, Clarence

Young stabbed another inmate, Cornell Wylie, while the two men were working in the mess hall. No reason was given for the attack.

The inmates were not the only source of violence in the prison. During this period, a shadowy group of guards known as the "goon squad" enforced order and discipline through "non-official" means. Though the squad disappeared after William A. Bannmiller became warden in 1965, it was nevertheless a major force within the penitentiary for punishment and retribution. The "goon squad" was overseen by Warden Walter Tees, whose antipathy toward rehabilitation and prisoner's rights made him a holdover from the militaristic style of the prison's earlier days.

The prison continued to see more than its share of riots during this period. In 1961, prisoners rebelled after a failed escape attempt. On December 24, 1960, inmate Richard Mayberry was discovered carrying a "zip gun," or a penitentiary-built weapon that uses a spring to propel projectiles, making it just as deadly as a real pistol. This was the first indication that an escape was planned, although Mayberry's capture pushed back the date. Two weeks later, after cleaning the officer's dining hall, inmate John Klauzenberg asked the guard on his cellblock, Donald Carr, to open another inmate's cell so that he could retrieve his guitar from his friend, Harry Shank. Although it was against the rules, Carr was new on the job and complied, taking Klauzenberg to Shank's cell. Once the door was open, both Klauzenberg and Shank subdued Carr, stabbing him in the process. Carr managed to escape from the cell, but the two inmates had taken his keys, which they used to free another inmate, Manny Madronal.

The three inmates, carrying sharp homemade knives, made their way to a guard post and took the four officers on duty hostage. One of the guards was Lieutenant William Richter, who, as senior officer, was in charge of the penitentiary. The inmates swapped clothes with three of the guards and moved to cellblocks one and fifteen, which were solitary, death row, and maximum security. The inmates likely assumed that the prisoners on these blocks, all of whom had histories of violent crime and breaking penitentiary rules, would prove ideal assistants in what was quickly becoming a riot.

Unfortunately for the rioters, Officer Carr, who hid after being attacked, managed to contact guards in the gatehouse, who in turn called Warden Brierly at home and informed him that some of the inmates were out of their cells in the penitentiary. Brierly, when he could not reach Lieutenant Richter inside of the prison, assumed that he had been taken hostage and set into motion a predetermined plan called "Operation Breakout." The plan was designed to coordinate the efforts of the Pennsylvania State Police, Philadelphia Police

Department, and Philadelphia Fire Department in order to contain – and bring to an end – any riot or escape that occurred. Once Klauzenberg, Shank, and Madronal realized that officials knew what was happening behind the prison walls, they decided to free all of the inmates, hoping that the ensuing chaos would provide the cover needed for them to escape. Dozens of prisoners flooded the corridors and cellblocks and in the melee that followed, both guards and fellow inmates were savagely attacked.

The riot lasted for only an hour and a half. By 10:00 p.m., Eastern State was flooded with four dozen guards and state policemen who began reasserting control. The warden and his troops made it as far as the garage, where the ringleaders were barricaded in with inmates carrying knives, zip guns, and Molotov cocktails made from bottles and gas cans. One of the ringleaders threatened to decapitate the guards they still held hostage and roll their heads out "like bowling balls" if anyone approached the garage. Brierly responded by having state troopers fire tear gas into the garage and then they stormed the building. The troops quickly overwhelmed the rioters, and all of the men in the garage were stripped naked and made to stand in the cold so that the guards could be separated from the inmates. Once that happened, the inmates were taken back to their cells, where they were severely punished.

Even though the riot was successfully contained, it was an embarrassment to both the penitentiary and the state legislature because it "spurred renewed criticism of the antiquated structure and its residential location." This was nothing new. Eastern State had been criticized for nearly half a century for being obsolete and a hazard to the city. After the riot in 1961, however, the public became aware of just how vulnerable the aging structure was and demanded a solution. The legislature funded a three-year study of the Pennsylvania penal system, which recommend sweeping changes, including moving Eastern State to a location outside of the city. But very few towns wanted a maximum-security prison located close to them and repeated attempts to procure land were defeated by town councils in those areas. For a time, Eastern State remained in operation, but it was clearly existing on borrowed time.

Although there was some talk of trying to renovate the old prison -- walls had crumbled in some locations and in others, ceilings were starting to collapse – the cost of repairing it turned out to be as high as building a new one. In 1970, Pennsylvania Governor Raymond P. Shafer announced that four new prisons would be built to replace Eastern State. Most of the men from Eastern State would be transferred to Graterford Prison, which would be located about 25 miles from Philadelphia. Construction began immediately on this institution to help relieve the overcrowding and the concern about the conditions at the old prison. When Graterford was completed in 1971, prisoners began to be sent there. By April 14, 1971, Eastern State was completely empty.

Though Eastern State housed a few hundred inmates following a riot at the city's Holmesburg Prison, by the end of 1971, the once world-famous institution was empty once more, a sad reminder of the hopes of a small group of men who once believed that the unique building had the ability to save men's souls.

Years of violence, bloodshed, riots, tragedy, pain, and despair left an indelible mark on these stone walls. Is it any wonder that people believe the place is haunted?

Hauntings at Eastern State

Whispers and rumors of ghosts had echoed from the prison walls for many years before the penitentiary was actually closed down. One of the oldest ghost stories of the prison is connected to its most famous former inmate – mobster Al Capone.

Capone, who was the undisputed boss of Chicago during the latter part of the 1920s, spent time at Eastern State after being arrested on a weapons charge in Philadelphia in May 1929. According to gangland legend, he was ordered to lay low by members of the emerging national crime Syndicate, headed by men like Charles "Lucky" Luciano and Meyer Lansky. For the Syndicate leaders, Mafia battles were a thing of the past, a holdover from the days of the ethnic gangs. They wanted a Syndicate in which each member controlled his own territory and no one person was in charge. Just months before, Capone had ordered members of Chicago's North Side gang to be shot down in a garage on North Clark Street – the St. Valentine's Day Massacre. Capone had intended to wipe out the gang's leader, George Moran, but had killed seven other men by mistake.

Luciana and Lansky decided that it would be a good idea for Capone to go to jail. Not only would it allow the heat from the St. Valentine's Day Massacre to continue to cool, but it might be just the thing to save Capone's life. George Moran, along with a few scattered remnants of his gang, was still plotting to kill Capone so he did the best thing he could – he had himself thrown in jail.

Capone had become friendly at the horse track the year before with a Philadelphia detective named James "Shooey" Malone, so he telephoned a friend in Philadelphia and asked him to get a message to Malone. He and a bodyguard, Frank Rio, then drove to the city and decided to go to the movies at a theater on Market Street. When they came out around 9:00 p.m., Malone and another detective, John Creedon, were waiting for them. When the detectives flashed their badges, Capone and Rio handed over their guns.

The police magistrate, before whom they were arraigned shortly after midnight, fixed bail at $35,000 each. They only had a few thousand bucks between them and the two lawyers that Capone had sent for, Bernard L. Lemisch and Cornelius Haggerty, Jr., accused the police of railroading their clients into jail. Capone just smiled – railroading was exactly what he wanted.

The judge imposed the maximum sentence of one year. As Capone was led off with the unlucky Frank Rio to Philadelphia's Holmesburg County Prison, he took a diamond ring from his finger and handed it to his attorney, instructing him to get it to his brother Ralph. Between arrest and imprisonment, only 16 hours had passed.

Holmesburg, with more than 1,700 prisoners jammed into cells built to hold 600, was one of the country's worst county jails. A few weeks before Capone entered it, the prisoners, rioting over bad food and brutal guards, set fire to their mattresses. The word went out from Chicago that a $50,000 fee awaited any attorney that could get Capone out of Holmesburg. None succeeded. The same fee was offered to the district attorney in Philadelphia, John Monoghan, as a bribe to procure Capone's release, but he turned it down.

Luckily for Capone, he was transferred in August to the city's larger and more orderly Eastern State Penitentiary. There, Warden Smith made him more comfortable, giving him a private cell and letting him furnish it with Oriental rugs, pictures, a chest of drawers, double bed, bookshelf, lamps and a $500 radio console. As his work assignment, he drew the comfortable job of library file clerk. Capone continued to conduct business from prison. He was allowed to make long-distance telephone calls from the warden's office and to meet with his lawyers and his brother, Ralph, along with high-ranking mobsters Frank Nitti and Jake Guzik, all of whom made frequent trips to Philadelphia. For ordinary inmates, visiting hours were limited to Sunday, but Capone's family and friends could come and see him any day. He also met often with reporters, who kept their readers up to date on Capone's schedule, daily life, and reading habits.

He bought $1,000 worth of arts and crafts made by his fellow inmates and mailed them to friends as Christmas presents. He also donated $1,200 to a Philadelphia orphanage. Such seemingly good-hearted deeds aroused a great deal of sympathy for Capone. A civil engineer from Chicago, a total stranger to Capone, who was in Philadelphia on business, got permission to visit him. He warmly shook his hand and told him, "Al, we're with you."

Shortly after arriving at Eastern State, Capone had to have his tonsils removed. The surgeon who performed the operation, Dr. Herman Goddard of the Pennsylvania State Board of Prison Inspections, could barely contain the admiration that he felt for his infamous patient. "In my seven years' experience," he said, "I have never seen a prisoner so kind, so cheery and accommodating."

But Capone was not always "cheery and accommodating" at Eastern State, especially at night, after the lights had gone out. It was at Eastern State Penitentiary, during those dark nights while he tossed and turned in the cot in his cell, that a terrifying memory of the St. Valentine's Day Massacre came back to visit Al Capone.

That memory's name was James Clark.

It was while he was incarcerated at Eastern State that Capone first began to be haunted by the ghost of James Clark, a member of the North Side gang and one of the men killed during the St. Valentine's Day Massacre. While in prison, other inmates reported that they could hear Capone screaming in his cell, begging someone whom he called "Jimmy" to go away and leave him alone. No one had any idea what he was talking about; Capone was alone in his cell. During the daylight hours, he refused to speak about it.

Later, that would change. After his return to Chicago, Capone would speak often about the ghost and about the "curse" that haunted his life. He even went so far as to hire a spirit medium to try and convince the ghost to leave. Was the ghost real? Did Capone imagine the whole thing, or was he already showing signs of the psychosis that would haunt him after his release from Alcatraz years later?

Capone certainly believed the ghost was real and over the course of the next few years, the haunting would become more intense, reaching a point when Capone was not the only person to encounter the vengeful spirit of James Clark.

But James Clark was not the only spirit rumored to haunt the prison. Clark's spirit – if it was real – likely departed with Al Capone. However, others were believed to linger behind.

By the time the building's last living prisoners were removed, anyone who had spent any time behind the stone walls was certain that something supernatural was taking place at Eastern State. It was said that when the last guards made their rounds through the prison, this last foray into the darkness caused them to utter chilling stories to one another -- and to anyone else who would listen and not think them insane. They spoke of the sounds of footsteps in the corridors, pacing feet in the cells, eerie wails that drifted from the darkest corners of the complex, and dark shadows that resembled people flitting past now-darkened doorways and past windows and cells. It seemed that the abandoned halls, corridors, and chambers were not so empty after all. Those who left the penitentiary on that final day had become convinced that a strange presence had taken over the building and most breathed a sigh of relief to be gone. But the prison would not be abandoned for long.

In the middle 1970s, the empty prison was designated as a National Historic Landmark and was eventually purchased by the city of Philadelphia to be used as a tourist attraction. The Pennsylvania Prison Society of Philadelphia was placed in charge of operating and promoting it as a historic site, and they continue to conduct tours of the penitentiary today.

And from these tours and forays into the prison, come more tales of ghosts and hauntings. Without question, the prison was designed to be a frightening place and, in recent times, it has become even more so. The prison still stands as a ruin of crumbling cellblocks, empty guard towers, rusting doors, and vaulted, water-stained ceilings. It is a veritable fortress and an intimidating place for even the most hardened visitors. But does the spooky atmosphere of the place explain the ghostly tales as merely tricks of the imagination? Those who have experienced the spirits of Eastern State say that it does not.

Greta Galuszka, a former program coordinator for the prison stated: "The idea of staying in this penitentiary alone is just overwhelming... I would not stay here overnight."

Over the years, volunteers and visitors alike have had some pretty strange experiences in the prison. In Cell Block 12, several independent witnesses have reported the hollow and distant sound of laughter echoing in certain cells. No source can ever be discovered for the noises. Others have reported the presence of shadowy apparitions in the cells and the hallways, as though prisoners from the past can find no escape from this inhuman place. Several volunteers believe that they have seen these ghostly figures in the "six block," while others have seen them darting across corridors and vanishing into rooms.

A locksmith named Gary Johnson was performing some routine restoration work one day when he had his own odd encounter. He recalled, "I had this feeling that I was being watched but I turned and I'm looking down the block and there's nobody there. A couple of seconds later and I get the same feeling... I'm really being watched! I turn around and I look down the block and shoooom.... this black shadow just leaped across the block!" Johnson still refers to the prison as a "giant haunted house."

Angel Riugra, who has also worked in the prison, agreed. "You feel kinda jittery walking around because you feel something there, but when you turn around, you don't see anything. It's kinda weird, it's spooky!"

One of the most commonly reported specters in the prison is encountered by staff members and visitors among the older cellblocks. The phantom is always described as being a dark, human-like figure that stands very still and quiet. The figure usually goes unnoticed until the visitor gets too close to it and it darts away.

The sightings never last for long but each person who has encountered the apparition state that it gives off a feeling of anger and malevolence. Could this be a prisoner who has remained behind in protest of the inhumane treatment that he and so many others received in this cruel and brutal place? Perhaps, but it's likely that this spirit does not walk here alone.

Another of the penitentiary's most frequently seen apparitions is a ghost that stands high above the prison walls in a guard tower. It has been assumed for many years that this was the spirit of a former guard who is still standing his post after all these years. One has to wonder why a guard, who was free to leave this place at the end of the day, would choose to remain behind at the prison. Perhaps this is the lingering spirit of Floyd Reynolds, the guard who was thrown to his death by escaping inmates in 1927. Or perhaps it is some other spirit who has no choice but to remain. We can only speculate as to what dark deeds this lonesome man may have been witness to, or perhaps had taken part in, during his years at the prison. Maybe he is now compelled to spend eternity watching over the walls that held so many men prisoner in days gone by.

As intimidating as this may sound, it's the history and the hauntings of the place that continue to bring people back. Many of the staff members, while unsettled by the strange events that sometimes occur are fiercely protective of the place and are determined to see that it is around for many years to come. Even so, they can't help but feel that forces are at work inside the prison. Greta Galuszka added: "So much did happen here that there's the potential for a lot of unfinished business to be hanging around. And I think that's my fear... to stumble upon some of that unfinished business."

2. A CELL DOOR KEY
OHIO STATE REFORMATORY

Looming on the outskirts of the small town of Mansfield, Ohio, is a gloomy, gothic structure that was for many years the Ohio State Reformatory. Designed as a prison for criminals who were too old for the Boys Industrial School in Lancaster and not hardened enough for the Ohio Penitentiary in Columbus, the reformatory saw untold thousands of prisoners during its years of operations. Once applauded as a place that could humanely reform first-time offenders, the conditions deteriorated to the point that it became known more for abuse, torture, and murder than for its early successes.

It's been closed down now since the end of the 1980s, but those who cross the threshold of this place can assure you that the prison is far from empty.

The campaign to build a prison in Mansfield began during the years of the Civil War, but it was not until 1884 that the state legislature actually approved the creation of a prison that would serve as an "intermediate" place of incarceration for Ohio lawbreakers. Using land that had served as one of Mansfield's two Civil War camps, the city raised $10,000 to purchase the land and the state acquired the more than 150 acres that adjoined it. The cornerstone of the prison was placed on November 4, 1886, and marked a day of great celebration in the city. A crowd of more than 15,000 turned out for the event, and it featured a parade that started in Mansfield, which was decorated with flags and bunting, and ended at the new building site. A number of dignitaries were present for the celebration, including former President Rutherford B. Hayes, Senator John Sherman, Governor J.B. Foraker and General Roeliff Brinkerhoff, the man who led the drive to have a prison built in Mansfield. Cleveland architect Levi T. Scofield was hired to design the reformatory, which was expected to cost about $1.3 million to build. According to reports, he based his design on sketches of castles in Germany.

Numerous funding problems in the years that followed caused so many delays that the reformatory was not able to accept its first group of inmates until 1896, a full ten years after work at the site began. The prison officially opened on September 17, when 150 inmates were transferred to the new facility from the Ohio Penitentiary. The transfer drew almost as much attention as the original groundbreaking did. Large crowds turned out in Columbus to watch the inmates, dressed in prison stripes, march from the penitentiary to the train station. The prisoners, entertained by the attention, waved and made jokes to the crowds as they passed. Men along the route even passed out cigars to the inmates as they walked by them. The train was greeted by another large crowd when it stopped in Galion, before continuing on to Mansfield. People in town cheered as the men were unloaded at the northwest corner of the reformatory and were taken directly to their cells. The inmates were immediately set to work. The reformatory was still far from finished and the convicts were used to complete the sewer system and other parts of the structure. Construction was not fully completed until 1910.

Reform, rather than punishment, was the main goal of the Ohio State Reformatory when it was conceived. Education was one of the focal points. Classes were held at the reformatory, and the students were taught the very fundamentals of education with the belief that so many of them had committed crimes because they lacked the basic knowledge needed to live an upstanding life. At one time, there were more than 1,600 men and boys who were students at the reformatory, and they were trained by 16 teachers, learning subjects like math, reading, English, economy, history, and geography. In 1925, Chief Engineer W.P. Close organized classes for drafting and engineering so that inmates could learn a solid skill or trade. In 1928, plumbing, welding, and steam-fitting were added to the curriculum. Other trade classes that were introduced included broom-making, brick-laying, stonecutting, and other activities. Extracurricular activities like music, debate, drama, and sports were also added to boost the young men's confidence and keep them from turning back to a life of crime. The Ohio State Reformatory's goal was to help a man develop his full character. Not every man could be reformed, of course, but all of them would be better prepared for life outside of the reformatory.

The inmates learned the various trades in shops that were scattered about the grounds of the reformatory. The initial work done by the inmates was the sewer construction that was mentioned previously. They also built a 25-foot stone wall behind the main building. As time went on, they were employed at farm work, building roads, and carrying out other improvements for the facility. All of the brick buildings added to the institution, as well as the steel cell blocks, were built by inmate labor. There were also five industries on the site that were involved in printing, making shoes, clothing, furniture, and machines.

The furniture factory opened in 1912 and produced high-quality items that were known for their expert handiwork and beautiful finishes. More than 150 inmates worked there at one time, and in 1931 alone, they produced over 18,000 pieces of furniture. The reformatory's print shop made many state college annuals and catalogs and employed 140 inmates. The machine shop, using at least 75 inmates, made chair clips used in the furniture factory, typewriter desk mechanisms, and steel beds for hospitals and institutions. The shoe factory made various types for men, women, and children with styles that ranged from oxfords to high heels for women and men's waterproof work boots. The clothing factory made regulation uniforms for the inmates, officer uniforms, and clothing for children's homes and orphanages across the state of Ohio. This industry employed about 250 inmates, and the building where it was located housed 85 sewing machines, steam-pressing equipment, and special machines for buttonholes and seams.

Some of the inmates worked at the farm dormitory, which was located between the reformatory and the barns. The farm dormitory was an outside annex to the main prison and usually employed about 250 trustees (prisoners given special privileges because of good behavior) who had duties to be carried out at the poultry farm, dairy, and hog barns. Much of the food for the reformatory was produced there. Although never full self-supporting, this industry grew rapidly and was praised by prison officials. By 1934, the reformatory was able to grow and raise most of the food needed for the inmates.

If an inmate was sick during his time at the reformatory, he visited the prison hospital. It was a 90-bed facility that employed a full staff of doctors, nurses, and other personnel like an anesthetist, several specialists, clerks, cooks, and surgical help. The hospital was three stories high and extended off the east cellblock in a northward direction. The kitchen was located on the first floor, along with a dentist's office, record office, and surgical dispensary room. On the second floor were doctor's offices, storage and drug rooms, an X-ray and surgical room, and more private rooms. On the third floor were private rooms, a large medical ward, baths, a linen area, and a room for highly contagious patients.

The contagious ward was frequently in use. The biggest health threat of the early twentieth century was the same as in many other facilities across the country at the time – tuberculosis. It was highly contagious and until the introduction of medicines that could treat the disease in the 1940s, it killed thousands of people every year. Hardest hit were large facilities where the illness went untreated until it was too late. The tuberculosis ward at the reformatory was large and airy (it was believed at that time that the best "cure" was fresh air) and was often filled with patients. Space there was usually at a premium. The death toll from the illness eventually began to drop after vaccines were developed to treat the disease.

One of the most important processes that the hospital was involved in was the initial exam of new inmates. Each new arrival would be stripped, bathed, deloused, and outfitted in a prison uniform after the exam was completed. Each man was checked for communicable diseases and physical ailments and a chart would be created for him. Blood tests for various diseases, disorders, and sexually transmitted diseases were performed. Any vaccines needed would also be administered at this time.

Large amounts of linens were used in the hospital and throughout the reformatory each week. By the 1930s, 72 inmates worked each day to wash the nearly 75,000 pieces of linen that were used each week.

The main dining room at the reformatory was another area that saw a tremendous amount of weekly activity. It could seat 1,760 prisoners at one time and tables could be cleared within 50 minutes. The baker could turn out 15,000 loaves of bread every day, and 12,000 pounds of butter were churned weekly. The food was plain, but it was substantial.

The men were fed well, cared for physically, and their needs were met spiritually, too. When a man entered the reformatory, his religious preference was noted and he was informed when church services were held for his faith. Each new inmate was presented with a book on the rules of conduct by the chaplain on staff. He was not only the spiritual advisor to the inmates, but he also wrote for and supervised the reformatory's newspaper, the *New Day*.

The reformatory had its own cemetery on the grounds. The more than 200 numbered headstones remain in place today. Many died of old age, disease, or worse. The cemetery also includes the graves of those who died from unnatural causes like murder and suicide, and those whose bodies went unclaimed by family after their demise.

Life at the reformatory changed over the years, mostly according to the type of inmate that it housed. The original purpose of the reformatory was to teach, enlighten, and reform young male prisoners so that they could be returned to society as hardworking, honest individuals who had been swayed toward the right side of the law. Unfortunately, this philosophy changed as the years passed by and more and more hardened criminals found themselves behind the reformatory's stone walls. For the first 50 years of its existence, the reformatory was praised as one of the best institutions of its kind in America. This changed by 1933, when overcrowding became an issue and conditions started to decline. This peaked in the 1970s with a legal case that cited the reformatory's "brutal and inhumane conditions." The early dreams of reform became a nightmare, and by 1990, the prison was closed for good.

But, of course, that would not be the end of the story.

Escapes, Suicides and Murders

Because the reformatory was an intermediate prison, designed for young offenders, it had few famous inmates during its history. At least one of them went on to great notoriety, however, proving that reform was not always possible with some offenders. The most famous former inmate was Henry Baker, one of the men convicted of pulling off the Brink's heist in 1950.

The Brink's robbery was one of the carefully executed, masterful jobs of the twentieth century. The robbery was planned over a two-year period as 11 middle-aged men from Boston worked out every detail imaginable to steal a fortune from the Brink's North Terminal Garage. They entered the garage at night and walked about in their stocking feet, measuring distances and locating and checking doors, all under the noses of unsuspecting guards. On one occasion, they even removed all of the locks from the doors, fitted keys to them, and replaced the locks. They even went so far as to break into a burglar alarm company in order to take a closer look at the alarm system used by Brink's. The robbery was carried out on January 17, 1950, and the bandits entered the garage wearing Brink's uniforms, rubber Halloween masks and rubber-soled shoes. They made their way to the counting room and relieved five very surprised employees of $2.7 million in cash, checks and securities. In less than 15 minutes, they had vanished.

The plan was to keep a low profile for six years, until the statute of limitations ran out, but one of the bandits, Joseph "Specs" O'Keefe, felt that he had not received his fair share and demanded more. The others refused and then started to worry that he might turn into an informant, so they hired a professional hitman, Elmer "Trigger" Burke, to take him out. Burke missed his first opportunity and ended up chasing O'Keefe through the streets of Boston, firing at him with a machine gun. O'Keefe was wounded in the arm and chest, but escaped before Burke could finish him off. Burke was soon arrested and O'Keefe, taking offense over the fact that his friends had tried to have him killed, started talking to the law. Thanks to O'Keefe, eight of the robbers, including former Ohio State Reformatory inmate Henry Baker, were convicted and received life sentences.

Some of the inmates at Mansfield didn't just commit crimes to get into prison, or after they got out. Some of them actually carried on criminal operations while they were still incarcerated. On August 21, 1921, two reformatory inmates, King Williams, age 18, and John Kmetz, age 17, were charged with carrying on a counterfeiting operation while behind bars. The plot came to the attention of the U.S. Secret Service from the superintendent of the reformatory, who acted on a tip from a trustee. The two young men had apparently been creating counterfeit bills and passing them to reformatory guards, who circulated them throughout the area. Assistant Superintendent Rowe had actually caught Williams in the act of putting the finishing touches on a bogus $5 bill. Williams and Kmetz were paroled in late 1921 and were immediately re-arrested by federal authorities, who charged them with counterfeiting.

But darker crimes have occurred in the history of the reformatory, as well. Two corrections officers have been murdered in the line of duty at the Ohio State Reformatory. On November 2, 1926, a paroled inmate named Phillip Orleck returned to the prison to try and help a friend escape. Early that morning, he encountered a guard named Urban Wilford in the guard tower and shot and killed him. Orleck fled before his escape attempt could fail, but was apprehended two months later. He met his end in the electric chair at the Ohio State Penitentiary the following year.

The second officer was Frank Hanger, who died after being beaten with an iron bar. Hanger tried to stop an escape attempt by a dozen prisoners in October 1932 and paid for it with his life. Two inmates, Merrill Chandler and Chester Probaski, were charged with the guard's murder and were sent to the electric chair in 1935.

Several attempts – both failed and unsuccessful – occurred during the reformatory's history. One inmate who worked in the shoe factory convinced his fellow inmates to nail him inside of a large wooden crate of shoes that was being shipped out by truck. No one searched the crate as it left the reformatory, and as the truck started down the highway toward Columbus, it seemed as though the escape was going to be successful. But that success turned out to be short-lived. The truck's destination was the Ohio State Penitentiary, where the inmate was quickly apprehended and traded a cell in one institution for a cell in another.

But most escapes were not so humorous, such as the one that occurred in 1936. After overpowering and beating a guard with an iron bar, five inmates attempted a daring escape on Friday, July 17. Guard A.H. Morris was making his rounds of E Dormitory around 10:00 p.m. when he was assaulted by four of the five prisoners involved in the escape attempt. Morris was restrained while the fifth inmate beat him over the head with the bar and then grabbed his keys. Leaving Morris unconscious on the floor, they used his keys to begin moving through the facility. Four prisoners fled the dormitory and ran toward the main building, while the fifth man ran toward the highway east of the reformatory's grounds. Within minutes, the four men were spotted and a volley of warning shots from the guards on duty quickly convinced them to surrender. The fifth man vanished into the darkness that night and, according to records, was never recaptured. Reformatory officials refused comment when asked the name of the prisoner's involved in the escape.

And this was not the first escape to occur at the Ohio State Reformatory. In November 1902, an inmate named John Gagnon escaped from the reformatory. After slipping out of the facility, he made his way into nearby Mansfield and snuck into Engine House #2 of the fire department. After bumping into several firemen – while wearing his conspicuous gray prison uniform – they started to chase him, until they realized that he might he armed. They called the reformatory and the police department instead and soon a chase took place through an area of warehouses and industrial factories on the edge of town. Gagnon's uniform was found discarded in a hobo camp, where he had switched clothes with someone and vanished. Trains were stopped and searched and reports were sent out on the telegraph wire, but it was all to no avail. John Gagnon escaped that night and was never seen again.

In May 1907, a prisoner managed to escape before he even officially arrived at the reformatory. Rudolph Kervinak, 18, had been convicted of grand larceny and was sentenced to do time at the reformatory. While traveling via train with escort Sheriff Robert Wells, the young convict escaped from the Pennsylvania Railroad passenger car by jumping from the train car window. Sheriff Wells secured a horse and buggy and began searching for the escaping prisoner, alerting locals as he flew through the countryside. After arriving in Lucas, Ohio, he questioned townspeople and railroad employees. One railroad operator recalled seeing a man of Kervinak's description in a nearby cemetery. When officers searched the burial ground, they found Kervinak asleep in a fenced corner with his swollen and bruised wrists still handcuffed together. He had been injured when he jumped from the train and landed on his hands and arms. Sheriff Wells shook him awake and placed him back into custody. The interrupted trip to Mansfield was completed that day, but Wells stayed very close to his prisoner during the remainder of the journey.

One of the most daring escapes occurred in 1910. On the night of Tuesday, September 27, three prisoners – Joseph Sterns, George Wilson, and John McDonnell -- cut their way through a steel bar to freedom. They sawed their way through a cell bar with a sharpened piece of metal bar that Sterns had smuggled out of the machine shop on the reformatory grounds. After being transferred from the machine shop to the laundry, Sterns went to work on the window bars in the laundry room restroom, which was rarely used. Following a carefully orchestrated plan, McDonnell received a pass to the hospital for the treatment of jaw pain that he had been experiencing at the same time that Wilson was "injured" in the blacksmith shop and had to visit the hospital to be patched up. The trio met up and ventured into the bathroom laundry. The window bar was removed and all three of them managed to wriggle through the opening. They dropped about 20 feet to the ground and made their way along the outside of the east wing. As they made their way across the property, their route took them right in front of the main building, but amazingly, no one saw them. They gained their freedom but were spotted by a crew member from one of the city streetcars that ran past the reformatory – who didn't report it until later. No one even realized the three men were missing until a guard in the blacksmith shop began to think that Wilson's "hospital visit" had lasted a very long time. After it was discovered that he was missing, the search was started, which resulted in a head count that revealed that Sterns and McDonnell were also gone. The alarm was sounded and the manhunt began, spreading to Mansfield and neighboring towns. It went on for more than a month and only one of the men was ever found. John McDonnell was captured in Buffalo, New York on October 25, but he escaped a short time later. His method? He sawed through the metal bars and slipped out into the night.

Inmate William Moore escaped from the reformatory on New Year's Day, 1953. Facing between one and 20 years for drug possession charges, he managed to slip past his captors after serving 22 years behind bars – apparently feeling like he had done all of his time. He walked off the prison grounds and was never heard from again.

On September 30, 1959, Frank Freshwater escaped after being sentenced on voluntary manslaughter charges. He was never apprehended and, technically, both he and William Moore are still wanted by the Ohio Department of Corrections.

Perhaps the darkest days in the history of the Ohio State Reformatory came with the parole of two inmates, Robert Daniels and John West – who would forever be immortalized in newspapers as the "Mad Dog Killers." In the summer of 1948, just days after being released from prison, the two young men went on a killing spree that ended with seven people dead, including a guard at the reformatory and his wife and daughter. They started the spree by killing a Columbus tavern owner named Earl Ambrose on July 10, followed by Frank Frech, an elderly tourist camp operator on July 11. After that, they drove straight to Mansfield and the Ohio State Reformatory. Robert Daniels, interviewed after he was captured stated that they had gone to the prison looking for a guard named "Red" Harris, but when they didn't find him, they went to the home of another guard, John Niebel. Daniels told authorities: "We planned the Niebel business three or four months ago. We planned to beat the hell out of him. While I was in OSR, Niebel treated me like a rat. At one time, Niebel slugged me. If they had given us just a little longer we'd have wiped them all out – all those sonsabitches at the reformatory."

Daniels and West arrived at the Niebel home around 1:30 a.m. and knocked on the door. When Niebel answered, they told him that their car had broken down and they wanted to use the telephone. He let them inside, but did not recognize the two men at first. It was not until Daniels pulled out a gun that Niebel realized the horror that he had allowed into his home. While West held a gun on Niebel, Daniels went upstairs forced Mrs. Nolana Niebel, and her 20-year-old daughter, Phyllis, to come downstairs. The family was forced into a light-gray automobile and was driven by Daniels and West through Mansfield, around Central Park, and then out of town to Flemings Falls Road. As they traveled, Daniels forced the Niebels to take off all of their clothes and throw them out the window.

Finally, the car was stopped and the family was forced out into the lonely cornfield that would become their death site. Daniels marched them through the knee-high corn and then, forcing them to stand in a line next to one another, shot each of them in the head with an old Mauser automatic. Daniels later reported, "I lined them up in the cornfield. I shot Niebel first, then I shot the girl, then I shot Mrs. Niebel. I never shoot people in the back, it's against my principles."

Daniels and West fled the scene and abandoned the car they were driving. A few hours later, they were captured when they attempted to shoot it out with police and sheriff's deputies at a roadblock north of Van Wert. The blockade was set up as part of what became one of the greatest manhunts in the state's history. The newspapers called the killing spree a "13-Day Reign of Terror." The killers claimed their last two victims just before they were caught, driving a stolen truck that was being used to haul four brand-new automobiles. James J. Smith, a newlywed farmer from Tiffin, was shot through the head when he refused to give up his driver's license. Less than an hour later, the body of another man, Orville Taylor, a truck driver from Niles, Michigan, was found in a roadside park near Tiffin. Taylor was believed to be the driver of the truck that the killers were driving when they were stopped. Shots were exchanged at the roadblock and Daniels and West managed to wound a Van Wert policeman named Leonard Conn and Frank Fremont, a conservation division employee, during the gunfight. It ended with West being shot dead and Daniels being taken into custody.

While in jail, Daniels bragged about his exploits, and when he was brought outside to pose for news photographers, an angry mob gathered and demanded that he be turned over to them to be hanged. Officials managed to get him safely back indoors, but not before Daniels cursed the police, the photographers, and the crowd. He was later tried and convicted for the murders and took a well-deserved seat in the Ohio State Penitentiary electric chair in January 1949.

If the inmates at the Ohio State Reformatory were not killing guards, they were killing each other – or themselves. In 1955, a guard discovered the body of an inmate who had hanged himself in his cell. A few years later, another inmate poured a can of turpentine over himself and lit a match, setting his clothing on fire. After a prison riot occurred at the reformatory in 1957, 120 prisoners were confined to a solitary confinement area known as "the hole." This was a dank, pitch-dark place of confinement where it was rumored that several inmates had gone insane. Because there were only 20 rooms in the hole, many of the men had to be locked into the solitary cells together for 30 days. During this time, at least one prisoner was alleged to have been murdered, his body hidden by another inmate under some bedding for several days.

Some blamed the condition of the prison on the mental state of some of the inmates. By the early part of the 1930s, the reformatory was already being criticized for being overcrowded and offering inhumane living quarters for the prisoners. As the years went by, the facility deteriorated even more. In the 1970s, the state declared that the Ohio State Reformatory no longer met the standards and guidelines for correctional institutes. Public outcry about the state of the prison was led by the Counsel for Human Dignity, a coalition of civic and church groups. In 1978, they filed a federal lawsuit on behalf of the 2,200 inmates at the reformatory, claiming that the prisoners' Constitutional rights were being violated because they were forced to live in "brutalizing and inhumane conditions." The lawsuit was finally resolved in 1983 with the filing of a consent decree in which prison officials agreed to improve conditions while preparing to close the cellblocks by December 31, 1986. The closing date ended up being extended for a few years, but by 1990, the reformatory was closed for good.

During the final years of the prison, the only people who seemed to appreciate the crumbling prison were Hollywood moviemakers. While the reformatory was still in operation, two movies – *Harry and Walter Go to New York* in 1975 and *Tango and Cash* in 1989 – used the prison for some scenes. However, it was not until 1994, when the film crew for *The Shawshank Redemption* arrived, that film crews began to realize that the Ohio State Reformatory was the perfect setting for prison films. The facility was widely featured in the film with more than 30 scenes shot in the prison or on the grounds. Several years later, scenes from *Air Force One* were also filmed at the reformatory. In recent years, there have also been a number of music videos produced at the prison, as well.

The reformatory continued to decline for a time after it closed but then, in an effort to save the place, the Mansfield Reformatory Preservation Society (MRPS) was formed. Today, steps are under way to restore the remaining structure to its original condition. The building was added to the National Register of Historic Places and the reformatory's six-tier east wing is listed in the *Guinness Book of World Records* as the world's largest free-standing steel cellblock. The MRPS continues its work today by offering guided tours and numerous events, and they have received several awards for their efforts to save this piece of Ohio history.

Hauntings at the Ohio State Reformatory
Since the closing of the reformatory in 1990, stories have circulated that the prison is haunted by the tormented spirits of former inmates, guards, and prison officials who have simply never left. According to the legends, they are trapped here behind these decaying stone walls and rusted iron bars by the violent and painful events of their individual pasts. The horror and death of years past seems to be replaying itself behind the gates of the Ohio State Reformatory. Visitors who come here today become quickly aware that the cellblocks and corridors of the prison are not as empty and silent as they first appear to be.

As recounted in the introduction to this book, I have had my own experiences at the Ohio State Reformatory. I have visited the place – and spent entire nights inside of its walls – on more than a dozen occasions, and I have truly come to believe that the place is haunted. My encounter in the former library was just one event that convinced me of this and there have been others that were just as unnerving. And I'm far from the only person to interact with the spirits of this place.

The hospital's infirmary is an area of the prison where strange experiences often occur. It was there that inmates were treated for influenza, tuberculosis, and a legion of other ailments and diseases caused by the poor conditions that plagued the prisoners. A number of men died of these illnesses during the years of the reformatory's operation and some believe their ghosts may linger at the last place where they suffered during their lifetimes. It has often been reported that video cameras, recorders, and electronic equipment behave erratically in this area and that shadows are often seen, moving about in the dim light. It is a part of the prison where few want to venture alone.

The prison's chapel is located just above the infirmary and it has its own tales of ghosts and hauntings. The most commonly reported incidents there seem to involve a man who has been seen peeking around the doors and peering into the room. He always ducks away when someone notices him. At first, visitors believe this is a real person, or someone from their own group, hoping to play on trick on them. But when they check the other side of the door, they discover that no one is there.

The prison's cellblocks have their own dark stories to tell. It was in these cells where the inmates lived, suffered, and sometimes died. Prisoners committed suicide, mutilated themselves, and committed horrific acts on one another. Beatings, stabbings, and rapes were not uncommon, and a brutal attack might be visited on another inmate for something as trivial as looking at someone the wrong way. Life in the reformatory could be agony, filled with hate, violence and insanity. Many of these men carried these emotions with them to the grave and their spirits, trapped within these walls, are still manifesting these feelings in death. The doors to the cellblocks may be standing open these days, but the spirits of the men who were once locked behind them remain imprisoned behind the rusted bars.

The lowest levels of the reformatory are perhaps the most frightening to visitors who come to the reformatory today. The basement is a maze of dark, twisting hallways and rumors persist that inmates were sometimes brought here to be beaten and tortured by guards. A number of people claim to have seen the ghost of a young inmate, allegedly beaten to death, wandering the dark hallways of the basement. The boy always vanishes, or runs away, after he is noticed.

But perhaps the most sinister location in the old prison is the infamous "Hole." There is no record of just how many prisoners were subjected to the terrifying conditions of this part of the prison, where they were jailed in total darkness and forced to sleep on bare, concrete floors – or how many of them may have been left behind as restless spirits. The "Hole" is a place that saw the darkest side of human nature and the most violent acts carried out within the reformatory's walls. One does not need to have any psychic abilities to feel the intense energies of this area. Those who visit the "Hole" say they feel goosebumps, cold chills and, on many occasions, become violently sick to their stomachs. Is it merely their imagination, sent into an overactive state because of the dark stories that are told about this place?

Perhaps, but if so, how do we explain the strange cries that have been recorded in these cells, the tapping footsteps, and the unshakeable feeling of being watched? The history that has been imprinted on the stone walls of this dank part of the prison seems to be making its presence known to a great many people who dare to come to this spot.

One of the most tragic events to occur during the reformatory's history – and which has left a haunting presence behind -- took place on November 5, 1950, in the administration wing of the prison. One section of this wing contained the home and offices of Warden Arthur L. Glattke, his wife, Helen, and their sons, Arthur, Jr. and Teddy. Warden Glattke was one of the most respected officials in the reformatory's history. By all accounts, Glattke was well liked by guards and prisoners alike. He instituted a series of reforms and was credited with piping radio music into the cells of the inmates.

On November 5, a Sunday morning, Mrs. Glattke was in her bedroom alone and was getting dressed to go out. It was believed that she reached up into a high shelf in her closet, trying to get her jewelry box, and moved a .32-caliber pistol out of her way. The gun had been placed in the residence for the family's protection. Dr. P.A. Stoodt, the attending physician, believed that Helen may have dropped the pistol and as it slipped out of her hands and hit the floor, it went off. The bullet struck her in the chest and penetrated her left lung.

When Warden Glattke heard the shot, he ran to the bedroom and discovered Helen bleeding on the floor. He summoned the reformatory physician, Dr. J.V. Horst, who, unable to treat her on site, had Mrs. Glattke rushed to the General Hospital. She never regained consciousness and died during the early morning hours of Tuesday, November 7. While rumors have swirled that there may have been more to her death than was originally reported, this does not seem to be the case. The death of Helen Glattke was a tragic, horrible accident that separated two young boys from their beloved mother. This may be the reason that her ghost is believed to linger behind in the administration wing.

Tragically, just nine years after Helen's death, Arthur Glattke died of a heart attack in his office, just steps away from where his wife died in 1950. It is believed that the ghosts of both Mr. and Mrs. Glattke haunt the reformatory. At certain times, visitors have reported feeling cold rushes of air in the administration wing and equipment failures are also common in the still-preserved rooms. The "pink bathroom" located in this wing is a spot where the ghost of Helen Glattke is said to most often make her presence known through the smell of perfume and the scent of fresh flowers.

Whichever of the Glattkes – if their ghosts truly linger – remain behind in their old apartment, I've seen first-hand how they can occasionally make their presence known. One night in 2012, I was spending the night at the Ohio State Reformatory with my friends, Chris and Angela Settles, and a group of other ghost researchers. While we were quietly exploring the administration building's apartment, we were disturbed by a distinctive metal clicking sound, which echoed loudly in the empty room that we were standing in – the same room where Mrs. Glattke had been shot when the pistol fell from the high closet shelf.

All three of us searched the room, listening closely, and trying to discover the source of the metallic sound. We found it at a window, just a few steps away from the leaning closet door. The wooden window frame had a metal lock on the top of the lower frame. By twisting it counter-clockwise, the window could be locked, which would make it impossible to be raised. As we stood there watching, all three of us saw that metal lock, turning rapidly back and forth, locking and unlocking – even though no one was touching it at the time. The lock twisted back and forth, twisting and turning over and over, for nearly a minute before it stopped in front of our startled eyes.

Whatever had been in that room that night, it certainly wanted to get our attention.

The Ohio State Reformatory can be a physically and mentally exhausting place. There are seemingly miles of rooms, offices, corridors and cell blocks to be explored and it's not a place for the faint of heart. Unexplained occurrences continued to this day and give evidence to the fact that sometimes escape simply isn't possible – even after death.

3. A WOODEN GUN
THE LAKE COUNTY, INDIANA JAIL

It's a jail made famous by the escape of one of the most legendary bank robbers of all time, but John Dillinger was far from the only bad man that called this place his temporary "home." The deputies of the Lake County, Indiana sheriff's department locked up rapists, killers, thieves, and psychopaths behind the steel bars and brick walls of the old jail – and some of them left a bit of themselves behind within this crumbling edifice of punishment.

In 1840, Crown Point was established as the county seat of Lake County, Indiana. A frame courthouse was built on Clark Street in 1849, containing a courtroom, jury room, and a sheriff's office. In 1851, a small, wooden jail was added to the structure. It was made from heavy wooden beams, cross-planked for security, and divided into cells by sheets of iron. As the county and town developed over the next three decades, a new brick and stone courthouse was erected at the intersection of Main and Joliet Streets in 1878. Due to a state law that required the sheriff to make his residence adjoining the jail, the first permanent structure of this type was built in 1882 at its present location, 226 South Main Street, at a cost of $24,000. The jail measured 36 by 48 feet and contained six steel cells for males, four for females, and strong steel corridors.

As the local population grew, a larger jail was needed. Around 1908, this jail was replaced with a larger structure, and in 1928, another addition was made that extended the length of the jail through the block to East Street. The combined residence and jail included all the facilities necessary for its purpose as a law enforcement institution. Located within the walls were the family's living area, warden's residence, department offices, 150 cells, maximum security accommodations, institutional kitchen, food storage, heating and cooling systems, barber shop, and a garage.

The jail in Crown Point was considered to be one of the finest in Indiana and thought to be escape-proof – a myth that John Dillinger proved was untrue on March 3, 1934 when he made a daring escape from the facility.

In the early 1930s, during the height of the Great Depression, John Dillinger was one of the most famous men in America. During this era of national poverty, many ordinary Americans saw bandits like Dillinger, Bonnie and Clyde, "Pretty Boy" Floyd, and others as folk heroes, getting revenge on the banks and government institutions that had brought the country to its knees. Stories made the rounds that some of these bank robbers stole from the rich and gave some of the money to the people who really needed it. And in the early 1930s, a lot of people really needed it.

Dillinger and his gang had wreaked havoc across the Midwest, robbing, shooting up towns, and emptying bank vaults of whatever cash they could find inside of them. Dillinger, an Indiana boy, rarely made too much trouble in his home state, and what finally got him locked up in Crown Point was likely for something he didn't do. Dillinger, his girlfriend, Billie Frechette, and several members of his gang spent part of the winter in Florida, playing cards, fishing, and listening to the radio. Bored, they soon packed up and traveled to Arizona. Between the time the gang left Dayton Beach and arrived in Tucson, the First National Bank of East Chicago, Indiana, was robbed by two unknown men. During the robbery, a policeman named Patrick O'Malley was machine-gunned to death. Dillinger and his friend, John Hamilton, were accused of the crime and Dillinger was said to have been the policeman's killer -- but he always denied it. He wasn't even in the state at the time.

The trip to Tucson turned out to be a disaster. Two of Dillinger's pals were arrested there after a fire broke out in their hotel. They paid a fireman hundreds of dollars to rescue their suitcases, but he became suspicious when he noticed one of the suitcases was extremely heavy. He opened it to find a machine gun and several pistols. Dillinger was soon identified and was extradited to Indiana to stand trial for the East Chicago robbery -- the one robbery that he probably didn't commit. Dillinger was to be jailed in Crown Point, Indiana, in the Lake County Jail, which was said to be "escape proof."

There were about 500 spectators on hand when Dillinger entered the jail. Armed citizens patrolled the grounds of the jail; ready and waiting in case any of Dillinger's friends decided to break him out. But all of Dillinger's friends were also in jail, so he would be breaking out on his own.

A festive atmosphere developed inside of the jail as a huge throng of reporters and lawmen drank beer and chatted with the friendly and talkative bank robber. Among those in the crowd were Lake County Prosecutor Robert Estill and Sheriff Lillian Holley, the widow of the former sheriff (who had been killed by a drunken farmer) and who was in charge of the Crown Point Jail. Dillinger, who told the reporters that he was innocent of the murder charges, said that he liked Estill and added, "Mrs. Holley seems like a fine lady." When the newspapers published photographs of Prosecutor Estill with his arm around Dillinger, who had his fingers cocked in the shape of a gun, there was national outrage and Estill's political career was ruined.

Dillinger was locked up in his new home, which was supposedly so "escape proof" – inmates had to pass through six steel doors – that it was thought that only master magician Harry Houdini might be able to make a successful breakout. With dozens of men with shotguns and machine guns surrounding the building, there seemed to be no way that even Dillinger could get out.

On February 8, Dillinger was identified by five men as the killer of Officer O'Malley. Again, this was an impossible robbery for Dillinger to have carried out, but they were convinced that he was the killer. The following day, he was arraigned in the courtroom of Judge William J. Murray. If he was convicted, Dillinger would receive a death sentence. Although his father had hired a lawyer for his defense, Dillinger chose another – flamboyant Louis Piquett, who was famous for his dramatic courtroom performances in which he dazzled the jury with emotional and melodramatic speeches. Piquett, who had not attended law school but had taught himself while working as a waiter and bartender, had to take the Illinois bar exam a dozen times before he passed it. He became the city prosecutor of Chicago and then a defense attorney.

Dillinger was quiet and well-behaved while in jail. He was placed in a cell with three other prisoners and played cards and read magazines and books. He was not given any newspapers. He was, however, allowed to write and receive mail from his father and sister. Several visitors were allowed to see him, including Billie Frechette; Piquett and two other attorneys from his office; and a few local friends.

More than anything, though, Dillinger thought about how he was going to escape. Estill attempted to have the prisoner moved to a more secure location, such as the state prison in Michigan City, but Judge Murray rejected the idea because he thought it would make the local officials look weak. Dillinger devised a plan whereby his gang, headed by John Hamilton, would dynamite the jail and set him free. He asked Billie to be his go-between, but when she returned, she said that Hamilton had rejected the idea. Most of the gang members were also in jail, and those who were not knew it would be suicide to attempt a breakout of the heavily fortified jail. Dillinger realized he would have to do it himself.

Through Piquett, Dillinger managed to bribe one of the jail officers (most accounts implicate Deputy Sheriff Ernest Blunk) to smuggle a wooden gun into the facility, and Edwin J. Saager, a garage mechanic, was to provide a fast car for the escape. By bringing a fake gun into the jail, a cover story could be devised that Dillinger had gotten a razor from a piece of wood, which he then darkened with shoe polish to make it look authentic.

With the bribes distributed, the breakout was originally planned for Friday, March 2. However, Piquett had not yet tracked down a wooden gun. It showed up at the office around noon that day and someone subsequently passed it to Blunk. Early on the chilly, gloomy morning of March 3, Blunk gave the wooden gun to Dillinger, who then began looking for his chance to get out of the "escape proof" jail.

Just after 9:00 a.m., attendant Sam Cahoon, carrying soup, and some trustees entered the lower tier of cells at the Crown Point jail as Dillinger and 14 other prisoners were exercising nearby. As the group passed by Dillinger, the bank robber thrust the wooden gun into Cahoon's side and took him hostage. Using Deputy Sheriff Blunk to summon Warden Lou Baker and several guards, Dillinger locked them in cells. Herbert Youngblood, a black man jailed while awaiting trial for murder, agreed to go with Dillinger. As they left the cell tier, they encountered trustee John Kowaliszyn, who offered no resistance and was taken prisoner.

After Dillinger took a full set of keys from the trustee, he, Youngblood, and Blunk entered the jail office, where guns and ammunition were stored. Dillinger walked up to a guard that was dozing in his chair with his back to the door, and put the wooden gun up to his head. With his other hand, he lifted a machine gun from a nearby rack, warning the now startled guard that if he moved a muscle, he'd "blow your head off your shoulders."

Dillinger told Youngblood to grab the machine gun that was in the guard's lap and doubled their fire power. With Youngblood, trailing behind, he swept through the first floor of the jail and released the prisoners, forcing them to march in front of him. When they encountered an Indiana National Guardsman on duty, he was relieved of his .45-caliber pistol. With too many hostages to handle, he sent the prisoners back to the cellblock. He, Youngblood, and Blunk went into the kitchen, where three more guards, the warden's wife, and her mother, Mary Linton, were taken prisoner. Dillinger put on a hat and overcoat that was hanging on the wall and took his captives back to the cellblock, after assuring the women that he wouldn't hurt them.

The women were locked in the basement laundry, and the guards were taken to the cellblock where Dillinger had left his other captives. A search of the jail turned up another five guards, who were locked in with the others. Dillinger, Youngblood, and Blunk went into the jail garage, where there were two cars, but the keys were missing. They went back inside and Dillinger went through the warden's desk and then returned to the cell where he had locked up the guards. He told them that he needed some money for his escape and took up a collection of $15. He then laughed and rapped the wooden gun on the cell doors so that they could see what he had used to escape. He told Warden Baker, "I'm sorry to have to do this to you, Mr. Baker. But you can see how it is."

The warden sighed. "Yes, John, I can see how it is."

After Dillinger locked several doors behind him, he, Youngblood, Blunk, and three trustees who had joined the group walked through the kitchen door and into a side yard. Dillinger and Youngblood, each still armed with machine guns, led the group through the yard and entered the back door of the Main Street Garage. No guards were around. They had apparently all been stationed in front of the jail, and yet, did not hear the clamor of more than 30 jail employees yelling from the windows to be let out.

On an interesting note, the sister of the garage's owner, Clyde Rothermel, was married to the brother of Dillinger pal John Hamilton. Rothermel knew there was going to be an escape attempt, but he wanted nothing to do with it, since he would be an obvious suspect, so he stayed home. Oddly, no one seriously investigated him in the wake of the escape. Mechanic Edwin Saager and Robert Volk, a mail truck driver, were the only people inside of the garage. Although Volk had a pistol, he offered no resistance when Dillinger walked in and demanded the fastest car in the garage.

Saager showed him to Sheriff Holley's Ford, which was gassed up and ready to go. Dillinger allowed the trustees to return to the jail, while he got into the car's passenger seat and forced Blunk to driver. Youngblood and Saager climbed into the back. Holding a machine gun across his lap, Dillinger ordered Blunk to drive out of the garage. He laughed, "Maybe I ought to go back and tell Mrs. Holley I'm leaving. She seemed like an awfully nice lady, and I don't want her to feel hurt about all this."

As the car sped away from the jail, Blunk came close to hitting a passing motorist and drove through a red light. He was moving so fast that Dillinger later said that he was tempted to rob the local bank with the officer as his getaway driver.

Meanwhile, mail truck driver Edwin Volk immediately called the police, then ran out of the garage and yelled at a volunteer guard who was stationed across the street, telling him what had happened. He was met with skepticism. He then hurried next door to the prosecutor's office, where numerous guards had been stationed to prevent a raid on the jail. Once again, no one believed him. But Volk was insistent and so several of the volunteers went next door and tried to get into the jail. The doors were all locked. It took more than 10 minutes for them to get inside and free the imprisoned jail employees. Sheriff Holley was first told of the escape by John Hudak, a trustee, and immediately notified the state police. She thought the escape was "too ridiculous for words." She couldn't believe that it could happen. The sheriff denied a report that she had a job that was too big for a woman. "Oh, hell's fire, of course not," she scoffed, adding, "If I ever see John Dillinger again, I'll shoot him dead with my own pistol."

As the escapees left Crown Point behind, Dillinger worried about roadblocks and sent Blunk off onto gravel roads. He had him stop once to remove the red light from the front of the sheriff's car, and instructed him to keep his speed down to thirty miles an hour so they wouldn't attract attention. Dillinger sang as they drove along muddy back roads. Along one muddy track about two miles from Peotone, Illinois, the car skidded into a ditch filled with water. It took Saager half an hour to put chains on the rear wheels so that the vehicle could get out of the ditch.

Once he was finished, Dillinger set his two captives free, giving them $4 for food and carfare. Dillinger apologized and told them that he would have given them more if he had it.

Suspecting that a white man and a black man traveling together would draw too much notice, Dillinger told Youngblood to hunker down in the back seat. Then, waving at the two men he'd left on the side of the road, he drove off toward Chicago.

A farmer later picked up Saager and Blunk and took them back into town, where they explained what had happened and called Sheriff Holley. Blunk later said, "I was never scared of Dillinger. I knew he wouldn't hurt me. He was too nice for that."

Since there was no extensive radio system that could quickly alert police throughout the region about the escape, Dillinger and Youngblood reached Chicago without incident. It didn't hurt that the authorities in Crown Point had given out the wrong license number for the sheriff's stolen car. The police were slow to find out what had happened. In fact, officials in Indianapolis learned about the escape from local newspapers.

Dillinger's lawyer, Louis Piquett, learned of the escape from a telephone call that morning, while Billie Frechette was in his office. That afternoon, Piquett met Dillinger and Youngblood for a few minutes on Belmont Avenue, after which Youngblood went off on his own. That evening, the attorney met Dillinger again, who was now with Billie and another woman, on Halsted Street, just a block away from the Town Hall police station. Naturally, Piquett assured the authorities that he tried to convince Dillinger to turn himself in. The bank robber assured him that he "would do it later."

Sherriff Holley's car was found abandoned on Chicago's North Side on March 5.

The newspapers were all about Dillinger in the days after the escape. Acting Police Commissioner Ira McDowell warned that, "If Dillinger sticks his head inside Chicago, he will be shot at first sight. Those are my orders."

Dillinger came and went many times from Chicago, but eventually, the law caught up with him – or so the official records say. In July 1934, just a few months after the escape, Dillinger was shot to death outside of the Biograph Theater on the city's North Side. Or at least that's what the FBI has always claimed. There are many who believe that it was not Dillinger who died on that hot July night, but that's a story for another time.

Suffice it to say, the escape of John Dillinger – using only a wooden gun – gave the Lake County Jail in Crown Point a notorious place in the annals of American crime. But Dillinger was not the only famous prisoner to spend time at the jail.

And he was definitely not the most depraved or bloodthirsty.

The Most Dangerous Man in Chicago

Perhaps the most psychotic prisoner to ever be locked up at the jail in Crown Point was James "Fur" Sammons, a killer who wreaked havoc in Chicago's gangland and a man so dangerous that even other criminals were afraid of him. He was a career criminal and became a "resident" of the old Lake County Jail in

November 1933, until he was convicted on bribery charges. As a career criminal, he drew a life sentence. That might have been Sammons' last arrest, but it was far from his first.

His record was long and varied. In 1900, at the age of just 16, he and four others kidnapped an eight-year-old schoolgirl, raped her, beat her, broke her nose, punched out one of her eyes, and stabbed her in the vagina with a pencil. Sammons, who showed no remorse over the attack, smirked at the girl's parents in court. He was given five years for his part in the crime and was paroled two years later. Two months after his release, Sammons was arrested for the murder of Patrick Barret, a saloon keeper. He was convicted and sentenced to be hanged. He was put into solitary confinement where it was said he was driven insane by the solitude. He remained on death row until June 1917, when he managed to escape and commit a series of robberies before being recaptured in October. Sammons received a new sentence of 50 years.

On July 28, 1923, though, Sammons was paroled by the infamously corrupt Illinois Governor Len Small, a longtime friend of gangsters. Sammons went right back to his old habits. In March 1926, he was the leader of a gang that stole the International Harvester Company payroll, netting more than $80,000. He was arrested for the crime, but release for lack of evidence. Soon after, he was arrested for carrying a revolver after a police chase in Lyons, Illinois, but was released on bond.

Around this same time, Sammons hired out as a gunman for the O'Donnell gang, which operated on the West Side of Chicago. Earlier in the summer, the Capone mob had accidentally murdered State's Attorney William H. McSwiggin, forcing Capone to lay low for a while. An attack on the O'Donnells had killed gunmen James Doughtery and Red Duffy, but also took the life of their drinking buddy, McSwiggin. The murder of a couple of hoods might now draw much in the way of public condemnation – their corpses were mere footnotes in the list of 64 other dead gangsters that year – but a dead public official was different. When the O'Donnells thought they had a chance to move against Capone's western interests, Capone retaliated with a machine gun attack on Sammons. Unfortunately, his gunmen missed.

In the winter and spring of 1927, Capone's holdings increased without much bloodshed. Sammons and Klondike O'Donnell were arrested on charges of siphoning whiskey from a government bonded warehouse. The charges stuck and both men pleaded guilty. Sammons was sentenced to 18 months in Leavenworth. He didn't return to Chicago until October 1928.

In 1930, he was convicted on vagrancy charges, but they were reversed on a technicality. In July, he was arrested as a "John Doe" after a traffic accident. The police hauled him in after he was found waving a pistol in the other driver's face and threatening to blow it off. He used the name "John Nolan" and claimed to be an electrician. He was again released on bond.

On October 31, Sammons was arrested again, this time in connection with the shooting and wounding of Sergeant James McBride of the Bellwood Police. Sammons was arrested in Riverside, Illinois at the home of long-time pal, "Three-Fingered" Jack White. Both White and Sammons had been paroled in 1923 by Governor Len Small, after paying a small fortune in bribe money to "Porky" Dillon, one of Small's bagmen. Dillon had an interesting background too. He had once been sentenced to serve 10 years in the state prison but managed to rig a pardon for himself from the same corrupt governor, Small.

When Sammons was arrested at White's house, he was with his girlfriend, Pearl Barry, and White's wife. When he was arrested, he was found with a revolver, a bulletproof vest, and a policeman's badge. Once again, the charges failed to stick – a familiar story for Sammons.

By February 1933, the gangster landscape of Chicago had changed dramatically. Capone had gone to prison on tax evasion charges and his Outfit was being run in his absence by men like Frank "The Enforcer" Nitti, who wanted to make sure that money was going to keep rolling in after the end of Prohibition and the lucrative illegal liquor trade. "Three Fingered" Jack White, Murray "The Camel" Humphreys, and Klondike O'Donnell emerged to lead efforts into the expanding field of racketeering. The new climate had made former enemies into allies. The chief prize to be won was control over the men who delivered the city's supplies: coal for heating, food, building supplies, even beer and ice. They all wanted the Teamster unions and only the gang run by Roger "Terrible" Touhy was strong enough to stand against Capone's Outfit.

"Three Fingered" Jack White was placed in charge of dealing with the Touhys. White was a competent and dangerous man. He claimed that he got his nickname when a brick fell on his hand on a construction site when he was a boy, crushing several fingers. It was a deformity he tried to hide with a glove, stuffing the empty fingers with cotton. In fact it's more likely that White lost the fingers in a bungled burglary attempt where he mishandled nitroglycerin, a common mishap for safecrackers of the day. White had a bloody job to do and for it, he recruited Sammons, a psychopath that was probably the most dangerous man in Chicago, if not in the United States.

White was an effective battle tactician. Now backed by Sammons' psychotic brutality, he was able to take back the upper hand in the battle against the Touhys in four quick and deadly blows. The first to die under the White-Sammons regime was Teddy Newberry, a bag man for Mayor Anton Cermak who plotted the shooting of Frank Nitti a short time before. Nitti survived, but Newberry did not. He was found lying face down in a ditch of frozen water in Porter County, Indiana.

Next they got Touhy's strongest ally, Paddy Barrell, the international vice president of the Teamsters. He was killed while he and his bodyguard, Willie Marks, were vacationing in Wisconsin. Marks, a former Moran gunner, had survived the St. Valentine's Day Massacre by being late for work. This time he wasn't so lucky. The killer, believed to be Sammons, caught Barrell and Marks by surprise while the two were fishing, standing knee-deep in a lake. The blast from the shotgun, fired only inches from the victims, nearly took off Barrell's head.

Another setback for the Touhys came when White and Sammons caught Matt Kolb at his saloon, the Club Morton. Kolb was standing in the hallway next to a roulette wheel. Walking up from behind him, Sammons greeted him and as Kolb reached out to shake hands, Sammons grabbed his hand and arm tightly as White pulled out an automatic and poured the six shots into the little fat man. As the killers started to leave, Sammons turned and fired another shot into Kolb's head – just to make sure he was dead.

The new blow came when Sammons gunned down Tommy Touhy, Roger's brother. It happened when Tommy and two cars of his men combed the streets of Chicago looking for Sammons, who was in an armor-plated car, looking for the Touhys. The two groups stalked one another for hours, until Touhy ordered his men to pull over at an intersection and wait for Sammons. Several minutes later Sammons brazenly pulled up alongside them. Touhy leaned out his window, machine gun in hand, and opened fire on Sammons, hitting his tires and radiator. Then, without taking his finger off the trigger, he climbed out of his car and stood on the bumper and fired into Sammons' windows. Sammons seemed unfazed by the flying bullets and shattered glass. He stepped on the gas, leaned out the window, and emptied a machine gun clip into Touhy's legs, driving with one hand and firing with the other. A squad car from the town of River Forrest pulled onto the scene and demanded that the gunmen throw down their weapons and get out of the car. The Touhys answered by shooting at the officers, who returned fire, but amidst the smoke and noise, Touhy and Sammons had vanished into the city.

In July 1933, Sammons was arrested again, this time on gun charges in Kansas City. He was returned to Chicago and charged with intent to murder in connection with the Touhy shootout. A few days later, he was released on bond with an order to appear in court on September 8. He never showed and an order went out for his arrest.

On November 6, he was arrested while intoxicated in Cedar Lake, Indiana, and locked up at the Lake County Jail in Crown Point to await trial. While in jail, he attempted to bribe the warden and found himself facing a new charge. He was found guilty on the bribery charge, and ruled a habitual criminal by the judge, he was sentenced to a life term in the state penitentiary.

Nearly 10 years later, in May 1943, Sammons was paroled from Indiana, but only on the condition that he be returned to the prison system of Illinois. By that time, his 1923 parole had been deemed illegal and he was now facing another 30 years in jail. He was locked up in Joliet, where he spent five years going blind. In 1948, at the age of 66, broken, and nearly blind, Sammons asked for a compassionate release from prison. He wept in court, but his release was refused until December 1952, when he was finally paroled.

He lived for eight more years, even if he didn't deserve them. On May 20, 1960, James "Fur" Sammons – once regarded as the most dangerous man in Chicago – was found dead in a hotel in Englewood.

Hauntings at the Lake County Jail

Meanwhile, the Lake County Jail in Crown Point continued to house and hold prisoners who served short sentences or waited for trial dates that would see them be locked up in prison or set free. Until 1958, state law required Indiana sheriffs to reside in a house adjoining the jail, but once the requirement was lifted, the sheriff's house was turned into offices. The last sheriff to live in the residence was Jack West. The house was used as an office until 1974 and has been empty ever since -- of the living anyway.

In 1974, the current county government complex was completed on North Main Street in Crown Point, and the sheriff's offices moved to that facility. During the late 1970s, some areas of the old residence and jail were used for retail purposes as part of a commercial complex. After they closed, the buildings remained unoccupied. In 1987, interest in restoring the facility grew and the Old Sheriff's House Foundation, Inc. was formed the next year. The Old Sheriff's House and Jail was placed on the National Register of Historic Places in 1989, and the property was acquired in 1990 and restoration plans began.

As restoration has continued over the last two decades, stories have emerged about a haunting at the jail. Apparitions have been seen in cells and corridors, strange photographs have been taken, footsteps have been heard in what seem to be empty corridors, cell doors open and close by themselves, lights turn on and off, and

81

disembodied footsteps and voices have often been reported by volunteers and visitors alike.

Personally speaking, I had heard about the old Lake County Jail being haunted as far back as the 1980s and more stories began to emerge after the foundation acquired the building in 1990. Once the restoration efforts started, the ghostly stories seemed to intensify, as they often do when old buildings with a lot of history are remodeled and renovated. One often told story involved the apparition of an inmate that continued to be seen among the cells on the top floor. Several different people told me about their sightings (and sightings by others) of a shadowy figure that was often glimpsed peering out from one of the cells. Each time he was seen, he ducked back out of sight, but a check of the cell always revealed that it was empty. Tradition stated that this was one of the jail's former inmates, still stuck here doing time, long after his physical body had been released.

In the spring of 2014, I had the chance to spend the night at the jail with a group of people from American Hauntings, as well as staff members and long-time friends Tom and Michelle Bonadurer, Maggie Walsh, and Lisa Taylor Horton. We spent hours roaming the old sheriff's house and the cellblocks of the jail. During the night, several people reported temperature changes that could not be explained, eerie noises, and inexplicable voices that were recorded, but not actually heard by the researchers.

With my small group, we only had one really strange incident that could not be explained. While up on the top floor of the jail, in an old dormitory area used for youthful offenders in the late 1960s, we had a curious incident occur with one of the electronic devices that we had brought with us to monitor the area for any sort of paranormal activity. The device is called a REM Pod and (not to get too technical) it was designed to track paranormal events that may distort the electromagnetic fields of a location. In the past, the only way to track a wide area was to use several different magnetic detectors at the same time. The REM Pod actually does the work for you, monitoring the environment and alerting ghost hunters to changes in the field (and the ambient temperature) with sounds and multi-colored lights. Many readers have likely seen this device used on television, but I can assure you that it's not usually as active as the television ghost shows would like you to believe. However, when the alarms do go off, they are loud, shrill, and certainly get your attention.

While investigating the dormitory upstairs, we had placed a REM Pod in the center of the floor and were exploring other sections of the large room. In addition, we had a recording device going on at the same time and questions were being asked in hopes that an unheard voice might end up on the recording when it was played back. As it happened, a name was spoken on the recording by a voice that none of us heard – "David," it said, apparently in response to a question about whether anyone there was present. More unnerving, though, was that at the same time the voice was recorded, the REM Pod reacted wildly to some sort of change in the atmosphere of the room. With flashing lights and a blaring alarm, it announced that something was present, and then went dark again. It never went off again for the rest of the night. But something – or someone – made its presence known to us that night and further convinced me that the history of the past remains behind at the Old Lake County Jail.

4. A METAL PRISON SHANK
THE JOLIET PENITENTIARY

The Joliet Penitentiary in northern Illinois was meant to be the last stop for many of the thieves, killers, and desperate criminals who found themselves locked behind the prison's ominous walls. It was not designed to be a place of hope or rehabilitation, but a place of punishment for the men who chose to ignore the laws of society. The Joliet Penitentiary broke the bodies and minds of scores of criminals over the years of its operations, and for many of those who perished there, the prison became their permanent home. There was no escape, these luckless souls discovered, even after death.

For more than 40 years, from Illinois' statehood in 1818 to around 1858, there was only one state penitentiary in Illinois, located in the Mississippi River town of Alton. The prison was completed in 1833, but soon deteriorated beyond repair, which was a major concern since the state's population was growing rapidly and, along with it, the crime rate. During his inaugural speech in 1853, newly elected Governor Joel Mattson, a Joliet native, spoke out for the need of a prison in northern Illinois. By the middle 1800s, the population center of the state had shifted from southwestern Illinois toward the expanding city of Chicago. In 1857, spurred by scandals involving the horrific conditions of the Alton prison, the Illinois legislature finally approved a commission to scout for locations for the new penitentiary.

Governor Mattson's friend, Nelson Elwood, a former mayor of Joliet, was appointed to the Board of Penitentiary Commissioners, and it was Elwood who convinced the members of the board to build a prison at a site that was then two miles north of the city of Joliet. The location boasted a fresh water spring, proximity to railroads and the Illinois & Michigan Canal, and the city of Chicago. But the greatest argument in favor of the site was the limestone deposits that were located under the 15-acre location. The deposits were so deep that no inmate could escape by tunneling out through them.

The penitentiary was designed by William Boyington in a style known as castellated Gothic. Boyington had also designed several Chicago landmarks, including the Chicago Pumping Station and the Water Tower on Michigan Avenue. The structures were all of similar style and reminiscent of medieval construction, evoking castles and, of course, dungeons. The walls of the prison would be 25 feet high, six feet wide at the base and two feet wide at the top. Turreted guard towers anchored each corner of the site. The cellblocks were to be constructed inside long row houses, holding 100 cells in each one.

Construction on the penitentiary began in 1858. The workforce consisted of 53 prisoners that had been transferred in from Alton. They lived in makeshift barracks while they mined the Joliet-Lemont limestone quarry, which was located just across the road from the building site. Local private contractors supervised the construction and the prisoners. Quarry drilling was done entirely by hand and the huge blocks were hauled by mule cart to the road. A conveyor belt was later built to transport rocks to the surface. As work progressed, more prisoners were transferred to Joliet and assigned to work on the construction. There was no shortage of stone or labor and, in 1859, the first building was completed. It eventually took just 12 years for the prisoners to construct their own place of confinement. By then, the Alton prison had been completely shut down and all of the state prisoners had been sent to Joliet.

The Joliet Penitentiary contained 1,100 cells – 900 for the general population, 100 for solitary confinement, and 100 to house female inmates. At the time it was finished, it was the largest prison in the United States and was adopted as an architectural model for penitentiaries around the world, including Leavenworth, the West Virginia State Penitentiary, and the Isle of Pines in Cuba.

Prisoners were housed in two-man cells that were 6 x 9-feet, with no electricity, plumbing, or running water. Each cell had a pitcher for fresh water and a bucket for waste. The stone walls of the cells were eight inches thick with only the door and a small ventilation hole for openings. The cellblocks were built running the length of the middle of the long row house, away from any natural light. The cells were grim, confined, dimly-lighted chambers that offered little hope for the men incarcerated in them.

Life in the new penitentiary was harsh and sometimes brutal. The plan for the Joliet prison was based on the dreaded Auburn System, which was created in Auburn, New York, in the early 1800s. The inmates at Joliet passed their days under a strict regime of silence, but were allowed to speak to their cellmates during the evening hours in quiet voices. Contact with the outside world was severely limited, and no recreational activities were offered.

Prisoners moved from place to place within the prison using a "lock step" formation, which was a sort of side step shuffle with one hand on the shoulder of the man in front of them. Inmates' heads had to be turned in the direction of the guards, who watched for any lip movement that signaled when someone was talking. The lock step formation also made it easier for one guard to watch over a larger number of prisoners. Floggings, stocks, and extensive time in solitary confinement were common punishments for those who broke the rules. The inmates wore striped uniforms all year round. Men who were deemed to be escape risks were shackled in irons.

Convict labor, under constant discipline, allowed the Joliet Penitentiary to initiate factory-style working conditions at a profit. Lucrative contracts were sold to the highest private bidder, who then sold the products manufactured in the prison on the open market. Under the constant scrutiny of the guards, the prisoners were put to work producing an array of goods: rattan furniture, shoes, brooms, chairs, wheelbarrows, horse collars, and dressed limestone. The prison was also self-sufficient in most aspects of daily life. It had a thriving bakery, a tailor shop, a hospital, and a library, which was administered by the prison chaplain.

A prisoner's day began at 6:00 a.m. when he was marched into the prison yard to empty his waste bucket into the sewage ditch. He then marched into the kitchen, then back to his cell for a breakfast of hash, bread, and coffee. When the dining hall was completed in 1907, prisoners were allowed to eat communally, but in silence. Prisoners in solitary confinement received a daily ration of two ounces of bread and water.

The prison buildings were impossible to keep warm in the winter and very hard to keep clean, which made it a breeding ground for lice, rats, and various diseases. Tuberculosis, pneumonia, and typhoid were the main causes of death among inmates. Unclaimed bodies were buried in a pauper's graveyard, called Monkey Hill, near the prison on Woodruff Street.

The strict silence, unsanitary conditions, forced labor, and harsh punishments gave the Joliet Penitentiary a reputation as the last possible place that a man wanted to end up.

Prison reform was first introduced at Joliet in 1913 with the appointment of Edmund Allen as the warden. By 1915, the striped uniforms and the lock step formation were gone, and the rule of silence ended. Prisoners were allowed recreation privileges and a baseball diamond was built. Warden Allen also started an honor farm on 2,200 acres located four miles north of the prison. Prisoners were allowed to work in the fields, and on the farm, as a reward for good conduct.

Allen was progressive in every sense of the word. His second wife, Odette, who was not only a striking beauty but was once a singer in New Orleans, supported him in his work and was a considerable influence in establishing the "honor system" at Joliet. With this system, inmates were graded on their conduct. Starting in a middle grade, they could be elevated by continued good conduct or could be demoted by bad conduct. Punishments could be handed out with the occurrence of offenses, but the honor system required continued good conduct as a method of obtaining better job assignments and privileges.

Ironically, though, Warden Allen, who lived in an apartment on the prison grounds with his wife, Odette, experienced personal tragedy, possibly at the hands of one of the trusted inmates. On June 19, 1915, Warden Allen and his wife planned to leave on a trip to West Baden, Indiana. Mrs. Allen's dressmaker had not quite finished two of her dresses, and Odette persuaded her husband to go ahead and leave without her. Early the next morning, a fire broke out in the Warden's apartment. When the prison fire department responded, they discovered Mrs. Allen dead, and her bed engulfed in flames. The fire was ruled as arson and a trustee, "Chicken Joe" Campbell, who had been Mrs. Allen's servant, was charged with the crime. Campbell was tried, convicted, and sentenced to death, despite the fact that the evidence against him was purely circumstantial. At Warden Allen's request, Illinois' Governor Dunne commuted his sentenced to life imprisonment. Allen continued to support the honor program and begged others not to judge all men by the actions of one man. He resigned several months after Odette's murder.

This tragic event, along with the increasing involvement by the United States in World War I, brought an end to the era of progress at Joliet. Reform would not be attempted again for many decades.

Construction on a new prison, called Stateville, began in 1916 on the land where the honor farm was located. It was originally intended to replace the older prison, but the national crime sprees of the 1920s and 1930s kept the old Joliet Penitentiary open for more than 80 additional years.

During its time in operation, the prison housed some of the most infamous and deadly criminals in Illinois history. Some of them were already well known when they walked through the front gates, but others gained their infamy inside the walls.

The first execution at the prison took place during the Civil War years. In the spring of 1864, George Chase, a convicted horse thief, attempted to escape from the penitentiary. When he was confronted by Deputy Warden Joseph Clark, Chase attacked him with a club and hit him so hard in the head that he killed the officer. Chase was recaptured, charged with murder, and sentenced to hang – turning a short sentence for stealing horses into the death penalty. Chase was hanged a short time later and became the first inmate to be executed at Joliet.

Famous Chicago gangster George "Bugs" Moran served three terms for robbery at Joliet between 1910 and 1923. After the murder of his crime mentor Dean O'Banion in 1926, Moran became the leader of Chicago's north side bootleggers. His time in power lasted until 1929, when seven of his men were slaughtered by the Capone gang in the St. Valentine's Day Massacre. Moran turned to a life of petty crime and died in Leavenworth in 1957.

Frank McErlane was considered one of the most vicious gunmen in Chicago and before being sent to Joliet, was credited with killing nine men, two women, and a dog. Arrested for his part in the murder of an Oak Park police officer in 1916, he served one year at Joliet before trying to escape. He was caught and served another two years for the attempt. Shortly after the start of prohibition, McErlane began running a gang with partner Joseph "Polack Joe" Saltis on Chicago's south side. Later, they allied with the Capone gang against the O'Donnell Brothers. During the war with the O'Donnells, McErlane introduced the Thompson machine gun to Chicago and with it, killed at least 15 men during the Beer Wars. McErlane suffered serious wounds during a gun battle with George Moran in 1930. While recovering, Moran sent two gunmen to kill him, but McErlane pulled a revolver from underneath his pillow and began firing, driving off the surprised gangsters. McErlane was wounded in the gunfight, suffering two wounds in his injured leg and one in his arm, but he recovered. In 1932, he became ill with pneumonia and died within days.

Nathan Leopold and Richard Loeb, two college students from wealthy families, were sentenced to life imprisonment at Joliet in 1924 after kidnapping and murdering 14-year-old Bobby Franks. They had been attempting to pull off the "perfect crime." Warden John L. Whitman was firm in his assertion that the young men received the same treatment as the other prisoners, but his claims were nowhere near the truth. Leopold and Loeb lived in luxury compared to the rest of the inmates. Each enjoyed a private cell, books, a desk, a filing cabinet, and even pet birds. They also showered away from the other prisoners and took their meals, which were prepared to order, in the officers' lounge. Leopold was allowed to keep a flower garden. They were also permitted any number of unsupervised visitors and were allowed to keep their own gardens. The doors to their cells were usually left open and they had passes to visit one another at any time. Loeb was stabbed to death by another inmate in 1936. Leopold was eventually released in 1958, after pleas to the prison board by poet Carl Sandburg. He moved to Puerto Rico – allegedly rehabilitated -- and died in 1971.

George "Baby Face" Nelson also served time at Joliet. In July 1931, he was convicted of robbing the Itasca State Bank and sentenced to one year to life at Joliet Penitentiary. He served two months before being sent to stand trial for another bank robbery. He was under armed guard and on his way back to Joliet when he escaped and went back to robbing banks with the Dillinger gang.

Another famous inmate was Daniel L. McGeoghagen, a racketeer, prohibition beer-maker and skilled safecracker. The McGeoghagen gang attempted to loot 300 safe deposit boxes in 1947, but when things went wrong, they ended up taking seven people hostage. A gun battle with the police ensued, leaving two people dead and two wounded. McGeoghagen was captured, tried, and sentenced to 15-20 years at Joliet. He was paroled in 1958.

Another infamous inmate at Joliet was serial killer John Wayne Gacy, one of Chicago's most notorious murderers. Between 1972 and 1978, Gacy tortured and killed 33 young men, burying 28 of them under his home. He was sentenced to death in 1980 and spent some of his time on death row in a cell at the Joliet Penitentiary.

The 1970s saw the rise of gang violence within the penitentiary's walls. The Gangster Disciples, the Vice Lords, the Latin Kings, and the P. Stone Nation all vied for power, leading to a riot in April 1975. A group of 200 P. Stone Nation gang members took 12 prison workers hostage and held a cell block for five hours. Herbert Catlett, a former member of the gang, attempted to intervene on behalf of the hostages. He was serving time for armed robbery and trying to turn his life around for when he was released. When the hostages were eventually set free, Catlett was found with his throat slashed.

In 2001, the Joliet State Penitentiary was closed down. The crumbling old prison had finally been deemed unfit for habitation and all of the prisoners were moved out. But, as many who came to the penitentiary were soon to discover – the prison may have been abandoned, but it was certainly not empty.

Ghosts at the Joliet Penitentiary

The first mention of ghosts connected to the old penitentiary was not a story about the prison itself being haunted, but rather one of the inmates. That man's name was Adolph Luetgert, Chicago's "Sausage King." Luetgert was a German meatpacker who was charged with killing his wife, Louisa, in May 1897. The two of them had a stormy marriage and when Louisa disappeared, detectives feared the worst and searched the sausage factory that was located next door to the Luetgert home. In one of the vats in the basement, they found human bone fragments and a ring bearing Louisa's initials and Luetgert was arrested.

His first trial ended with a hung jury on October 21, after the jurors failed to agree on a suitable punishment. Some argued for the death penalty, while others voted for life in prison. Only one of the jurors thought that Luetgert might be innocent. A second trial was held and, on February 9, 1898, Luetgert was convicted and sentenced to a life term at Joliet. He was taken away, still maintaining his innocence and claiming that he would receive another trial. He was placed in charge of meats in the prison's cold-storage warehouse and officials described him as a model inmate.

By 1899, though, Luetgert began to speak less and less and often quarreled with the other convicts. He soon became a shadow of his former self, fighting with other inmates for no reason and often babbling incoherently in his cell at night. But was he talking to himself? Or to someone else?

According to legend, Luetgert began to claim that he was talking to Louisa in his cell at night. His dead wife had returned to haunt him, intent on having revenge for her murder. Was she really haunting him or was the "ghost" just the figment of a rapidly deteriorating mind? Based on the fact that residents of his former neighborhood also began reporting seeing Louisa's ghost, one has to wonder if Luetgert was seeing her ghost because he was mentally ill – or if the ghost had driven him insane.

Luetgert died in 1900, likely from heart trouble. The coroner who conducted the autopsy also reported that his liver was greatly enlarged and in such a condition of degeneration that "mental strain would have caused his death at any time."

Perhaps Louisa really did visit him after all....

The "Joliet Singer"

In 1932, the Joliet Penitentiary gained statewide attention, and great notoriety, for a strange ghostly phenomenon that was allegedly occurring at Monkey Hill, the old pauper's burial ground on the property.

In the 1930s, the prison maintained a large field behind the compound for grazing cattle and a limestone quarry that served to provide the prisoners with hard labor. Nearby was the pauper's graveyard where the unclaimed dead were buried. The graveyard was a desolate place that was largely ignored by those who lived nearby. It probably would have never been talked about at all, if not for the fact that an unexplained voice began to be heard in the cemetery in July 1932.

On July 16, the night of a full moon, a woman named Mrs. Dudek was standing in her backyard, which adjoined the potter's field. As she was enjoying the cool night air on that summer evening, she began to hear a beautiful baritone voice singing what sounded like Latin hymns from a Catholic mass. She called to her daughter, Genevieve, and the two of them took a flashlight and pointed it in the direction the voice was coming from. They saw nothing there.

The next evening, Mrs. Dudek's son, Stanley, and her husband, George, both of whom had been away the night before, also heard the singing. They searched the cemetery, but found no one. They were unable to determine where the sound was coming from. News of the voice spread through the neighborhood and those who came to listen to what the Dudeks claimed to hear went away stunned. They quickly realized that the voice was not coming from someone's loud radio. It was a ghost, they said -- a ghost in the old prison cemetery.

News of what was assumed to be a specter in the potter's field spread throughout Joliet and soon people from all over town were coming to hear the Latin hymns. Lines of cars filled Woodruff Road and then turned into the prison field, where neighborhood boys directed them to parking places. The procession began early in the evening each night since the voice began to sing around midnight.

After about 10 days of this, the enigmatic voice had become news all over the Chicago area. Curiosity seekers came from the city, from Indiana, and from the nearby cities of Plainfield, Lockport, Aurora, and Rockdale. The story was picked up in the local newspapers, and then in Chicago and Indiana, and, finally, across the country. The people of Joliet had a genuine mystery on their hands.

People soon began to come from as far away as Missouri, Wisconsin, and Kentucky to hear the singing. According to the local newspaper, a man named Joshua Jones from Sickles Center, Missouri, was sent by a local contingent from his town. "Folks in my town read about this in the newspapers but they won't believe it until they hear it from me," Jones told a reporter.

The visitors to the old cemetery started off numbering in the hundreds and the groups of thrill-seekers soon began to grow into the thousands. From the beginning, the tourists attempted to uncover the source of the "ghostly" sounds, or at least the whereabouts of the person pretending to be a ghost. Whenever the singing began, the searchers rushed into the field, looking behind bushes, in trees, and even below ground for any hidden caverns. They looked for wires, loud speakers and concealed microphones, but found nothing. In spite of this, the singing persisted night after night and each night it was the same, the low, mournful calling of Latin hymns.

The skeptics who came in search of a reasonable answer just went away confused. People soon began to accept the genuineness of the phenomenon, as all attempts to prove it as a hoax had failed. Each night, thousands of people drove to the field and climbed the hill to what had once been a lonely graveyard. They sat on the flat grave stones, spread their blankets in the grass and brought along picnic baskets and thermoses of coffee. The crowds waited expectantly for the eerie voice and, for a time, were not disappointed.

Eventually, though, the voice began to miss its nightly performance. And when it did come, it was sometimes as late as 4:00 a.m., several hours after it had originally started. The faithful stayed and waited for it, though, huddled in blankets and sleeping in the chilly air of the early morning hours. They claimed the voice was offended by those who came only for thrills. It waited for the quiet, attentive listeners, who received a performance of prayerful hymns.

However, even the most devoted still searched for an explanation for the voice. Was it some sort of heavenly visitor? The ghost of a deceased prisoner? No one knew, but in late July, officials at the prison announced that they had an explanation for the singer. They claimed that it was merely an Irish-German prisoner, a trustee named William Lalon Chrysler, who was singing in joy about his upcoming parole. Chrysler had been convicted of larceny and had served four years of his term before becoming eligible for parole. Toward the end of his sentence, he had been placed in charge of late night inspection of water pumps at the nearby quarry. It was said that the "mysterious" singing was Chrysler intoning Lithuanian folk songs in English to relieve the monotony down in the depths of the quarry. The prison officials reported that the bare stone walls of the quarry were a perfect sounding board for enhancing and throwing his voice to the hilltop, which was more than a quarter mile away. They added that if there were a wind from the north, it would sound as though the voice was right inside the cemetery, where the crowds had gathered. The case was closed – there was nothing supernatural about the voice, they said, it was merely a trick of sound and the wind.

Many people went away convinced that this "official" story was the final word on the subject, but others were not so sure. Many believed that the prison officials were more concerned about getting rid of the crowds than with solving the mystery of the voice. For the entire month of July, thousands of people had encroached on the prison's property. The barbed wire fence that had surrounded the prison field was broken down and the cow pasture had been turned into a parking lot.

To make matters worse, Joliet police officers were unable to deal with the massive numbers of people who came to hear the voice. Local criminals began preying on the tourists, picking pockets and breaking into cars, while some of the less savory neighborhood youths began a car parking racket that extorted money from those who parked in the field. They began threatening motorists with broken windshields if they didn't pay protection money to keep their autos safe. The situation had become a far cry from the first days of the phenomenon, when neighborhood children were helping to direct traffic.

Since the prison officials were unable to stop the voice from being heard, they discredited it instead. William Chrysler provided the perfect solution. He was assigned to the sump pumps at the quarry, so he was outside, and he was due for parole at any time, which meant that he wouldn't chance offending prison officials by denying that his voice was the one heard singing. The officials named Chrysler as the unexplained voice and they closed off the fields to trespassers for good.

The Joliet Singer had been given an official solution, but did the explanation really measure up to the facts in the case? Not everyone thought so in 1932, and not everyone does today either. In the official version of the "facts," Chrysler was at the bottom of a quarry when he sang and his voice was transported to a hilltop that was about a quarter mile away. He had to have had a light with him in the bottom of the quarry, because it was otherwise pitch dark, and yet no one who searched the area reported seeing a light.

Another problem with the story is how Chrysler's voice could have been heard over such a distance. The "quarry as a sounding board" theory does make sense, but it is unlikely that the sound could carry anywhere other than inside the quarry and to a short distance around it. No one who searched the area ever reported hearing the singing coming from the quarry, which means that Chrysler would have had to have been purposely hoaxing the crowds using ventriloquism. However, magicians and ventriloquists who were interviewed in 1932 stated that this would have been a very difficult, if not impossible, trick, especially for someone with none of the necessary skills. Chrysler readily admitted that he had never been trained in magic or in the art of throwing his voice.

And finally, strangest of all, why did no one ever report hearing the sump pumps at the quarry? According to the official story, Chrysler was out in the field because he was manning the pumps, singing to himself. If this was the case, then how could his voice be heard so clearly, but not the much louder sounds of the mechanical pumps?

Even with these lingering questions, though, it must be admitted that the singing voice was never heard again after Chrysler's "confession" and the closing of the field. Was the whole thing really a hoax? Or was it simply that the voice was no longer heard singing because people stopped coming to listen for it?

"Prison Break" Haunts

After the Joliet Penitentiary closed in 2001, questions remained as to what would become of the old building. It sat empty for the next several years and then became the setting for the Fox television series, *Prison Break*. Standing in as the fictional "Fox River Penitentiary," the Joliet Prison became the setting for the first season of this innovative television show. In the series, actor Wentworth Miller played Michael Scofield, a structural engineer who gets himself thrown into prison to try and save his brother, Lincoln Burrowes (played by Dominic Purcell), who was framed for murder and is scheduled for execution. Scofield has the blueprints for the prison cleverly disguised in the tattoos on his body and created an elaborate plan to help his brother escape – which, of course, goes awry along the way.

Shortly after the large cast arrived for filming at Joliet, they began to realize there was something not quite right about the old prison.

Lane Garrison, the actor who played "Tweener," a young convict, on the show, stated that standing in the shadow of the prison walls made it easier for him to get into his character. He recalled, "My first day here, I walked through those gates and a change happened. You see the walls and the razor wire, and you feel the history here. It's not a positive place. We do some stuff in Gacy's cell, which is really scary."

Rockmund Dunbar, who played the inmate called "C-Note," was usually the most unnerved member of the cast and referred to the prison as "stagnant." He often refused to walk around in the cell blocks by himself. "You're expecting something to come around the corner and grab you. I don't go into the cells. I just don't want to get locked in there." He was also the first cast member to admit that he believed the prison was haunted. "There were stories of neighbors who called, saying 'stop the prisoners from singing over there' – and the prison was closed!" he said.

Perhaps the one cast member to talk most openly about his strange experiences and haunted happenings at Joliet was Dominic Purcell, who played the ill-fated Lincoln Burrowes. Purcell's office on the set was John Wayne Gacy's former cell, which Purcell said was not a nice place, and "a little creepy." He added, "If I let my imagination run away with me, I can start to pick up on some stuff. I don't like to spend too much time in there, knowing that one of the world's most notorious serial killers was lying on the same bunk that I'm lying on. It ain't a comfortable feeling."

Purcell confessed that many members of the cast and crew believed that the spirits of former prisoners still lingered at Joliet. He described one weird incident that he personally experienced. "I had something touch me on the neck. I looked around and thought, 'It's weird', and blew it off and didn't think about it too much. Then, in the afternoon, one of the other actors came to me and said 'Did you just touch me on the shoulder?' No.... Then I went back to my little thing and said 'Hmmm', and the crew was starting to talk about the weird stuff that's going on. Some said the prison's known to have been haunted for a long time," he said.

Purcell, like Lane Garrison, admitted that it was easy to get into character after setting foot inside the prison's walls, but when the time came to wrap up filming for the day, he was always ready to leave. "I am always relieved to leave, always. You never want to hang out there by yourself. The corridors are long, so far, and you get creeped out exploring. There's a section in the yard where they used to do hangings, and you can see the foundations of what they used to use. That place left a brutal impression on me. It ain't a place for the faint-hearted," he concluded.

Today, the Joliet Penitentiary still stands, slowly crumbling as the years pass by. What will become of this old place? Many locals consider it an eyesore and embarrassment, but still others see it as an important place in Illinois history. It's been a target for the wrecking ball, and been named as a possible historic site, but, for now, its future remains a mystery.

Do the ghosts of the past still linger in this place, trapped here in time as they were trapped in the cells that once held them? Many believe this to be the case, leading them to wonder what will happen to these mournful spirits if the prison that holds them is lost. Only time will tell.

5. THE ELECTRIC CHAIR
THE WEST VIRGINIA PENITENTIARY

When the state of West Virginia was admitted to the Union in 1863, breaking away from Virginia and the Confederacy, there were no penal institutions of any kind within its borders, save for small county jails. It would not be until 1866 that the legislature would select a site for a penitentiary near the town of Moundsville. The tract of land took up about five acres, with a 300-acre farm located about a mile from the prison, fronting on Jefferson Avenue and located directly across from Grave Creek Mound, a Native American burial site.

The prison would remain in operation for 129 years until it closed in 1995. During that time, the stone walls saw all manner of horror, desperation, disease, death, and depravity. It became the last home for West Virginia killers like Trout Shue, the murderer of Zona Heaster Shue, a victim who allegedly testified from the grave, and Harry Powers, the "Bluebeard of the Quiet Dell."

But perhaps, most infamously, it became known for its executions. Between 1899 and 1959, 94 men went to their deaths at the West Virginia Penitentiary. Hanging was the method of execution until 1949 with 85 men meeting that fate. Up until 1931, the hangings were open to the public. However, on June 19, Frank Hyer was executed for murdering his wife and when the trap door beneath him was opened, and his full weight was put onto the noose, he was instantly decapitated. After that, a hanging could be attended by invitation only.

Starting in 1951, the electric chair – known as "Old Sparky"—became the method of execution. Ironically, the chair was built by a prison inmate, Paul Glenn, and it sent nine men to their deaths before the state outlawed executions in 1965.

With a reputation for torture, strict punishments, brutality, murder, and insanity, the West Virginia Penitentiary may be one of the darkest and most haunted locations within these pages. It will come as no surprise to the reader to learn that the prison is believed to be infested by the spirits of those who were locked behind these walls. It is not a place for the faint of heart.

After seceding from Virginia at the height of the Civil War, West Virginia had a shortage of various public institutions, including prisons. From 1863 to 1866, Governor Arthur I. Boreman lobbied the West Virginia Legislature for a state penitentiary but was repeatedly denied. The Legislature at first tried to direct him to send the prisoners to other institutions out of the state, and then they directed him to use existing county jails, which turned out to be inadequate. After nine inmates escaped in 1865, the local press took up the cause, and embarrassed the politicians into taking action. Soon after, the land in Moundsville was purchased. The town was located only about 12 miles from Wheeling, which was the state capital at the time, making it an attraction spot.

During that first summer, the state built a temporary wooden prison to give officials time to assess what prison design should be used. In the end, they decided to model it off the Gothic Revival architecture of the prison in Joliet, Illinois, which exhibited "as much as possible, great strength and conveyed to the mind a cheerless blank indicative of the misery which awaits the unhappy being who enters within its walls." In other words, prisoners who found themselves inside were told to abandon all hope – only punishment awaited them.

The first building constructed on the site was the North Wagon Gate, built from stone quarried in the surrounding counties. The state used prison labor during the construction process, and work continued on this first phase until 1876. In addition to the North Wagon Gate, there was now north and south cellblock areas. South Hall had 224 cells and North Hall had a kitchen, dining area, hospital, and chapel. A four-story tower, the administration building, connected the two and it included space for female inmates and personal living quarters for the warden and his family. The facility officially opened that year, and it had a population of 251 inmates, including some who had helped construct the very prison that now held them. After this phase, work began on prison workshops and other secondary facilities, as well as improvements throughout the prison. More cells were added in the 1890s; the wooden floor in the front entrance was changed to tile in 1886; stone steps were installed outside in 1888; an elevator was added in 1894, as well as a revolving cage on the first floor of the administration tower.

Improvements were also made for the health of the prisoners with steam heat recommended by the prison doctor in the 1870s, and the small oil lamps used in the cells being replaced by electricity in 1900. Bricks that had been intended for a new mess hall were used instead for brick walks and roads inside the penitentiary yards. This eliminated the mud and standing water, improving the sanitary conditions of the yard.

In addition to construction, the inmates had jobs to do in support of the prison. In the early 1900s, some industries within the prison walls included a carpentry shop, a paint shop, a wagon shop, a stone yard, a brickyard, a blacksmith, a tailor, a bakery, and a hospital. At the same time, revenue from the prison farm and inmate labor helped the prison financially. It was virtually self-sufficient. A prison coal mine located a mile away opened in 1921. This mine helped serve some of the prison's energy needs and saved the state an estimated $14,000 a year. Some inmates were allowed to stay at the mine's camp under the supervision of a mine foreman, who was not a prison employee.

At the start of the twentieth century, the prison was generally praised as an example of a well-managed facility. According to a warden's report, "both the quantity and the quality of all the purchases of material, food and clothing have been very gradually, but steadily, improved, while the discipline has become more nearly perfect and the exaction of labor less stringent." Education was a priority for the inmates during this time. They regularly attended class. Construction on a school and library was completed in 1900 to help reform and educate inmates. The West Virginia Penitentiary was one of the most lauded penal operations in the country – or so it seemed.

Death and Disease
While the public records often spoke of how conditions at the penitentiary were being constantly improved for the prisoners, the death and medical records told a different story. Disease ran rampant at the prison in the days before antibiotics,

proper hygiene, and sterilized medical instruments. Death records at the penitentiary show a range of illnesses and conditions, including enlarged liver, heart disease, syphilis, smallpox, influenza, tuberculosis, cancer, epilepsy, anemia, and malnutrition. Many died during various epidemics that swept through the prison.

There were two hospitals at the prison for many years: one for general use and one for tuberculosis patients. Each had its own steward, nurses, kitchen, dining room, and cook. There were two doctors normally kept on staff, although they both served only part-time, with outside practices to manage.

A few of the deaths listed in the penitentiary's records sound especially painful, like that of Samuel Elliott, who died from a bowel blockage so severe that his intestines burst in 1938. In 1940, a man named Ernest Burrell died from a strep infection of the penis and scrotum. Inmate Lewis Campbell died in his cell from a perforated stomach ulcer in 1932. A toxic goiter claimed the life of Monroe Conley in 1939.

And while many inmates died horrific deaths from disease, there were many others who succumbed to the violence that was endemic to the penitentiary.

Torture, Murder, and Violence

As was the case with so many American prisons, conditions at the West Virginia Penitentiary slowly worsened. In time, it would be ranked by the U.S. Department of Justice as one of the "Top Ten Most Violent Correctional Facilities" in the country. One of the more infamous locations in the prison, with reports of gambling, fighting, and rape, was a recreation room known as "The Sugar Shack".

But violence had long been a part of the prison's history. Suicide, murder, and harsh punishments contributed to the deaths of scores of inmates. There were 36 recorded homicides that took place during the years of the prison's operation, but poor record-keeping in the facility's early days may hide many more during its shadowy past. In addition, there were hundreds of suicides.

Since prisons were first built, floggings were an acceptable form of punishment. There were several methods used. In some penitentiaries, prisoners were tied to a post and lashed with a whip or with leather harness straps, or paddles. The officials at the West Virginia Penitentiary were more creative, however.

As early as 1886, prison officials were exposed in the newspapers for hiding whips and other items, used to punish incorrigibles, from the state inspectors. But after one of the superintendent's resigned from the prison, he did a "tell all" interview with the *Cincinnati Enquirer*, exposing the violence and torture on inmates by prison officials. He described some of the torture devices that were used by prison guards, like the "Kicking Jenny." He explained, "It is an instrument invented and built in the prison. It is made somewhat in the shape of a quarter-circle, with the highest end about three or four feet above the platform upon which it is set. The prisoner is stripped naked and bent over upon the machine. His feet are fastened to the floor with ropes, while his hands, which are stretched over the upper end, are tied with ropes attached to small blocks, by which a tension so strong that the frame of the prisoner can almost be torn in two can be made with a slight pull. After the prisoner is placed in position, the Superintendent, or whoever does the whipping, takes a heavy whip, made of sole leather, two pieces of which, about three feet long, are sewed together and the ends scraped slightly rounding, the lash being three inches broad at the handle, tapering to a point. With the whip the prisoner is beaten until he is almost dead, or the strength of the man who is doing the whipping gives out."

As bad as that sounds, it was not the only torture device that the prison officials invented. Another was called the "Shoo-Fly," an instrument that was arranged so that the victim could be placed with his feet in the stocks, his arms pinioned, and his head fastened so that he couldn't move it. While strapped in this position, a guard would take a water hose and turn it full on into the prisoner's face. This early version of "water-boarding" went on until the man was nearly drowned.

In time, punishments changed. Officials shackled the men to a ball and chain or forced them into a lock-step march, a tiresome method of repetitive marching with a hand placed on the shoulder of the man in front of the prisoner in line. To break the line, or cause any disturbance of it, resulted in punishment. Eventually, physical punishments were replaced by solitary confinement and a loss of privileges, punishments that would have their own sets of consequences when prisoners rioted or acted out.

For while many died from disease and torture, many others committed suicide or were murdered by other inmates. Men were stabbed to death, beaten to death, burned to death, and poisoned by fellow prisoners. Although there were others, Ben Thorp was stabbed to death in 1929, as was David Lee Poole in 1963, Jesse Taylor in 1964, David Larry Painter in 1970, Kent Slie in 1986, Ronald Vance in 1985, and Robert Quimby in 1995.

Some deaths were more mysterious. In 1929, Arthur Perry "fell down" and died and in 1942, inmate Benjamin Legg died from "self-inflicted skull injuries." In 1989, John Perry's death was also caused by a crushed skull. Tony Santas, Jr. died from "accidental poisoning" in 1968, which was also the cause of death for Johnathan Jenkins two years later. Paul Wayne Short died from "self-induced poisoning" and Jesse James McNeely "drowned" in 1953.

There were also numerous suicides. Irving Trolley starved himself to death in 1929 and Frank Otero did the same in 1952. Inmate James Edward Jones cut his own throat in 1962. Virgil Hall also sliced his own neck in 1969. Thomas Gerald Steele swung from a homemade rope in 1959, as did Oley Holsclaw in 1964. John Henry Thomas, Jr. also hanged himself in 1969, followed by Jerry Moss in 1982, and Charles Phillips in 1988. Earl Heavner committed suicide by drinking antifreeze in 1943. In 1948, Ross May perished after drinking hydraulic brake fluid.

And, of course, there were also those who died within the penitentiary's walls from execution by the state.

At the End of a Rope

The West Virginia Penitentiary held executions behind its walls from 1899 until 1965, when the death penalty was abolished in the state. The last execution at the prison took place in 1959. Hangings were the first method of execution, and while most went just as planned, mistakes occasionally happened, with the condemned strangling to death or, in one horrific incident, being decapitated.

The first execution at the penitentiary occurred on October 10, 1899, with the hanging of Shep Caldwell. The previous June, he was found guilty of murdering his mistress, Rose Henshaw, after discovering her with another man. The 25-year-old black laborer went to the gallows in front of 50 spectators at just after 1:00 a.m. A select number of people had been allowed to attend the execution, but members of the general public gathered on nearby bleachers.

The first hangings took place at the North Wagon Gate, the penitentiary's original structure. Trap doors were installed on the second floor of the building that drop the condemned to their deaths. In the 1920s, death row cells, as well as the execution room, were moved to the Main Hospital Building. When the electric chair was put into use, a new building called the Death House was constructed. It contained four death row cells and an execution room on the first floor. The second floor contained a chaplain's office, library, and a guard's dining room. The Death House was torn down in 1965.

The second man to be executed at the penitentiary was Frank Broadenax. Like Caldwell, he was an African-American farm worker. He had been scheduled to be executed at the same time as Caldwell but, in his case, fate delayed his death. After a personal meeting with the prisoner, Governor Atkinson delayed the hanging for 30 days to allow further investigation into whether or not the murder of Sherman McFadden, of which Broadenax was convicted, was premeditated. At the time of the murder, Broadenax was the constable of a local "law and order organization," formed in response to the lawless state of the town of Kimball. During the 30-day

101

review, the courts ruled that the shooting had not been accidental, as Broadenax claimed. He went to the gallows on November 9, 1899, and before he was hanged, he warned the spectators, "Let bad whiskey and bad women alone. I have made my peace with God and I will soon be with Him."

During the years when the gallows were in use, there were a number of notable hangings at the penitentiary:

Hugh Bragg

Liquor led to murder and the gallows for Hugh Bragg, who was only 21-years-old when he accidentally shot Deputy Sheriff John Dennis Morton on January 12, 1920. Morton was serving a worthless check warrant that day and Bragg shot him on his doorstep. Sadly, the two men were friends, but Bragg had been drinking for hours when the deputy arrived. Oddly, Bragg had no legs. He had lost them in a railroad wreck a few years before.

Bragg was arrested in the wake of the murder and was taken to the Webster County Jail. When news spread of the shooting, Morton's brother rushed to the jail intent on carrying out revenge against Bragg. His pistol misfired and Bragg escaped death, but only for a short time. He was sentenced to death on January 27, and was executed three months and three days later on April 30.

Harry Sawyers

In 1926, Sawyers, an African-American migrant worker, was convicted of the robbery and assault of Mrs. Cullen Amburgy, the wife of a local dentist. He attacked her along some railroad tracks near the Williamson Ice and Cold Storage Company. After beating and choking her into unconsciousness, he raped her and stole her jewelry, which was worth about $1,000. It was not the robbery that sent him to the gallows -- it was the rape of a white woman.

After he was arrested, Sawyers immediately confessed to the crime and was sentenced to hang. His trial, which only lasted for five minutes, was said to be the shortest in the history of Mingo County. He was taken by special train to Moundsville and executed on April 19, just days after his sentence was passed.

Frank Hyer

Until June 19, 1931, the hangings that were carried out at the West Virginia Penitentiary were open to the public. But it was on this date that an execution went horribly wrong.

Frank Hyer, who had beaten and murdered his wife at the restaurant that they owned together in Durbin, was arrested, convicted, and sent to death row. There was nothing out of the ordinary in the minutes that led up to his death. There were 23 spectators who had gathered to watch Hyer be executed for a tragic, yet ordinary, crime. When he was led up the steps to the gallows, he addressed the small crowd. "Booze is the cause of this whole thing," he said. "But I have made my peace with Jesus Christ and am ready to go. I was drunk when I did it but will make the sacrifice and shed my blood for my crime which I confess. You can have my body but my soul shall go to God."

The trap door was sprung at 30 seconds past 9:00 p.m. and he dropped to his death. But rather than have the rope snap his neck, as it was supposed to do, his full weight hit in just the wrong way and he was instantly decapitated – much to the shock of the onlookers. Warden Scroggins, who had never seen anything like that happen in his career, later told newspapers that the trap had been tested earlier, as was common practice. For whatever reason, though, Hyer was beheaded. Luckily, the prison physician stated, death was "instantaneous and no pulse was found immediately after the incident occurred."

Harry Powers

There is no death row inmate from the penitentiary's history that earned the infamy of Harry Powers, the so-called "Bluebeard of Quiet Dell." Although largely forgotten today, he remains West Virginia's most famous mass murderer. He was hanged at the penitentiary on March 18, 1932, bringing an end to a story that shocked the entire country.

Powers, a pudgy, bespectacled little man, claimed his victims through "lonely hearts" classified advertisements in newspapers. Claiming to be a wealthy farmer in his ads, he must have seemed appealing to widows and spinsters during the desperate years of the Great Depression. After his arrest, a trunk was found in his home that was full of letters from women all over America. He was charged with the murders of two women and three children – Dorothy Lemke of Massachusetts and Asta Eicher and her three children from Illinois. The bodies were found at Powers' farm in Quiet Dell. A search revealed a torture chamber of sorts in an outbuilding and the personal effects of his victims in his home. He had lured the women to West Virginia with letters and his claim of being a well-to-do civil engineer. (The full story of Harry Powers is included in my book *Fear the Reaper*, which was co-written with Rene Kruse)

Powers' lurid story garnered the attention of the nation. His trial in December 1931, generated so much interest from reporters that it had to be moved from the courthouse in Clarksburg to Moore's Opera House, the only auditorium in town that was large enough to hold the crowd. It took the jury less than two hours to convict him. While he claimed to be innocent during the trial, he later confessed in prison and boasted about the women he had murdered. The authorities at the time suspected that he may have killed as many as 50 people, based on missing person's reports and circumstantial evidence. While on death row, Powers vaguely admitted that there had been other murders, but never offered any proof of them.

There was a circus-like atmosphere in Moundsville on the day of the execution. Outside of the prison, a crowd gathered on the sidewalks and cars were lined up for blocks. State and prison officials gathered with doctors and policemen to await the summons that would take them to the Death House in a remote corner of the prison. Powers, as he waited to be hanged, was dressed in a black pin-striped suit that hung poorly on his five-foot, three-inch frame.

The trap was sprung on the gallows at 9:00 p.m. Doctors declared him dead 11 minutes later. His body was never claimed and he lies today with all of the other unclaimed inmates in Whitegate Cemetery on Tom's Run Road just north of Moundsville.

Orville Adkins

Frank Hyer was not the only botched execution in the penitentiary's history, but the hanging of Orville Adkins was not nearly as grisly. Adkins was convicted of kidnapping and waited only three months to go to the gallows. His accomplices in the crime, John Travis and Arnet Allan Booth, were hanged the same day. They had all been charged with the kidnapping of Dr. James Seden, a minister and missionary to Japan, from Huntington.

The trio took Dr. Seden from his home and imprisoned him in a Wayne County coal mine. Soon after, they sent a $50,000 ransom note to his worried family. Dr. Seden had been abandoned in the mine, but was rescued by Albert and Edgar Ronk, who discovered the minister suffering from pneumonia and partial paralysis. The kidnappers were captured the following day and confessed to their crime. Seden died a short time later of pneumonia and a brain hemorrhage.

The three men met the hangmen on March 21, 1938. When Adkins took his turn on the trap door, it was sprung before the noose could be placed on his neck and he crashed headfirst to the concrete below. He was seriously injured in the fall, but this didn't stop the execution. The guards carried him back up the stairs on a stretcher, placed the noose correctly around his neck, and he plunged down again – this time to his death.

The last man to hang in the state of West Virginia was inmate Bud Peterson, who was sentenced to death for killing a woman over a poker debt. He went to the gallows in 1949, and just before the trap door was sprung, he addressed the 10 people who had gathered to watch him hang. "Look what sin has brought me," Peterson said. "You folks should stay on this side with Jesus."

After this hanging, the Death House fell silent for a time. In March 1951, it was announced that the next execution at the prison would be carried out using the more "humane" method of the electric chair.

Taking a Seat in "Old Sparky"

The electric chair began to be developed in the 1880s, after the state of New York established a committee to look for a more humane method of execution than hanging. Alfred P. Southwick, a member of the committee, developed the idea of running electric current through a condemned man after hearing a case of how relatively painless and quickly a drunk man died due to touching exposed power lines. Southwick, who was a dentist, was used to performing procedures on patients in chairs and developed the idea of a chair that could be electrified.

The first electric chair was produced by Harold P. Brown and Arthur Kennelly. Brown was an employee of Thomas Edison, hired for the purpose of researching electrocution and developing the electric chair. Kennelly, Edison's chief engineer at the West Orange facility, was assigned to work with Brown on the project. Brown intended to use alternating current (AC), then emerging as a potent rival to direct current (DC), which was further along in commercial development. The decision to use AC was partly driven by Edison's claim that AC was more lethal than DC.

To prove the danger of AC electricity, which was then being developed by George Westinghouse, and its suitability for executions, Brown and Edison publicly killed many animals with AC for the press in hopes of associating alternating current with electrical death. Most of their experiments were conducted at Edison's West Orange, New Jersey, laboratory in 1888. The demonstrations of electrocution apparently had their intended effects, and the committee adopted the AC electric chair in 1889.

On August 6, 1890, convicted murderer William Kemmler became the first man to be executed in the electric chair at the Auburn State Prison in New York. Kemmler murdered Matilda "Tillie" Ziegler, his common-law wife, with a hatchet on March 29, 1889, and was sentenced to death in the electric chair. His lawyers appealed, arguing that electrocution was cruel and unusual punishment. Westinghouse, who backed the AC current that would eventually become standard and which then powered the electric chair, actively supported Kemmler's appeal. The appeal failed, partly due to the even greater financial support of the powerful financial tycoon, J.

P. Morgan. Morgan was backing Thomas Edison and wanted to use the execution to show that Edison's direct current was a much safer way to provide electric power.

Witnesses remarked that Kemmler was composed at his execution; he did not scream, cry, or resist in any way. He sat down on the chair, but was ordered to get up by the warden so a hole could be cut in his suit through which a second electrical lead could be attached. This was done and Kemmler sat down again. He was strapped to the chair, his face was covered and the metal restraint put on his bare head. The generator was charged with the 1,000 volts, which was assumed to be adequate to induce quick unconsciousness and cardiac arrest. The chair had already been thoroughly tested; a horse had been successfully electrocuted the day before. Current was passed through Kemmler for 17 seconds. The power was turned off and Kemmler was declared dead by Dr. Edward Charles Spitzka.

However, witnesses noticed Kemmler was still breathing. The attending physicians, Dr. Spitzka and Dr. Charles F. Macdonald, came forward to examine Kemmler. After confirming Kemmler was still alive, Spitzka reportedly called out, "Have the current turned on again, quick — no delay."

In the second attempt, Kemmler was shocked with 2,000 volts. Blood vessels under the skin ruptured and bled and some witnesses erroneously claimed his body caught fire. This was likely not true, but witnesses did report the smell of burning flesh and several nauseated spectators unsuccessfully tried to leave the room.

In all, the entire execution took approximately eight minutes. The competitive newspaper reporters covering the Kemmler execution jumped on the abnormalities as each newspaper source tried to outdo each other with sensational headlines and reports. A reporter who witnessed it also said it was "an awful spectacle, far worse than hanging." Westinghouse later commented: "They would have done better using an axe."

Despite the "awful spectacle," as one paper called it, New York executed four more men in the same manner in 1891.

The electric chair at the West Virginia Penitentiary – dubbed "Old Sparky" as so many were in the American prison system – was partially built by an inmate named Paul Glenn, who served as the heard carpenter for the job. Legend claims that Glenn was later removed from the prison's general population after word got out that he built the infamous chair. The design of the chair was supervised by the carpentry shop foreman, Bob Harness, who spent seven years as a guard at the prison. For years, he had overseen hangings at the penitentiary and he recalled them as "gruesome," with some men taking "21-23 minutes to die." The electric chair, which promised a "more humane" death, seemed a viable alternative to what was viewed as an obsolete method of execution.

106

The chair had some unusual features. It was bolted to a platform that had once covered the trapdoor of the prison's gallows. It had a control apparatus that was designed in such a way that three buttons were to be pressed simultaneously by three members of the execution team. Only one of the buttons actually completed the circuit and the execution team members never had any idea which one of them it was.

The First Electric Chair Executions

The first inmates to be put to death by electrocution at the West Virginia Penitentiary were Fred Painter and Harry Burdette, both convicted of the murder of Edward C. O'Brien. They had kicked the soft drink salesman to death in a parking lot in downtown Charleston and were sentenced to die on March 26, 1951. Painter had to be jolted twice after physicians on hand found that he was still breathing after the first attempt. He was pronounced dead after nine minutes in the chair. Burdette had died after only three.

At the same time that all of this was going on, two inmates took advantage of the chaos and managed to escape from the prison during Painter and Burdette's executions.

Larry Fudge

On the bitterly cold night of January 4, 1958, Mrs. Inez Booth of Huntington was discovered dying from multiple stab wounds. Before she expired, she named her attacker for police – Larry Fudge, a paroled convict who had been released just three weeks earlier from federal prison, where he had been serving time for extortion.

Mrs. Booth had been forced to leave her home at knifepoint after she answered a knock on her door. She was then pushed into a car and was driven to a "wooded place" where she was assaulted and stabbed. Larry Fudge was in custody within an hour after the attack took place. He was arrested at his parents' home, where police found him with a bloodstained knife in his possession. He entered a guilty plea at his trial on March 12, 1958, and was sentenced to die in the electric chair on July 1.

Fudge's last day was spent in his death row cell. He ordered steak for his noon lunch, and leading up to the execution, a prison quartet sang religious songs in the prison's north yard. No one knows whether or not Fudge could hear them from his windowless cell. He was executed that night at 9:00 p.m.

As bluesman Blind Lemon Jefferson wrote, "Wonder why they electrocute a man at night? Because the current is much stronger, when the folks has turned out the lights."

The Last Execution

Only six other men would meet their unfortunate ends in the electric chair at the West Virginia Penitentiary before the state abolished capital punishment altogether. The last man to die in the electric chair was a 43-year-old man named Elmer Bruner. He was the second oldest of six children in a poor family from Huntington. His blind father sold newspapers and pencils on a street corner when Bruner was growing up, hoping to make ends meet. However, they rarely did.

Elmer allegedly worked as a handyman, but had been deemed incorrigible as a youth and was locked up three separate times in the local jail for burglary. He never made it past the fifth grade in school. On May 27, 1957, one of his robberies went bad and he beat 58-year-old Ruby Miller to death when she caught him inside of her home. Her body was discovered the next day. Her eyes and mouth were covered with tape, her hands were bound, and a stocking was knotted around her throat. She had been hit in the head at least a dozen times with the claw end of a hammer. Items taken from her home, along with her automobile keys, were found in a locker that belonged to Bruner.

He was convicted of the murder, but maintained his innocence to the end. He had broken into the Miller home, he admitted, but hadn't meant to kill anyone. He was ransacking a bedroom when Mrs. Miller confronted him with a shotgun. In his statement, he said that he "wrestled the gun from her and picked up something and began hitting her with it." He claimed that he was only protecting himself, but the jury wasn't swayed by his pleas. They found him guilty of murder in the first degree without recommendation for mercy, making the death penalty mandatory.

On April 3, 1959, Elmer enjoyed his last meal, which was ham, mashed potatoes and gravy, jello, salad, biscuits, peaches, and coffee. He took an afternoon nap and later that evening, took his last walk to the execution room. A hood was placed on his head and eight minutes later, he was dead. His family learned of his execution during a radio broadcast. They were too poor to afford a trip to visit him.

"Old Sparky" had taken its last life. Bruner's case had been appealed twice to the Supreme Court of West Virginia and once to the U.S. Supreme Court, but all of his appeals were rejected. The state decided that it was taking no more chances. West Virginia abolished the death penalty in 1965. No one has been executed since Bruner's death and "Old Sparky" has been sitting dark and silent ever since.

But do any of the chair's victims still linger behind?

The Husband of the "Greenbrier Ghost"

During its years of operations, the West Virginia Penitentiary saw more than its share of notorious inmates, most of which were known mainly within the borders of the state. But there was one inmate whose story remains one of the oddest in the annals of the supernatural. The court case that sent him to prison remains the only one in American history in which a ghost helped to solve the crime and convict the killer.

The story of Erasmus Stribbling Trout Shue begins with his meeting with Zona Heaster in October 1896. Zona was born in Greenbrier County, West Virginia, around 1873. Little is known about her life before she met Trout Shue, a drifter who came to Greenbrier County to work as a blacksmith and to start a new life for himself. He began working in the shop of James Crookshanks and Shue became well-known for his work.

Zona became acquainted with Shue a short time after he arrived in town. The two of them were attracted to each other and soon were married, despite the animosity felt towards Shue by Zona's mother, Mary Jane Robinson Heaster. She had taken an instant dislike to him and often told her daughter that she felt there was something the otherwise amiable man was hiding.

The Shues lived together as man and wife for several months and then, on January 23, 1897, Zona's body was discovered inside of their house by a young boy that Shue had sent there on a contrived errand. He had asked him to run to the house from the blacksmith shop and see if there was anything that Zona needed from the store. The boy, Andy Jones, found Zona lying on the floor at the bottom of the stairs. She was stretched out, with her feet together. One hand was on her abdomen and the other was lying next to her. Her head was turned slightly to one side and her eyes were wide open and staring. Even to this small boy, Zona Shue was obviously dead. Andy, not surprisingly, ran home to tell his mother. The local doctor and coroner, Dr. George W. Knapp, was summoned to the house, although he didn't arrive for nearly an hour.

By that time, Shue had carried his wife's body upstairs and had laid her out on the bed. Contrary to local custom, he dressed the corpse himself. Normally, it was the proper thing for ladies of the community to wash and dress a body in preparation for burial. However, Shue took it upon himself to dress Zona in her best clothing. A high-necked, stiff-collared dress covered her neck and a veil was placed over her face. While Dr. Knapp examined her and tried to determine a cause of death, Shue stayed by his wife's side, cradling her head and sobbing. Because of Shue's obvious grief, Knapp gave the body only a cursory examination, although he did notice some bruising on her neck. When he tried to look closer, Shue reacted so violently that the physician ended the examination and he left. Initially, he listed her cause of death as "everlasting faint" and then as "childbirth." It is unknown whether

Zona was pregnant or not, but for two weeks prior to her death, Knapp had treated her for "female trouble."

Dr. Knapp sent someone out to notify Zona's parents, but word of the young woman's death quickly spread through the community. By late afternoon, two young men who were friends of Zona's, volunteered to ride out to an area called Meadow Bluff and tell the Heaster family what had happened. The Heasters lived in an isolated area, about 15 miles away, where a small scattering of homes and farms were nestled against the side of Little Sewell Mountain. When she was informed of the news of her daughter's death, Mary Heaster's face grew dark. She reportedly said, "The devil has killed her!"

On Saturday, January 24, Zona's body was taken by carriage to her parents' home. A handful of neighbors presided over the funeral entourage and they brought Trout Shue along with them to the mountain farm. He showed extraordinary devotion toward the body, keeping a vigil at the head of the open coffin as the wagon traveled over the rutted and bumpy roads. The body was displayed in the Heaster's house for the wake, an event that lasted all day Sunday. It gave neighbors and friends the opportunity to pay their last respects to the dead, visit with one another, give solace to the bereaved, and bring food for the family. A few local ladies sat up with the body throughout the night and until the time of the burial on Monday.

Those who came to pay their respects during the wake pointed out the bizarre behavior of Trout Shue. His grief swung back and forth between overwhelming sadness and manic energy. He allowed no one to get too close to the coffin, especially while he was placing a pillow on one side of her head and a rolled-up cloth on the other. He explained that these items were to help Zona "rest easier." In addition, he tied a large scarf around her neck and explained tearfully that it "had been Zona's favorite." When it came time to move the corpse to the cemetery, though, several people noticed that there seemed to be a strange looseness to Zona's head. Needless to say, people started to talk and speculation began about how Zona had really met her untimely demise.

Mary Jane Heaster did not need to speculate about whether or not Trout Shue had some part in her daughter's death; she was convinced that he had. She had disliked the man from the start and had never wanted Zona to marry him. She was sure that he had murdered her, but there was no way that she could prove it.

After the wake, Mary Jane took the sheet from inside the coffin and tried to return it to Shue, but he refused it. Folding it back up to put it away, she noticed that it had a peculiar odor, so she washed it out. She came to believe that what happened next was some sort of strange omen. Mary Jane dropped the sheet into

110

the wash basin and when she did, the water inside turned red. Strangely, a few moments later, the sheet turned pink and the color in the water disappeared. Mary Jane then boiled the sheet and hung it outside for several days but the stain could not be removed. She interpreted the eerie "bloodstains" as a sign that Zona had been murdered.

After this strange incident, she began to pray. Every night for the next four weeks, Mary Jane prayed fervently that her daughter would return to her and reveal the truth about how she had died. According to her story, a few weeks later, her prayers were answered.

Over the course of four dark nights, the spirit of Zona Shue appeared at her mother's bedside. She would come as a bright light at first and then an apparition would take form, chilling the air in the entire room. She woke her mother and explained over and over again how her husband had murdered her. Trout Shue had been abusive and cruel, and had attacked her in a fit of rage because he thought she had not cooked any meat for supper. He had savagely broken her neck and to show this, the ghost turned her head completely around until it was facing backwards.

Mary Jane had been right. Shue had killed her daughter and the word of her spirit proved it!

A short time later, Mary Jane went to the local prosecutor, John Alfred Preston, to try and convince him to re-open the investigation into Zona's death. She offered the visitations from her daughter's spirit as evidence that a miscarriage of justice was taking place. By all accounts, Preston was both polite and sympathetic to Mrs. Heaster. The two spoke together for "several hours" and at the end of the meeting, Preston agreed to dispatch deputies to speak with Dr. Knapp and a few others involved in the case. While it seemed unlikely that he was willing to take another look at the case because of the statement of a ghost, the investigation did get re-opened. Local newspapers reported that Mrs. Heaster was not the only one in the community who was suspicious about Zona's death. There were also "certain citizens" who had started to ask questions, as well as the growing "rumors in the community."

Preston himself went to see Dr. Knapp and the physician admitted that his examination of the dead woman had been cursory and incomplete. The two of them agreed that an autopsy was needed to answer the questions about Zona's death once and for all. If Trout Shue was innocent of any wrongdoing, this would clear his name.

A few days later, an exhumation was ordered and an inquest jury was assembled. The autopsy was performed in the Nickell School House, which was just a short distance away from the Soule Methodist Church graveyard where Zona had been buried. The schoolchildren were dismissed on the day of February 22, 1897, and Zona Shue's grave was opened. It was reported in the local newspaper that Trout Shue "vigorously complained" about the exhumation but it was made clear to him that he would be forced to attend the inquest if he did not attend willingly. He replied, "They will not be able to prove I did it." This was a rather odd and careless statement for a man who claimed to be innocent.

The autopsy lasted for three hours under the uncertain light of kerosene lanterns. The body of the dead woman was "in a near state of perfect preservation," thanks to the cold temperatures of February, making the work of the doctors much easier to complete. A jury of five men had been assembled to watch the proceedings, and they huddled together in the cold building with officers of the court, Trout Shue, Andy Jones (the boy who had found the body) and other witnesses and spectators. The autopsy began and the doctors quickly found what they were looking for. One of the doctors turned to Trout Shue, "We have found your wife's neck to have been broken."

Shue's head dropped and an expression of despair crossed his face. He whispered, "They cannot prove that I did it."

The autopsy findings were quite damning to Shue. A report on March 9, stated, "The discovery was made that the neck was broken and the windpipe mashed. On the throat were the marks of fingers indicating that she had been choken [sic]. The neck was dislocated between the first and second vertebrae. The ligaments were torn and ruptured. The windpipe had been crushed at a point in front of the neck."

The findings were made public at once, upsetting many in the community. Shue was arrested and charged with murder. He was locked up in the small stone jail on Washington Street in Lewisburg, and in spite of the fact that the evidence against him was circumstantial, at best, he was indicted by a grand jury and was formally arraigned for murder. He immediately entered a plea of "not guilty."

While he awaited trial, information about Shue's unsavory past began to surface. Zona had been his third wife. His first marriage to Allie Estelline Cutlip had produced one child but had ended in divorce in 1889 while Shue was in prison for horse stealing. His wife alleged in the divorce decree that Shue had been violent and had frequently beaten her. In 1894, Shue had married again, this time to Lucy Ann Tritt. Lucy died just eight months later under circumstances that were described as "mysterious." Shue claimed that Lucy fell and hit her head on a rock, but few believed him. Before any action could be taken against him, he packed up and left the area. In the fall of 1896, he moved to Greenbrier County.

In jail, Shue remained in good spirits, and reported that his grieving for Zona had ended. In fact, he announced that he had a lifelong goal of having seven wives.

Since Zona had only been his third, and he was still a young man, he had a good chance of realizing such a worthwhile ambition. He repeatedly told reporters that his guilt in the matter could not be proved.

The trial began on June 22, 1897, and numerous people from the community testified against Shue. The highlight of the trial, of course, came with the appearance of Mary Jane Heaster. Preston put her on the stand as both the mother of the dead woman and also as the first person to notice the unusual circumstances of Zona's death. He wanted to make sure that she appeared both sane and reliable. For this reason, he skirted the issue of the ghost because it was bound to make her appear irrational and also because it was inadmissible evidence. The teller of the story, in this case Zona Shue, could obviously not be cross-examined by the defense and so her testimony would be hearsay under the law.

Unfortunately for Shue, his attorney decided to ask Mrs. Heaster about her ghostly sighting. It seemed obvious that he was doing it to try and make Mary Jane look ridiculous to the jury. He characterized her "visions" as a mother's ravings and worked hard to admit that she might have been mistaken about what she allegedly saw. He continued to badger her for quite some time, but Mary Jane never wavered in her descriptions of Zona's ghost – nor about what the specter had told her about Shue's guilt. When the defense counsel realized that the testimony was not going the way that he wanted, he dismissed her.

By that time, though, the damage was done. Because the defense, and not the prosecution, had introduced the testimony about the spirit, the judge had a hard time telling the jury to exclude it. It was apparent that most of the people in the community believed that Mary Jane had seen her daughter's ghost. Despite Shue's eloquent testimony in his own defense, the jury quickly found him guilty. Ten of them even voted that he be hanged, which spoke volumes about Mrs. Heaster's believability as a witness. Without a unanimous verdict of death, though, Shue was sentenced to life in prison.

The sentence did not satisfy everyone in Greenbrier County. On July 11, 1897, a citizen's group of anywhere from 15 to 30 men assembled eight miles west of Lewisburg to form a lynching party. They had purchased a new rope and were well armed when they started towards the jail. If not for a man named George M. Harrah, who alerted the sheriff, Shue would have surely been lynched. Harrah contacted Deputy Sheriff Dwyer at the jail. It was said that when Shue was informed of this threat against his life, he became "greatly agitated" and was unable to tie his own shoes. Dwyer hid him in the woods a mile or so from town until deputies were able to disband the mob and return them to their homes.

Shue was moved to the West Virginia State Penitentiary on July 14, where he lived for the next three years. He died on March 13, 1900, from one of the epidemics that swept through the prison that spring. At that time, the prison commonly buried unclaimed remains in the nearby Tom's Run Cemetery, for which no records were kept until the 1930s. Thanks to this, no trace of Trout Shue can be found today.

Mary Jane Robinson Heaster lived to tell her tale to all who would listen. She died in September 1916, without ever recanting her story about her daughter's ghost.

And as for Zona, her ghost was never seen again, but she has left a haunting, historical mark on Greenbrier County. It is one that is still being felt today. In fact, a roadside marker along Route 60 still commemorates the case. It reads:

Interred in nearby cemetery is Zona Heaster Shue. Her death in 1897 was presumed natural until her spirit appeared to her mother to describe how she was killed by her husband Edward. Autopsy on the exhumed body verified the apparition's account. Edward, found guilty of murder, was sentenced to the state prison. Only known case in which testimony from ghost helped convict a murderer.

A Fading History of Horror

The reputation of the West Virginia Penitentiary began its slow decline in the early part of the twentieth century. As with so many American institutions, overcrowding became a serious problem in the 1920s. By the end of the decade, the state decided to double the size of the penitentiary. The 5 x 7-foot cells were too small to hold three prisoners at a time, but until the expansion, there was no other option. Two prisoners would sleep in the bunks with the third sleeping on a mattress on the floor. The state utilized prison labor once again and completed this phase of construction in 1959. Most of the delay had been caused by steel shortages during World War II.

By the middle of the twentieth century, the penitentiary had earned its notoriety as one of the most violent prisons in the country. In February 1968, a riot erupted that left two inmates seriously injured. At least 39 prisoners started a fire that burned the former female quarters. A few months later, another disturbance occurred, leaving two guards injured.

The first large riot occurred in 1973. Chaos ensued when five guards and two prisoners were hospitalized and one inmate was left dead after a fire was started by angry prisoners. A full-scale riot and fire followed, involving threats, bullets, and five guards being held hostage before it was all over.

The riot was triggered by a group of convicts overpowering a guard and taking the keys to the solitary confinement section of the prison. They released Bobby Gene Jarvis, an indicted convict who was awaiting trial for the murder of a prison guard, along with a number of other prisoners. Soon after, the guards were taken hostage. The prisoners barricaded themselves in the solitary confinement section and threatened to kill the five hostages if any shots or tear-gas were fired into the area. Tensions mounted before a long series of demands from the prisoners were addressed, eventually leading to an end of the riot.

This was the prison's first major riot. It would not be the last.

By 1986, conditions at the prison had continued to decline. Security had become extremely loose in all areas. Regarded as a "con's prison," most of the locks on the cells had been picked and inmates roamed the halls freely. Bad plumbing and insects caused rapid spreading of various diseases. The prison was now holding more than 2,000 men and crowding became an issue once again. Another major contribution to the success of the riot was that it occurred on a holiday – January 1, New Year's Day. Many of the officers had called off work, which fueled the prisoners to carry out their plans on that specific day.

Around 5:30 p.m., 20 inmates stormed the mess hall. Within seconds, six officers and a food service worker were tackled and slammed to the floor. Inmates put knives to their throats and locked them into their own handcuffs. Even though several hostages were taken throughout the day, none of them were seriously injured. However, over the course of the two-day upheaval, three inmates were slaughtered for an assortment of reasons. Governor Arch A. Moore, Jr. was sent to the penitentiary to converse with the inmates. This meeting set up a new list of rules and standards on which the prison would build over the rest of its history, but with little success.

The end came for the West Virginia Penitentiary in 1995. Toward the end of its time, the facility was marked with not only the riots, but many instances of violence, and several escapes. In the 1960s, the prison reached a peak population of about 2,000 inmates, but those numbers had declined to just over 600 by 1995. The fate of the prison had been sealed by an earlier Supreme Court ruling that stated that the 5 x7-foot cells were cruel and unusual punishment. A few years later, the penitentiary was closed. The remaining inmates were transferred to the Mt. Olive Correctional Complex in Fayette County and about 30 employees stayed behind to literally lock the doors and turn out the lights.

By April 1995, the old West Virginia Penitentiary was dark and silent. It stood empty and eerie for a time, only to re-open again as a historic site, offering tours and events to the public and offering instruction for prison guards on the science of preventing prison riots.

When the lights are turned off for the day, though, many who work in the crumbling old structure have come to believe that the former prison is not as empty as it appears.

Hauntings at the West Virginia Penitentiary

Death, violence, murder and suicide...

Each of these can contribute to the haunting of a location, but combine all of them and you have the setting for a truly terrifying spot – like the West Virginia Penitentiary. There seems to be no doubt among those who have spent time here after dark that the prison is a very haunted place. Visitors claim to have experienced the sound of phantom footsteps, voices and noises that have no explanation, inexplicable cold chills, overwhelming feelings of panic, elusive shadowy figures, and much more.

The penitentiary, which covers more than 20 acres, once housed the worst criminals in the state, and almost every surviving section of the facility seems to be linked to some sort of ghostly activity.

Just inside of the main entrance, facing Jefferson Avenue, is a unique addition to the prison. Inside of the first room, where prisoners entered and were searched, was a large wheel by which the prisoners were escorted to their cell. A small opening in the hallway allowed the guard to operate the double, circular cage that was installed in 1894. There was a single entrance to the center cage, which was then spun for the front of the hallway to the corridor. This wheel prevented the prisoners from making a break for freedom down the hall and out the main doors. This is one of the first haunted places in the prison that many present-day visitors will encounter. Although it is chained and locked up, there have been many reports of it attempting to still operate under its own power. The metal grinds, some say, and the chains clank as it tries to admit another prisoner to spend eternity within the prison's dank stone walls.

The North Hall area, dubbed "the Alamo," was where the worst of the worst prisoners were kept. Inmates were usually sent to this area after committing a crime or causing chaos in the cellblocks. During the later years of the prison's operation, when things had deteriorated to the point that it was nearly out of control, prisoners in this section reported that they literally had to fight to stay alive. This is a section of the prison where visitors report an overwhelming feeling of panic and occasionally, some will claim a shortness of breath as if crushed by the weight of the atmosphere.

116

There are two spots in this section that are said to be the most haunted. One of them is Cell #2, which belonged to Danny Lehmann, the spokesperson for the inmates during the 1986 riot. He was stabbed to death during the riot and his tormented spirit is believed to linger behind in this cell. The other haunted cell belonged to William "Red" Snyder, who was convicted of murdering his father and a neighbor in 1968. In 1992, Snyder was brutally murdered by another inmate and stabbed more than 40 times in his cell. That chamber today is a place of terrible despair – and not for the faint of heart. A number of people have reportedly lost consciousness in that cramped cell and some say they have been choked by unseen hands.

The "Alamo" is an almost unbearable area for many visitors and a number of ghosts are believed to be trapped here, including Eddie Fielder, who hanged himself in 1975 in a cell that has since been removed. A convict who was once housed in that cell claimed that he awakened one night to find a headless man who was holding him by the throat.

The former contact visitation section of the prison is another place that is haunted by the past. It was once a cell block area in the South Hall in the 1870s, but later became the main dining room and kitchen. In 1988, a new dining area was completed and this became a contact visitation room. Even today, the walls are still marked with colorful paintings, created by inmates to help children who came to visit their incarcerated relatives feel more comfortable. But underneath that bright paint, lurks a dark history. It was in this room on January 1, 1986, that the bloody riot began that led to the death of three inmates and many employees being taken hostage.

Did that leave an impression behind? Many believe that it did and have reported strange sounds, rushing footsteps, banging noises, cries, and screams. One visitor even left this section of the prison after feeling as though someone had grabbed hold of her arm. There was no one there, but witnesses stated that a bright red handprint appeared on her arm and remained there for several hours after the incident took place.

On the second floor of the main building is the medical infirmary and the psychiatric ward. The original hospital and tuberculosis ward were located in separate buildings out in the yard, but later, the hospital was moved into this space. Many visitors claim that the sights, sounds, and smells of the past often make themselves known in this section. Once jammed with beds, the hospital was often filled to more than capacity, housing men who were sick and dying from all sorts of illnesses. Doors have been heard to rattle in this area and even slam shut without

117

assistance. Voices, cries, and moans have been heard and recorded in the former wards.

Perhaps the most sinister haunted spot in the prison is the "Sugar Shack," a dark area of the basement that was used for indoor recreation when the weather outside was too severe. During the latter days of the prison, the inmates were pretty much left to their own devices in this large section. A guard checked on them periodically, but little was done to protect the weaker inmates from the savages and monsters among them. Even though no one was ever reportedly killed in the Sugar Shack, there was a lot of violence and injuries that occurred there. Men were beaten and raped, and the trauma suffered there imprinted itself on the atmosphere of the basement, leading to a terrifying haunting. There have been scores of reports from visitors of eerie voices, cries, and shuffling footsteps. In addition, there are more apparitions seen in this area than in any other part of the prison. Staff members and visitors have seen shadowy figures, as well as full-bodied forms. One guide recalled leading a group of 11 people on a tour of the prison, but when she counted heads on the way out of the Sugar Shack, realized there were 12 people behind her. The last man in line suddenly vanished in front of her eyes.

Another ghost that haunts the basement is a former maintenance man. Believed to be a "snitch" by the inmates, who informed on the prisoners to the warden and guards, was murdered in revenge. Stabbed to death while sitting on the toilet, his spirit now wanders through the basement and had allegedly been seen dozens of times over the years.

Located along the north side of the prison is the North Wagon gate, a narrow building that temporarily housed both men and women prisoners when it was the starting point of the penitentiary in the middle 1860s. The wooden trap doors on the second floor were used for hangings in the early days, before the electric chair was put into use. This is an area that is also said to be home to a number of lingering spirits. Visitors have reported seeing apparitions, as well as hearing disembodied voices and unexplained sounds in the old building.

But these short glimpses into the haunted history of the prison can't begin to capture the eeriness of this place. One of the chambers in the prison still houses "Old Sparky," the prison's electric chair. Originally, all executions were held in the Death House, a separate building that was located in the north recreation yard, but it is believed that those who went to their deaths in the chair still remain attached to the place where their lives ended. The maximum security area was located to the north of the main entrance, and had two levels of cells. The upper row of cells was constructed to hold inmates who were given less time outside. They rarely left the cells and were even forced to eat there. Like the dreaded "Hole," such solitary conditions often led to suicide – and, not surprisingly, to hauntings.

And the list goes on. As stated earlier, the West Virginia Penitentiary possesses what is undoubtedly the darkest history of any of the prisons on this list. It earned its reputation as one of the most dangerous and violent facilities in the country during its last years of operations and since its closure, has gained another reputation altogether – as one of the most haunted prisons in America.

6. A PLASTER HEAD

ALCATRAZ

"The Rock," the name given to Alcatraz Penitentiary, was the ultimate American prison. It was the place where scores of the country's worst criminal offenders, bloodletters, badmen, and escape artists called the end of the line. For 29 years, the damp, fog-enshrouded prison kept America's most notorious lawbreakers away from the rest of the world on a small island in San Francisco Bay. The heavy mist, the cold wind, freezing water, and ominous foghorns made Alcatraz the loneliest of prisons. During its almost three decades as a federal prison, its steel doors clanged shut on more than a 1,000 convicts. It was a place of total punishment and minimum privilege. Those who survived this place often did so at the cost of their sanity -- and in some cases, their souls.

Alcatraz Island, located in the mist off the coast of San Francisco, received its name in 1775 when the Spanish explorers charted San Francisco Bay. They named the rocky piece of land *La Isla de los Alcatraces*, or the Island of Pelicans. The island was totally uninhabited, plagued by barren ground, little vegetation, and surrounding water that churned with swift currents. In the late 1840s, the island was taken over by the U.S. military. It was a prime location for the establishment of a fort, and a lighthouse was desperately needed there because of the all of the ships that were coming to San Francisco during the Gold Rush. Topographical engineers began conducting geological surveys and by 1853, a military post was started. One year later, a lighthouse was established (the first on the Pacific Coast) to guide ships through the Golden Gate.

A few years later, a fort was erected on the island and in 1859, Alcatraz saw its first prisoners, a contingent of court-martialed, military convicts. Then in 1861, Alcatraz started to receive Confederate prisoners, thanks to the fact that the island was so isolated from the mainland. Until the end of the Civil War, the prison population varied, consisting of soldiers, Confederate privateers, and southern sympathizers. They were confined in the dark basement of the guardhouse and conditions were grim. The men slept side-by-side, head to toe, lying on the stone floor of the basement. There was no running water, no heat, and no latrines. Disease and infestations of lice spread from man to man and, not surprisingly, overcrowding was a serious problem. They were often bound by six-foot chains attached to iron balls, fed bread and water, and confined in sweatboxes as punishment.

After the war ended, the fort was deemed obsolete and was no longer needed. The prison continued to be used, though, and soon, more buildings and cell houses were added. In the 1870s and 1880s, during the American Indian Wars, native chiefs and tribal leaders were incarcerated on Alcatraz. They shared quarters with the worst of the military prisoners. The island became a shipping point for incorrigible deserters, thieves, rapists, and repeated escapees.

In 1898, the Spanish-American War sent the prisoner population from less than 100 to over 450. The Rock became a holding pen for Spanish prisoners brought over from the Philippines. Around 1900, Alcatraz again became a disciplinary barracks for military prisoners. Ironically, it also served as a health resort for soldiers returning from the Philippines and Cuba with tropical diseases. The overcrowding caused by a combination of criminals and recovering soldiers resulted in pardons to reduce the number of men housed on the island.

By 1902, the Alcatraz prison population averaged around 500 men per year, with many of the men serving sentences of two years or less. The wooden barracks on the island had fallen into a ramshackle state, thanks to the damp, salt air, and so, in 1904, work was begun to modernize the facility. Prisoner work crews began extending the stockade wall and constructing a new mess hall, kitchen, shops, a library, and a wash house. Work continued on the prison for the next several years and even managed to survive the Great Earthquake of 1906. The disaster left San Francisco in shambles and a large fissure opened up on Alcatraz, but left the buildings untouched. Prisoners from the heavily damaged San Francisco jail were temporarily housed on the island until the city's jail could be rebuilt.

Construction of the new buildings was completed a few years later and, in 1911, the facility was officially named the "United States Disciplinary Barracks." In addition to Army prisoners, the Rock was also used to house seamen captured on German vessels during the First World War. Alcatraz was the Army's first long-term prison and it quickly gained a reputation for being a tough facility. There were strict rules and regulations with punishments ranging from loss of privileges to solitary confinement, restricted diet, hard labor, and even a 12-pound ball and ankle chain.

Despite the stringent rules, though, Alcatraz was still mainly a minimum-security facility. Inmates were given various work assignments, depending on how responsible they were. Many of them worked as general servants, cooking and cleaning for families of soldiers housed on the island. In many cases, the prisoners were even entrusted to care for the children of officers. However, this lack of security led to a number of attempted escapes. Most of those who tried for freedom never made it to the mainland and were forced to turn back. Many others were never seen again. They had either made it to shore – or had drowned in the harsh waters of the bay.

During the 1920s, Alcatraz gradually fell into disuse. The lighthouse keeper, a few Army personnel, and the most hardened of the military prisoners were the only ones who remained on the island. The mostly empty buildings slowly crumbled, but this period would not last for long. A change was coming to Alcatraz that would make it the most formidable prison in American history.

America's "Devil's Island"

The social upheaval that began in America during Prohibition and continued into the Great Depression brought new life to Alcatraz. President Roosevelt and the newly empowered FBI began a national "War on Crime" to deal with the gangsters, kidnappers, and bandits that were "terrorizing" the country. Attorney General Homer Cummings supported J. Edgar Hoover and the FBI in creating a new, escape-proof prison that would send fear into the hearts of criminals. They decided that Alcatraz would be the perfect location for such a penitentiary. In 1933, the facility was officially turned over to the Federal Bureau of Prisons and the Attorney General asked James A. Johnston of San Francisco to take over as warden of the new prison. He implemented a strict set of rules and regulations for the facility and selected the best available guards and officers from the federal penal system.

The Rock became largely Warden Johnston's creation. New construction was started on the project and practically the entire cellblock building was built atop the old Army fort. Part of the old Army prison was used but the iron bars were replaced by bars of hardened steel. Gun towers were erected at various points around the island, and the cellblocks were equipped with catwalks, gun walks, electric locks, metal detectors, a well-stocked arsenal, barbed and cyclone wire fencing, and even tear gas containers that were fitted into the ceiling of the dining hall and elsewhere. Apartments for the guards and their families were built on the old parade grounds and the lighthouse keeper's home was taken over for the warden's residence. Alcatraz had been turned into an impregnable fortress.

Wardens from prisons all over the country were polled and were permitted to send their most incorrigible inmates to Alcatraz. These included inmates with behavioral problems, those with a history of escape attempts, and even high-profile inmates who were receiving privileges because of their status or notoriety. Each train that came from the various prisons seemed to have a "celebrity" on board. Among the first groups were Al Capone, Doc Barker, George "Machine Gun" Kelly, Robert Stroud (who would later become notorious as the Birdman of Alcatraz), Bonnie and Clyde driver Floyd Hamilton, and kidnapper Alvin "Creepy" Karpis. When each of these men arrived on Alcatraz, they ceased to exist as the people they once were and simply became numbers.

When Warden Johnston conceived of the idea behind Alcatraz prison, he did not even pay lip service to the principle of rehabilitation. This was a place of punishment, plain and simple, and nothing that these men had done or accomplished in the past mattered now. Inside, there would be no rewards for good behavior; it was simply expected and demanded. There were no trustees, only punishment for breaking the rules. Johnston believed that a policy of maximum security, combined with few privileges and total isolation would serve as a deterrent to America's public enemies and those who emulated them. In the end, though, it would deter them no more than the electric chair, the hangman or the gas chamber did. In fact, despite the propaganda coming from the Attorney General's office, comparatively few big-time gangsters ever went to Alcatraz. There were not enough of them who were captured alive to fill the cells. What the FBI called a "notorious mail robber" was more likely to be a small-time loser who broke into some postal boxes. Unbelievably, some inmates were first-time offenders. If the new prison profited anyone, it was the wardens who were able to empty some of their cells to populate Alcatraz. No court could sentence criminals to Alcatraz. Only those already serving terms could be transferred there, if the warden recommended it and the Bureau of Prisons approved the transfer.

Alcatraz became a brutal place of penitence. It was a place where the inmates had only five rights – food, clothing, a private cell, medical care, and a shower once each week. Any, and all, of those rights could be taken away for even a minor infraction.

Each of the cells in Alcatraz measured 4 x 8-feet and had a single fold-up bunk, toilet, desk, chair, and sink. A prisoner's day began at 6:30 a.m. with the clanging of a bell and bright electric lights. He had 20 minutes in which to dress and make his bed. If he wanted to shave, he had to shove a matchbox through the bars of his cell. A guard would place a razor blade in it and allow three minutes before returning to reclaim it. At 6:50 a.m. the bell sounded again and the floor guard took the morning count. A third bell would clang when all prisoners were accounted for. A fourth bell sounded when it was time for breakfast. The turnkeys, standing inside locked cages, pulled back a lever and all of the heavy steel cell door locks pulled back simultaneously. The prisoners then marched in a single file line to the mess hall. The prisoners ate 10 men to a table, with the black prisoners segregated. They all sat facing the same direction and all of them ate in silence. The first years of Alcatraz were known as the "silent years" and during this period, the rules stated that no prisoner was allowed to speak to another, sing, hum, or whistle. Talking was forbidden in the cells, in the mess hall, and even in the showers. The inmates were allowed to talk for three minutes during the morning and afternoon recreation yard periods and for two hours on weekends. This rule of silence was later relaxed.

The food was served cafeteria-style from a steam table. Bad food had caused more prison riots than anything else in history, so Warden Johnston was determined to serve three palatable meals each day. Typical breakfast fare consisted of oatmeal with milk, fried bologna sausage, cottage fried potatoes, toast with margarine, and coffee. Prisoners were required to clean their plates, and if they did not, they received no food the following day. Johnston also issued three packs of cigarettes each week, and for heavy smokers, he installed tobacco and paper dispensers in each cell so that inmates could roll their own. However, he did not approve a commissary, as most prisons had, where the men could buy candy, chewing gum and soda pop with the few cents they earned each day in the prison workshops.

After breakfast, the prisoners were lined up again and marched back to their cells for another count. No prisoner was allowed to wear a watch. Bells told the time and they rang almost every half hour for one reason or another. After the next count, prisoners were lined up again according to their assigned workshop. Aside from breaks and lunch, the prisoners worked for most of the day, until 9:30 p.m. when lights were turned out. The methodical routine never varied, except on Saturday and Sunday. On Sunday mornings, time was allowed for religious worship and on

124

Saturday, the men were allowed their weekly shower. Both days offered two hours of free time exercising in the yard or pursuing indoor hobbies.

In their cells, before lights out, prisoners could read books or magazines borrowed from the prison library, but to intensify their isolation, Johnston denied them newspapers or radios. Correspondence was also severely limited. A prisoner could write one letter a week to a relative, and from his family, receive no more than three. He could correspond with no one outside of his family except for his lawyer. Censors read all incoming and outgoing mail, deleted any part of it that did not confine itself to family affairs, and sent a typed copy of what remained. There were no set visiting days. Each monthly visit, limited to 45 minutes, had to be arranged through Johnston. A pass was then issued and instructions were given on where and when to board the boat to the island. A sheet of plate glass, which ran from floor to ceiling, separated the visitors from the inmates. At head level were two strips of steel, a few inches apart, which had small holes drilled into them. Visitors and prisoners could speak through these holes, but they were designed to be so small that nothing could be passed through them. Guards were also present and could hear every word that was exchanged. They interrupted if forbidden topics were broached.

The guards at Alcatraz were almost as hardened as the prisoners themselves. There was one guard for every three inmates, which was stunning considering that most prisons were staffed at about one guard to every 12 inmates. Gun galleries had been placed at each end of the cell blocks and as many as 12 counts each day allowed the guards to keep very close tabs on the men on their watch. Because of the small number of total inmates at Alcatraz, the guards generally knew the inmates by name. Although Warden Johnston forbid corporal punishment as a general rule, the guards did not hesitate, when met with any resistance, to knock a man senseless with water from a high pressure hose, break an arm or a leg with their clubs, or truss a prisoner up for days in a straitjacket. The usual punishment, though, was solitary confinement in the punishment cells. While the cells in which the prisoners lived were barren at best, they must have seemed like luxury hotel rooms compared to the punishment cells. In those cells, the men were stripped of all but their basic right to food, and even then, what they were served barely sustained the convict's life, let alone his health.

One place of punishment was the single strip cell, which was dubbed the "Oriental." This dark, steel-encased cell had no toilet and no sink. There was only a hole in the floor that could be flushed from the outside. Inmates were placed in the cell with no clothing and were given little food. The cell had a standard set of bars, with an expanded opening to pass food through, but a solid steel door enclosed the prisoner in total darkness. Men were usually kept in this cell for one or two days. The cell was cold and completely bare, save for a straw sleeping mattress that the guards removed each morning. This cell was used as punishment for the most severe violations and was feared by the prison population.

The "Hole" was a similar type of cell. There were several of them and they were all located on the bottom tier of cells. They were considered to be a severe punishment by the inmates. Mattresses were again taken away each morning and prisoners were sustained by bread and water, which was supplemented by a solid meal every third day. Steel doors also closed these cells off from the daylight, although a low-wattage bulb was suspended from the ceiling. Inmates could spend up to 19 days here, completely silent and isolated from everyone. Time in the Hole usually meant psychological and sometimes even physical torture. Usually, convicts who were thrown into the Hole for anything other than a minor infraction were beaten by the guards. The screams from the men being beaten in one of the four Holes located on the bottom tier of D Block echoed throughout the block as though being amplified through a megaphone. Sometimes when men emerged from the darkness and isolation of the Hole, they would be totally disoriented and would end up in the prison's hospital ward, devoid of their sanity. Others came out with pneumonia and arthritis after spending days or weeks on the cold cement floor with no clothing.

And there were even worse places to be sent than the Hole. Located in front of unused A Block was a staircase that led down to a large steel door. Behind the door were catacomb-like corridors and stone archways that led to the sealed-off gun ports from the days when Alcatraz was a fort. Fireplaces located in several of the rooms had not been used for warmth, but to heat up cannonballs so that they would start fires after reaching their targets. Two of the other rooms located in this dank, underground area were dungeons. Prisoners who had the misfortune of being placed in the dungeons were not only locked in, but also chained to the walls. Their screams could not be heard in the main prison. The only toilet they had was a bucket, which was emptied once each week. For food, they received two cups of water and one slice of bread each day. Every third day, they would receive a regular meal. The men were stripped of their clothing and their dignity as guards chained them to the wall in a standing position from morning until night. In the darkest hours, they were given a blanket to sleep on. Thankfully, the dungeons were rarely used, but the dark cells of D Block, known as the "Hole," were regularly filled.

Alcatraz could test the limits of men's endurance, both physically and mentally. Over the years, a number of inmates attempted suicide, and a few succeeded. Those who failed always wound up in the Hole. A counterfeiter named John Standig tried to kill himself before he even got to Alcatraz by jumping from the train taking him there, but he survived. At the prison, where he made another attempt, he told a fellow inmate, "If you ever get out of here, tell them I wasn't trying to escape. I was trying to kill myself." An inmate named Jimmy Grove, a former soldier imprisoned after raping an officer's daughter, was saved by a blood transfusion after he cut the arteries in both of his arms. In April 1936, a prisoner named Joe Bowers was taken to the Hole after he broke his eyeglasses and tried to cut his own throat with the glass. When he was released from solitary, he scaled the fence surrounding the work area, knowing that the guards would shoot him. They did, and his body fell 75 feet into the waters of the bay below. Ed Wutke, a former merchant marine who was serving 27 years for murder at sea, was found dead in his cell one day after severing his own jugular vein with the blade from a pencil sharpener.

In 1937 alone, 14 of the prisoners were medically diagnosed as insane, and that did not include the men who slowly became "stir crazy" from the brutal conditions of the place. To Warden Johnston, mental illness was nothing more than an excuse to get out of work. If a man was capable of functioning physically, without disruption to the general population, a madman was ignored. If he was uncontrollable, he was confined to the hospital ward. A consulting psychiatrist visited the island at irregular intervals, but offered little help to the inmates. One prisoner from Leavenworth screamed every time an airplane flew over the island. Another kept his head wrapped in towels to protect him from invisible assailants. Another one, nicknamed "Rabbit," was a docile prisoner until he scooped up every object in his third-tier cell, wrapped them in a bundle, and then hurled it all over the railing when his cell door was opened again. He was dragged clawing and howling to the medical ward and never returned to the cell blocks.

And then there was prisoner no. 284, Rube Persefal. A former gangster and bank robber, Persefal was assigned to work on the dock detail. One day, he picked up a hatchet, placed his left hand on a block of wood and, while laughing maniacally, began hacking off the fingers on his hand. Then, he placed his right hand on the block and pleaded with a guard to chop off those fingers as well. Persefal was placed in the hospital, but was never actually declared insane.

In 1941, inmate Henry Young went on trial for the murder of fellow prisoner Rufus McCain, his accomplice in a failed escape attempt. The two men, along with three other inmates – Doc Barker, William Martin and Dale Stamphill – had slipped out of the prison on the foggy night of January 13, 1939. An alarm sounded and the men were discovered on the beach trying to fabricate a crude raft. Two of the men started to flee and guards fired, killing Barker and wounding Stamphill. Young and McCain surrendered peacefully and were kept in solitary for almost a year. After

127

they were returned to their cells in November 1940, the two argued on several occasions. McCain was assigned to the tailor shop and Young to the furniture shop, located directly downstairs. On December 3, Young waited until just after a prisoner count and then, when a guard's attention was diverted, he ran downstairs and stabbed McCain. The other man went into shock and he died five hours later. Young refused to say why he had killed the man.

Young's attorney was able to explain it, however. During the trial that followed, his attorney claimed that, because of the terrible conditions at the prison, Young could not be held responsible for his actions. He stated that the Alcatraz guards frequently beat his client and that he had endured long periods of extreme isolation. This cruel and inhumane treatment had caused Young to become insane and his responses to hostile situations had become desperately violent. The attorney literally put Alcatraz itself on trial. He subpoenaed Warden Johnston to testify about the prison's conditions and policies and in addition, several inmates were also called to recount the state of Alcatraz. The prisoners told of being locked in the dungeons and of being beaten by the guards. They also testified to knowing several inmates who had gone insane because of such treatment. The jury ended up sympathizing with Young's case, and he was convicted of a manslaughter charge that only added a few years onto his original sentence.

After the trial, Young was transferred to the Medical Center for Federal Prisoners in Springfield, Missouri. After serving his federal sentence, he was sent to the Washington State Penitentiary and was paroled in 1972. He had spent nearly 40 years in prison. After his release, Young vanished into history and whatever became of him is unknown.

Capone on the "Rock"

Chicago mobster Al Capone arrived at the prison in August 1934. Upon his arrival, he quickly learned that while he may have once been famous in the Windy City, he was only a number on Alcatraz. He made attempts to flaunt the power that he had enjoyed at the federal prison in Atlanta, where he was used to the special benefits that he was awarded by guards and wardens alike. He was arrogant, and unlike most of the other prisoners, was not a veteran of the penal system. He had only spent a short time in prison and his stay had been much different than that of most other cons. Capone had possessed the ability to control his environment through wealth and power, but he was soon to learn that things were much different at Alcatraz.

After Capone and the prisoners who arrived with him were unloaded from the train, they were taken to a low barge that brought them across the water to Alcatraz.

The guards who had transferred him from Atlanta took off his leg irons, but not his handcuffs. Capone walked with the rest of the men onto the boat, across the bay, and then up the steep, spiraling roadway to the top of the island.

Warden Johnston had a custom of meeting new prisoners when they arrived to give them a brief orientation. When Capone entered the rear of the cell house, Johnston sat at a desk. When he called out the names of the prisoners, a guard removed their handcuffs and brought them to the desk. Johnston later wrote in his memoirs that he had little trouble recognizing Capone when he saw him. Capone was grinning and making comments to other prisoners as he stood in the lineup. When it became his turn to approach the warden, Johnston ignored him and simply gave him a standard prison number, just like all of the other men. Johnston wrote: "It was apparent that he wanted to impress other prisoners by asking me questions as if he were their leader. I wanted to make sure that he didn't get any such idea. I handed him a ticket with his number, gave him the instructions I had given every other man, and told him to move along."

The guards led Capone to the bathhouse to be stripped, medically examined, and his ears, nose, mouth and rectum probed for contraband. For weekday wear, he was issued pants and a shirt made of gray denim, and for Sunday, a blue denim uniform. For cold weather, he was given a wool-lined pea coat. The fronts and backs of his clothing were stamped with Capone's number, 85, that could be seen from 20 yards away. He was then given sheets, a pillowcase, towel, comb, and a toothbrush and taken to his cell, where he would spend about 14 hours out of every 24, seven days a week. Capone drew the fifth cell from the right, third tier, block B. The entire process must have been quite a shock to the crime boss, from the clothing to the accommodations. Even in Atlanta, he had been used to special treatment, his own clothing, special food and drink, and even silk underwear. He quickly discovered that Alcatraz was not the same sort of prison.

Warden Johnston had a policy to listen to any prisoner who wanted to speak with him and when, on the day after he arrived, Capone requested an interview, Johnston had him brought to his office. He asked what the interview was about and Capone explained, "Well, I don't know how to begin but you're my warden now and I just thought I better tell you that I have a lot of friends and expect to have lots of visitors and I want to arrange to see my wife and mother and my son and brothers."

Johnston explained to him that, like all of the other inmates, Capone had very limited visiting privileges, extending to blood relatives only, except for his brother, Ralph, who had a prison record. None of his "friends and business associates" were allowed to visit. No rules were going to be bent for any of the inmates, no matter who they were.

Capone smiled feebly as he said, "It looks like Alcatraz has got me licked."

Johnston granted another interview request from Capone the following week, where Capone again tried to plead his case for special visitors. He explained that among his important friends were big businessmen who depended on him for help and advice. Johnston again sent him on his way.

Capone may have struck out with the warden but he was determined to try and gain the kind of leadership within the prison that he had enjoyed at Atlanta. Capone tried to dispense favors to his fellow prisoners, offering to have money sent to their relatives and to buy musical instruments for those who, like himself, wanted to play in the prison band. Johnston thwarted all of his efforts. When it became apparent that Capone could not obtain even the smallest consideration, he lost respect, as Johnston intended, among the inmates, especially among the minor criminals who made up the majority of the prison population. He soon found that his safety was in danger.

It was deprivation of news from the outside world that led to Capone's first punishment. He spent a full 19 days in the Hole for attempting to bribe a guard to bring him a newspaper. He also did two 10-day stretches in the Hole for talking to other inmates when the rule of silence was in effect. Each time that Capone was sent to the Hole, he emerged a little worse for wear.

Capone was assigned to work in the prison's basement laundry room, to which the Army posts around the bay area sent their wash. The laundry room was damp and badly ventilated, and when an Army transport ship anchored in the bay with an accumulation of wash, the work load became backbreaking. In January 1935, Capone was at his usual station when 36 of his co-workers walked off the job in protest. The strikers were quickly surrounded, separated and sent to the Hole. Because Capone took no part in it, he aroused a great deal of hostility from the other workers. A month later, one of the strikers, Bill Collier, was catching laundry as Capone fed it into the machine. He complained that it was coming to him too fast, but Capone ignored him. Finally, Collier picked up a sopping bundle and flung it into his face. Before the guards could stop the fight, Capone blacked both of his attacker's eyes. Both men spent eight days in the Hole for the altercation.

Another strike, this time a general one, took place without Capone in January of the following year. The immediate provocation was the death of a prisoner with a stomach ulcer, whom Johnston had refused medical treatment because he thought he was pretending to be sick. Capone stuck to his post again, once more incurring the wrath of the strikers. But it was not cowardice that kept him from striking; he knew the odds and knew there was nothing to be gained by going up against the guards. He asked to be excused from work and allowed to remain in his cell until the strike ended. Capone was not alone in his idea. Nearly all of the prison's high-profile inmates – felons like Doc Barker, George "Machine Gun" Kelly, kidnappers Albert Bates and Harvey Bailey, and train robber and escape artist Roy Gardner – shared Capone's prudence and likewise incurred the dislike and hatred of the strikers.

Capone's request was granted. On his first day back at work, after the strikers were starved into submission, an unknown person hurled a sash weight at his head. Roy Gardner saw it coming and threw himself at Capone, shoving the other man aside. The weight still managed to strike Capone's arm, inflicting a deep cut. After that, he was transferred to the bathhouse cleaning crew. The bathhouse adjoined the barbershop. On the morning of June 23, five months after the second strike, Jim Lucas, a Texas bank robber, reported for his monthly haircut. When he left, he grabbed a pair of scissors, slipped up behind Capone, who was mopping the bathhouse floor, and drove the blades into his back. Capone recovered after a week in the hospital and Lucas went to the Hole.

After this incident, a San Francisco lawyer, representing wife Mae Capone, appealed to the Attorney General to have Capone incarcerated somewhere else, but all of the requests were refused. Other attempts followed to kill or maim the "wop with the mop," as his enemies now referred to him. His friends exposed a plan to doctor his coffee with lye one morning and on his way to the dentist, he was jumped and almost strangled before he broke his attacker's hold and knocked the man down.

During this time, Capone still longed for news from outside. The best way to get it was from new arrivals, whom most of the inmates would work tirelessly to get close to and befriend. If they succeeded, they had to hold their conversations out of the earshot of the guards. A newcomer whom Capone managed to befriend was Alvin Karpis. The two had an initial conversation one day while sitting in the recreation yard with their backs against the wall. Capone asked him if he needed money and Karpis told him that he didn't. They discussed their personal lives, and since Karpis was able to play guitar, he joined the prison band at Capone's suggestion. Capone had become quite adept at the tenor banjo. The two men talked for the next few Sundays, as they bent their heads together over a music stand, pretending to study the sheet music that had been placed on it. Karpis turned out to be the first of several new arrivals who kept Capone abreast of recent developments in the underworld, including the murder of Capone's friend "Machine Gun" Jack McGurn; the expansion and operation of the Chicago Outfit; and his wife's struggles to retain their house in Florida after lawyer's fees, trial costs, and taxes. It was not much, but it was the best that Capone could hope to hear while confined within the daunting prison's walls.

The attempts on Capone's life, the days of silence, trips to the Hole, grinding daily routine, and likely what was, by now, an advanced case of syphilis, began to take their toll on Capone. Eventually, he stopped going into the recreation yard and practiced his banjo instead. Once practice was over, he returned immediately to his cell, avoiding all of the inmates except for a few of his closest friends. Occasionally, guards reported that he would refuse to leave his cell to go to the mess hall and eat. They would often find him crouched down in the corner of his cell like an animal. On other occasions, he would mumble to himself or babble in baby talk or simply sit on his bed and strum little tunes on the banjo. Years later, another inmate recalled that Capone would sometimes stay in his cell and make his bunk over and over again.

When the guards decided that the weather was cold enough for the inmates to wear their pea coats, they indicated the decision with three blasts of a whistle. The morning of February 5, 1938, started off unseasonably warm and no whistle blew. Capone, nevertheless, put on his pea coat. For a year, he had been on library duty, delivering and collecting books and magazines. Alvin Karpis, who occupied the second cell to the left of Capone and always followed him in the line to the mess hall, had a magazine to return and he tossed it into Capone's cell as he passed it. Seeing Capone standing there in his winter coat, including a cap and gloves, he called to him that he didn't need his jacket that day. Capone seemed to neither hear nor recognize him. He simply stood there, staring vacantly into space.

He failed to fall into line when ordered to do so, a breach of discipline ordinarily punished by a trip to the Hole, but the guards sensed something was seriously wrong and watched without disturbing him. He finally left his cell and entered the mess hall last in line. A thread of drool dripped down his chin. As he moved mechanically toward the steam table, a deputy warden, Ernest Miller, spoke to him quietly and patted his arm. Capone grinned strangely and for some reason, pointed out the window. Then, suddenly, he started to choke and retch. Miller led him to a locked gate across the hall and called to the guard on the other side to unlock it. They helped Capone up a flight of stairs to the hospital ward.

To the prison physician, and a consulting psychiatrist that he sent for, Capone's symptoms suggested damage to the central nervous system characteristic of advanced syphilis. When Capone, after a return to lucidity, understood this, he finally agreed to a spinal puncture and other medical tests that he had refused at the penitentiary in Atlanta. The fluid was rushed to the Marine Hospital in San

132

Francisco for analysis. Warden Johnston later stopped by his bed to ask him what had happened to him that morning. Capone replied, "I dunno, they tell me that I acted like I was a little whacky."

The report from the Marine Hospital confirmed the doctor's diagnosis. Word of it reached the press, and newspapers from coast to coast painted a picture of Capone as a man driven insane by the horrors of Alcatraz. Mae Capone pleaded with Warden Johnston by telephone, imploring him to free her husband, an act that was far beyond his power. The hardened warden must have taken some pity on the former "King of Chicago," though. Capone was never returned to the cellblock and spent the remainder of his sentence in the hospital ward, subjected to injections of arsphenamine, shock treatments, and induced fever. His disease was slowed down but not stopped. He alternated between lucidity and confusion, coming to the brink of total insanity. He spent most of his time sitting by himself, plucking at the strings of his banjo, unaware of his surroundings.

His last day on Alcatraz was January 6, 1939. He was then transferred to the new federal prison at Terminal Island near Los Angeles. When he was paroled, he became a recluse at his Palm Island, Florida, estate and died in 1947.

But did he actually leave Alcatraz?

Escape from Alcatraz

During the 29 years that Alcatraz was in operation, there were at least 14 escape attempts in which 34 men risked their lives to try and make it off The Rock. Almost all of the men were either killed or recaptured. Only one of the men was known to have made it ashore. John Paul Scott was recaptured when he was found shivering in the rocks near the Golden Gate Bridge. As for the men who vanished, it was believed that most of them succumbed to the cold water and the always-churning currents that moved past the island. Although no bodies were ever recovered, the authorities assumed that the men had drowned and marked the cases as closed.

Of all of the escape attempts, though, two of them left a lasting mark on the history of the island. The most dramatic and violent of them took place in 1946. It was later dubbed the "Battle of Alcatraz." It began as an organized, carefully planned breakout from the "escape-proof" prison, but it soon deteriorated into a bloody disaster about which one unknown prisoner left graffiti behind, etched into a steel bar, which read: "Hell broke loose – May 1946."

The accounts of what happened on Alcatraz in May 1946 vary in detail, but May 2 marked the beginning of events that would lead to the deaths of two guards and three inmates on the island. On that day, six inmates captured a gun cage, obtained prison keys, and took over the D block cell house in less than an hour. The breakout attempt might have succeeded if not for the fact that a guard, Bill Miller, didn't return one of the keys to the gun cage as soon as he finished using it, as was required by prison regulations. The strange twist of fate completely disrupted the escape attempt. When the cons captured the gun cage, they found all of the keys except for the one that would let them out of the cell building. This was the key that Miller failed to return to the guard cage. The breakout was grounded before it even began.

But the prisoners, Bernard Coy, Joe Cretzer, Marvin Hubbard, Sam Shockley, Miran Thompson, and Clarence Carnes, would not give up. Unable to get out of the cell house, they began trying to kill some of the tower guards, and Coy succeeded in wounding one of the officers. As officers broke into the cell house, the inmates captured them and put them into two cells, 402 and 403 (which were later changed to C-102 and C-104). Half-crazed, Sam Shockley shouted, "Kill all the sonsabitches! Kill the bastards! Kill them all! Don't leave any witnesses!" Urged on by his fellow escapee, Joe Cretzer opened fire with one of the captured rifles, firing wildly into the two cells. His shots critically wounded two officers, Miller and Corwin, wounded three other officers, and left the others pretending to be dead on the cold concrete floor. They had no idea what the convicts would do next. Their inability to escape from the cell house had created a tense situation, leaving them trapped and desperate. They had no idea that, by this time, Officer Miller had dropped the key that would let them out of the building into the toilet in cell 403.

Warden Johnston knew how serious the situation had become and he began organizing all of his back-up systems. Bureau of Prisons Director James V. Bennett in Washington received a teletype from Johnston that read:

Serious trouble. Convict has machine gun in cell house. Have issued riot call. Placed armed guards at strategic locations. Most of our officers are imprisoned in cell house. Cannot tell extent of injuries suffered by our officers or amount of damage done. Will give you more information later in the day when we get control.
J.A. Johnston, Warden

A radio message was sent to the Coast Guard and the San Francisco police, informing them of the trouble and asking that their boats form a perimeter around the island. All of the officers were called into duty and messages were sent to the press. As the story made headlines, thousands of spectators lined up to watch from San Francisco as the police and Coast Guard boats began encircling the island. Dramatic headlines appeared in the newspapers, and stories filled with rumors and exaggerations drew even bigger crowds on the mainland to watch events unfold on Alcatraz.

Other inmates in the facility were gathered and marched into the yard to be guarded, first, by Alcatraz guards, and then by U.S. Marines, who offered help by sending a detachment of men from a nearby base. Fear swelled on the island, not only among guards and officials, but also with the other inmates, who by their own choice did not want to be involved in what was going on. Once the alarms had sounded, everything began to happen very fast and the inmates knew there would be no careful selection of targets; all of them were in danger. Most of them had returned to their cells once the alarms had sounded, only to be marched into the yard a short time later. They were kept out there all night before being taken into cellblock A. The inmates were cold, tired, and hungry, but most of all, they were scared. But they could not have been as terrified as the prisoners who had no part in the rebellion and yet were trapped inside of the cell house with the six escapees. One inmate recalled, "They were more scared than anything else. They thought the whole place might go up in flames and smoke any minute. There was shrieking and cursing all night long."

The warden's main concern was to get to the guards who were being held hostage in cells 402 and 403. After that, he concentrated on isolating the armed prisoners. The guards, Marines and special personnel surrounded the building, keeping close aim on all of the doors and windows of the cell block. Gas was fired into the cells and rifle grenades were launched into D block. One of them went off target, fell to the ground, and started the grass on fire. From San Francisco, it must have looked like Alcatraz was burning. The cellblock continued to be barraged with bullets, mortars and grenades. The helpless inmates inside the building took refuge behind water-soaked mattresses and tried to stay close to the floor and out of the path of the bullets that riddled the cells. But even after realizing that they could not get away, the six would-be escapees decided to fight it out.

The fighting lasted for two days. With no place to hide from the constant gunfire, Cretzer, Coy, and Hubbard climbed into a utility corridor for safety. The other three men returned to their cells, hoping they would not be identified as participants in the attempt. They had no idea that one of the guards had scrawled their names on the wall of one of the cells.

In the bloody aftermath, Cretzer, Coy, and Hubbard were killed in the corridor from bullets and shrapnel from explosives. Thompson and Shockley were later executed in the gas chamber at San Quentin and Carnes received a sentence of life, plus 99 years. His life was spared because he helped some of the wounded hostages. The cell building was heavily damaged and took months to repair.

The May 1946 riot may have been the most violent escape attempt from Alcatraz but it is, by all means, not the most famous. The classic "Escape from Alcatraz" occurred in 1962, and was carried out by three bank robbers who were serving long terms: Frank Morris and two brothers, Clarence and John Anglin. No one knows how long they planned their escape, but it must have taken them several months to put it all together. Early that year, a fellow prisoner named Allen West helped the trio to devise a clever plan to construct a raft, inflatable life vests, and human-like dummies that could be used to fool the guards during nighttime head counts. Over a period of several months, the men used tools stolen from work sites to chip away at the ventilation shafts in their cells. They fabricated the life vests, the rafts, and the dummies, and they also created ingenious, duplicate grills that hid the cement that had been chipped away from around the vents. The quality of the human heads and faked grills was remarkable, as they used only paint kits and a plaster created from soap and concrete powder to make them. They also collected hair from the barbershop to make the plaster heads look more lifelike.

These painstaking preparations paid off on the night of June 11, 1962. Immediately after the lights-out head count at 9:30 p.m., Morris and the Anglins scooted through the vents and scaled the utility shafts to the upper levels. Once they reached the roof, they climbed through a ventilator duct and made it to the edge of the building. After descending pipes along the cement wall, all three climbed over a 15-foot fence and made it to the island's shore, where they inflated the rafts and vests. They set out into the cold waters of the bay and were never seen again.

The escape was discovered the next morning when Morris failed to rise for the morning count. A guard jammed his club through the cell bars to wake him up and to his shock, a plaster head rolled off the bunk and landed on the floor. Alarms were sounded but by then, it was too late. The FBI pursued the case for a time but never found any active leads. Prison officials maintained that the trio drowned in the 34-degree water of the bay. A watertight bag was found floating in the bay four days later by a patrolling Army Corps of Engineers debris boat. The contents of the bag belonged to Clarence Anglin and mostly contained photos of a woman. A search was conducted for the three men's bodies, but they were never found. More than 40 years later, it is still unknown whether or not the trio made a successful escape – but legend holds that they did.

After this last escape attempt, the days of the prison were numbered. Ironically, the frigid waters around the island, which had long prevented escape, were believed to be the leading ruin of the prison. After the escape of Morris and the Anglins, the prison was examined because of the deteriorating conditions of the structure, caused mostly by the corrosive effects of the salt water around it. In addition, budget cuts had recently forced security measures at the prison to become more lax. On top of that, the exorbitant cost of running the place continued to increase and over $5 million was going to be needed for renovations. According to U.S. Attorney General Robert Kennedy, the prison was no longer necessary.

On March 23, 1963, Alcatraz closed its doors for good. After that, the island was essentially abandoned while various groups tried to decide what to do with it. Then, in 1969, a large group of American Indians landed on the island and declared that it was Native American property. They had great plans for the island, which included a school and a Native American cultural center. The Indians soon had the attention of the media and the government and a number of meetings were held about the fate of Alcatraz.

The volume of visitors to the island soon became overwhelming. Somehow, during the talks, the island had become a haven for the homeless and the less fortunate. The Indians were soon faced with the problem of no natural resources and the fact that food and water had to be brought over from the mainland. The situation soon became so desperate that island occupants were forced to take drastic measures to survive. In order to raise money for supplies, they began stripping copper wire and pipes from the island buildings to sell as scrap metal. A tragedy occurred around this same time when Yvonne Oakes, the daughter of one of the key Indian activists, fell to her death from a third story window. The Oakes family left Alcatraz and never returned.

Then, during the evening hours of June 1, 1970, a fire was started and raged out of control. It damaged several of the buildings and destroyed the Warden's residence, the lighthouse keeper's home, and even badly damaged the historic lighthouse itself.

Tension now developed between federal officials and the Indians as the government blamed the activists for the fire. The press, which had been previously sympathetic toward the Native Americans, now turned against them and began to publish stories about beatings and assaults that were allegedly occurring on the island. Support for the Indians disintegrated, especially in light of the fact that the original activists had already left Alcatraz. Those who remained were seen as little more than squatters. On June 11, 1971, the Coast Guard, along with 20 U.S. Marshals, descended on the island and removed the remaining residents.

Alcatraz was empty once more.

In 1972, Congress created the Golden Gate National Recreation Area and Alcatraz Island fell under the purview of the National Park Service. It was opened to the public in the fall of 1973, and has become one of the most popular of America's national park sites. During the day, the old prison is a bustling place, filled with tour guides and visitors but at night, the buildings are filled with the inexplicable. Many believe that some of the men who served time on The Rock remain behind, lingering here for eternity. Alcatraz, they feel, is a very haunted place – a place where strange things can, and do, happen.

Hauntings on the Rock
Hauntings have been widely reported since Alcatraz has been closed down. Despite a "no ghosts policy" (meaning that ghost stories from staff members are not allowed) park service employees and visitors to Alcatraz report weird, ghostly happenings in the crumbling old buildings. Inexplicable clanging sounds, footsteps, and disembodied voices are commonly reported. Others say that they have heard screams coming from empty corridors and long-abandoned cells. Some guides have reported strange events in certain areas of the prison, like the infamous Hole, where prisoners suffered and sometimes died, during the years of the prison's operation.

Every visitor who arrives by boat on Alcatraz follows the same path once walked by the convicts who came to do time on The Rock. The tourists who come to the island prison pass through the warden's office and the visiting room and eventually enter the cell house. After passing the double steel doors, a visitor can see just past C Block. If they look opposite the visiting room, they will find a metal door that looks as though it was once welded shut. Although the tour guides don't usually mention it, behind that door is the utility corridor where Coy, Cretzer, and Hubbard were killed by grenades and bullets in 1946.

It was also behind this door where a night watchman heard strange, clanging sounds in 1976. He opened the door and peered down the dark corridor, shining his flashlight on the maze of pipes and conduits. He could see nothing and there were no sounds. When he closed the door, the noises started again. Again, the door was opened, but he still saw nothing that could be causing the sounds. The night watchman did not believe in ghosts, so he shut the door again and continued on his way. The sounds continued to be heard in the years that followed and the door was eventually welded shut. It is still regarded today as one of the most haunted locations on Alcatraz.

Noises coming from behind the metal door are not the only strange sounds heard in this cell house. Other night watchmen who have patrolled the building, long after the last tourist boats have left for the day, say they have heard the sounds of men running in the upper tiers. Often thinking that an intruder is inside the prison, they have investigated the sounds, but always find nothing, and no one, out of place.

One National Park Service employee reported (off the record, of course) that she had been working one rainy afternoon when the sparse number of tourists were not enough to keep all of the guides busy. She went for a walk in front of A Block and was just past the door that led down to the dungeons when she heard a loud scream from the bottom of the stairs. She ran away without looking to see if anyone was down there. When asked why she didn't report the incident, she replied, "I didn't dare mention it because the day before, everyone was ridiculing another worker who reported hearing men's voices coming from the hospital ward and when he checked the ward, it was empty."

Several of the rangers and guides have also expressed a strangeness about one of the cells in the infamous Hole, number 14D. Several spoke of a feeling of sudden intensity in the cell that seems to come over anyone who spends much time there. One guide said, "That cell, 14D, is always cold. It's even colder than the other three dark cells. Sometimes it gets warm out here - so hot that you have to take your jacket off. The temperature inside the cell house can be in the 70s, yet 14D is still cold... so cold that you need a jacket if you spend any time in it."

Tour guides and park rangers have not been the only ones to have strange experiences in that particular cell. One former guard, who worked at the prison while it was still in operation, told of several eerie incidents that occurred in the Hole, particularly in Cell 14D. During the time when the guard was working at Alcatraz in the middle 1940s, he recalled an incident that took place when an inmate was locked in the punishment cell for some infraction. According to the officer, the inmate began screaming within seconds of being locked in. He claimed that some creature with glowing eyes was locked in with him. As tales of a ghostly presence wandering the nearby corridor were a continual source of practical jokes among the guards, no one took the convict's cries of being "attacked" very seriously.

The man's screams continued on into the night until finally, there was silence. The following day, guards inspected the cell and they found the convict dead. A horrible expression had been frozen onto the man's face and there were clear marks of hands around his throat. The autopsy revealed that the strangulation could not have been self-inflicted. Some believed that he might have been choked by one of the guards, who had been fed up with the screaming, but no one ever admitted it. A few of the officers blamed something else for the man's death. They believed that the killer had been the spirit of a former inmate. To add to the mystery, on the day following the tragedy, several guards who were performing a head count noticed that there were too many men in the lineup. Then, at the end of the line, they saw the face of the convict who had recently been strangled in the Hole. As the guards stood staring at the man in stunned silence, the figure abruptly vanished.

139

It may come as no surprise to most readers, but this same cell was where Henry Young was confined after his attempted escape in 1939. He was confined there in the darkness for months, and when he emerged, he was allegedly insane from the horrible isolation that he endured. Days later, he murdered Rufus McCain in the prison shop. Young found sympathy with the jury because they believed that his time in the Hole had deprived him of everything about him that was spiritual and human. Did Henry Young leave a piece of his insanity behind in Cell 14D – or did something that already inhabited that grim place give a little of itself to Young?

If, as many believe, ghosts return to haunt the places where they suffered traumatic experiences when they were alive, then Alcatraz must be loaded with spirits. There have been claims made that many of the guards who served at the prison between 1946 and 1963 experienced strange happenings on Alcatraz. The guards often spoke to one another of voices sobbing and moaning, inexplicable smells, cold spots, and spectral apparitions of prisoners and soldiers inhabiting every part of the island, from the cellblocks to the prison yard and on down to the caverns beneath the buildings. Phantom gunshots were known to send seasoned guards ducking to the ground in the belief that some of the prisoners had escaped and had obtained weapons. There was never an explanation. A deserted laundry room would sometimes fill with the smell of smoke, even though nothing was burning. The guards would be sent running from the room, only to return later and find that the air was clear.

Even Warden Johnston, who did not believe in ghosts, once encountered the unmistakable sound of a person sobbing while he accompanied some guests on a tour of the prison. He swore that the sounds came from inside the dungeon walls. The strange sounds were followed by an ice-cold wind that swirled through the entire group. He could offer no explanation for the weird events.

And since the prison has been closed down, the ghostly happenings seem to have intensified. Weird noises and eerie apparitions continue to be encountered and one of the most prominent ghosts still lingering on the island may be one of the most famous men to have served time there: Al Capone. It's not uncommon for rangers and guides to sometimes hear the sound of banjo strings being plucked on the cell block or in the bath house, where Capone once cleaned and became known by the derogatory nickname of the "wop with the mop." Many who have experienced these strange sounds have no idea that Capone once played the banjo, and one ranger even surmised that perhaps it was a ghostly echo from the time when Alcatraz was a military fort. Other have come to believe that the sound of the banjo is the only lingering part of a man who left his sanity behind on the island. Is it

140

merely an imprint from the past, or is Al Capone still here on Alcatraz, a lonely and broken spirit still plucking the strings of a spectral banjo that vanished decades ago?

Or could it be merely another of the countless ghosts who continue to haunt this place, year after year, still serving time on The Rock?

AMERICAN HOSPITALS

In the early years of the nineteenth century – and for more than a century to come – most Americans gave birth, endured illness, and even underwent surgery at home. Our ancestors belonged to a largely rural society and few among them ever had the opportunity to visit a hospital.

Hospitals in America emerged from institutions, notably poorhouses, which provided care for the ailing poor. Rooted in this tradition of charity, the public hospital traces its roots back to the city's efforts to shelter and care for the ill, deprived, and disabled. A six-bed ward founded in 1736 in the New York City Almshouse became, over the course of the next century, Bellevue Hospital.

Bellevue was founded at a time when New York City did not extend much further north than Wall Street. It was established in what was then a mostly unpopulated section of Manhattan in order to quarantine the sick. The hospital would even have a great effect on how the streets of the city were laid out. When the grid system of streets was established in 1811, the survey had to take the location of Bellevue into account, and the placement of First Avenue on the grid is mainly due to the location of Bellevue.

Bellevue would literally shape the medical history of the city. In 1819, New York University began to conduct clinical instruction for doctors at Bellevue Hospital and in 1849, an amphitheater for clinical teaching and surgery was opened. Bellevue physicians promoted the "Bone Bill" in 1854, which legalized dissection of cadavers for anatomical studies. The nation's first nursing school, based on principles developed by Florence Nightingale, was founded in 1873. Bellevue also had the nation's first maternity ward in 1799; the first children's clinic in 1874; the first emergency room in 1876; and a ward for the insane —an approach considered revolutionary at the time—was erected within hospital grounds in 1879.

By 1867, Bellevue physicians were instrumental in developing New York City's sanitary code, the first in the world. One of the nation's first outpatient departments connected to a hospital (the "Bureau of Medical and Surgical Relief for the Out of Door Poor") was established at Bellevue that year. In 1868, Bellevue physician Stephen Smith became first commissioner of public health in New York City; he initiated a national campaign for health vaccinations. A year later, Bellevue established the second hospital-based, emergency ambulance service in the United States.

Bellevue Hospital would go on to set new standards for health and psychiatric care into the twentieth century, but it was not alone in its desire to aid the sick and dying. The original Charity Hospital in New Orleans opened its doors the same year that Bellevue was established. The oldest hospital in Tennessee, located in Memphis, was founded in 1829. Similar origins exist for other public hospitals – places where the "care of strangers" grew from modest origins into the institutions that we think of in the modern era.

The American hospital as we know it today emerged over the course of about 60 years, beginning around the time of the Civil War. During the war, emergency field hospitals were established on the battlefields, in tents, barns, private homes, and just about anywhere that shelter could be found. Although hastily arranged and seldom able to provide anything other than adequate treatment, field hospitals were modeled after the treatment centers that had started to emerge in the major cities of the country. In turn, the hospitals that followed the war were patterned after those that treated the wounded and dying on the fields of war.

Hospitals staffed with physicians and professional nurses were products of the growing American cities and the economic expansions that came with the Industrial Revolution, together with waves of immigration and large strides in medicine and surgery. By about 1880, asepsis (sterilizing) opened broad new horizons for surgeons, who began to see fewer and fewer patients dying on the operating table – or from the infections that too often followed. This brought on even greater advances and hospitals became symbols of hope for their communities.

During the first few decades of the twentieth century, new types of hospitals emerged to treat – or at least quarantine -- the victims of specific illnesses, like tuberculosis and influenza. These public and private facilities, although sometimes short-lived, were modeled after the "pest houses" of the past, where contagious patients could be treated and isolated so that the illness did not spread to nearby communities. Thousands died in such hospitals around the country, cementing their place in the haunting stories found in the pages that follow.

By the 1920s, the American hospital was a place where one could hope illness might be treated and even cured. Most hospitals were not-for-profit at this time and many of them began reducing their traditional charitable role in favor of creating prestigious institutions, attractive to an upper middle-class clientele. The remaining public hospitals continued their commitment to the poor, though, and began to be faced with even greater challenges than in the past.

All hospitals before the 1920s had operated without much money. Physicians donated their time, and costs for nurses and staff tended to be low. Around this time, hospitals began to require significant funds. Doctors and surgeons began to be paid larger salaries and as nurses and support staff began to become professionals, they also required better pay. Public hospitals that were not connected to churches were often forced to establish affiliations with universities and medical schools to continue operating and to continue the mission of treating everyone, including the poor.

The years of the Great Depression brought an even greater challenge to public hospitals. Their patient load increased substantially during the 1930s and so did their costs and yet, there was no additional money to be found.

Things began to change after World War II. The population boomed and advances in medicine saw the advent of penicillin for a host of diseases, streptomycin as a cure for tuberculosis, and the Salk vaccine for polio. The economy was booming, unemployment was at a record low, and millions of Americans moved from cities to suburbs. Soon, their health needs began to be met largely by private insurance companies. For a time around 1950, the future of city and private hospitals seemed bright in various ways. In spite of persistent lack of funds, many were well-staffed and affiliated with medical and nursing schools. However, although they benefited from, and helped to implement many medical advances, public hospitals were hurt by the population shift from city to suburbs. Within only a few years, tax bases eroded in the large cities were the public hospitals were located. The poor and the unemployed continued to seek treatment in hospitals that had no money left for services.

Things grew worse in the 1960s. Hidden beneath the prosperity that followed World War II was an impoverished underbelly that could not be ignored. Health care for the poor was sorely lacking in a society that was regarded as the wealthiest on earth. This problem hit the public hospitals especially hard. Doctors, nurses, and hospital staff struggled to provide adequate care in deteriorating facilities that were often ill-equipped, obsolete, and poorly supplied.

Health and hospital insurance was another issue that emerged during the downward spiral of the public hospital system. Across the country, many employers typically covered the insurance needs of their employees. However, this system, which eventually fell apart for almost all Americans, left the poor and elderly without insurance at a time when medicine had grown capable of treating thousands of illnesses in new and effective ways. Although President Truman had planned a national health system in 1949, it proved politically impossible to forge into law.

During President Lyndon B. Johnson's "War on Poverty" and the "Great Society" in 1965, Congress enacted Medicaid and Medicare to provide some access to care for those who couldn't afford it. These government programs, which largely enabled patients to apply to hospitals of their own choosing, proved to be of great assistance for most, but not all, patients. They only covered a portion of medical costs, which left the indigent still faced with massive medical bills, and created even greater costs for the public hospitals.

By the 1970s, many local governments began divesting themselves of their public hospitals, putting them under control of corporations, turning them over to medical schools or other organizations, or shutting them down completely. Federal cuts in the 1980s caused even more closures as many public facilities simply couldn't afford to operate. In many cases, the gap caused by the loss of these hospitals was filled with private institutions, but in far too many towns and cities, their local hospitals were lost altogether.

The American hospital today is a far cry from the poor houses and institutions of centuries ago. Surgeons are many steps away from operating in barber shops, as they did before the Civil War, and robbing graves because it was illegal to purchase bodies for anatomy dissections. Modern medicine has managed to disconnect us from death in ways that our ancestors would have never imagined. People were sick, were treated, and often died, at home – not in a hospital room.

145

So, are the ghosts that linger in our modern hospitals of a more recent time? Is the same confusion, trauma, and suffering still present when someone dies in such a sterile environment, leaving a troubled spirit behind?

The reader will have to decide from the items that were collected for the pages ahead.

7. A BODY IN A COPPER TUBE
MCDOWELL MEDICAL COLLEGE

The city of St. Louis is today considered one of the most outstanding medical training centers in the United States. Over the years, dozens of medical schools have flourished here, along with many excellent hospitals, but not since Dr. Joseph McDowell's college and hospital was closed just before the Civil War has there been another school like the one he founded in 1847. It was a place where wild rumors, lurid stories, and tales of the owner's eccentricities were often told.

Unfortunately most of those stories were true.

It was also a place that became explicitly tied to the Civil War and, in fact, if the hauntings in the building were not connected to the grave robbing, deaths, illnesses, and other strange events that occurred during its first decade or so of existence, they were certainly connected to the hospital's time as a Civil War prison.

St. Louis was a city torn apart by the Civil War. Although St. Louis was largely pro-Union, it had to deal with the rest of Missouri, which was sympathetic to the Confederacy. Among those sympathizers was Missouri's governor, Claiborne Jackson, who came from a family of wealthy Kentucky slave owners. He grudgingly respected the state's decision in March 1861, to remain in the Union, but when war began a month later and President Lincoln called for four regiments of volunteers from Missouri, Governor Jackson called the request "illegal, unconstitutional and revolutionary." He refused to respond to the call for volunteers, and four days later, Union leaders ordered Captain Nathaniel Lyon to muster four regiments into public service. Before nightfall, Lyon had his troops at the St. Louis Arsenal, supplied with both arms and ammunition.

The confusion continued for months. Secessionists met at the capital in Jefferson City so they could organize a state militia to defend against a Union invasion, while Union leaders met in St. Louis to discuss the defense of the city against the Confederates. In the end, battles were fought throughout the state, while St. Louis remained a Union stronghold, supply point and base of operations along the Mississippi River. Under the command of General Henry W. Halleck, St. Louis saw thousands of soldiers from both sides of the war swell its population to record numbers. The Federal men were there to train, convalesce, or to protect the city, but the Confederate soldiers were not so lucky. Those men arrived as prisoners and were subjected to the conditions of one of the worst prison camps of the Civil War – a place that had once been dedicated to the study of treating the sick.

The McDowell Medical College was founded in 1840 as the Medical Department of Kemper College. The head of the medical school was Dr. Joseph McDowell, and it became the first to be successfully established west of the Mississippi. McDowell's school remained connected with Kemper College until 1847, when financial problems forced Kemper to drop the program. At that point, McDowell struck out on his own and constructed a building to house the school at Ninth and Gratiot Streets.

It became one of the most prominent buildings in the city, but its fame was often overshadowed by the eccentric reputation of the school's founder. Joseph McDowell was considered to be one of the finest doctors of his day. He was thought of as an excellent physician and a very capable surgeon in a city where medical standards were high. Many graduates of other medical schools in St. Louis would attend lectures at McDowell's school as part of a graduate course. He came from a distinguished medical family, as his uncle, Ephraim McDowell, was known as the first doctor to successfully perform an ovariotomy (a surgical incision into an ovary).

In spite of this, it was McDowell's unusual personality traits that often made him the subject of local gossip. He was described as having "an erratic temperament that approached insanity" and was horribly jealous of other doctors. He was also an ardent secessionist and believed strongly in the rights of the Southern states and in the institution of slavery. To make his volatile political positions quite clear, he often placed a loaded revolver on the table in front of him when discussing issues of slavery, states' rights or secession. While known for being generous in his treatment of the poor, he was also known for his hatred of immigrants, African Americans, and Catholics. He would lecture on those subjects on street corners to anyone who would listen. After receiving numerous death threats, he made a breastplate of armor and wore it with his regular suit every day.

The castle-like building on Gratiot Street was erected to McDowell's specifications. It was designed with two large wings and flowed outward from an octagonal tower. The tower had been fitted with an unusual deck around which six cannons had been placed to defend the school against possible attack. He also kept the school stocked with muskets that could be handed out to the students in case of emergency. During patriotic holidays, McDowell would pass out the rifles and march the students into the field along Seventh Street. After a short speech, he would give the command to fire off the guns and to set off the cannons in the direction of Mill Creek. The staff and students at the Christian Brothers College next door always made a hasty retreat when they saw the medical students assembling on the lawn.

The building had other unusual elements. The central column of the tower had niches that were intended to hold the remains of the McDowell family members after their deaths. The bodies were to be placed in alcohol-filled copper tubes. The building also included a dissecting room, a chemical room, a lecture hall, a laboratory, and a hospital dispensary where the poor were treated free of charge. There was also a rooftop observatory and offices for the doctors on staff. A massive anatomical amphitheater was fitted with six large windows so that dissections would be done in natural light. McDowell also opened a museum that contained more than three thousand specimens of birds and animals from North America. There were also minerals, fossils and antiquities, all of which could be viewed for a 25-cent admission. Clergy and physicians were admitted for free.

McDowell was famous for his surgical skills and he emphasized anatomy in his classes. Students were required to take part in the dissection of human cadavers, a practice that would bring even more notoriety to the school and hospital. In those days, it was nearly impossible for medical colleges to get bodies for research because dissection was against the law. To obtain cadavers for study, McDowell and his students were forced to go on nighttime forays into the city's cemeteries. In this way, they introduced "body snatching" to St. Louis.

When rumors of grave robbing reached local residents, they were duly horrified. For the most part, the school began to be avoided as a cursed or haunted place, but occasionally, the more courageous citizens were stirred into action. On one occasion, the disappearance of a German immigrant woman started a riot at the McDowell College when rumors spread that she had been killed and her body dissected by medical students. Everyone knew that McDowell hated immigrants, so he was quickly regarded as a suspect. The woman was later found wandering the streets of Alton, Illinois, in a demented state.

It would be an incident involving one of McDowell's stolen corpses that would cause him to start to believe in the possibility of ghosts and life after death. The incident so unsettled him that he turned away from his religious upbringing as a strict Calvinist and became an ardent Spiritualist. At one time, McDowell was an outspoken critic of anyone who believed in ghosts or other "such frauds without foundation," but that was before the spirit of his dead mother saved his life.

A German girl who lived in the neighborhood died of an unusual disease, and McDowell and some of his students stole her body and hid it away in one of the laboratories. News spread of the theft and many of the local Germans became angry and vowed to break into the school and find the body.

McDowell received a letter that warned him that the locals planned to break into the school that night so he went to the college to hide the body. When he arrived, all was quiet and he went into the dissecting room with a light. He lifted the girl's corpse onto his shoulder, planning to carry it to the attic and conceal it in the rafters, or perhaps to hide it in a cedar chest that was out of sight in one of the closets.

"I had ascended one flight of stairs," he later wrote, "when out went my lamp. I laid down the corpse, and re-struck the light. I then picked up the body, when out went my light again. I felt for another match in my pocket, when I saw distinctly my dear, dead mother, standing a little distance off, beckoning to me."

McDowell said that he saw her rise up a little in front of a window and then vanish. Shaken, he nevertheless climbed the steps to the attic, where he hid the body. He came back downstairs in the darkness and when he reached the window, he saw two Germans talking. One of them had a shotgun and the other carried a revolver. The doctor eased down the staircase and when he got to the door of the dissecting room, he looked down the stairs into the hallway below. There he saw another five or six men, and one of them was lighting a lamp. "I hesitated a moment as to what I should do," wrote McDowell, "as I had left my pistols in the room where I took

150

the body. I looked in the room, as it was my only chance to get away, when I saw my spirit mother standing near the table from which I had taken the corpse. I had no light, but the halo that surrounded my mother was sufficient to enable me to see the table quite plainly."

Suddenly, footsteps sounded on the staircase below and McDowell darted into the room. He lay down on the table where the girl's body had been and pulled a sheet up over himself. The men came into the room to look for the dead girl among the other bodies that had been placed there. Sheets were lifted from the faces of the corpses, and when they passed the table where McDowell was hiding, one of them commented on the freshness of the corpse and that he had died with his boots on. However, they did not look under the sheet. McDowell was terrified that he would be discovered but claimed that he heard a soft voice in his ear, urging him to be still.

The Germans searched the building, but found neither the girl's body nor Dr. McDowell. When he finally heard them depart from the school, he breathed a sigh of relief. He had been saved and he gave the credit for his safety to the spirit of his mother.

After that, McDowell's newfound respect for the spirit world often affected the decisions he made and the ideas that he came up with. Of pressing concern to him were the eventual deaths of his family. He hated to think of their decay after death, so he planned to have them encased in copper tubes and installed in the niches of the medical school's tower when they died. Later though, he tried to have the bodies placed inside of Mammoth Cave in Kentucky in hopes that the cool air of the cave might preserve them. He eventually settled on a cave closer to home, however.

The cave he purchased was near Hannibal, Missouri, and it was there that the body of his 14-year-old daughter was placed when she died. Her body was encased inside one of the copper, alcohol-filled tubes and she was hidden away in the cave. In his book *Life on the Mississippi*, Mark Twain, who grew up in Hannibal, mentioned the cave and its curious occupant. He stated that "there is an interesting cave a mile or two below Hannibal. In my time, the person who then owned it turned it into a mausoleum for his daughter, age 14. The body was put into a copper cylinder filled with alcohol and this was suspended in one of the dismal avenues of the cave".

Unfortunately, though, his daughter did not rest here in peace, for some of the locals pried the iron door off the cave and often went inside to peer at the girl as a curiosity. Perhaps because of this, McDowell purchased a mound across the river, near Cahokia, and when his wife died, he had a tomb for her built atop it. It was said that he would sometimes watch the tomb with his telescope from a cupola on top of his home.

At the beginning of the Civil War, McDowell's son, Drake, joined the Confederate Army under the command of General Meriwether Jeff Thompson. He took two of the school's cannons with him. McDowell also went south to serve the Confederacy as medical director for the Trans-Mississippi Department.

In November 1861, General Henry W. Halleck took over as a commander of the Union Army's Department of the West, headquartered in St. Louis. Provost Marshall George E. Leighton seized the abandoned medical college and it was taken over by the Union military. The building was first used as a recruiting office for St. Louis and then it was converted into barracks for arriving soldiers. Finally, Confederate prisoners of war began being housed in the building to help relieve the overcrowding at a smaller, nearby prison, a hellish place known as Lynch's Slave Pen.

The job of converting the medical college to a prison was given to a Major Butterworth. In December 1861, 50 men, including 15 former slaves, were put to work renovating the hospital and cleaning out what the medical students had left behind. The former slaves were given the distasteful task of removing the three wagon-loads of human bones and the assorted medical specimens that were found in the basement. Cooking stoves and sleeping bunks were constructed and McDowell's dissecting room was converted into a dining hall. General Halleck placed Colonel James M. Tuttle in charge of the prison's operations.

The first prisoners arrived on December 22. A large crowd of curious spectators gathered at the train depot to watch them come in, but before the train arrived, the crowd became unruly and two regiments of soldiers from Iowa and Indiana had to be dispatched to the station to maintain order. As the train stopped, the Indiana regiment formed two lines from the cars to the prison. A military band, which had assembled at the scene, began to play "Yankee Doodle" as the men climbed from the train and "Hail Columbia" as they were forced to march off to the prison. The Confederates were in sorry shape when they arrived. They had no uniforms and what little clothing they had was tattered and torn. The officers' clothing was in better shape, but not by much.

The soldiers were taken to the Gratiot Street Prison and it was soon obvious that the prison had been poorly planned and prepared. The building's capacity was about one-third of the number that arrived on the first day. The holding areas were badly ventilated and unsuited for large numbers of people. The waste buckets that had been placed in the rooms were insufficient for the number of men who had to use them, as was the trench latrine in the yard area. In an effort to keep the prison as clean as possible, Colonel Tuttle issued an edict that would make the prisoners responsible for the cleanliness of their quarters. They were to sweep the rooms each morning and scrub them every two weeks. Unfortunately, though, the overcrowded conditions made this impossible. When the scrubbing details were enforced, water sloshed around on the floor and seeped into the lower rooms, making the situation even worse.

Conditions were chaotic because of the lack of organization of prisoners. Prisoners of all types could be housed in the same rooms. Held within the walls were not only Confederate prisoners of war, but suspected Southern sympathizers, bush whackers, spies, Union deserters, and Union soldiers who had been arrested for criminal activity. The prison even held women accused of harboring fugitives or sympathizing with the South.

Discipline was harsh, especially in the beginning when St. Louis was still embroiled in the riots, murders, and shootings that marked the early days of the war. Guards were ordered to shoot anyone who not only tried to escape, but even those who simply stuck their heads or other body parts out of a window. There were reports that some of the guards took potshots at prisoners just to practice their aim.

One prisoner, Captain Griffin Frost of Missouri State Guard, who was captured in Arkansas, noted in his journal that "the officers of the regiment now guarding us are perfect devils - there is nothing too low, mean or insulting for them to say and do... we are surrounded by bayonets and artillery, guarded by soldiers who curse, swear and fire among us when they please, and resort to balls, chains and dungeons for the slightest offense." Another prisoner, Henry M. Cheavens, who was captured after the battle at Wilson's Creek, wrote "one night, the guards shot at one [prisoner] because he refused to put out the light."

The prison was a filthy, horrifying place. The population soared and sanitary conditions and food rations further declined. The hospital was always filled, so the sick and dying were left lying on the floor. The dawn of each new day would reveal from one to four dead men stretched out on the cold stone. One prisoner wrote, "All through the night can be heard coughing, swearing, singing and praying, sometimes drowned out by almost unearthly noises, issuing from uproarious gangs, laughing, shouting, stamping and howling, making night hideous with their unnatural clang. It is surely a hell on earth."

During the prison's occupations, there were outbreaks of measles, pneumonia, vermin infestations, and the war's most accomplished killer, chronic diarrhea. The *St. Louis Republican* newspaper called the hospital "filthy and unhealthy."

In March 1863, a smallpox epidemic raged through the close quarters, and the polluted conditions in the cellblocks declined further. Lice and bed bugs invaded the prisoners, their clothing, and everything else. Men died at an alarming rate, largely due to new outbreaks of dysentery and typhoid.

In April 1863, the Western Sanitary Commission, a private agency that operated in the West during the war to help the army deal with sick and wounded soldiers, appointed two physicians to look into the situation at the prison. Among other things, they found that the bunks for the men were spaced so tightly together that a man could scarcely pass between them and that the prisoners' bedding had been reduced to scraps of blanket and pieces of carpet. The floors were so encrusted with filth that the stone had started to resembled dirt flooring. They concluded their report with, "It is difficult to conceive how human beings can continue to live in such an atmosphere."

A great many of them did not continue to live. Constant new inmates, many of whom were dead on arrival or died soon after, propelled the population at Gratiot Street to new highs in 1864. Horrified at the rate of death and illness within the prison walls, Union Surgeon General George Rex reported that despite the attention that has been called to the problem of overcrowding, the "evil still continues unabated." The prison remained open until the end of the war. By then, the conditions inside had collapsed beyond imagination.

By the summer of 1865, the prison had closed down, and not long after, Dr. McDowell returned to St. Louis to re-establish the hospital and medical school. He cleaned and renovated all of the rooms, except for one, which was left just as it had been when the prison was open. He called that room "Hell" and most likely, the description was a fitting one.

McDowell died from pneumonia in 1868, and the medical school was left vacant for years. As for McDowell, his body turned out to be safer than those whose corpses were disinterred and ended up on his dissection table. He was buried in the city's Bellefontaine Cemetery, next to the graves of his family. The plot includes the body of his wife, removed from her tomb in Illinois, and that of his daughter, who was retrieved from the cave near Hannibal and finally laid to rest.

The abandoned hospital fared much worse. In June 1878, the south wing was condemned as being unsafe and was demolished by order of the fire department. The octagonal tower and the north wing remained until 1882, when they were torn down. Nothing remains of the building today, and it is merely a forgotten spot on the Ralston-Purina company's back lot.

But for years after the building closed down for good, it was anything but a forgotten place for the people who lived in the neighborhood around the old college. To them it was a haunted and forbidding place, and not only because of the horrific experiments they believed had once been conducted by Dr. McDowell and his ghoulish students. The people in the area were convinced that the ghosts of men who died at the Gratiot Street Prison remained behind at the site.

According to the stories, cries and screams were often heard coming from the crumbling walls of the old prison. If anyone searched inside, they would find the place empty and abandoned. What could they have been hearing? Could it have been an eerie replay of the cacophony that was described by prisoners during the war? One of them wrote that on many nights, it was impossible to sleep because of the sounds that came from the lower levels of the prison. The natural sounds of incarcerated men were "sometimes drowned out by almost unearthly noises... laughing, shouting, stamping and howling, making night hideous with their unnatural clang."

Could these have been the sounds described by the terrified local residents as coming from an empty building that had once housed almost unimaginable horrors?

8. A WHEELCHAIR

WAVERLY HILLS SANATORIUM

When it comes to the places known as "the most haunted in America," it's often hard to tell the difference between truth and fiction. It seems that the more haunted the location appears to be, the more desperate people become to try and provide a reason for the lingering ghosts. The former Waverly Hills Sanatorium is a place of myth, legend, and exaggeration – and yet, there is no question that it's very haunted. Over the years, many have told stories of deaths at the old hospital that number into the tens of thousands, of deceased staff members that never existed, of deaths that never occurred, and ghostly tales that are nothing but pure invention.

And yet, it is one of the most haunted places that I have ever visited and where I even got my first glimpse of an actual ghost.

With this item – a rusty wheelchair that once positioned tuberculosis patients in front of the large windows to take in the sun and fresh air – we'll try to separate the fact from the fiction at one of my favorite haunted places in America.

"No Spitting in Public Places"

During the 1800s and early 1900s, America was ravaged by a deadly disease known to many as the "white death": tuberculosis. But the illness had been with mankind since antiquity, manifesting in various forms and under a variety of names. The most common form of the disease was pulmonary tuberculosis, which affected the lungs and was spread from person to person through airborne droplets. This terrifying and very contagious plague, for which no cure existed before antibiotics were discovered, claimed entire families and occasionally entire towns.

While the history of tuberculosis may conjure up images of health-restoring sanatoriums and pale-faced, slender, and romantic men and women of the Victorian Age, the truth of the disease was a bitter one. The terminal stages of the "white death" – so named for the characteristic pallor of its victims -- meant a violent, bloody cough, breathlessness, pain, night sweats, and a slow, insidious wasting away of young and tormented bodies.

In the nineteenth century and the first half of the twentieth century, tuberculosis killed millions of people. It was a plague that was as devastating as the "black death" in Europe during the Middle Ages, but it did not come and go in epidemic waves. It was always present, sapping the energy and destroying the lives of young men and women, and even children, across the country. Tuberculosis, along with a host of other "crowd" diseases, wiped out generation after generation of people in the prime of life – depriving children of parents, families of breadwinners, and lovers of sweethearts. Life expectancy in some places was a little over 30 years, and tuberculosis ranked high as a leading cause of death in the nineteenth century. Even in the early part of the twentieth century, it killed more people than any other infection.

In 1882, Dr. Robert Koch discovered the tubercle bacillus that caused the disease and managed to quash some of the older theories as to how it was spread, which included a hereditary "consumptive disposition," the "indigent habits" of the poor, and the "sorrowful passions" of young lovers. The fact that Koch showed tuberculosis to be an infectious bacterial disease confirmed what many believed all along: the disease hit hardest at those whose lives were blighted by poverty and poor nutrition, and worked in badly ventilated, overcrowded, cold, damp, or dusty conditions. It was now clear that the bacilli spread rapidly and easily when people lived or worked in close proximity, breathing in one another's coughs, sneezes, and spittle. Those most likely to succumb to the symptoms were people with little resistance to fight off infection.

Public health campaigns began to appear that instructed people on how to avoid contracting or spreading tuberculosis. One clear directive was "no spitting in public places," and spittoons were provided to try and limit the spread of airborne bacilli. In New York City, spitting became a punishable offense, and by 1916, nearly 200 American cities had rules in place against spitting in public.

Many tuberculosis patients were advised to seek out drier climates in the west, which brought relief for many. Because of their warm, dry climates, California, New Mexico, and Arizona became known as the "Land of New Lungs."

Isolating the infected and giving them the opportunity to rest became the preferred way of dealing with the disease, for which there was no cure. The old idea of seeking "healthy airs" – whether in spas, by the seaside, or in the cold, dry mountains – gave rise to an expansion of sanatoriums. And it was not just the wealthy "lungers" who benefited; the contagious poor were also encouraged or even pressured into entering one of the state or charity-run sanatoriums. The movement became the most popular in the early twentieth century. Rest, sun, fresh air, rich food, and moderate exercise were part of the patients' daily routine.

But a cure was still decades away and no matter how well-intentioned the methods of the scores of tuberculosis sanatoriums across the country, there was little that could be done to save the lives of those afflicted by the disease. As a result, hundreds of thousands of people perished within the walls of the hundreds of hospitals, which could be found in almost every town, county, and state across America.

There are many such hospitals where the ghosts of the past are said to linger behind, but none as famous as the former sanatorium that overlooks the city of Louisville, Kentucky.

Waverly Hills

In 1900, Louisville, Kentucky, had one of the highest tuberculosis death rates in America. On low swampland, the area was the perfect breeding ground for disease. To try and contain the disease, plans were made for a two-story wooden sanatorium on a windswept hill in southern Jefferson County. The land where the hospital was built had been purchased by Major Thomas H. Hays in 1883, and he constructed his family home on the hilltop. Since it was far from any existing schools, Hays decided to open a local school that his daughters could attend. Lizzie Lee Harris was hired as the teacher, and due to her fondness for the Sir Walter Scott's Waverley novels, she named the schoolhouse Waverley School. Major Hays liked the peaceful-sounding name, so he named his property Waverley Hill.

When the Board of Tuberculosis bought the land and opened the sanatorium, they kept the name. It is not known exactly when the spelling changed to exclude the second "e" and became Waverly Hills; however, the spelling fluctuated between both spellings many times over the years.

In 1910, construction was started on the hospital. The initial construction featured an administrative building and two open air pavilions that could accommodate between 40 and 50 "early case" patients. On August 31, 1912, all tuberculosis patients from the City Hospital were relocated to temporary quarters in tents on the grounds of Waverly Hills pending the completion of a hospital for advanced cases. The new building was completed in December of that same year. In 1914, a children's pavilion added another 50 beds to the hospital, making the official capacity around 130. The children's pavilion was not only for sick children, but also for the children of tuberculosis patients who could not be cared for properly otherwise.

But this was still not enough. Due to constant need for repairs on the wooden structures, need for a more durable structure, and a demand for more beds so that the sick would not be turned away due to lack of space, a new five-story building was designed that could hold more than 400 patients.

Construction on Waverly Hills started in 1924 and it opened two years later. Built in the collegiate gothic style, it was considered the most advanced tuberculosis sanatorium in the country. Even so, many of the patients succumbed to the disease. There was no medicine available at that time to treat the infection and so patients were offered rest, fresh air, and large amounts of healthy food. Patients were placed in front of wide, open windows on the upper floors, on sun porches, and the roof, no matter what the season. Old photographs show patients lounging in chairs, taking in the fresh air, while literally covered with snow.

Sadly, though, the main use for the hospital was to isolate those who had come down with the disease and to keep them away from those who were still healthy. Families were tragically divided with parents, and even children, forced into the sanatorium with little contact with their loved ones.

Treatments for tuberculosis were sometimes as bad as the disease itself. Some of the experiments that were conducted in search of a cure seem barbaric by today's standards but others are now common practice. Patient's lungs were exposed to ultraviolet light to try and stop the spread of bacteria. This was done in "sun rooms," using artificial light in place of sunlight.

Other treatments were less pleasant --- and much bloodier. Balloons would be surgically implanted in the lungs and then filled with air to expand them. Needless to say, this often had disastrous results, as did an operation where muscles and ribs were removed from a patient's chest to allow the lungs to expand further and let in more oxygen. This blood-soaked procedure was seen as a "last resort" and many patients did not survive it.

While the patients who survived both the disease and the treatments left Waverly Hills through the front door, many others left through what came to be known as the "body chute." This tunnel was constructed at the same time as the main building and it traveled 500 feet to the railroad tracks at the bottom of the hill. One side of the tunnel had steps that allowed workers to enter and exit the hospital without having to walk the steep hill. The other side had a set of rails and a cart powered by a motorized cable system so that supplies could be easily transported from the railroad stop to the hospital on top of the hill. Air ducts leading from the roof of the tunnel to above ground level were incorporated every hundred feet to let in light and fresh air.

In time, the tunnel was used to not only bring up supplies, but to send out the dead as well. Legend has it (since this has not been stated in hospital records) that the sight of the dead being taken away was not good for patient morale. With that in mind, staff members began using the motorized cart to discreetly lower the bodies to the bottom of the hill and into waiting hearses, or onto a passing train.

There are many inaccurate reports as to how many people died during Waverly Hills' decades of operation. Some claim that tens of thousands (the highest claim is 62,000) died within the walls of the hospital, but this number is greatly exaggerated. According to Dr. J. Frank Stewart, a former assistant medical director at the hospital, the highest number of deaths to occur at Waverly Hills in a single year was 152. Stewart noted that the worst time for deaths was at the end of World War II, when troops were returning from overseas with advanced cases of tuberculosis. By 1955, the death rate had dropped to as low as 42 deaths and it has been estimated (based on death certificates that were filed) that approximately 6,000 patients died there, dating all of the way back to the original hospital records from 1911. While far short of the numbers being tossed about in the legends, it's still a tremendous number of deaths to have occurred in a single structure.

The End of Waverly Hills

The sanatoriums, the public notices, and the discovery of X-rays that could provide a clear picture of the lungs of tuberculosis sufferers helped to keep the disease from spreading out of control; however, the search for an effective vaccine or therapeutic drug continued to be problematic.

Development of a vaccine was eventually achieved in 1921 by two French scientists, Albert Calmette and Camille Guerin. The vaccine was widely used in many countries after World War II, although it was less popular in the United States.

160

It was followed in the mid-1940s by the discovery of the first antibiotic effective against tuberculosis – streptomycin. Selman Waksman, a Ukrainian-born American, found the compound in a mold growing in the throats of chickens that had been raised in a field that was filled with manure. Two other drugs – para-amino-salicylic acid and isoniazid – were subsequently combined with streptomycin as a way of preventing resistance to any single drug. This triple therapy, developed by Sir John Crofton and his team in Edinburgh in the 1950s, became known as the Edinburgh Method. It proved extremely successful in treating tuberculosis, and over the following decades, saved millions of lives. The threat of tuberculosis continued to decline over the decades and by the 1980s, was no longer considered a public health threat in the West.

But oddly, historians have noted that the dangers of tuberculosis had already begun to subside before the development of the Edinburgh Method in the 1950s. The reasons for this continue to be a mystery today. If vaccines and medicines played no role in the early stages of the decline in tuberculosis, what caused the decline? Some believe that it might have been improved nutrition, the isolation of the sick, the concerted efforts to stop the spread of the disease, or social improvements that led to better housing and working conditions for the poor.

Regardless, tuberculosis began to decline worldwide in the late 1930s, and by the 1940s, new medicines had largely eradicated the disease in the United States. A small jump in new cases did occur after World War II and many soldiers returning from the war were housed at Waverly Hills. Dr. J. Frank Stewart noted in his autobiography that many of the soldiers had cases that were so advanced that they did not live for more than a week after arriving at the hospital.

New cases of tuberculosis continued to dwindle over the next decade. It reached a point that it was no longer cost effective to operate a hospital the size of Waverly Hills. The remaining patients were eventually sent to nearby Hazelwood Sanatorium, and by 1961, Waverly Hills was closed down for good.

A year later, the hospital re-opened as Woodhaven Geriatrics Sanitarium. There have been many stories told and allegations made about patient mistreatment and unusual experiments during the years that the building was used as an old age home. Most of these tall tales have turned out to be false, but others have unfortunately turned out to be true. Electroshock therapy, which was considered to be highly effective in those days, was widely used for a variety of ailments. Budget cuts in the 1960s and 1970s led to both horrible conditions and patient mistreatment, and in 1982, the state closed the facility for good.

Is it any wonder, after all of the death, pain, and agony within these walls, that Waverly Hills is considered to be one of the most haunted places in the country?

161

Waverly Hills: One of America's Most Haunted

The buildings and land were auctioned off and changed hands many times over the course of the next two decades. In 1983, a developer purchased the property with plans to turn it into a minimum-security prison for the state of Kentucky. Plans were dropped after neighbors protested and a new idea to turn the former hospital into apartments was devised. A lack of financing caused this plan to be abandoned.

In March 1996, Waverly Hills and the surrounding land was bought by Robert Alberhasky, who ran Christ the Redeemer Foundation, Inc. He had plans to construct the world's tallest statue of Jesus on the Waverly Hills site, along with an art and worship center. The statue, which was inspired by the famed Christ the Redeemer statue in Rio de Janeiro, was to be situated on the roof of the hospital at a cost of about $4 million. The next phase of his plan was to convert the sanatorium into a chapel, theater, and gift shop for another $8 million. Donations to the project fell far short of what was expected. During the first year, only $3,000 was raised towards the effort and the project was scrapped in December 1997.

Alberhasky abandoned the Waverly Hills property and then, in order to recoup some of his costs, tried to have the property condemned so that the buildings could be torn down and the land redeveloped. This plan was blocked by the county and according to rumor, demolition work was then done around the southern edge of the building in order to undermine the structural foundations and collect insurance money. This scheme also failed, and in 2001, Waverly Hills was sold to Charlie and Tina Mattingly, the current owners of the property.

By 2001, the once stately building had been nearly destroyed by time, the elements, and vandals who came looking for a thrill. Waverly Hills had become the local "haunted house." It was also a magnet for the homeless looking for shelter, and teenagers, who broke in looking for ghosts. The former hospital soon gained a reputation for being haunted and stories began to circulate of resident ghosts, like the little girl who was seen running up and down the third floor solarium, the little boy who was spotted with a leather ball, the hearse that appeared in the back of the building dropping off coffins, the woman with the bleeding wrists who cried for help, and others. Visitors told of slamming doors, lights in the windows when no power was running through the building, strange sounds, and eerie footsteps in empty rooms.

Other legends told of a man in a white coat who was seen walking in the kitchen and the smell of cooking food that sometimes wafted through the room. The kitchen was a disaster, a ruin of broken windows, fallen plaster, broken tables and chairs, and puddles of water and debris that resulted from a leaking roof. The cafeteria had not fared much better. Even so, a number of people reported hearing footsteps in the room, seeing a door swinging shut under its own power, and the smell of fresh baked bread in the air.

The "death chute" on the property was another location that attracted those looking for spirits. It's believed that the number of bodies moved through the tunnel over the years of the hospital's operations left a residual energy behind. Many of the alleged experiences that have occurred in the tunnel – from feelings of being touched and pushed, strange sounds, and voices – can be explained away by the darkness and the claustrophobic atmosphere of the passageway. But can they all? Those who have experienced these sensations state definitively that they are real.

Perhaps the greatest – and most controversial – legend of Waverly Hills was connected to the fifth floor of the building. This area of the old hospital consisted of two nurses' stations, a pantry, a linen room, a medicine room, and two medium-sized dormitories on both sides of the two nurses' stations. One of these, Room 502, is the subject of many rumors and legends and just about every curiosity-seeker that had broken into Waverly Hills over the years wanted to see it. This is where, according to the stories, people have seen shapes moving in the windows, have heard disembodied voices and, if the legends are to be believed, some have even jumped to their deaths.

There are a lot of legends about what went on in this part of the hospital, but perhaps the biggest misconception was that this was a floor used to house mentally-ill tuberculosis patients. This was not the case. The patients here were not insane, nor were they confined to their rooms. They were free to move about, just like patients on all of the other floors of the hospital. This floor, thanks to its design, allowed patients to still benefit from the fresh air and sunshine that was believed to cure, or at least extend the lives, of those with the disease. It was centered in the middle of the hospital and the two wards, extending out from the nurses' station, were glassed in on all sides and opened out onto a patio-type roof.

According to the stories, a nurse was found dead in Room 502 in 1928. She had committed suicide by hanging herself from the light fixture. She was said to have been 29-years-old at the time of her death, unmarried, and pregnant. It is unknown how long she may have been hanging in this room before her body was discovered. And this would not be the only tragedy said to be connected to Room 502.

In 1932, stories say, another nurse who worked in the same room jumped from the roof patio and plunged to her death. No one seems to know why she would have done this, but many have speculated that she may have been pushed over the edge. There are no records to confirm this, but the rumors continue to persist.

Those are the stories anyway.

As with so many legends, no records exist to say that any of this actually happened. There are also conflicting accounts as to how the pregnant nurse managed to hang herself. Some say that she did it from the light fixture, others from a pipe over the door, and some say from the rafters. There are some issues with these stories. There are no rafters in Room 502, the pipe over the door was part of a sprinkler system installed in 1972, and the light fixture is hung on a light decorative chain that would not hold the weight of a person. There is no actual documentation of either death, although some claim the stories were verified by a former staff member named John Thornberry, who died in 2006. According to his obituary, Thornberry was born in 1922, which would have made him six and ten-years-old at the time of the alleged deaths in Room 502. This makes his "verification" more than a little problematic.

So, what happened in Room 502 that could cause so many people to claim paranormal experiences there? Overactive imaginations, or is it something real? It's hard to say, but it seems likely that something occurred in that room to cause the legend to take root in the first place. What that might have been, no one knows. The story of Room 502 may have been loosely based on some forgotten facts, but the truth remains buried under speculation and rumor.

In spite of this, strange things continued to be reported. Over the course of the next year, volunteers working toward the restoration of the building experienced ghostly sounds, heard slamming doors, saw lights appear in the building when there should have been none, had objects thrown at them, were struck by unseen hands, saw apparitions in doorways and corridors, and much more. But none of the stories that I had been told could have prepared me for my first visit to Waverly Hills.

The first time that I visited the hospital was in September 2002. I was in town for a convention and a friend of mine, who had been working with the owners at Waverly Hills, offered to take me to see the place that I had been hearing so much about. At that point, the old hospital had been opened for tours but had not reached the level of "infamy" that it has today. There were yet to be any television shows, books, or websites dedicated to the place.

It was literally a dark and stormy night when we arrived at the hospital and it had been raining all day. I was looking forward to seeing the place, no matter what the weather, and not because I was convinced that I would meet one of the former patients face to face – I simply wanted to experience the place for myself. By this time, I had traveled all over the country and had been to hundreds of places that were alleged to be haunted. I had felt just this same way before exploring all of them, so Waverly Hills was no different. To me, it was just an old, spooky building with a fascinating history. The fact that it was alleged to be haunted simply added to the experience. I had long since abandoned the idea of expecting too much.

After meeting with the owners, we went inside and started our exploration of the building. It was almost silent. All I could hear was the sound of our own footsteps, our hushed voices, and the drip of rain as it slipped through the cracks in the roof and splashed down onto the floor. I was given the full guided tour and saw various rooms: the treatment areas, the kitchen, the morgue, and on and on. We climbed the stairs to the top floor and I saw the legendary Room 502, as well as the lights of Louisville as they reflected off the low and ominous-looking clouds that had gathered above the city.

The only floor that we skipped over was the fourth. My friend explained that this was the only floor in the building to which the entrance was kept locked and he had saved it for last. When we finally arrived on the fourth floor, I got the distinct feeling that something strange was in the air. I make absolutely no claims of any psychic ability whatsoever, but there was just something about this floor of the hospital that felt different than any of the others. What had been nothing more than an old ramshackle, broken-down building suddenly seemed different. I can't really put into words what felt so strange about it, but there almost seemed to be a tangible "presence" that I had not encountered anywhere else in the place.

And apparently, I have not been the only person to feel this way. Since my first trip to Waverly Hills, I have read about (and witnessed) other people's experiences on the fourth floor. There are tales of footsteps, whispers, knocking and banging, and more. Tradition holds that this floor was used to house the sickest of the patients – leading to dangerous surgeries and the highest number of deaths. Many believe that this floor has a heavy atmosphere, filled with sadness and misery (I would have to agree) and there have been many reports of shadowy figures that have been seen in the long corridors. A few years after my initial visit to the hospital, I was with a group of authors and guests from a convention who were touring the place and witnessed a heavy metal door on the fourth floor slam shut by itself. There was no earthly way to explain it.

But on that first night, I felt a chill as I walked out onto the fourth floor and right away, eerie things started to happen.

We had entered the floor in what I believe was the center of the building. Behind us was a wing that I was told was not safe to enter. Sections of the floor had collapsed and this area was off-limits to tours and visitors. The strange thing about it was that both of us clearly heard the sounds of doors slamming from this part of the building. I can assure the reader that it was not the wind. The wind was not

165

strong enough that night to have moved those heavy doors and it clearly sounded as though someone was closing them very hard. When I questioned my friend about who else could be up there with us, he said we were the only ones because the floors were unsafe in that section. I investigated on my own and determined that he was correct -- there was no one walking around on that part of the fourth floor.

I switched off my flashlight and we walked down the corridor using only the dim, ambient light from outside. The hallway runs through the center of the building and on either side are former patient rooms. Beyond the rooms is the "porch" area that opens to the outside. It was there that patients were placed to take in the fresh air. There was never any glass in the huge outer windows, which has left the interior of the floor open to the elements. On this night, the windows also illuminated the corridor, thanks to the low-hanging clouds that glowed with the lights of Louisville. We walked down through the dark and murky corridor and I began to see shadows that flickered back and forth. I was sure that this was trick of the eye, likely caused by the lights or the wind moving something outside. But it was where the corridor angled to the right that I got a look at something that was definitely not a trick of the eye!

In order for the reader to understand what I saw, I have to explain that the hallway ahead of us continued straight for a short distance and then turned sharply to the right. In the early 1900s, most institutions of this type were designed in this manner. It was what was dubbed the "bat-wing" design, which meant that there was a main center in each building and then the wings extended right and left, then angled again so that they ran slightly backward like a bird, or bat, wings. Directly at the angle ahead of us was a doorway that led into a treatment room. I only noticed the doorway in the darkness because the dim light from the windows beyond it had caused it to glow slightly. This made it impossible to miss since it was straight ahead of us.

We took a few more steps and then, without warning, the clear and distinct silhouette of a man crossed the lighted doorway, passed into the hall, and then vanished into a room on the other side of the corridor. I got a distinct look at the figure and I know that it was a man and that he was wearing something long and white that could have been a doctor's coat. The sighting only lasted a few seconds, but I knew what I had seen.

And for some reason, it shocked and startled me so badly that I let out a yell and grabbed hold of my friend's jacket. I am not sure why it affected me in that way; perhaps it was the setting, the figure's sudden appearance, my own anxiety -- or likely all of these things. Regardless, after my yell, I demanded that my friend turn on a light and help me to examine the room the man had vanished into. After my initial fright, I became convinced that someone else was on the floor with us. My friend assured me we were the only ones there but he did help me search for the intruder – in an empty room with only one way in or out. There was no one there. Whoever that figure had been, he had utterly and completely vanished.

I doubt that I was the first person to see this mysterious apparition on the fourth floor and it's unlikely that I will be the last. However, this sighting convinced me that Waverly Hills is haunted. Usually, for me to declare a place to be haunted, I must have my own unexplainable experience that goes beyond a mere "bump in the night" or spooky photograph. In this case, I had actually seen a ghost and at the time, I could count my personal ghost sightings on two fingers.

Waverly Hills is haunted and for me, seeing was believing.

9. A SYRINGE OF STREPTOMYCIN
ESSEX MOUNTAIN SANATORIUM

There is likely no place as worthy of legend and lore in Northern New Jersey than the Essex Mountain Sanatorium, which once stood outside of the city of Newark. It became a place of strange stories, tall tales, and ghostly encounters before being destroyed in the 1990s, utterly wiped out, and replaced by a nature preserve. But the stories of the place still linger…

Created by the untiring efforts of two women and first filled with patients under the cover of darkness, the sanatorium had one of the greatest survival rates of any tuberculosis hospital in the country. And yet, even in this place, the "white death" held sway over the lives of the tired and broken, and scores of people died.

While the hospital was still standing, those who did not survive their battle with tuberculosis lingered within its walls. And while the sanatorium may be gone, their stories remain.

"Four Women and a Sanatorium"

The history of the Essex Mountain Sanatorium began long before the first walls of the hospital were built. It began with the Newark City Home, which was established in Verona, New Jersey in 1873 on property that today is part of the Verona High School. The goal of the home was to both reform the children of Newark who were "treading the downward path" and to serve as an orphanage. On the night of January 9, 1900, the main building of the children's home was destroyed by fire. Luckily, no one was injured or killed. An engineer on a passing train had sounded his whistle to alert the sleeping residents of the fact that the building was on fire.

After the fire, the trustees of the home decided that the institution should be changed from one large building to house the children to the "cottage" system, which had recently been adopted for other types of institutions around the country. Under this system, a new administration building would be needed, along with a kitchen and utility building, and separate buildings for boys and girls. In late 1900, a location was chosen for the girl's building about a quarter-mile northwest of the boy's cottage.

The cornerstone for the "Newark City Home for Girls" was laid on the crest of the second Orange Mountain (known today as Second Mountain) at the highest point in Essex County, on October 30, 1900. The cottage was completed and opened in January 1902, but the number of delinquent girls was small, and in most cases, homes for orphaned girls could be secured with private families. Just four years later, in 1906, the girl's cottage was phased out and the building stood vacant.

A completely different string of events would begin a new history of the abandoned building. In 1906, there were at least 3,000 cases of tuberculosis in the city of Newark. By the early months of the year, 842 had already died. Because there were no proper facilities to cope with the disease, the Board of Health was helpless to deal with it.

One of those who had become ill with tuberculosis was the husband of a laundress who worked for the family of Edwin Prieth of Montclair. Concerned about the family of her employee, Mrs. Prieth and a neighbor, Miss Mary Wilson, applied to the Newark Board of Health on the family's behalf. The laundress and her husband and children lived in Newark where, as mentioned, there were no facilities for treating tuberculosis. The Board was sympathetic, but had nothing to offer. But the two ladies were not content to let the matter alone. They appealed to the president of the Board, Dr. Herman C.H. Herold, who took the problem to the city council. Once again, though, there was sympathy, but little that could be done.

169

Mrs. Prieth and Miss Wilson began to investigate the problem and found that things were worse than they first imagined. Not only were there no facilities designed to treat tuberculosis patients in the city, they found that indigent patients were suffering under deplorable conditions. One consumptive man was living in the basement of a downtown restaurant. He was unattended, had no money, and only survived on the food that was given to him by the owner of the restaurant. The Board of Health, however, had given him a blanket. Moved to tears by his plight, the two women paid for his stay at one of the few hospitals that had paid beds for tuberculosis patients.

At that point, they decided to find out why Newark could not provide for poor tuberculosis sufferers. The chief need, they discovered, was for a plan as to where they would be placed and how to get them there. It was Miss Wilson who found the solution to both questions. She explained, "I had gone for a walk along the ridge near the Montclair Hotel. Looking across the valley, my attention was suddenly held by the glorious colors of the evening sunset as reflected in the windows of the abandoned girl's home. Like an inspiration, the conviction came. That is the answer. The building is unoccupied. It is owned by the city. The location is ideal, so why not?"

There turned out to be a number of official reasons as to "why not?" but two women forged ahead. The Board of Health was quick to rally to their side and soon, Dr. Herold was back before the city council, which agreed to apply to the legislature for funding. Mrs. Prieth and Miss Wilson were also present to urge action, which was considered highly unusual for the time. Women simply did not appear in political forums in 1907, and it was not something that was encouraged. But Miss Wilson in particular stunned the council with a litany of practical facts and figures about the building, needs for the hospital, and the surrounding acres of land. By the time that they were finished, a health officer declared that the city would become the "next Denver for beneficial results" when it came to treating tuberculosis.

Things started smoothly, but that didn't last for long. The legislation was introduced in Trenton and Mrs. Prieth and Miss Wilson traveled there to support the bill. They were turned away at the doors to the chamber and told they would not be allowed inside. They were graciously reassured and sent home with an explanation that no difficulties were anticipated in getting the bill passed. Weeks passed and soon the legislature was within one week of adjournment. Concerned about the fate of the bill, the ladies inquired only to be told that it had failed almost as soon as it was introduced several weeks before.

With this news, the women began their battle for the sanatorium. They hurried to Trenton and made a plan to corner and speak with every assemblyman in the capital. The young women quickly schooled themselves in politics and learned that they couldn't vary their appearance too much or they would be forgotten. They adopted a "uniform" of sorts – a gray-tailored suit with a gray hat that was decorated with an ostrich feather. Whenever a member of the committee on municipal corporations showed himself, he was cornered by one of the young women and forced to discuss the legislation. They discovered that they were fighting an uphill battle. Property owners in the area were protesting the hospital and, at one point, a bribe was offered to try and get the women to go away. The word was out for the political machine to kill the bill, but the machine was battling a new force in politics – two women who were determined not to back down.

The intensive campaign waged by Mrs. Prieth and Miss Wilson finally succeeded in getting the bill before the House where, under dramatic circumstances, it passed by one vote. It then went to the Senate, where they were warned, it could never pass. But their fight had won them friends in high places and leading congressmen began winning votes on their behalf. It ended up passing through the Senate unanimously. When it was over, Mrs. Prieth (Miss Wilson had been called home because an in illness in her family) carried the bill to the governor. He signed it and sent the pen to Miss Wilson. A provision was now made for the "Newark City Home for Consumptives."

Exhausted by their efforts to secure the funding for the hospital, Mrs. Prieth and Miss Wilson stepped back from the fight. The work they had set out to do was finished and they felt it would be wise to withdraw from any active participation in the affairs of the institution whose existence they had assured. Miss Wilson soon married, and while the ladies remained interested in the development of the sanatorium, they left the work for two other women to carry on.

Their efforts had thoroughly inspired the physicians and health authorities, and they lost no time in setting about providing care for the consumptives of the city. Unfortunately, though, the fight to establish the hospital was not yet over. Although there were no legal obstructions to turning the girl's cottage into a sanatorium, the plan drew strong opposition from the citizens of nearby Verona. A campaign was started to keep the sanatorium out. Threats were made that an injunction would be sought in the courts to stop the opening.

Before any direct action could be taken by the protesters, the first few patients were admitted into the building under the cover of darkness in November 1907. At midnight the transfer of the property became official and Newark's city sanatorium came into existence. To evict the physician and his patients would require more court proceedings at that point and they were not pursued.

Those first few patients of the "Newark City Home for Consumptives" did not stay long, however. The former girl's building needed extensive repairs because it had been allowed to deteriorate during its vacancy. A hurried remodeling job was done, and on January 21, 1908, the sanatorium received the first two patients of the 129 that were treated there during its initial year.

Over the next decade, tuberculosis gradually began to be considered a county problem. Legislation followed, which placed responsibility for the care of the sick with the county. The Newark Board of Health suggested in 1917 that the Board of Chosen Freeholders take over the institution and enlarge it to handle the needs of the 4,012 persons suffering from tuberculosis in Essex County's communities. The county acquired the hospital in 1917, and initiated a building campaign, which led to the construction of 11 new buildings. They were completed and opened to patients in 1922.

It was at that time that a third woman stepped into an important role in the treatment of tuberculosis in Essex County. It came about because of a national event – the passing of the nineteenth amendment, which allowed women to vote. The women of Essex County elected Mrs. Elizabeth Harris, a well-known supporter of many social causes, to serve on the county board. She took her place on the board in January 1922 and was made chairman of the sanatorium.

She discovered that the hospital was being seriously taxed by the demands placed on it by new cases of tuberculosis. Additional beds were needed, even after the expansion, and since the office of the superintendent had recently become vacant, a new head was urgently needed. Dr. B.M. Harman, a graduate of the University of Pennsylvania Medical College, who had long experience in hospitals and relief work and was himself a victim of tuberculosis, was chosen for the position. All of this was taking place in the midst of the completion of a new 250-bed unit for the sanatorium and the organization of all of the tuberculosis cases in the county. The new unit was completed in 1926 – just before 100 more beds were requested by various organizations. Mrs. Harris spearheaded an expansion of the wards, along with more service facilities, such as the kitchen, laundry, and housing for the staff. She also organized the building of a chapel, a community building, and housing for children who were stricken with the illness before her term as the chairman of the hospital came to an end in 1930.

Four years after Mrs. Harris' term ended, another woman was elected to the county board and was placed in charge of the sanatorium. Mrs. Edith Hyde, who worked in public service during her husband's career in state and national politics, took over the affairs of the sanatorium. Under her chairmanship, the development of the hospital continued. More beds were added in 1936 by converting the sun

172

rooms of the hospital building into wards. She also oversaw the development of surgical treatments for tuberculosis, gaining permanent positions for two staff members to carry out the extreme methods used to try and provide some relief to chronic patients.

For its time, the sanatorium was a state-of-the-art facility. During its years of operation, it boasted a 50-percent recovery rate and was regarded as one of the finest treatment center in the country. Its location on the mountain, with its pure air and water, was considered the "Colorado Springs of the east." In addition to treating patients from all over America, the sanatorium became a haven for veterans of World War I who had suffered from lung injuries during the war.

During the middle years of the twentieth century, great advancements were made in the treatment of tuberculosis. With the discovery of streptomycin, an antibiotic that essentially cured the disease, the number of patients at the sanatorium began to swiftly decline in the 1950s. Within two decades, most of the sanatorium's buildings had fallen into disuse and the county struggled to find ways in which to utilize them.

In the early 1970s, the vacant wards were used to house the overflow of mental patients from nearby Overbrook, a psychiatric hospital. The building once used for the hospital's staff began to be used to house doctors from Overbrook and their families. Turning Point, a drug and alcohol rehabilitation center, was established in the male employee housing in 1975. Also, much of the sanatorium's vast farmland was used as a compost site for Essex County.

It would be science's victory over tuberculosis that would eventually seal the fate of the sanatorium. The eradication of the disease meant the end of a need for the sanatorium. In 1977, the last patient was released and the sanatorium officially closed its doors and ceased all operations. The gates to the property were locked on December 1, 1982, and the county officially abandoned the complex.

The Essex Mountain Sanatorium was left silent and dark on its hilltop, but soon, stories emerged that claimed that the crumbling building was not as empty as it seemed.

Hauntings at the Sanatorium

Almost from the time that the sanatorium closed its doors, strange stories began to be told about the abandoned structure. It became a magnet for teenagers, vandals, trespassers, and well-intentioned "urban explorers" who hoped to hold onto the memory of the place through photographs and accounts of their wanderings on the property. All who came there found the place remarkably – and eerily – preserved.

The closure of the sanatorium almost seemed like a hurried event, as if the staff had simply walked away one day and left everything behind. The beds, equipment, gurneys, medical supplies, and patient files had all been left behind, and rumors swirled about the final days of the hospital. There were tales of the mistreatment of the overflow patients from the mental institution that had been housed there, whispers of bizarre experiments, and stories of the *real* reason the hospital closed down – missing money. In actuality, none of those stories were true, and yet, the rumors became legend and took on a life of their own.

More legends began to surround the buildings now that they had been abandoned. Trespassers claimed to find brains, fetuses, and body parts stored in jars. They allegedly encountered former patients living in the tunnels under the hospital. Satanic rituals were said to take place in the building's darkest corners.

And then, of course, there were the ghosts.

Mixed in with the wild stories of escaped lunatics and devil worshippers were tales of eerie encounters with shadowy figures that vanished, disembodied voices, slamming doors, phantom footsteps, unexplained lights, and more. Could many of these stories be dismissed as nothing more than urban legends, natural sounds that were mistaken for something otherworldly, or the result of drinking too much alcohol? Of course, but mixed in with the tall tales were strange accounts that were not so easy to dismiss.

One account from an "urban explorer" recalled a visit in the late 1980s when he and two friends decided to check out the sanatorium they had heard so much about. They walked in, took a lot of photos of the buildings and water towers, and then went inside. They knew they were alone, and yet, several times as they walked, they heard the distinct sound of footsteps behind them. They checked several times down the shadowy corridor they had passed through, but there was no one there. Finally, all three young men came to a sudden halt, only to hear the footsteps continue! That was enough to convince them to flee. As they ran out of the building, the witness claimed that they heard a scream and then a loud, deep voice that warned them not to return. They sprinted the rest of the way down the mountain. The witness later added, "For me, the scariest part was still hearing the footsteps behind us while we were running. One of my friends also claims to have seen a figure in black running towards us. That one to the hospital visit was my last. I had nightmares for a long time."

Another explorer entered the hospital with a couple of friends on a night in 1986. It was a dark and rainy night and they took flashlights along as they trudged through the woods to the ruins. After going into the building and roaming around for a while, he saw something move out of the corner of his eye. He checked to see

174

if it was his friends, but they were on the other side of him. He slowly got their attention and then they saw it too -- an old wheelchair that was moving on its own. He noted, "The creepy thing was, there was no wind that night, not even a slight breeze. We all hightailed it out of there very fast."

One local resident with vivid memories of the old sanatorium visited the place as many as a dozen times while growing up in Verona between 1981 and 1989. He heard about the place from a friend's older brother, who used to go up there and have parties. According to the older boy, it had been an abandoned mental asylum and everything had been left in its place, like hospital beds, paperwork, gurneys, X-ray machines, like something out of a horror movie. Intrigued, he planned a trip to see the place with five of his friends on the last day of their eighth grade school year.

After hiking up the mountain with a baseball bat in hand (his friend's brother told him that some of the former patients still roamed the ground), he was awed by the size of the place – and by the fact that the stories of its abandonment were true. There were hundreds of hospital beds, hospital clothing, gurneys, syringes, and medical supplies all over the floor. There was broken glass, peeling paint, and patient files everywhere. Eerily, there was still some electricity to the building since the exit signs above some of the doors were still working. He also found that other stories were also true. In a room on the top floor of the main building, they found body parts that had been stored there in jars – a brain, a heart, a slice of a lung, and a tapeworm that was removed from a 40-year- old woman, or at least that's what it said on the side of the jar. They were resting there, preserved in formaldehyde, on a shelf, untouched. This discovery added to the feeling that the sanatorium had been evacuated overnight.

The first exploration lasted only a short time longer. As they started to make their way downstairs, they began to hear loud noises coming from the darkened rooms. Was someone else in the building? They didn't know, but they quickly left. Despite the scare, this was not enough to keep him away from the place. Over the summer, he told other friends about the hospital and returned three more times before school started again. He even asked some of his older neighbors if they knew anything about the hospital, but after all of those years, few remembered that it had once served to care for tuberculosis patients in the county. Most only knew the recent stories of mental patients, abuse, and black magic rituals. Eventually, his hospital expeditions were discovered by his parents and the sanatorium was made off limits.

Several years later, though, he went back and found that little had changed. That last visit occurred in 1989 and by then, he was in college and working a summer job. He met a girl who was into the supernatural and enjoyed anything scary. Once he

175

told her about the old hospital, she had to see it. One day after lunch, they took a ride up to the crumbling old building. As they entered the property, they drove around the main building to where it connected to the infirmary, and parked almost directly underneath a crosswalk that was used to get from one building to another. He was telling his girlfriend about his experiences there when, suddenly, he looked up and they both saw what looked like a nurse walking very slowly across the bridge that went from one building to the next. The witness recalled, "It was in broad daylight and as clear as day. I proceeded to drive away as fast as I could. I never went back there --ever."

As the years have passed, stories of the old hospital are still recounted and belief remains strong that it was haunted until the end by the spirit of the souls who died there. First-hand accounts tell of seeing clear figures of doctors and patients, of hearing the sounds of babies crying, and of a voice that came over an intercom that hadn't worked in decades.

Was it truly haunted? Perhaps, which leads us to an even bigger question – what happens to the ghosts when the buildings they haunt are destroyed?

The End of Essex Mountain Sanatorium

Despite what many felt was a clear need to preserve the hospital for its place in American history, it was never added to the National Register of Historic Places or offered any sort of protection against destruction. Although the sanatorium buildings were deemed structurally sound, county officials gave little thought to rebuilding them for other uses. Consequently, in August of 1993, the main complex of the sanatorium was destroyed and its memory was laid to rest, ending an era in local, state, and national history.

A few years later, the remaining buildings, structures, and foundations were also wiped out. Essex County opened a new 240-acre wooded reservation and nature preserve, effectively erasing the sanatorium from existence.

It had been the development of a vaccine that could treat tuberculosis that first doomed the hospital, but it had been progress that finally banished it from history.

10. OLD MEDICINE BOTTLE

YORKTOWN MEMORIAL HOSPITAL

Contributed by April Slaughter

There is nothing about Yorktown Memorial Hospital that is overtly ominous. It sits in the middle of a small Texas town, where few would ever know of its existence, had it not gained a reputation for being one of the most haunted places in the state.

The hospital first opened in 1951. Donations from various individuals and organizations made it possible to erect the facility in an area of Texas desperately lacking adequate medical resources. The Felician Sisters, an order of Catholic nuns, ran the hospital and also called it their home and place of worship.

As with any hospital, death was ever-present at Yorktown. Nearly 600 individuals were reported to have died within its walls in a six year period; not a

177

slight number considering the low population of the area. It was a difficult task to keep the hospital staffed with doctors and nurses, and as a result, many were admitted to the hospital seeking help only to end up the alleged victims of neglect or malpractice. Dr. Leon Nowiersky had the longest tenure at Yorktown, but was reportedly responsible for a great deal many medical mistakes that either further complicated the lives of patients or ended them prematurely. One such patient was said to have suffered a botched thyroid surgery, in which his throat was cut and he died as a result of severe blood loss. Dr. Nowiersky practiced well into his 90's until he was forced to retire. He died shortly afterward.

In 1986, Yorktown closed its doors following the opening of a new hospital in the nearby town of Cuero. In the years that followed, the building briefly served as a rehabilitation facility. Death was not finished with Yorktown, however, as a double homicide occurred in a love triangle gone horribly awry. A female caretaker had become involved with both a patient and a co-worker, and upon being discovered with her patient in the basement of the hospital, she was fatally stabbed to death by the male employee. The rehab facility was later shut down for its inability to properly care for and control its patients.

Yorktown Memorial Hospital sat vacant and abandoned for many years until it was privately purchased, cleaned of debris, and opened to paranormal investigators to explore. Various medical items, both original to the hospital and brought in from other locations, were placed throughout the building to help it more closely resemble its original state. As it sits today, Yorktown Memorial Hospital appears almost functional, but has an air about it that sets many who visit on edge, including myself.

My first visit to the site was in October of 2010, with a group of individuals interested in seeing how Instrumental Transcommunication (ITC) might work in the hospital. ITC is the use of modified electronic devices to facilitate two-way real-time communication with ghosts and/or spirits. It is a controversial practice, and one I had been quite familiar with for many years prior.

As with any new location or investigative technique, I was highly skeptical. I have become all too familiar with the claims of those who had little to no data to back them up. The stories behind Yorktown's paranormal activity certainly sounded intriguing, but I was unconvinced. When the invitation was extended to experience the location for myself, I accepted with a bit of hesitation.

My expectations were admittedly low, but within only a matter of minutes inside the hospital, I knew something was keenly aware of our presence. A small group of people had gathered in the front lobby of the hospital and were fumbling with various pieces of equipment to prepare for the investigation. I brought very little along with me, and felt well enough prepared with my flashlight and digital audio recorder in hand. As I waited for the others, I stood by the main floor nurse's station and fixed my gaze down one of the extending hospital hallways. No one had yet ventured away from the lobby, yet I watched as two distinct figures exited a room on the left side of the hallway and walk directly into a room on the right. I did not alert anyone else to what I had seen, and slowly walked down the hallway. As I approached the room I'd seen the figures walk into, the room blackened and the air immediately felt several degrees colder around me. It didn't cause me to feel frightened, however, I felt an overwhelming sense of sadness. It must have been only a matter of moments before the room lightened again and the feeling was gone.

The next hour or so proved rather uneventful, but as the entire group assembled in the basement of the hospital, there was a palpable shift in the energetic environment around us. I kept my observations to myself, but heard several others make mention of how odd they were feeling. An individual leading the group's attempt at spirit communication with a modified EMF induction amplifier asked that we gather as closely as we could as he sat in a basement storage closet and began working with the device. For several minutes, he called out to the spirits of the hospital, the amplifier remaining silent.

Just as my patience for the attempt was growing rather thin, a voice emanated from the device clearly saying, "Hello." When the individual was asked to provide their name, the male voice responded, "I'm Doug." This exchange was not recorded and discovered upon playback. Whoever was speaking to us was doing so as if he were standing right there in the room with us, and I was beginning to believe he was. As the conversation wore on, this man described relayed his awareness of no longer being among the living. He said he was comfortable in his surroundings, and even joked a little about wishing he had access to a bottle of whiskey. He was asked if there were others he was aware of in the hospital, and he said there were but he did not interact with them.

While the exchange was interesting, and even a little unnerving, it was not yet enough to convince me that the hospital was necessarily haunted. People have often manufactured 'evidence' to convince others that what they are experiencing is paranormal in nature when in fact they are just being cleverly deceived. I had not yet made up my mind as to whether or not I believed the experience to be authentic.

Two more unseen individuals would speak through the amplifier over the next couple of hours, one of them claiming to be the spirit of Dr. Leon Nowiersky. He seemed unaware that the hospital was no longer functioning as it had been when he was alive, and made several references to the responsibilities he needed to attend

179

to. As the amplifier once again fell silent, I felt the need to break away from the group and continue exploring the hospital on my own.

Nothing of note would happen for the remainder of my time at Yorktown that evening, but enough had occurred to pique my interest, and a return visit with a trusted group of friends and fellow investigators was planned.

When next I entered the hospital, I had the overwhelming sense that I would not leave with the same measure of skepticism I had before, and I was right. In the time that had passed between my first and second visits, I had acquired a modified EMF amplifier of my own, and was eager to attempt contact with the spirits of Yorktown without having to blindly trust another individual to make a legitimate connection.

My group and I gathered in the area of the basement called the four-way, where all of the walkways intersect. We sat in a circle with our audio equipment running, idly talking. The caretaker of the property, a man named Mike, agreed to sit with us and discuss some of the recent events in the hospital that he believed were the result of spirit activity. As I switched on the EMF induction amplifier, the group fell quiet and I began to ask questions in hopes someone would approach to talk to us. A slight buzzing was heard through the device, and remained constant for several minutes before growing slightly louder.

While no voices came from the device, it was obvious to us all that something was energetically affecting its functioning, as if something or someone was approaching that we could not see. I had not moved, nor had anyone else. There was no explanation for the device to be reacting the way that it was. At the point when the buzzing grew its loudest, a loud crash was heard down one of the hallways. It sounded as if an entire shelf of glass bottles had crashed to the floor. We were all quite startled by the event; even more so when we went to investigate the source, only to find the shelf of glass medical bottles entirely intact and undisturbed.

Mike began to grow restless, and had to excuse himself from the group to take in a bit of fresh air outside. He was fairly used to having things occur around him while in the hospital, but he had never grown as faint as he had while sitting with us in the four-way that evening. He did not feel well, and was unsure why, but he was convinced we had not been the only ones in the basement of the hospital. While I was never under the impression that we were unwelcome, several members of my group expressed an overwhelming sense that we should leave.

As we were gathering up our equipment, I noticed a child's plastic ball sitting up against one of the walls. Barely visible, as the hallways were nearly completely dark, I kicked the ball quite forcefully down the hallway directly in front of me. I could hear the ball bounce a distance away before stopping altogether, but I could not see where it had come to rest. Thirty seconds or so later, the ball was bounced right back towards the group, with the same force, as if someone had been standing at the other end and returned it to us in play. A friend and I walked down the hallway together, peering in each of the rooms on either side, but our invisible playmate went undiscovered. A second attempt at kicking the ball down the hallway proved fruitless, and it was not returned to us as it had been before.

Before calling it a night, several of us in the group wanted to walk through the building one final time to see what if anything we could capture on our equipment. As I made my way to the hospital operating room, I began hearing the sounds of glass breaking once again, as if a hundred or so feet behind me, someone was knocking bottles to the floor one by one. None of us ever discovered any evidence that this had actually happened, but the sounds were recorded and clearly unmistakable. Just as I was about to shut down my audio recorder and lock up for the night, I captured an EVP of a male voice in the lobby that said, "Goodnight, April."

My group and I had arrived at Yorktown that evening a group divided in our beliefs. Some of my friends were absolutely convinced that nothing supernatural was possible and simply came along for the ride. We left a group united in the idea that we had witnessed several things that simply had no other explanation.

In all of my visits to Yorktown, no two incidents have ever been identical in nature, but one thing has remained consistent; there has never been a time when I left feeling disappointed or left with the impression that the hospital was just a spooky old abandoned building and nothing more. There are individuals who still walk the halls of Yorktown, who are aware of it when we enter their space, and who interact with the living in a myriad of ways. Who they are, why they have chosen to remain, and how long they will stay is anyone's guess.

11. A COOKING SPOON
RIVERSIDE HOSPITAL
NORTH BROTHER ISLAND, NEW YORK

The year 1906 marked a turning point in American medicine. It was the year when the new science of bacteriology gained public attention when it was used in the investigation of a typhoid outbreak in New York City. It was a strange case that led the authorities to a healthy woman who was unknowingly spreading the disease. As these same authorities struggled to convince her that she was infecting the people she worked for, they eventually quarantined her for 26 years.

The story of "Typhoid Mary" has had a lingering effect on American history. Her name alone has become a metaphor for fear of contamination from contagious disease and her plight now symbolizes the need to balance the civil liberties of disease-carrying individuals when the population at large is at risk. Her story has had other lingering effects as well, namely on the place of her confinement, a now abandoned hospital on New York's North Brother Island. Is one of the ghosts that still walks the hallways of the hospital that of "Typhoid Mary"? Perhaps, for hers was a strange history to tell...

"A Foul and Fatal Fever"

Typhoid fever is one of the great plagues of mankind. Spread when food and water become contaminated by human feces, it was a disease that no one wanted to discuss and in the nineteenth century was believed to be an illness that only the poor were stricken with. And it was true that it seemed to be most prevalent in poverty-stricken, immigrant neighborhoods, largely due to the fact that the causative agent was a bacteria that spread rapidly in places with poor sanitation and inadequate hygiene.

Typhoid causes a range of symptoms, including abdominal pain, blinding headache, a rash, and a high fever. If left untreated, it could be fatal in about 10 to 20 percent of cases. The disease has undoubtedly been around for centuries, but historically speaking, it is difficult to separate typhoid from many other "fevers" of the past. Improvements in public health, water supply, and food hygiene have helped to reduce its prevalence in industrialized nations. However, it remains an often deadly disease in third-world countries.

Typhoid really entered the historical record of the nineteenth century with the death of Britain's Prince Albert in 1861. At that time, Queen Victoria was on the throne and was deeply in love with her husband. There had been, a few years earlier, a fever scare at the royal castle in Windsor, but it had come to nothing. Britain was moving into the modern age of flushing toilets and industrial innovation. In 1851, Prince Albert had spearheaded the Great Exhibition at the Crystal Palace, where for the first time visitors had enjoyed an opportunity to "spend a penny" in one of the latest attractions of the age – the paying public toilet. Back home, Prince Albert had tried to sort out 53 overflowing cesspools at Windsor Castle, but whenever the Thames rose and saturated the grounds with raw sewage, the royal gardeners had simply raked up the filth and shoveled it back into the river.

Three years later, Prince Albert was fighting for his life. He was running a high fever and was violently sick, while on his torso there appeared a collection of red spots. The royal physicians, Sir James Clark and Sir William Jenner, were in constant attendance. They diagnosed a "bowel fever" (likely typhoid), but they could do little for him. On December 14, 1861, Prince Albert died at the age of only 42. Queen

Victoria was inconsolable and dressed in mourning black for the remainder of her life.

Most cities in America were no better than London at that time. Fevers, it seemed, accounted for a great many deaths – both among the rich and the poor. Just a little over a year after the death of Prince Albert, a young boy in America was also stricken with a fever that was undoubtedly typhoid. His name was Willie Lincoln and he was the son of the President of the United States, Abraham Lincoln. In January 1862, both Willie and his brother, Tad, became seriously ill. Although Tad recovered, Willie's condition grew worse by the day. The most likely cause of the illness was typhoid, contracted from contaminated drinking water. At that time, the White House drew its water from the Potomac River, along which thousands of soldiers and horses were camped. Gradually Willie weakened and then died on February 20, 1862.

Both parents were deeply affected. His father did not return to work for three weeks. Willie's younger brother, Tad, cried for nearly a month over his lost brother. Mary was so distraught that Lincoln feared for her sanity. In time, both of the Lincolns turned to Spiritualism to ease their pain, igniting a revival of the American movement based on communication with the dead.

The deaths of Prince Albert and Willie Lincoln proved that typhoid was dangerous to everyone, not just the poor. The fevers could attack anyone, but what caused them? And were they all from the same source?

There were many fever-related diseases at that time. Some, like smallpox and yellow fever, were reasonably well-recognized and defined (if not understood), but many others were lumped together or described by their feverish symptoms and fatal effects rather than by what actually caused them. For many physicians, the overpowering stench of many locations where illnesses ran rampant suggested that the real cause of most fevers must lie in the noxious vapors, or "miasmas," emitted by stagnant marshes, cesspools, raw sewage, and the animal and human waste that contaminated the fields, streets, and water of towns across the country. Even the air that was exhaled by people who were sick were blamed for the spread of disease. Not the sewage and contaminants themselves, though, just the smell of them. The "miasmatic theory" of disease was so in fashion with many scientists in the nineteenth century that the term "mal'aria" (from the Italian, "bad air") began to be used as a catch-all description for the cause of disease.

Two diseases that became especially muddled and mired in this "miasmic" mess were typhoid and typhus, both of which were clearly associated with filth, poverty, poor sanitation, and, above all else, poisonous odors. Thanks to the scientists who studied the differences between them – American physician William

Wood Gerhard, British royal physician William Jenner, and British epidemiologist William Budd – it was discovered that typhoid was not caused by smells, but by contaminated water. He was proven correct in the 1880s when the typhoid bacteria was identified and cultured by a group of German scientists. This was one of the first discoveries of a bacterial agent as a cause of disease. It took some additional time for the cause of typhus (transmitted by body lice) to be discovered.

By the end of the nineteenth century, the germ theory of disease (first put forward by Louis Pasteur decades before) had finally become more widely accepted. Within a few years, it was recognized how typhoid was transmitted. The bacteria responsible moved from the infected individual through feces or urine, which then contaminated food and drinking water, and entered the mouth of the next victim. In principle, stopping typhoid should have been simple. Since only humans carried it, it could be stopped by strict hygiene – for example, washing hands before touching food, providing pure water, keeping fecal-carrying flies away from food, and insuring that no human waste gets into the water supply.

But there was one intriguing mystery about the infectious nature of typhoid and that was that no doctor could pinpoint the time when a fever patient was contagious enough to pass the illness along to another person. It was realized that recovering patients were still carrying the disease, even after their symptoms had stopped. In an era when there was no treatment, the key question was how long such survivors could continue to be a source of infection. And stranger yet, could a seemingly healthy person still be a carrier of the disease?

In time, campaigns to clean up the deplorable states of many American cities, along with information on the proper care and handling of food and education on hygiene, led to a reduction of the disease. However, it remained a threat in times of war, including the Boer War in Africa, Spanish-American War, World War I, and World War II. By the late 1940s, an effective drug – chloramphenicol – had been developed to treat the disease. As mentioned, it still remains a problem in developing countries, but has largely been eradicated in most parts of the world today.

But it's possible that the disease would not have been understood when it was if not for an infamous series of incidents that took place in New York City in the early years of the twentieth century. It is a strange story and one that left an indelible impression on the history of death and disease in America.

"Typhoid Mary"

The tale of "Typhoid Mary" began in the summer of 1906, when New York banker Charles Henry Warren rented a summer home for his family in Oyster Bay,

Long Island. The house was leased from George Thompson and a large staff was hired, including a working-class Irish immigrant named Mary Mallon, who was employed as a cook.

On August 27, one of the Warren's daughters became ill with typhoid fever. Soon after, Mrs. Warren and two maids also became stricken with the same symptoms of high fever, diarrhea, vomiting, chills, and a rash. Days later, another daughter became sick, as did the Warrens' gardener. In all, six of the 11 people in the household came down with typhoid.

Since the most common way that typhoid was spread was through food and water sources, the owners of the house feared that they would not be able to rent the property again without first discovering the source of the outbreak. The Thompsons hired investigators to look into the situation, but they were unsuccessful in finding the cause. Then, they hired George Soper, a civil engineer who had experience with typhoid fever outbreaks. It was Soper who believed that the recently hired cook, Mary Mallon, was the cause of the sickness. Mallon left the Warrens about three weeks after the outbreak and went to work for another wealthy family. Soper began researching her employment history, looking for clues.

Mary Mallon had been born on September 23, 1869, in Cookstown, County Tyrone, Ireland. According to what she told friends, Mary came to America at the age of 15. Like many Irish immigrant women, she found work as a domestic servant. Regarded for her skills, she became a cook, which paid better than most domestic service positions.

Soper traced Mary's employment history back to 1900, and found that typhoid outbreaks had followed her from job to job. From 1900 to 1907, Soper found that Mary had worked at seven jobs in which 22 people had become ill, including one young girl who died, with typhoid shortly after Mary came to work for them.

Soper was convinced that this was not a coincidence, and yet, he needed stool and blood samples from Mary to prove that she was a carrier. The idea that someone could be healthy and still carry a disease – and spread it to others – was a concept that had been only recently suggested by scientific discoveries. Mary Mallon, Soper knew, might be the first such person discovered by science.

In March 1907, Soper found Mary working as a cook in the home of Walter Bowen and his family. Soper needed samples from Mary and he confronted her at her place of work. She was shocked, as anyone would have been. As far as she knew, she was quite healthy and now she was being approached by a stranger who not only told her that she was spreading some sort of disease that was killing people, but wanted her to give him samples of her blood and her feces. Mary not only refused, she became quite angry.

186

Soper later wrote:

I had my first talk with Mary in the kitchen of this house. . . . I was as diplomatic as possible, but I had to say I suspected her of making people sick and that I wanted specimens of her urine, feces and blood. It did not take Mary long to react to this suggestion. She seized a carving fork and advanced in my direction. I passed rapidly down the long narrow hall, through the tall iron gate . . . and so to the sidewalk. I felt rather lucky to escape.

But Soper was relentless in his pursuit. He followed Mary to her home and tried to approach her again. This time, he brought an assistant, Dr. Bert Raymond Hoobler, for support. Again, Mary was enraged and made it clear that they were unwelcome. She cursed at them as they made a quick retreat. Soper, now realizing that it was going to take more persuasiveness than he was able to offer, handed his research and theories over to Hermann Biggs at the New York City Health Department. Biggs agreed with Soper's theories and sent Dr. S. Josephine Baker to talk to Mary.

After Soper's clumsy attempts to obtain blood and stool samples from her, Mary was now extremely suspicious of doctors and health officials. She refused to listen to Baker and sent her away. Baker returned a short time later, this time with five police officers and an ambulance. When they arrived at the house, Mary met them at the door with a long kitchen fork in her hand and lunged at Dr. Baker with it. As Baker stepped back, colliding with police officers behind her and knocking them down the steps, Mary slammed the door shut and made a run for it. By the time they got the door open and followed in pursuit, Mary had disappeared. Baker and the policemen searched the house, but found nothing. Eventually, footprints were discovered leading from the house to a chair placed next to a fence. Mary had apparently escaped into a neighbor's yard – or so they thought at first.

They searched both properties for the next five hours until, finally, they found what Dr. Baker later described as "a tiny scrap of blue calico caught in the door of the areaway closet under the high outside stairway leading to the front door." Mary was dragged from the closet "fighting and swearing," and even though Dr. Baker spoke to her calmly about the specimens that she needed, Mary refused to listen. Dr. Baker wrote, "By that time, she was convinced that the law was wantonly persecuting her, when she had done nothing wrong. She knew she had never had typhoid fever; she was maniacal in her integrity. There was nothing I could do but take her with us. The policemen lifted her into the ambulance and I literally sat on her all the way to the hospital; it was like being in a cage with an angry lion."

187

Mary was taken to Willard Parker Hospital and there, the specimens were finally taken. Laboratory results showed that Mary indeed had typhoid bacteria in her stool – she was a carrier of typhoid fever. As the first healthy typhoid carrier in New York City, Mary was made an example of by public health officials and was punished for her resistance to their tests. She was promptly detained and was quarantined on North Brother Island, located in the East River near the Bronx, which housed hundreds of individuals infected with highly contagious tuberculosis and other conditions. The otherwise healthy Mary Mallon was confined in a cottage on the island, making newspaper headlines and creating her infamous nickname of "Typhoid Mary."

Mary had been taken by force and was held against her will without a trial. She had not broken any laws, but because of the fact that she was a lowly Irish immigrant with no money or political clout and also because she was infected with an illness that people dreaded at the time, she found few to rally to her cause. Mary believed that she was being unfairly persecuted. She could not understand how she could have spread disease and caused a death when she, herself, seemed healthy. She wrote, "I never had typhoid in my life, and have always been healthy. Why should I be banished like a leper and compelled to live in solitary confinement with only a dog for a companion?"

Public officials felt they had every right to lock up Mary indefinitely, basing their power on sections 1169 and 1170 of the Greater New York Charter, which read:

The board of health shall use all reasonable means for ascertaining the existence and cause of disease or peril to life or health, and for averting the same, throughout the city. [Section 1169]

Said board may remove or cause to be removed to [a] proper place to be by it designated, any person sick with any contagious, pestilential or infectious disease; shall have exclusive charge and control of the hospitals for the treatment of such cases. [Section 1170]

The charter was written before anyone knew that "healthy carriers" – people who seemed healthy but carried a contagious form of disease that could infect others – could even exist. But the health officials of the early 1900s believed that healthy carriers were even more dangerous than those who were sick with a disease because there was no way to visibly identify a healthy carrier so that they could be avoided or quarantined. For this reason, they had no issues with locking Mary away for as long as they deemed necessary.

Mary was initially confined for two years on North Brother Island, during which time she wrote letters and filed a legal suit pleading for her freedom and release from the island.

During the time of her confinement, health officials had taken and analyzed her stool samples about once a week. The samples mostly came back positive with typhoid, but not always. For nearly a year, Mary also sent samples to a private lab, which tested all of her samples negative for typhoid. Feeling healthy and with her own lab results in hand, Mary believed that she was being unfairly held.

But in truth, Mary did not understand much about typhoid fever and, unfortunately, no one tried to explain it to her. Not all people have a strong bout of typhoid fever; some people have such a weak case that they only experience flu-like symptoms. Because of this, Mary could have had typhoid fever but never knew it. Though commonly known at the time that typhoid could be spread by water or food products, people who are infected by the typhoid bacteria could also pass on the disease by not washing their hands after using the bathroom. For this reason, infected cooks (like Mary) or food handlers had the most likelihood of spreading the disease.

In 1909, Mary argued to the Supreme Court that she was never sick and was never given due process before her confinement. The court ruled against Mary, setting the precedent for the courts to rule in favor of public health officials when individual liberties were at stake. "Typhoid Mary" was remanded to the custody of the Board of Health of the City of New York and went back to her isolated cottage on North Brother Island with little hope of ever being released.

In 1910, however, the new health commissioner of New York decided to release Mary as long as she agreed to regularly report to the health department and to promise that she would never work as a cook again. Anxious to regain her freedom, Mary accepted the conditions. On February 19, she was let free.

Mary vanished into obscurity after her release – but not for long.

In January 1915, the Sloane Maternity Hospital in Manhattan suffered a typhoid fever outbreak. Two people died during the outbreak and 23 others became sick. During the investigation, evidence pointed to a recently-hired cook, Mrs. Brown – who was actually Mary Mallon using a false name.

Some believe that Mary never had any intention of following the conditions of her release, but most likely she found that not working as a cook forced her into domestic positions that did not pay as well. Feeling healthy, Mary still did not believe that she could spread typhoid. Mary first worked as a laundress and a few other jobs, but for some reason that has never been documented, she eventually went back to working as a cook.

If the public had shown Mary any sympathy during her first period of quarantine because she was an unknowing typhoid carrier, that sympathy vanished after she was locked up again. This time, "Typhoid Mary" knew of her carrier status – even if she didn't believe it – and so she willingly and knowingly caused suffering and death to her victims. The fact that she had been using a false name made her look even more guilty.

Mary was sent back to her cottage on North Brother Island and she remained there, imprisoned on the island, for the next 23 years. The exact life that she led on the island is unclear, but it is known that she helped around the island's Riverside Hospital, earning the title "nurse" in 1922. In 1925, she began helping in the hospital's lab.

In December 1932, she suffered a stroke that left her paralyzed. She was then transferred from her cottage to a bed in the hospital's children's ward, where she stayed until her death six years later on November 11, 1938.

In the years that followed her death, "Typhoid Mary" stopped referring specifically to Mary Mallon and became a term for anyone with a contagious illness. But how did Mary become such a legend? Yes, she was the first healthy carrier to be found, but she was not the only one discovered at the time. An estimated 3,000 to 4,500 cases of typhoid fever were reported in New York City alone and it was estimated that about three percent of those who had typhoid became carriers, creating more than 90 new carriers a year. Mary was also not the most deadly. There were 47 cases of typhoid connected to Mary, while Tony Labella (another healthy carrier) caused 122 people to become sick and five deaths. Labella was only isolated for two weeks and then was released. Mary was also not the only healthy carrier who broke the health officials' rules after being told of their contagious status. Alphonse Cotlis, a restaurant and bakery owner, was told not to prepare food for other people. When health officials found him back at work, they agreed to let him go free when he promised to conduct his business over the phone.

So, why did Mary become so infamously remembered as "Typhoid Mary?" Why was she the only carrier isolated for life? These questions are impossible to answer. Some historians believe that it was prejudice that contributed to her extreme treatment by health officials. She was Irish, she was a woman, uneducated, a domestic servant, had no family, and was basically a "nobody." She didn't have the money or the position to fight back and when she did, she was dismissed by the courts for all of the same reasons. Even though Mary was temperamental and flagrantly violated the conditions of her release, one has to wonder if the "crime" really deserved the punishment she was given.

The question remains unanswered today, which is perhaps the reason why her spirit still lingers at an abandoned hospital where she spent her final days.

Haunting of Riverside Hospital

North Brother Island is a place of ghosts.

It is a 13-acre piece of history that lies just southwest of Hunts Point in the East River and a remnant of a long-forgotten era in New York history. It has been abandoned since 1963, when the city closed down Riverside Hospital, which had opened in 1886 to treat and isolate victims of contagious diseases. It gained its notoriety during the tenure of "Typhoid Mary" and remains a mysterious place today, off limits to the public because it is the nesting place of a species of rare black-crowned herons.

It is, without question, a spooky place – and some say a haunted one. Time seems to have bypassed North Brother Island's gaslight-lined streets, brownstone hospital buildings, crumbling doctor's houses, and sandy beaches littered with cookware and heavy glass tonic bottles.

Tragedy first bloodied the island's history in June 1905, when the *General Slocum* disaster took the lives of 1,141 people, most of them German immigrants from the Lower East Side. They were on their way to a Sunday picnic on Long Island when the overcrowded steamer was accidently set ablaze. The ship ran aground on North Brother Island and doctors and patients from the hospital ran to try and save the hundreds of passengers who had jumped from the burning ship. For hours after the tragedy, bodies continued to wash up on the island's shore and the beaches were strewn with victims.

And for decades after, island residents spoke of seeing the ghosts of these victims as they wandered the grounds of North Brother Island, weeping for the lives and loves they lost in the disaster.

Perhaps these spirits do not walk alone...

Riverside Hospital was closed as a quarantine hospital in 1942. It was abandoned for a short time before briefly being used as housing for World War II veterans who were studying at New York colleges. It was serviced by two ferries that regularly stopped at the western slip, but this proved inefficient and expensive, and when cheaper housing was found for these men, the island was abandoned again.

In 1952, it opened again, this time as an experimental juvenile drug treatment facility that was offered as an alternative to going to jail. The tuberculosis pavilion of the hospital (which was built in 1942 and never actually used to house tuberculosis patients) became a dormitory and then a main residence and treatment building for the program. The doors of many of the rooms were retrofitted into seclusion rooms with sheet metal reinforcement and heavy deadbolts that could be used for withdrawal management.

The experimental plan would take a patient, newly arrived and addicted to heroin, and place him or her in one of these rooms with no conveniences except for a bare mattress and a mess bucket. He or she would be forced to undergo withdrawal in the seclusion room without any kind of medicine. After several days, when withdrawal was complete, the patient would be introduced into the general population. It was believed that this harsh return to reality, followed by a stay of no less than 90 days on the island, and bolstered by athletics and education, would provide the best chance against relapse.

All of the buildings on the island were renovated. The services building became the school, the nurses' residence became the girls' dormitory, and the tuberculosis pavilion became the admissions hospital and boys' residence. The building next to the tuberculosis pavilion – originally the hospital's children's ward, where Mary Mallon spent her final days – was turned into a library and annex to the school.

The grand experiment was a failure. Recidivism rates were extremely high, and even at the isolated island hospital, patients still found means of obtaining and using drugs. There are accounts of boyfriends making the trip to the island in order to visit in the middle of the night; accounts of orderlies getting paid in cigarettes to smuggle heroin on the ferries; and accounts of physical and sexual abuse of and by patients. The hospital was shuttered and the island was abandoned in 1963 for the final time.

The lost souls of this era certainly left an indelible mark on the island, but the most famous troubled spirit that may linger is that of "Typhoid Mary" herself. Mary was first quarantined on the island in 1907, after causing a number of outbreaks of typhoid fever. She was set free in 1910, but returned to the island five years later after an investigation into an outbreak of typhoid at a Manhattan hospital revealed that Mary was once again working as a cook, although under an assumed name. She was sent back to her cottage on the island, this time for good.

Mary never understood that she was a carrier of a possible deadly disease. Instead, she felt she was a victim of persecution at the hands of officials who could neither prove that she was the source of these outbreaks nor explain to her why she felt so healthy and why she seemed free of any of the typical symptoms of typhoid. In 1938, she died on the island due to complications from a stroke she had suffered six years earlier.

Mary's cottage was demolished after her death – officials felt that it was unsafe for habitation – but she spent much of her time working, and later dying, at Riverside Hospital, where her ghost is still believed to walk.

Over the years, visitors to the island – who brave the river and the warnings against trespassers – have reported the spirit of a woman who wanders the corridors of the crumbling old hospital. She has been seen a number of times by a wide variety of people, including staff members at the hospital during the era when the drug treatment program was in place. One account details an orderly who followed the woman down a corridor, only to see her walk into one of the rooms. Thinking that one of the inmates had gotten out of her room, the orderly hurried down the hall and entered the exam room – only to find there was no one there!

Was this woman one of the many tragic spirits of North Brother Island, or could it have been the ghost of Mary Mallon, unable to rest after nearly three decades of punishment that she never felt that she deserved?

No one will likely ever know for sure.

12. BRICK FROM THE RUINS
LEHI HOSPITAL, UTAH
Contributed by April Slaughter

There is an empty lot located on State Street in Lehi, Utah where a building near and dear to my heart once stood. Originally erected in 1891 as the Lehi Commercial & Savings Bank, this building eventually became the Lehi Hospital in 1926 and operated as such until 1967. For a brief period of time during the 1970's, it housed a few small residential apartments. At one point, the building was also home to a small mechanic's shop, but as the building fell into disrepair, it was left vacant and abandoned.

I had grown up within just a few miles of the building, and had never taken much notice of it until I was an adult. It piqued my interest at a time when researching paranormal phenomena had become a priority in my life, largely due to the fact that I'd had no shortage of strange experiences that I simply could not explain. My childhood home was (and remains) an active place, for reasons I still have not discovered. If unexplained phenomena were prevalent in my home, they certainly had to be occurring in other locations as well.

While driving down State Street one afternoon in October many years ago, I passed the Lehi Hospital and noticed that hanging haphazardly on the side of the building was a handmade wooden sign that read Haunted Hospital. It appeared that the building was being run as a haunted house attraction for the fall season, and I wondered if it had been transformed into one due to supernatural occurrences or if it was simply a convenient and available location. After doing a little digging, and being unable to locate any helpful information, I decided to make inquiries with the individuals working there.

I approached the building one evening, and was allowed access to the front foyer by a small group of teenagers practicing their parts. As was common for me, I entered with my digital audio recorder running, just in case. I was only inside a matter of minutes when the owner entered the building and promptly asked me to leave the premises. In later discussions with him, I realized he had only been dismissive because he had been under the impression I was an employee from a rival attraction out to see what surprises and tricks were being rigged in the building.

As soon as I had returned home that evening, I played back my short recording, and was astonished to hear I'd captured something clearly disembodied. Seconds before the owner entered and demanded I leave, a clear voice said, "Get out quick! Haaaaa…" It's as if whomever was in the room with me knew my presence would not be welcome, and attempted to warn me before I was discovered. After hearing this, I felt I needed to approach the owner and clearly explain my intention. I desperately wanted to spend time in the building, and would treat it with the utmost respect. I was subsequently allowed access to the building whenever I wanted it.

Weeks passed, and a great deal many people became interested in the time I spent at the hospital trying to experience and record various phenomena. The local paper asked if they could accompany me one evening to witness the process for a Halloween piece they were going to run, and I obliged. Nothing of note happened in the first couple of hours, but as I escorted them into what I believed to be the most active room in the building, they all began to feel a little on edge.

Across the room from us hung a mirror original to the hospital. I was casually chatting with one of the reporters when another brought something to my attention. He pointed toward the mirror and said, "Are you seeing this?" We all stood frozen in place as we gazed at the mirror. A menacing face materialized, seemingly out of nowhere. It looked as though the mirror were a pane of glass with someone peering at us through the other side, as if peeking into a window. The face moved, pulled back, and reappeared several times at different angles. When it ceased to be visible, the crew insisted that they examine the mirror for any possibility that it had been rigged or tampered with to create the illusion of something supernatural. Of course, nothing had been done to it. I'd spent countless hours in this particular room and had never before witnessed anything like it. In the weeks that followed, nothing occurred with the mirror at all.

I'd have the occasional friend with me during my visits to the hospital, but most of my time there was spent alone. In the beginning, it felt unsettling, but as time wore on, I began to feel that I was welcome. Oftentimes, I would review my audio recordings and discover voices saying things like, "Hi April," and "Missed ya." It was a strange sensation, at least in the beginning, to feel as though I were recognized every time I returned.

There was only one incident on the property when I ever felt threatened in any way. My friend James and I had made our way down to the basement crematorium one evening. It was an area I'd often heard strange noises in, including the sound of someone whistling. The ceiling was low and the room almost completely pitch black, so it had an ominous vibe about it anyway. James snapped several photos in the basement, and long streaks of an orange-hued light unseen by the naked eye appeared to be moving around the two crematory ovens. They were not photographs of orbs. I dismissed a majority of photographs containing orbs as nothing more reflections off of moisture and/or dust. These anomalies were far different than anything I had seen before.

As we scrolled through the pictures on the LCD screen, he and I walked toward an opening leading to a crawl space underneath the hospital. Just as we'd finished reviewing the pictures, I was pushed into the wall. Seconds later, I felt someone's breath on my right ear followed by a loud hissing sound. James had witnessed the entire thing, and was certain it was a sign that he and I needed to get out of the basement. I hesitated for a moment, trying to get a grip on what had just happened, but upon his insistence, we quickly walked toward the stairs leading back up to the main floor. As he and I were approaching the steps, a cold breeze went quickly through the room, a black shadow passing briefly between us and the staircase. Neither of us had any real desire to spend any more time in the hospital that night.

I returned to the building days later, however, as I didn't believe there was anything I truly needed to fear. One afternoon, while it was still light out, I wandered through the hallways of the hospital for no other reason than just to pass some time. All throughout the building, doorways were draped in black plastic sheeting, separating one room from the next, and as I approached one of these doorways, I noticed someone standing on the other side of the sheeting about ten feet in front of me. All I could see was their legs up to about the knee. Whoever it was wore sneakers and a pair of jeans. Initially, I thought someone had broken in, as kids often did out of curiosity. It wasn't uncommon for me to discover a group of kids hiding out in one of the rooms, trying to psych each other out.

"Hey! Who's there?" I shouted.

They made no response. I took a couple of steps forward, and watched as the individual turned right and disappeared. Moments afterward, I pulled the black sheeting aside to follow them, only to find a wall where they had vanished. Their presence had been as plain as day, and seen in the middle of the afternoon, yet they were nowhere to be found.

I relayed much of what I had experienced to the owner, who had no real interest in hearing the stories. He knew his building had a reputation for being haunted, and he'd had a few unnerving experiences himself, but he left me to my own devices and didn't ask questions. One afternoon, he'd come to the hospital to work on a few needed repairs for the haunted house attraction. I came to the front entrance, only to find it locked, so I knocked loudly on the door for several minutes, hoping he'd pause long enough to let me in. Eventually, the door opened and I was greeted by a little boy. He looked to be no more than seven or eight years old, had an olive complexion, and dark brown eyes.

"Is Todd here?" I asked.

He nodded.

"Mind if I come in and talk to him for a minute?"

He opened the door a little wider and stepped aside to let me by. He closed the door behind me and pointed toward the farthest hallway. I followed the sound of hammering, and found Todd putting up a panel of drywall.

"Why on earth would you have a little boy in here, Todd? This place is falling apart; a little dangerous for a kid to be wandering around, don't you think?"

"What are you talking about? I don't allow little kids in here. I've been here alone all day," he said.

"Liar. Who is the kid that just let me in the front door then?" I asked.

"April, there is no little boy here. I assure you. How did you get in, by the way? I locked the front door."

I tried explaining to him that the young man had unlocked the door for me, but he wasn't buying it, and muttered that he must have left it unlocked after all. I never made mention of my experiences after that. He granted me unlimited access to his building because he trusted me, but he didn't want to hear about the things I experienced there.

I must have spent months altogether in that hospital. I catalogued hundreds of hours of audio, often discovering Electronic Voice Phenomena (EVP) that were far clearer than anything else I had recorded before.

"Wait... she thinks we're all dead."

"Michael, Michael! Momma, Michael's dead!"

"Where's the way out?"

"I want to hold your hand."

"Why can't I sleep?"

"When can I go home?"

And these were just a few.

The Lehi Hospital had become a second home to me. When I married and moved out of state, it was quite difficult for me to leave it behind. My family and close friends knew how much I treasured my time there, and as bizarre as they thought my fascination was, they knew I would be devastated to learn that city condemned the building shortly after I had moved. Despite his best efforts to raise enough money to save the building, Todd could not make the repairs required to keep the hospital standing. It had been successfully listed on the National Register of Historic Places, but it was subsequently demolished in stages.

Unbeknownst to each other, several of my friends made a point to visit the site, and when no one was around to witness it, they each picked up one of the hospital's bricks. About once a week for a period of a little more than a month, packages containing these bricks made their way to my front door in Texas. The hospital had never officially belonged to me, but everyone who knew me felt that if anyone should own a piece (or pieces) of it, it should be me.

Many lives were brought into the world at the Lehi Hospital, just as many others came to an end within its walls. There is a history there that demolition cannot erase. A new structure will inevitably inhabit the site in the future, and when that day arrives, so too will a few unexpected guests.

AMERICAN ASYLUMS

If spirits are truly the personalities of those who once lived, then wouldn't these spirits reflect whatever turmoil might have plagued them in life? And if hauntings can sometimes be the effects of trauma being imprinted on the atmosphere of a place, then wouldn't places where terror and insanity were commonplace be especially prone to these hauntings? As an answer to both of these questions, we need point no further than to the crumbling remains of the former state hospitals that dot the landscape of America.

We tend to think of mental hospitals of the past as places of terror, halls of chaos and misery, squalor, abuse, and brutality. Most of them are now shuttered and abandoned and are places about which we experience a shiver of horror as we contemplate being confined in such a place. Before the middle nineteenth century, the mentally ill were hidden away from the rest of us, kept out of sight from the "decent folk," and often hidden in cold basements, locked in cages or chained to walls. Mental health care barely existed. In those days, anyone suffering from a mental disorder was simply locked away from society in an asylum. Many of these hospitals were filthy places of confinement where patients were often left in straitjackets, locked in restraint chairs, or even placed in crates or cages, if they were especially disturbed. Many of them spent every day in shackles and chains and even the so-called "treatments" were barbaric.

Not surprisingly, such techniques brought little success and patients rarely improved. In those days, before psychiatry and medication, most mental patients spent their entire lives locked up inside of an asylum. There was little preparation for them to return to life outside, because no one ever expected them to be freed. After years in the asylum, residents became "institutionalized," and no longer desired, or could no longer face, the outside world. They lived in the state hospitals for decades, died in them, and were buried on the grounds. Under such conditions, it was inevitable that the asylum population would grow and individual asylums, often large to begin with, came to resemble small towns. It was inevitable, too, that with a large inmate population, and inadequate funding and staffing, that state hospitals fell short of their original ideals. By the latter years of the nineteenth century, they had fallen into states of squalor and neglect and were often run by inept, corrupt, or even sadistic bureaucrats – a problem that persisted into the twentieth century.

But most state hospitals did not start out to be places of squalor and fear. The first hospitals were often palatial buildings with high ceilings, lofty windows, and spacious grounds, providing abundant light, fresh air, exercise, and a varied diet. Most asylums were self-supporting and grew and raised their own food. Inmates would work in the fields and dairies, work being considered a form of therapy for them, as well as supporting the hospital. There were gigantic kitchens and laundries and, like the gardens and livestock, provided work and therapy for the patients, as well as an opportunity to learn life skills. These were things that many, withdrawn into their illnesses, might never have acquired before. Community and companionship, too, were vital for patients who would be otherwise isolated in their own mental worlds, driven by their own obsessions or hallucinations. Thanks to this, even when things became so dismal in the 1950s, some of the good aspects of asylum life could still be found in them. There were often, even in the worst hospitals, pockets of human decency and kindness. By the start of the twentieth century, asylums were no longer places of isolation, but rather meant to be places of comfort and safety for the mentally ill.

And often they were. These asylums enjoyed a sort of "golden age" between the latter part of the nineteenth century and into the years of the Great Depression. But things would change, and conditions, in many hospitals began to deteriorate, declining back to the days when mental illness was a stigma and when the insane were kept away from the "normal people."

The 1950s brought the advent of specific antipsychotic drugs, which seemed to promise, if not a "cure," at least an effective alleviation or suppression of psychotic symptoms. The availability of these drugs strengthened the idea that hospitalization need not be for life. If a short stay in a hospital could "break" a psychosis and be followed by patients returning to their own communities, where they could be maintained on medication and monitored as outpatients, then it was felt, the prognosis, the whole history of mental illness, might be transformed and the vast and hopeless populations of asylums drastically reduced.

During the 1960s, a number of new state hospitals were built with this idea in mind, dedicated to short-term admissions. Sadly, though, the new hospitals found themselves soon overwhelmed by the influx of patients from older hospitals that were now being closed down. Legal changes followed, now making it illegal for the patients to work. This meant that instead of doing useful activities in the laundry, or outdoors, they were now left sitting zombie-like in open wards, in front of now never-turned-off televisions. With many patients filled full of drugs, their complacency allowed them to be released, or "deinstitutionalized," to use one of the psychiatric catch-phrases of the day. And what started as a trickle of released patients in the 1960s became a flood in the 1980s, even though it was clear by then that it was creating as many problems as it solved. Every major city was filled with daily reminders of those problems in the form of untreated patients wandering the streets. There was no way to deal with the hundreds of thousands of inmates who had been turned away by the few state hospitals that remained. Most of the hospitals had, by then, been closed down by federal budget cuts that swept the nation.

By the 1990s, it was clear that the system had overreacted and that the wholesale closure of state hospitals had proceeded far too rapidly, with no alternatives in place. It was not closure that the hospitals needed, but fixing: a plan to deal with overcrowding, understaffing, negligence, and brutality. Simply treating the problems with drugs was not enough. The benign aspects of the asylum had been forgotten, and they had stopped offering the safe haven that the first state hospitals were meant to provide.

For those first state asylums were meant to offer a place of safety to those which society had deemed to be "mad." From the mid-nineteenth century to the early twentieth century, close to 300 institutions for the insane were built across the United States. In 1840, there were only 18 asylums, but by 1880, that number had jumped to 139. Even in the midst of the Great Depression and World War II, when shortages of resources, funding, and qualified staff burdened the system, the hospitals survived and continued to be filled beyond capacity.

For more than half of America's history, vast mental hospitals were prominent architectural features across the country's landscape. Practically every stated could claim to have at least one. The catalyst for their creation was schoolteacher-turned-reformer Dorothea Dix, who, beginning in the early 1840s, traveled across America lobbying states to build hospitals for the proper care of the "indigent insane." She knew just how bad things were. Her tours of America's asylums revealed that people with mental illness were often treated no better than criminals and were often kept in jails and cages. The insane asylums that did exist were a slightly better option, but offered no treatment.

Dix's humanitarian appeals were persuasive and they were well timed: expansionist America was eager to create large civic institutions that would serve as models to an enlightened society. Public schools, universities, prisons and asylums were all part of this agenda, though the high-minded rhetoric was not always matched by the less-than-altruistic motives of politicians. Regardless, Dix bullied and cajoled one state legislature after another until they bent to her will.

Dix was the catalyst for the first wave of asylum building, but it was Thomas Story Kirkbride who provided the blueprint for their expansion. Kirkbride, who served as the superintendent of the Pennsylvania Hospital for the Insane in Philadelphia, drew on his own experience and travels in Europe to devise the model asylum. As a skilled administrator, he was obsessed with asylum design and management. He believed that a well-designed and beautifully landscaped hospital could heal mental illness. If the insane were placed in a peaceful, structured environment, he believed, they had a much better chance of returning to the outside world as an improved individual. His belief – and the design that he created – helped to spread the idea that lunacy could be cured in a hospital, not at home.

The asylum building was the cornerstone of Kirkbride's idea. It consisted of a central administration building flanked symmetrically by linked pavilions, each stepping back to create a "V, like a formation of birds in flight, or as some have called it, a "bat-wing design." The layout was designed by sex, illness, and social class. The most disturbed patients were housed in the outermost wards, while those more socially adjusted lived closer to the center, where the staff lived. The stepped arrangement of the wards made the hospital easier to manage, while at the same time, admitted an abundance of light with views of the outdoors. The location of the planned asylums was meant to be in the country, away from the city, offering privacy and land for farming and gardening. The land immediately around the

202

asylum was used for pleasure, where the patients could take a relaxing stroll and admire picturesque views.

The "Kirkbride Plan" was an American invention. For the residents of many smaller towns, especially those who had never been to a major city, the Kirkbride building on the state hospital grounds would be the largest building they would ever see. Building the asylum required enormous state expenditures and an army of workers who lived on-site during the construction. It was a technological marvel of the time, offering modern amenities, such as fireproof construction, central heating, plumbing, and gaslight. But it was not a hospital in the modern sense of the word. On the outside, it exuded grandeur, but inside, it resembled a dormitory. Each pavilion in the structure was three stories high, with one ward per floor. The ward consisted of a long, wide hallway, lined by small bedrooms. Each ward also contained a dining room, a parlor or sitting room, bathrooms, storage closets, and rooms for attendants. Patients spent most of their time in the hallways or common areas, not in the bedrooms, which were locked during the day and used only for sleeping. Period photographs often show well-appointed interiors, with plants, rugs, framed artwork, and rocking chairs – all the comforts of a Victorian home. Their outward similarity to the great resort hotels of the era is obvious.

But they were certainly not resorts. Like so many lofty ideals, the asylums failed to live up to their expectations. They soon became so overcrowded by the influx of the urban poor, many of them immigrants, who did not respond well to the "moral treatment" envisioned by Kirkbride and others like him. In other words, the "lower classes" could not be expected to get any better. The elderly and the chronically ill – two groups that would never get better – began filling the wards. As the patient populations grew larger, the need for control prevailed, and treatment began to swing from the curative to the custodial. Moreover, state hospitals were held accountable to the state legislatures and were subject to fiscal pressures. The financial panics of 1873, 1893, and 1907, as well as periods of recession, all took their toll, leading to budget cuts and staff shortages. Low wages, high turnover rates, and inexperienced attendants led to patient abuses and corruption. But the asylums remained popular, even as their quality of care declined, and they remained important to the public because they offered a convenient solution about what to do with the insane.

As the patient populations grew, so did the hospitals. Many of them reached monumental proportions. Kirkbride's initial design called for a hospital of 250 patients, but planners later agreed to increase the size to 600 patients. Construction of the asylums could not keep pace with admissions, and it was often the case that after a state built its first one, subsequent hospitals were built soon after – not to meet future needs, but to relieve pressure on existing institutions. Still, the Kirkbride Plan persisted until well into the late nineteenth century, long after the initial methods of treating insanity with peaceful environments had fallen out of fashion. It had become the status quo, and the growing psychiatric profession was not eager to give up its leading symbol of prestige and authority. Ironically, as the reputation of asylums waned, generous expenditures continued to be lavished on their design. Some of the grandest Kirkbride buildings were built during the latter period of the 1870s and 1880s, ignoring the fact that their golden age had come and gone.

The Kirkbride asylums were not easy to abandon: their planning and construction took years, sometimes decades. State committees had been formed, land purchased, architects chosen, plans approved, contractors hired – with every group often representing a different political power base. But with no cure for mental illness in sight, it became increasingly difficult to justify the need for large, expensive asylums.

Two new models, Willard and Kankakee State Hospitals, offered alternatives that incited a debate within the profession. Willard State Hospital in upstate New York, was built specifically for the chronically ill and by this focus on those who would never get better, actually predicted the custodial role that asylums would assume. Kankakee State Hospital, first known as Illinois Eastern Hospital for the Insane, included a Kirkbride building, along with outlying dormitories. Proponents of both styles claimed that some patients required less attention and would benefit from a less formal atmosphere, while the elderly and chronically ill – the incurables – simply needed a comfortable place to live. Critics protested, saying everyone should be housed under one roof for better supervision and quality of care. Anything less, they claimed, was an admission of failure – that insanity was incurable.

The dormitories at Kankakee State were less ornate and cheaper to build, and they helped pave the way for the adoption of the "Cottage Plan," which called for clusters of separate buildings that were organized like a college campus. The breakup of the asylum into smaller pieces was inevitable after the Kirkbride structures had grown in size to an almost absurd point of impracticality (Buffalo State Hospital was more than one-third of a mile long). Most institutions with existing Kirkbrides just built new structures off to the side to meet the demands for additional space. Although the Cottage Plan appeared to create a freer environment, it was still an institution, operating along the same lines as before.

The harshest criticism of the asylums came from professional ranks. After the Civil War, medical advances forged on the battlefield led to a new medical specialty – neurology, the study and treatment of disorders of the nervous system. These new specialists saw their future in science and had little inclination to tend to the chronically ill. They had little use for the antiquated methods of asylum doctors, who they criticized for being bureaucratic and corrupt. At the turn of the twentieth century, in keeping with the times, and making an effort to assimilate psychiatry into mainstream medicine, "insane asylums" were renamed as "state hospitals," although eventually this, too, became a derisive term.

The last wave of state hospitals, which were built up until World War II, looked nothing like the structures of the Victorian era. The ornate architecture was gone and so were the prominent architects who once lobbied to present their designs. The hospitals had a decidedly institutional, functional feel, looking more like Depression-era public housing than the resort hotels of a bygone age. Yet some essentials remained the same – they were located in rural areas where land was cheap, they operated as near self-sustaining communities, producing almost everything they needed, including food, water, and power. Despite ever-shrinking budgets, hospitals were able to stay afloat because of the large pool of inmate labor. They helped to construct the buildings, grow crops, raise dairy cattle, pigs, and chickens, and make furniture and clothing. The state hospitals, with thousands of residents and staff, and hundreds of acres, became more like work farms than medical facilities.

After new psychotropic drugs were introduced in the 1950s, commitment laws began to change, leading to a steady decline in patient populations. It was followed by the era of deinstitutionalization, which ultimately resulted in the loss of patient labor. This dealt a fatal blow to the economic viability of the state hospitals. In the 1970s, agricultural and industrial programs were closed down, services were contracted to the private sector, and farms were sold off to help pay for mandated services. Buildings already in disrepair were left to deteriorate further, too expensive to renovate and bring up to code. As patient numbers plummeted, the hospitals shut down, one by one, though many still remain, even though most people with mental illnesses today are treated in their own communities. For those who are committed, their stays are usually numbered in days instead of months and years. Hospitalization these days is considered a last resort.

After the hospitals were closed, they were largely abandoned to ruin and became surplus property to be sold to developers who prized the land but had little interest in preserving the architecture. A few of the hospitals have been converted successfully into residential, commercial and even academic uses, while others have been reopened as prisons. This is ironic since so many of the former patients who were left to fend for themselves on the streets when the hospitals closed down now find themselves incarcerated as prisoners. In their cases, one institution was traded for another.

Today, only a few of the Kirkbride buildings still serve their original function. The very qualities that made them so appealing in the first place – their massive size, heavy construction, and distinctive floor plan – have made them difficult to adapt to a new purpose. In addition, as preservationists struggle to find new uses for the decaying structures, they also have to grapple with the stigma attached to them. As vestiges of a less enlightened era, the Kirkbrides don't elicit the same kind of nostalgia that other historic structures do, even though the builders originally envisioned the asylums as places of refuge and healing. That side of their history has been lost over the decades.

Of course, to those with an interest in America's more macabre history, which includes ghosts and the supernatural, the notoriety of the old asylums is not a stigma at all. Many are drawn to such places, searching for the lingering spirits of the past. The trauma experienced by so many troubled people within the walls of the buildings have left an impression behind at such places. The damaged souls of those who lived and died in the old asylums have stayed behind, forced to relive their monotonous days of agony over and over again. In addition, the madness, forced treatments, and all too frequent abuse have left residual impressions within these buildings' walls, leaving the asylums to be haunted by their history.

America's old asylums have long been places where the spirits of the dead are believed to linger. Are they actually the lost souls of those who perished within – the tangled personalities of those who once lived in the agony caused by their illness? Or are they merely the flickering images of the past, imprinted on the atmosphere of the place like an old movie scene, destined to fade away someday?

The reader will have to decide that. But if the opportunity ever arises for you to spend the night within the walls of any of the old hospitals that still stand today, accept any invitation to do so with care. If spirits truly are the personalities of those who once lived, then the spirits who remain in such places are sure to be restless ones indeed.

13. AN AUTOPSY TABLE
DIXMONT HOSPITAL FOR THE INSANE
Contributed by Rene Kruse

"I proceed, Gentlemen, briefly to call your attention to the present state of Insane Persons confined within this Commonwealth, in cages, stalls, pens! Chained, naked, beaten with rods, and lashed into obedience."

This began the report by Dorothea Dix on the state of the insane poor in the jails and almshouses of Pennsylvania in the first half of the nineteenth century. She appealed to state legislatures to "act and appropriate funds to construct facilities for the care and treatment of the insane." She worked tirelessly to bring the plight of the insane to the public, the press, and the lawmakers of individual states. Many states responded to her call and dedicated facilities and treatments by building dozens of asylums to fulfill her mandate.

Many of Dix's philosophies and concepts about how best to house and treat the nation's mentally ill citizens were mirrored by those of Dr. Thomas Story Kirkbride, a Philadelphia physician and asylum superintendent. Drawing from the philosophies of both Dix and Kirkbride, institutions for the insane (as they were historically referred to), were designed and built across the United States.

One of these institutions was built just outside of Pittsburgh, Pennsylvania. In 1848, the Western Pennsylvania Hospital, located in the heart of Pittsburgh, was a general hospital for all sorts of illnesses, but it also became one of the first hospitals in the country to also provide treatment for the insane. It soon became clear that the few beds set aside for insane patients was not sufficient and plans for the construction of a new facility were begun. Dorothea Dix herself was consulted in preparation for this new facility. The building was to be constructed following the Kirkbride plan and Dix was to choose the location. Wishing to keep to a rural, wooded setting, Dix chose a 407 acre plot of land in Kilbuck Township, along the Ohio River. The facility was to carry the name "Dixmont" in honor of Dorothea Dix, however, she would only allow the Dix name to be used if it was in memorial of her beloved grandfather, also named Dix.

The new hospital, saddled with the ridiculously long name of Department of the Insane in the Western Pennsylvania Hospital of Pittsburgh, opened its doors and began admitting patients in 1862. Before long, 113 patients were calling the new hospital home. Dorothea Dix frequently stayed there as well, as a guest of Dr. Joseph Reed, the hospital's first superintendent and namesake of the Kirkbride building, which housed the administrative offices and the patients. This was to be a pleasant place for the insane of western Pennsylvania to live out their lives in peace, or as close to peace as they could get.

In the 1800s, the definition of "insane" was loosely translated as anything that might cause a person to act in an abnormal manner. These included everything from alcoholism to postpartum depression, from masturbation to epilepsy, from retardation to what we now know as autism, old age senility, brain tumors, and dementia. Of course, you could also find patients with schizophrenia, bipolar disorder and various other "manias." In some cases, if a man could afford to pay the price, a nagging wife or illegitimate child might also find themselves committed to a mental asylum.

Dixmont was, in its day, a cutting edge facility, designed to provide a humane setting and respectful treatments. Social reformers believed that "restful quiet and country air of rural institutions" created the best possibility for a cure, or at the very least, a positive effect on its patients. Dixmont certainly fit that bill, so much so that within a very few years, the patient population swelled by hundreds and several new buildings needed to be added. Some of the buildings were to provide patient rooms, but most were in support of the facility or to provide support for the patients. Dixmont was to be as self-sufficient as possible, with its own water treatment plant, sewage treatment plant, water reservoir, heating systems, and later, its own electrical power plant. In time, they had their own post office and dentist office and industrial arts building. The medical staff, and many of the support staff also lived on the grounds.

At its peak, there were nearly 80 buildings on the Dixmont site, a site that was conveniently kept from the public eye by a secluded setting and a grove of trees. Even though social changes had brought about a more progressive understanding of a variety of mental illnesses, a strong stigma was attached to insanity – or even having a mentally ill family member. Therefore, it was best for the mentally ill to be kept from view of the general public. Thousands of people might travel past Dixmont without even noticing it was there. Even members of the social and financial elite of Pittsburgh felt it safe enough to spend a summer in Dixmont for "rest and medical care," as long as they were able to pay for the privilege.

The grounds and the facility continued to make changes as the years passed. Recreational activities for the staff and patients, including croquet, billiards, tennis courts, a baseball field, and winter sleigh rides. The hospital received the only slightly less cumbersome name of Western Pennsylvania Asylum for the Insane at Dixmont. In 1885, Dr. Henry A Hutchinson became the new superintendent, bringing with him his own philosophies for the hospital in the form of work therapy. He believed that the patients should be given the opportunity, if they were able, to work or to make things. He felt that through work, the patients could maintain focus, gain a sense of accomplishment and personal value. Patients made the clothing for many of the other patients, repaired shoes, cooked, cleaned, did landscaping, cared for livestock, and worked in the massive gardens that helped feed the patients and staff. In this way, Dixmont became even more self-sufficient. Additionally, many patients did crafts and sold their wares to visitors to help with the finances of the hospital.

The Dixmont doctors and staff really were trying to help the patients, though many of their methods sound barbaric, or even torturous, by today's standards. Most of these treatments were being tested and used across the country, and at the time, believed to be helpful. Hydrotherapy was popular for decades. The patients were immersed in tubs of ice water, or at times, hot water. Others had the top, sides and back of their heads packed in ice, rather than full body submersion. Another popular practice involved covering the patient's eyes and ears to induce sensory deprivation. Still another popular treatment, though no stretch of the imagination can explain how anyone might think it helpful, was to spray a patient with cold water from a hose. From the 1800s into the early 1900s, doctors didn't really know what might help and it seemed as though they were willing to try just about anything to "cure" a case of insanity.

By the turn of the century, the facility was given a new name, Dixmont Hospital for the Insane. The population at Dixmont continued to grow, receiving more than 1,000 patients, along with several thousand support and medical staff. More buildings were added, the largest of which was the Dietary Building, located directly behind Reed Hall (the Kirkbride building). The Dietary Building had a large cafeteria where those patients able to move about and feed themselves took their meals. The long, narrow building also housed the new kitchens, food storage rooms, loading dock, cleaning supply storage and several large freezers. (After Dixmont closed, a room in the basement of this building held a very large cage, large enough to hold several dozen patients, or so many trespassers believed -- creating all sorts of scenarios about torture and punishment. The reality of this cage was that it was built to store fresh fruits and vegetables. The bars and lock were found necessary to keep some of the more crafty patients from making off with the food for the next day's or week's meals). On the top floor of the building was another example of the support and humane care of the patients: a large auditorium. This beautifully appointed room, with a large stage and stately pillars, was designed so that the patients and staff could showcase their talents, put on plays and skits, ceremonies, and musical performances.

Dixmont peaked in 1920, reaching a patient population of 1,700. The staff admitted as many patients as the hallways and attic could hold, with nearly 300 of these patients sleeping on the floor. At this point, the administration halted admissions for a time, until the number of patients began to drop. The reason for the patient surge was the end of World War I. Many of the soldiers began suffering "mental issues" upon their return home and either checked themselves in, or were committed to asylums for the insane. They were suffering from what was then called "shell shock," a disorder we now know as PTSD (Post Traumatic Stress Disorder). This phenomena was not exclusive to Dixmont, but presented in asylums across the country.

Eventually, the patient population declined to a manageable number and it seemed that things would return to normal. However, this was not to be. After a decade of struggling to care for an inordinate number of mentally ill patients, the country was hit by the Great Depression. As the country went, so did Dixmont.

With very little money coming in and gross understaffing, the administration found it impossible to pay the wages for most of their staff. As a result, they offered free room and board in lieu of money. Some left, but most stayed and Dixmont carried on.

By the 1940s, treatment of the mentally ill was moving into a new phase. Most reputable asylums had moved past treatments involving hydrotherapy, sensory deprivation, and hose spraying. Now, a host of new and innovative treatments were being introduced and practiced in mental institutions. In the spirit of attempting to do what they could, the doctors at Dixmont embraced these new methodologies for behavior modification, including electroshock therapy, insulin therapy, physical restraints, and barbaric lobotomies, all of which will be explored in the chapters to come.

In 1954, the Hutchinson Building was opened at the hospital. This building housed the infirmary. Within the infirmary was the intensive care unit, the X-ray facility, a small cafeteria, a barber shop, isolation units, physical therapy areas, observation rooms, and instrument sterilization equipment. On each floor, there were patient rooms on each end, with a nurses' pod between so they could observe both sides. In this building, electroshock therapy, insulin shock therapy, and lobotomies were performed. Within these patient areas, the men were housed on one side and the women on the other. One women's and one men's ward was for patients receiving electroshock or insulin shock therapies. One additional men's ward was labeled the "untidy ward." It was here that extremely violent or unruly men were restrained with rawhide handcuffs and leg cuffs, tied to their beds. Despite these seemingly barbaric therapies, many former employees – as well as former patients -- stated that they believed the medical staff truly cared for them and were trying to help.

Also housed in the Hutchinson Building was the laboratory, a four drawer morgue, and autopsy facilities. Although most of the patients at Dixmont were there for mental issues, and not health related issues, thousands died while housed there. A majority of the patients, once admitted to Dixmont (and other asylums around the country), spent the rest of their lives at the hospital. For the most part, insanity was not considered as a curable illness. Occasionally, people would leave, walking upright, but for most people; once they arrived, Dixmont would be the only home they would ever know. Most of the patients who left Dixmont, did so through the morgue.

But for many, they never actually left. One other service performed on the Dixmont grounds was their burial. About one acre of the 407 acres making up the Dixmont complex was set aside for a cemetery. The Dixmont cemetery is the final resting place for over 1,300 souls. Most were buried in long wicker baskets and a few in plain pine boxes. Each has a simple stone marker, inscribed with just a number. No name or any other information was on the marker. All burial information was recorded in a log book. Some of these people had no one left to see to their burial, but most were simply abandoned by their families once they were admitted. The stigma of mental illness was so strong, that many families, once notified of their relative's demise, refused to claim their body. And thus, the cemetery continued to fill.

The hospital on the hill went through two more major changes. The ownership of the facility was transferred to the state and the name was changed to Dixmont State Hospital. The second major change was yet one more paradigm shift in treatments and treatment theories. By the 1960s, fewer and fewer lobotomies were being performed, until the procedure was no longer supported by the Dixmont doctors. Moving into the 1970s, major changes were taking place. The concept of "deinstitutionalization" was gaining support across the country as states moved toward shifting the care of mentally ill citizens from large asylums to mainstreaming them in the general public. Sadly, for many former patients, they were released into a world they hadn't lived in for many years, and with no place to go. For some of those released, and many of the patients still living in institutions, the use of psychotropic drugs, such as Thorazine, became the treatment of choice. Rather than house mentally ill patients in asylums for long periods of time, the new system was to admit, diagnose, find the right drug and dosage, and send them back out into the world. Many former patients joined the ranks of the homeless, while others wandered back to their former home, living on the fringes of the asylums or moving back in if the facility was closed.

Dixmont was in decline. The state drastically reduced funding, patients were no longer allowed to work without pay, and major repairs were needed on many of the buildings. As patient population declined, buildings no longer needed were demolished. By 1983, only 177 patients remained, most of them elderly. Most of the Reed Building was closed off and only 50 of the remaining patients still lived there. Of the 80 buildings once used, all but 22 had been demolished, most of them smaller utility or storage buildings. The only main buildings remaining were the Kirkbride building (Reed Hall), the Dietary Building, the Hutchinson Building (infirmary), and the Industrial Arts Building, by then just an empty shell. The remaining patients were transferred to other institutions or released to the public.

On June 30, 1984, after 122 years caring for the insane and mentally ill of Southwestern Pennsylvania, the Dixmont State Hospital closed its doors for good.

Only one building, the Cammarata Building (also the newest building), remained in use by the Holy Family Institute to care for elderly patients.

It didn't take long for the closed and relatively abandoned asylum to become a hot spot for other sorts of activities. Vandals were soon breaking windows and spray painting any surface they could get to. Many homeless people, several of which were believed to be former residents who had nowhere to go when released, moved into Reed Hall, where the rooms were still fitted with beds and other furnishings. Urban explorers migrated to the location from all over the country to wander the halls of the empty buildings. There were amateur film makers, with or without permission, using the site for cheesy horror movies. And last but not least, the site became a highly sought after venue for psychics and ghost hunting groups. After all, Dixmont just had to be haunted – didn't it?

The state tried to keep a handle on the property while ideas were bounced about as to what to do with the old white elephant. At one point, an area hospital wanted to buy the property, renovate Reed Hall and a few of the buildings, and use them for an independent living facility for elderly patients. It would be perfect as the property was almost entirely self-sustaining, with its own power plant, water treatment and sewage treatment facilities. However, shortly before the transaction, many of the buildings, including the utility buildings, were found to have flooded basements, rendering them useless for the hospital's plans.

Next, the state wanted to demolish all of the buildings and build a new county jail on the cleared property, but after law suits and local opposition, the plan was dropped. And so Dixmont was left abandoned and empty – well, not entirely empty. There were still the squatters, the explorers, and the ghost hunters. Every plan for the campus hit too many obstacles or just failed for one reason or another. The future of the property remained in limbo. In the meantime, alarm lines were being cut and the lines to the reservoir were cut, leaving the structures with little protection from fire. The local fire chiefs, in Kilbuck and Pittsburgh, became concerned that Dixmont might become a prime target for arson. And soon, their fears were realized.

On June 7, 1995, an arsonist broke a window in the Reed Building and set four fires in four locations. The security guard at the entrance to the campus failed to notice the fire, but motorists driving below the hillside on Route 65 saw smoke rising above the trees, and called in the fire. Despite having no functioning fire hydrants and poor roads for the fire trucks, the fire department was able to save most of the building. Both wings were left largely unscathed, but the central administration section was totally destroyed. It was rendered an empty shell, with the beautiful entry façade reduced to a blackened and crumbling ruin.

After news reports of the fire were broadcast on all three Pittsburgh television stations, news of the large, mostly forgotten, abandoned buildings became common knowledge. A few weeks after the fire, a group of scrap salvagers snuck onto the property and removed every window in the Reed Building. They were specially designed blind style windows meant to make escape difficult. Once inside the building, the salvage crews removed metal fixtures and furniture and sold them off before anyone knew they were missing.

Eventually, the state gave up the idea of making something out of the old campus. After the fire and flooded basements, property that had been worth many millions was rendered almost worthless. The state put the whole 407 acres, minus the one-acre cemetery, up for auction. There were few bidders, but Ralph Stroyne, who owned a small farm which adjoined the property, won the site at auction. He purchased the entire campus for $757,000. At first, Stroyne had several ideas, but most of them fell through or didn't work out for one reason or another. He was able to renovate the Cammerara Building, which is now a Montessori School and office space. He was generous with historical artifacts and records, making them available to the public, or donating them to the Senator John Heinz History Center in Pittsburgh. He allowed the Dixmont Cemetery burial records to be accessed online, free of charge. He made a little money selling some of the hospital items outright – including the porcelain autopsy table from the Hutchinson Building to a fellow who apparently wanted to make it into a bar for his home.

Stroyne and his family cleaned up around the area but did little else. With the Reed Building open to the elements, and the windows smashed in most of the other remaining buildings, the deterioration of the structures accelerated. Soon, a criminal element moved into the ruins. Roving gangs of teenagers, and some older gangs, moved in and used the buildings for parties and drug deals, vandalizing what was left, smashing windows, and breaking open doors. Dixmont became a scary place to be at night and sometimes even in the daytime, but this didn't keep the urban explorers and the ghost hunters from venturing inside.

In 2002, Stroyne decided to divide up the property and sell some of it. He worked out a deal to sell 75 acres to a corporation that builds Walmart stores. This deal seemed to be the best solution all around. The construction company was going to demolish all of the buildings, clear 75 acres of trees, and start work on one of the larger stores and an adjoining strip mall. With only a short time left for the hospital to be explored before it was demolished, I was very interested in seeing if the place was really as haunted as so many people claimed.

But I was unsure if the many legends had any basis in fact. As far as anyone could discover, no hauntings or ghost stories had ever been recorded throughout

Dixmont's 122 years of active history. But does that necessarily mean that it wasn't? A very old, historical insane asylum seems like a structure ripe for a haunting. Remembering that this was a mental institution, imagine the reaction of the staff if a patient related seeing someone walking into their room and then disappearing through a wall, or seeing someone long dead gliding down a hallway. Who would notice disembodied voices, wails, sobs, bangs, or crashes in a building that would normally be filled with such sounds? What staff member would readily admit to others that *they* had seen something out of the ordinary? Might they be worried about moving from staff status to patient status in that very asylum? It is not hard to believe that strange things might have been going on and no one wanted to go on record as having experienced them.

Dixmont had been a place of great joy and happiness, and in turn, great sorrow, pain and confusion. Even those patients not on the receiving end of often torturous treatments were likely stressed with feelings of social isolation, shame, and family abandonment, on top of mental illness. Thousands of people expressed great emotion and energy. Since the facility closed, there were stories that filtered out about strange things going on in and around some of the buildings, such as phantom nurses escorting a phantom patient down a hallway. Even down in the service tunnels, connecting most of the remaining buildings, there were rumors of strange shadowy figures seen moving about in the distance, but without making any sounds or disturbing the dust on the floors.

It was hard to judge which stories, if any, were supernatural in origin, and which came from the fertile imaginations of individuals who, wandering dark tunnels and long deserted corridors, were hoping to see or hear a ghost. I cannot speak for anyone else who roamed the Dixmont campus, but I can speak for myself and a few trusted friends. During the summer of 2002, shortly before the sale was to be completed, three experienced paranormal researchers and myself received permission from Ralph Stroyne to investigate the entire Dixmont campus -- twice. Both times, we spent the entire afternoon exploring in the light and the evenings, investigating in the dark. We walked into every building still standing and wandered the underground tunnels, which were very spooky indeed. We chose not to stay too late, having been warned about the gangs who made the buildings their domain late at night.

Given enough time, we could have explored for a week and still wanted more. The place was just massive and most of the time, we were in awe of the derelict site and the wonder of the history surrounding us. For most of our time exploring, both in the light and in the dark, each building and each room seemed peaceful. We did not experience any of the feelings or events that might have alerted us to a haunting presence -- until we entered the Hutchinson Building. This was the only building that remained secure, but we had been given the key. Much of the building was a jumbled-up mess, with vintage medical equipment and random paraphernalia strewn about. An old wheelchair was tipped over on its side. An IV stand was propped up in a corner, its wheels twisted to one side. A curtain, used to draw around a patient bed for privacy, was torn and hanging from the last two hooks. In the basement, we found the morgue, all four doors to the body drawers stood ajar, one on twisted hinges. In the center of the room stood the white porcelain autopsy table. It looked as if it had been used just the day before. The day was extremely hot and, yet, that autopsy table was cold to the touch. One would expect it to feel a bit cool, but it was icy cold! As we stood around the table, all of us feeling the cold, we heard a loud bang directly above us, as if someone had taken something made of heavy metal and struck the floor with great force. We immediately moved to see what could have made the noise, but found nothing and no one. We went up to the top floor, which was made up of one large infirmary ward, divided in the center by what appeared to be a nurses' station. This room had many large windows all around the perimeter, all beaming in the scorching afternoon sunshine. It was too hot to stay there long, but while in the room, two of us felt something blow on the back of our necks. Were these experiences the result of over-excited imaginations or was something there with us? Impossible to know for sure, but it certainly left an impression.

On the second night, the whole place was very quiet. As far as we could tell, we were the only living people on the grounds. My friend Edgar and I had set our video cameras to record in one of the larger rooms in the Dietary Building, far down the central hallway from where we were waiting outside the building on the loading dock. After 30 minutes or so, we decided to go back in to retrieve our cameras. The walk down the hall was slow and tedious. The ceiling over the hall was suspended, and it appeared that someone had pulled down every single ceiling panel and dropped them to the floor, where they were now soggy with moisture, making it a bit difficult to walk safely by flashlight. Edgar had always been a believer in ghosts, but had never felt or seen anything personally. When we finally got to the room with our cameras, we were calmly chatting with each other as we started to collapse our tripods. Edgar suddenly went silent. At the same time, every hair on my body stood up and I felt a cold chill move past me. I suddenly became very agitated and felt panic setting in. Edgar said for me to just grab the camera and tripod and run; something was wrong. He didn't have to tell me twice. I suddenly couldn't wait to get out of that room and out of that building. Edgar was the sort of fellow who remained calm no matter what happened, but not that night. As we made our way

216

down that soggy hallway, hanging on to our equipment, he kept walking faster and faster. Soon, he had ahold of my arm and was pulling me even faster. It is shocking that we both didn't stumble and fall face first into the stinky mush on the floor. We made it to the double doors on the loading dock and rejoined our two friends. Just as the doors swung closed, we heard a massive sound coming from the other end of the building -- the other end of that same hallway. A gang of boys had just burst into the building, yelling and screaming and cursing. We heard windows shattering and what sounded like steel bars slamming against the walls. They were moving through the building, smashing everything they saw. We were near our van and decided that was our cue to quickly leave. We did not stay long enough to see the boys make it through to our end of the building, but we did see more windows being smashed from inside the building, and parts of a chair go flying out of a window. It was a terrifying experience, and to this day, we are convinced that someone was in that building with us who did not want us to get hurt, and took steps to get us out before the gang could see us.

Did we have a guardian spirit with us that night? We believe we did, and we were grateful for the protection. Were there other spirits roaming the grounds and derelict buildings of Dixmont? I can't say for sure, but if there weren't, it would be a surprise. If any one place was meant to be haunted, it was Dixmont.

And perhaps the resident ghosts made one last attempt to make their presence known before the hospital vanished forever.

Between the winter of 2002 and 2005, the smaller utility buildings and plants were demolished one by one, and hauled away. During the winter of 2005-2006, the last two buildings suffered the same fate, including the once beautiful Reed Hall. During the spring and summer, the remaining debris was taken away, every tree was cleared, and heavy equipment began leveling the land in preparation for the Walmart shopping center. On September 19, 2006, something major happened, and some people believe that the spirits of Dixmont might have had a hand in it. Half a million cubic yards of hillside suddenly collapsed onto the railroad tracks below and across the four lanes of Route 65. No one was injured, but it took several weeks to clear the soil and reopen the railroad and the last two lanes of the highway. Engineers were called in to check the stability of the land, and work was resumed.

But this was not the end of it. Shortly after the work resumed, a second, smaller land slide slammed down onto the road. All work on the property was stopped and the engineers returned. In early 2007, less than a year later, Walmart announced that it was abandoning the project but not the land. To their credit, they stayed to begin work stabilizing the hillside. The stabilization work continued for the next 6 years and the engineers stated that nothing could be built there for many years to

217

come. Walmart has pledged to plant 7,000 trees on the site and to let nature have its own way again.

Dixmont is gone, but only trees will mark the spot. No shopping center and parking lot. The cemetery remains intact according to state law.

Maybe the land slide that halted the construction project was just a coincidence, but at the same time, isn't it interesting that a massive building stood on the same site for 144 years – along with 80 other buildings – and the hillside held fast? Obviously, we will never know for sure, but one can't help but wonder if the spirits of Dixmont were using whatever means necessary to insure that their eternity passed in peace.

14. ORBITOCLAST LOBOTOMY TOOL
DANVERS STATE HOSPITAL

The Danvers State Hospital in Massachusetts is a place that is very closely connected to fictional horror. It was an institution so monstrous in size and reputation that it inspired horror writer H.P. Lovecraft to model the Arkham Sanatorium in his writings after it. The 1958 horror film "Home Before Dark" used Danvers as a location and most infamously, the abandoned hospital became the setting for one of my favorite horror films, "Session 9."

But tragically, Danvers State had just as close of a connection to real-life horror. It was an institution that saw abuse and even death for some patients, terrible and ineffective treatments that were closer to torture than cure, and, notoriously, it became known as the "birthplace of the prefrontal lobotomy," because of its use and refinement of this now discredited procedure.

Is it any wonder that the asylum became known as a haven for ghosts -- even after the hospital was transformed into an upscale condominium complex?

"The Castle on the Hill"

What would become Danvers State Hospital was constructed on a hill that belonged to the Francis Dodge family in the mid-nineteenth century. In the 1870s, when the Commonwealth of Massachusetts decided to build an additional psychiatric hospital to house the state's growing mentally ill population, it was decided that the hill on Dodge's farm would make the perfect location and he was persuaded to sell his land.

The Gothic-style building was constructed in 1878 and was designed by Nathaniel J. Bradlee according to the theories of mental health advocate Thomas Kirkbride, who believed in the compassionate care and treatment of the mentally ill. This meant that the new Kirkbride building would have ornate interiors, private rooms, and long, rambling wings to allow the sunshine in. It totaled 700,000 square feet in size and was nicknamed "the castle on the hill" by locals. It consisted of a main center building with four wings radiating off both sides of the structure that allowed each ward adequate ventilation and views of the surrounding land. This would, Kirkbride believed, help cure more patients and eliminate the "darkest, most cheerless and worst ventilated parts" of the hospital.

When the State Lunatic Asylum at Danvers opened, it was meant to be an appealing place with interiors that promoted the health and well-being of the patients and at the time, Danvers was considered a leader in humane treatment. The patient's daily regimen involved exercise and the creation of elaborate gardens. The hospital was incredibly self-sufficient. A pond on the grounds provided water for the buildings, and farms on the property provided work for the patients, along with food for the tables. Over the course of many years, over 40 buildings and structures were built on the property, including separate buildings for tuberculosis patients, two nursing homes, housing for staff, the Bonner medical building, machine shops, pump house, a cemetery, several cottages, a gymnasium, auditorium, and solarium, as well as an elaborate labyrinth of underground tunnels connecting all of the buildings. The tunnels, commonplace in most hospitals of the era, allowed for discreet patient transfers, employee passage, storage, and a tactful removal of the dead.

It was a one-of-a-kind facility and unlike just about every other asylum of its type at the time. The hospital administration refused to use physical restraints on the inmates and emphasized curing patients rather than merely hiding them away from the public. But some difficult patient populations brought problems with them. A large and unwanted influx of criminals brought chaos to the hospital for a time, but the 1886 construction of a hospital for the criminally insane in Bridgewater, Massachusetts, alleviated many of those issues. Another difficult group to treat were those suffering from "intemperance" and "dipsomania" – the nineteenth century terms for alcoholism and drug abuse. In addition, developmentally disabled patients mixed in with the general population, not being moved to their own unit until 1980.

Unfortunately, as the years passed, the "moral treatment" envisioned by Kirkbride was present at Danvers only in the main building's floor plan. The reality was that Danvers had become just another "snake pit." The structure was originally meant to contain no more than 600 patients, but in 1939, it had a daily population of 2,360, and the staff, whose size had remained relatively stable, was at a loss for how to control the patients, who were sick and dirty from their lack of care. Earlier superintendents had warned of "the evils of overcrowding," but their warnings had gone unheeded and requests for additional state funding were ignored. Crumbling plaster, wall stains, and holes created a general sense of physical decay. Barely clothed, and sometimes naked, hordes of inmates wandered about aimlessly on the wards, lying on dirty cement floors, or sitting slumped against the cracked, paint-chipped walls. Sometimes the patients died out of the staff members' sight, and weren't discovered until days later, rotting away in some forgotten room. Eventually, all of the nightmarish trappings of asylums were introduced: solitary confinement, straightjackets, electroshock therapy, and, of course, the lobotomy.

The Lobotomy

Although derided today as a barbaric procedure, the lobotomy started out with good intentions. It was believed that severe forms of mental illness could be treated by changing the way that the brain worked. Doctors believed that by severing the connections that the frontal lobes, or prefrontal cortex, had to the rest of the brain, they could calm patients' emotions and stabilize their personalities without doing away with their intelligence and motor functions.

A person's prefrontal cortex serves a number of complex functions in the brain, including higher-level decision-making, reasoning and understanding, personality expression, creativity, and behaving in a socially acceptable manner. The brain is essentially composed of two different types of matter: gray and white. Gray matter includes the neurons, or brain cells, along with their blood vessels and extensions. White matter comprises the axons, or nerve fibers, that connect the areas of gray matter and carry messages between them through electrical impulses. So a lobotomy was intended to sever the white matter between different areas of gray matter.

The first lobotomies were performed in 1935 by Portuguese neurologists Dr. Antonio Egas Moniz and Dr. Almeida Lima. Initially, they drilled holes in the skull on either side of the prefrontal cortex and injected the connecting fibers with alcohol to destroy them. However, this procedure resulted in too many complications, including damage to other parts of the brain. Moniz then decided to use a tool called

221

a leucotome. After drilling holes in the skull, the doctor pressed on the back of the tool, which extended a wire or metal loop inside. By extending and then retracting the leucotome, he could remove portions of white matter.

The first prefrontal leucotomy in America was performed at the George Washington University Hospital in 1936 by the neuropsychiatrist Walter Freeman and his friend and colleague, the neurosurgeon, James W. Watts. Freeman had encountered Moniz at a medical conference and became fascinated with his new procedure. He soon modified it. Instead of removing portions of brain matter, Freeman's procedure severed the connection between the frontal lobes and the thalamus. Because Freeman lacked a license to perform surgery himself, he enlisted James Watts as a research partner. One year after the leucotomy at George Washington University, Freeman directed Watts through the very first prefrontal lobotomy in the United States on housewife Alice Hood Hammatt of Topeka, Kansas. By November, only two months after performing their first lobotomy surgery, Freeman and Watts had already worked on 20 cases, including several second, follow-up operations. By 1942, the duo had performed over 200 lobotomy procedures and had published results that claimed 63 percent of their patients had improved after the surgery, 23 percent were unchanged and 14 percent were worse.

Perhaps their greatest failure was the lobotomy performed on Rosemary Kennedy, the sister of future president, John F. Kennedy. Rosemary was born with intellectual disabilities, though this remained a family secret for decades. Although placid and easygoing as a child, Rosemary became assertive and rebellious as a teenager. She was also reportedly subject to violent mood swings. Some observers have since attributed this behavior to her difficulties in keeping up with siblings who were expected to perform to high standards, as well as the hormonal surges associated with puberty. In any case, the family had difficulty dealing with her stormy moods and reckless behavior. Rosemary Kennedy had begun to sneak out at night from the convent school in Washington D.C. where she lived. Her erratic behavior frustrated her parents, especially her father, Joseph Kennedy, Sr., who feared Rosemary would bring shame and embarrassment to the family.

In 1941, when Rosemary Kennedy was 23, doctors told Joseph P. Kennedy, Sr. that a new neurosurgical procedure, a lobotomy, would help calm her mood swings and stop her occasional violent outbursts. Without informing his wife, Rose, of his decision, he decided that Rosemary should have the lobotomy performed by Watts and Freeman. She was awake when they opened her skull and made a small incision in her brain, near the front. Using a flat-bladed instrument, Watts cut while Freeman asked Rosemary to perform simple tasks like reciting the Lord's Prayer, singing

"God Bless America," and counting backwards. When she began to become incoherent, they stopped.

After the lobotomy, it quickly became apparent that the procedure was not successful. Rosemary's mental capacity was diminished to that of a two-year-old child. She was immediately institutionalized, where she remained for the rest of her life. In 1949, she was moved to Jefferson, Wisconsin, where her father built a private cottage for her on the grounds of the St. Coletta School. Because of her condition, she was largely detached from her family. Her father did not visit his daughter at the institution and Rose Kennedy did not visit her for 20 years. While her older brother John was campaigning for re-election for the Senate in 1958, the Kennedy family explained away her absence by claiming she was reclusive. At one point, a rumor circulated that Kennedy was too busy working as teacher for disabled children to make public appearances. The Kennedy family did not publicly explain her absence until after John was elected as President of the United States in 1961. Even then, they did not reveal that she was institutionalized because of a failed lobotomy, but instead said that she was deemed "mentally retarded."

After her father died in 1969, Rosemary was occasionally taken to visit relatives in Florida, Washington, D.C., and Cape Cod. By that time, she had learned to walk again – an ability erased by the lobotomy – but did so with a limp. She never regained the ability to speak clearly. She died from natural causes in 2005.

Meanwhile, Moniz's methods were also being modified by other physicians in Europe. The most notable one occurred in 1937, when Amarro Fiamberti, the medical director of a psychiatric institution in Italy, first devised the "transorbital lobotomy," in which the frontal lobes were accessed through a patient's eye sockets. His method was to puncture a thin layer of the orbital bone at the top of the socket and then inject alcohol into the white matter of the frontal lobes through the opening. This innovation would prove inspiration in the United States, where the transorbital lobotomy would become infamous – thanks to Walter Freeman.

After several years of performing lobotomies, Freeman heard of Fiamberti's method of operating on the brain through the patient's eye sockets, allowing him to access the brain without drilling through the skull. In 1945, after experimenting with an icepick from his own kitchen on grapefruits and cadavers, he formulated a new version of the transorbital lobotomy. The procedure, often known as the "icepick lobotomy," was performed by inserting a metal pick into the corner of the eye-socket and moving it back and forth, severing the connections to the prefrontal cortex in the frontal lobes of the brain. His first procedure was performed on a severely depressed housewife named Sallie Ellen Ionesco. After rendering her unconscious through electroshock, Freeman inserted an ice pick above her eyeball, banged it through her eye socket into her brain, and then made cuts in her frontal lobes. When he was done, he sent her home in a taxi cab. According to reports, the surgery was a success, which must have convinced Freeman that mental illness could be easily cut out of a patient's brain.

Since his new methods didn't require a neurosurgeon and could be performed anywhere without the use of anesthesia, Freeman was able to broaden the use of the procedure. He saw it as a way that he could bring help and relief to psychiatric hospitals all over the country that were overpopulated and understaffed. By curing the mentally ill with lobotomies, he could alleviate many of the problems that were plaguing these hospitals. But not everyone agreed with his methods. In 1950, Freeman's longtime friend and partner James Watts left their practice and split from Freeman due to his opposition to the cruelty and overuse of the transorbital lobotomy.

Following his development of the "icepick lobotomy," Freeman began traveling across the country visiting mental institutions in his personal van, which he called the "lobotomobile." He toured the nation, performing lobotomies and spreading their use by educating and training hospital staff members so that they could perform the operation on their own. Freeman charged just $25 for each procedure that he performed. He never wore gloves or a mask during the procedures. During his career, he performed more than 3,400 lobotomies in 23 states. The "icepick procedure" was used at least 2,500 times – despite the fact that he had no formal surgical training.

In February 1967, Freeman performed his final procedure on a woman named Helen Mortensen. She was no stranger to Freeman and, in fact, it was the long-term patient's third lobotomy from Freeman. She died from a cerebral hemorrhage – as did as many as 100 other of his patients – and he was finally banned from performing the procedure.

The ban came too late for many who suffered through one of Freeman's lobotomies. Some had to be re-taught to feed themselves and to use the bathroom. Relapses were common and, as mentioned, many died. In 1951, one patient at Iowa's Cherokee Mental Health Institute died when Freeman stopped for a photograph and the surgical instrument penetrated too far into the patient's brain. During his career, he lobotomized 19 minors, including a four-year-old child.

At age 57, Freeman retired and opened up a modest practice in California. He died on May 31, 1972, leaving a legacy of horror behind.

The Haunting of Danvers State Hospital

After Freeman performed the first transorbital lobotomy in 1946, many large psychiatric hospitals adopted the procedure, using it to treat everything from daydreaming and backaches to delusions and major depression. Danvers is often given the dubious title of the "birthplace of the prefrontal lobotomy" for its use and refinement of the procedure.

Discredited and banned almost everywhere today, the lobotomy was seen as the answer to numerous problems at overcrowded and understaffed hospitals like Danvers. Far too many patients were deemed "incurable" and as wards of the state, had very little input about their care. Many administrators and staff members knew that these patients would never be released and it was better to have them relaxed instead of disruptive. Since lobotomies were known for calming the patients, it seemed the perfect answer to all of the hospital's problems. While some patients certainly saw stunning benefits from this so-called miracle treatment, many others had adverse effects. Visitors to the hospital in the late 1940s described many patients as aimlessly wandering the halls, or vacantly staring at walls, often a result of the hastily arranged "icepick lobotomy."

As time went on, conditions at the hospital grew worse and worse as the administration's pleas for more funding fell on deaf ears. The massive building started to decay and crumble from the lack of upkeep, and entire wards were closed down one by one as patients were shipped off to other facilities. Portions of the hospital were shuttered starting in 1969, with most of it closed by 1985. The Kirkbride building was abandoned in 1989 after the remaining patients were moved to the Bonner Medical Building. Finally, the state closed Danvers State Hospital down in 1992.

The hospital, which was listed on the National Register of Historic Places, remained abandoned for 13 years as it continued to fall into disrepair. Danvers' most famous moment during this time came after director and writer Brad Anderson drove past the decaying structure and was inspired to write the film "Session 9," about an asbestos removal crew that goes into the hospital to prepare it for renovations – with horrific results. The atmospheric thriller used the eerie building to chilling effect, and during the filming, Scottish actor Peter Mullan (Gordon) even reported an unsettling encounter with what he believed was a ghost. While standing in one of the former patient's rooms, preparing for his next scene, a distinct voice whispered his name. Mullan described the whisper as having the tone of a "request," as if someone was trying to get his attention so that he would do something. Assuming that it was a crew member calling him back to the set in a quiet voice, Mullan turned to answer and found no one was there. He was very unsettled by the incident and was clear about the fact that he was not a believer in the supernatural – until he came to Danvers State. Actor David Caruso (Phil) noted in an interview that the cast and crew felt like the building was "alive." It was not a pleasant place to be during work on this disturbing film.

Once the filming wrapped, though, the historic building was once again left to crumble on the hilltop. In 2005, the hospital was purchased by Avalon Bay Development for $12 million with the plan to turn it into an apartment building. Against the wishes of the local preservation community, six of the original eight wards of the Kirkbride building were demolished during the construction. The remaining two wards and the center building were gutted, leaving only the building's facade.

But all would not go well during the construction. Things were seriously delayed in 2007 after a mysterious fire broke out on the property and burned down most of the newly constructed building and some of the construction trailers on site. The fire was so intense that it could be seen 17 miles away in Boston. A webcam that had been installed for security purposes by Avalon Bay to provide a live feed of the construction area suddenly stopped working at 2:03 a.m. – just before the fire started. The feed somehow cut out, disabling the camera. An investigation revealed nothing. There was no evidence of foul play and every reason for the fire – wiring, fuel, arson, or construction issues – was ruled out. The cause of the blaze remains unknown.

In 2008, Avalon Bay finished construction and residents began to move in shortly after. Since then, the building's management has been hit with a flood of complaints from tenants about the poor construction quality of the building. In July 2014, Avalon Bay sold the property to DSF Group, which released plans for major renovations of the property.

Today, the initial outward appearance of the hospital's Kirkbride building remains preserved. There isn't much left inside of it, although the cemeteries, some blocked-off tunnels, and the D and G wings remain – and that might not be all.

Over the years, those who spent time at the abandoned hospital claimed that it was haunted by the countless spirits of former residents. Trespassers reported strange banging sounds, eerie shapes, disembodied footsteps, screams, and even full-bodied apparitions of men and women in hospital clothes, their eyes empty and cold. Even the cast and crew of "Session 9" reported unusual happenings taking place during the shoot.

When the Avalon Danvers Apartments were finally opened, the condominiums quickly filled, and while there were the mentioned complaints of shoddy construction, more complaints were filed about how the buildings were always cold.

The chill was unbearable in the winter, some residents said. There were numerous problems with the plumbing and electrical systems. Sinks turned on and off, toilets flushed, and lights flickered and went out with no explanation. Some residents complained of hearing footsteps walking up and down the hallways at night. Others reported the sounds of someone screaming in the corridor. Another claimed that invisible hands pulled the sheets off the bed at night.

Something seems to be lingering in the old Danvers State Hospital – or at least in what's left of it. Is it possible that the former patients of this tragic place have simply never left? Have they remained behind to express their displeasure about what has happened to the only home that so many of them ever knew? Or are they merely unaware of the fact that they died many years ago and simply refuse to leave?

Time will tell, as perhaps more accounts of the old hospital will emerge as the years go by.

15. STRAITJACKET
TRANS-ALLEGHENY LUNATIC ASYLUM

The story of the Trans-Allegheny Lunatic Asylum, formerly Weston State Hospital, is a familiar one in the long line of woeful tales from American asylums. It was a place designed to provide a safe place for the mentally ill, and like so many others, began with good intentions, only to become overcrowded and undesirable in the twentieth century. But if there is one thing that sets this place apart from others like it, even those with a reputation for being haunted, is that the place once known as the Weston State Hospital is said to be infested with ghosts.

A Refuge for Lost Souls
The Weston State Hospital, known as the Trans-Allegheny Lunatic Asylum, was authorized by the Virginia General Assembly in the 1850s. Following consultations with Thomas Story Kirkbride, then-superintendent of the Pennsylvania Hospital for

the Insane, a building in the Kirkbride Plan was designed in the Gothic Revival and Tudor Revival styles by Richard Snowden Andrews, an architect from Baltimore. Construction on the site, along the West Fork River opposite downtown Weston, began in late 1858. Work was initially conducted by prison laborers and a local newspaper noted "seven convict negroes" as the first arrivals for work on the project.

Construction on the state asylum in Weston began when the region was still part of the larger state of Virginia. It was a volatile time in our nation's history with the fight over slavery raging between the southern states and the northern abolitionists. As tensions increased, it boiled over into what became the most calamitous event in American history. The Civil War not only divided the country, but it tore apart families and friendships, especially in Border States like Virginia.

When the war broke out in April 1861, the Weston State Hospital was still in the early stages of construction. At that time, the southernmost wing had been finished, along with the basement and foundation of the massive central structure. In June, Virginia's secession from the Union brought all work that was not related to the war effort to a halt. Following its secession from the United States, the government of Virginia demanded the return of the hospital's unused construction funds for its defense, but before this could occur, Weston was invaded by the Seventh Ohio Volunteer Infantry.

On June 30, the Union troops, led by Colonel Erastus Bernard Tyler, an Ohio furrier who sold his products to the people of the town and Lewis County before the war, swept into town. Tyler ordered his troops to sweep through the town and seize any individuals suspected of Confederate sympathies. More importantly, though, he wanted the asylum construction funds that were sitting in the Weston branch of the Exchange Bank of Virginia. The bank held almost $30,000 in gold, which had been deposited by the state government of Virginia to provide wages for the men building the new asylum. The vault opened and troops removed $27,000 in gold coin, leaving $2,371.23, which the books established was due to creditors. The money was taken to Wheeling, where it was put toward the establishment of the Reorganized Government of Virginia, which sided with the northern states during the war.

The partially-built asylum, and its surrounding grounds, became known as Camp Tyler, establishing Weston as a military post. The southern wing of the hospital provided barracks for the soldiers and the foundation of the main building was used as a stable for horses. The Federal troops used the position to control the area's roads, but not without difficulty. The area changed hands several times during the war. Confederate raids in 1862 and 1863 temporarily drove off the Union troops and in 1864, Confederate attackers emptied the local bank's vaults and confiscated all of the clothing that was intended for the hospital's first patients.

In the midst of the fighting, the Reorganized Government appropriated money to resume construction in 1862. Following the admission of West Virginia as a state in 1863, the hospital was renamed the West Virginia Hospital for the Insane.

Construction resumed in earnest after the war. While many other towns were financially ruined by the conflict, and would remain destitute for at least the next decade, Weston did not experience a post-war depression. Area business boomed as the asylum established itself as the town's primary economic resource. It would remain so until 1994, when the hospital closed down.

The Trans-Allegheny Lunatic Asylum was finally completed in 1881. At that time, it was the largest hand-cut stone building in the United States, and second in the world next to the Kremlin in Russia. Like other Kirkbride buildings, the sprawling, staggered wings and connected structures were designed to open up to all of the fresh air and sunlight that was possible. Kirkbride's theory of "a building as a cure" was obvious at the newly completed asylum.

Over time, a 200-foot central clock tower was added in 1871, as well as separate buildings for women, children, and African-Americans. The hospital was meant to be self-sufficient with a farm, dairy, and waterworks located on the grounds. A cemetery was added, which eventually grew to 666 acres, and a gas well was drilled on the grounds in 1902. Its name was changed to Weston State Hospital in 1913 in an effort to remove the stigma caused by the words "lunatic" and "asylum."

Originally designed to house just 250 inmates in peaceful solitude, the hospital held 717 patients by 1880. The numbers continued to climb into the 1950s, when more than 2,600 patients were packed into filthy, overcrowded conditions. A 1938 report by a survey committee organized by a group of North American medical organizations found that the hospital housed "epileptics, alcoholics, drug addicts, and non-educable mental defectives" among its population. The first to have been admitted were criminally insane men and women, but over time, they had added orphans, homosexuals, derelicts, and just about any other person that a family might deem undesirable. A series of reports by the *Charleston Gazette* in 1949 found poor sanitation and insufficient furniture, lighting, and heating in much of the complex.

The asylum was overcrowded, which led to other problems, including violence. There were a number of methods employed to control the violent patients, like straitjackets, solitary confinement, restraints, and the always popular lobotomy, which was widely used starting in the 1940s. After electroshock therapy was administered, the sharp tip of the orbitoclast was inserted at the corner of the eye until it reached the frontal lobes of the brain. With a few short sweeping motions, the frontal lobe had been disconnected – and the patient's life had been changed forever. With an overcrowded hospital and a staff that had little control over the horde of patients, the lobotomy gained popularity. Over the course of the hospital's history, over 3,500 lobotomies were performed using Walter Freeman's "icepick" method.

With hundreds and hundreds of the mentally ill living in a constant state of nightmarish insanity and with no help to be found, the inmates lived in a daze of anguish, pain, and utter hopelessness. It is no wonder that the imprint of their terror and madness has seeped into the walls and floors of the Weston State Hospital.

One of the most tragic sections of the hospital was the children's wing, an area where orphans and unwanted children were placed because they had no parents or because they had been given up to the state. Tragically, though, with so little control over the overcrowded hospital, the inmates were rarely separated. The patients were allowed to roam the hospital wings, and it was fairly common for the mentally ill to mingle with the children. Women were separated from the men in different wings, but the children's wing was adjacent to the men's wing – likely with often terrible consequences.

By the 1980s, the hospital's population was finally reduced due to changes in the treatment of mental illness. Those patients that could not be controlled, though, were often locked in cages. In 1986, Governor Arch Moore announced plans to build a new psychiatric facility and convert the Weston hospital to a prison. Ultimately, the new facility, the William R. Sharpe Jr. Hospital, was built in Weston and the old Weston State Hospital was simply closed in May 1994.

Time and vandals were not kind to the former asylum. It fell prey to trespassers, and in 1999, all four floors of the interior of the building were damaged by several city and county police officers playing paintball, three of whom were dismissed over the incident.

Efforts began to be made to preserve the structure and proposals were made to convert it into a Civil War Museum and a hotel and golf course complex. A non-profit organization, the Weston Hospital Revitalization Committee, was formed in 2000 for the purpose of aiding in preservation of the building and finding appropriate tenants. Three small museums devoted to military history, toys, and mental health were opened on the first floor of the building in 2004, but were soon forced to close due to fire code violations.

Finally, in 2007, the West Virginia Department of Health and Human Resources auctioned off the building. Joe Jordan, an asbestos demolition contractor from Morgantown, was the high bidder. He re-named the structure the Trans-Allegheny

Lunatic Asylum and began to renovate the crumbling building, eventually offering historic and ghost tours of the structure.

After the construction work began – and the tourists began to arrive – those who spent any amount of time in the asylum began to realize that the living were not alone in the old hospital. The dead were present – and they were making themselves known.

The Haunted Asylum

The Trans-Allegheny Lunatic Asylum, in the traditional style of the Kirkbride buildings, was made up of different wards to facilitate the treatment of various kinds of patients. On the third floor, Wards C and F held the more physically violent men and women, with only a single locked door separating the two wards from each other. Many who have visited Ward F have reported being touched, pinched, had their clothing pulled, being touched on the shoulder, whispers and, most eerily, the sound of the creaking wheels of gurneys being pushed down the empty corridors.

In Ward 2, located on the second floor, victims of a double suicide and a brutal stabbing have been said to wander the dark hallways, their dragging footsteps clearly being heard as they shuffle along the dark passageway. Witnesses claim to experience an icy grip of cold as the footsteps brush past, only dissipating when the sound is no longer heard.

On the first floor, in Ward 1, the most antagonistic of the asylum's ghosts is said to linger. Her name was "Ruth" and for many years, she lived in Ward C. When the violent women of Ward C became too much for the frail and elderly Ruth to withstand, she was transferred to Ward 1, where she continued to claw, bite, and scream obscenities at nurses, orderlies, and visitors. She became so hard to deal with that she spent much of her time strapped into a wheelchair, still shouting and screaming at anyone within earshot. When she died, it's believed that her spirit has remained behind to hit, push, and scratch people since her voice is no longer being heard.

One section of the hospital was long ago dubbed the "Civil War Wing" because it first admitted patients that had returned to their families from the war in such states of madness that no therapy of the time seemed able to reach them. "Shellshock," as it was called in those days, and many other forms of psychosis, as well as physical impairments like tuberculosis were common. It was also the very first in a series of wings that would make up the numerous, twisted hallways of the hospital.

Visitors to this area of the asylum have heard male laughter, coughing, voices, and have even been threatened by disembodied voices, warning them to leave the building. But the most famous story of this section involves a spirit that has been dubbed "Jacob," a Civil War soldier who was sent to the hospital after the war ended and has never left. He continues to roam the hallways and grounds, just as he did before he died. More than anything, Jacob seems to be attracted to young women who are brave enough to venture into the "Civil War Wing." They seem to get his attention, feeling touches, caresses, and a distinct feeling of a presence nearby.

Over time, many of the staff members at the asylum simply refuse to enter this wing alone or at night. Many of them have reported being chased by the hurried footsteps of a man who cannot be seen. They also report the intense feeling of being watched, but searches of nearby rooms and hallways reveal that no one – no one visible anyway – is present.

If there is a single floor that is more infamous than all others, it's the fourth floor, which was reportedly haunted even in the days when the Weston State Hospital was still in operation. The sounds of banging, footsteps, maniacal laughter, and haunting screams have been heard all over the floor. It is a place known to be so eerie that hospital workers refused to go up to the fourth floor without an escort. One former psychiatric worker admitted, "I knew that the fourth floor as haunted because I used to have to go up there after medical records. I could hear them following me."

Heavy footsteps trudged down the halls, accompanied by the sounds of distant crying, screaming, and moaning. Doors opened and closed on their own, banging sounds echoed off the pipes and door frames, and even the muted sound of conversation between two people have been heard – and recorded. There was no one present at the time. Some have even reported seeing gurneys and wheelchairs slowly rolling down the corridors or across rooms by themselves.

One of the haunts of the fourth floor is said to be the spirit of a nurse. Legend has it that she was murdered decades ago by a patient who hid her body in an unused stairwell for nearly two months before her body was discovered.

The Electroshock Therapy room and the hospital's morgue are also very active places, with reports of screams, the sounds of gurney wheels rolling across the broken tile floors, and the moaning gibberish of a patient who endured the tortured treatment of days gone by. Apparitions of both patients and doctors have been seen coming in and out of rooms and roaming the abandoned halls, still on their rounds, going about their routines. They appear to be as real and solid as you and I and, then suddenly, they vanish without a trace.

Without a doubt, the most famous lingering spirit of Trans-Allegheny Lunatic Asylum is that of the young girl that has come to be called "Lilly." Who she might have actually been remains unknown, but she appears to be a child, perhaps three or four-years of age. She wanders the hallways of the old hospital and seems particularly active when visitors ask her to play.

Where did this young spirit come from? No one knows, although numerous legends surround this lost little soul. Some believe that she was an orphan, an abandoned child left in the care of the state and placed in the orphanage located on the site. The stories say that she lived for a few years and then died from pneumonia or tuberculosis, common killers of children in those days. Others claim that Lilly's mother was a patient at the hospital, a mad woman who gave birth to a child while she was locked away. If so, Lilly may have been left in the care of the orphanage since her mother would likely never be cured.

However she ended up in the hospital, she died at some point and her spirit remained behind. After all these years, her ghost wanders the halls of the abandoned asylum, perhaps seeking the mother who left her, or perhaps just looking for anyone who wants to entertain a lonely little girl. Candy and small toys are often left behind for Lilly and just as often, they are found in places other than where they were left by visitors. Some reports the sounds of running and giggling whenever Lilly's spirit is around, while others have claimed to see the fleeting glimpse of a small girl in an old-fashioned dress as she hurries around a corner or vanishes up a staircase. Occasionally, she interacts directly with those from whom she seeks attention. A tour guide playfully rolled a ball down a hallway for her one night, only to have it abruptly change directions and return to them by some unseen force.

Suicide, murder, insanity, and natural deaths brought on by abuse, neglect, and disease claimed the lives and souls of hundreds of people during the asylum's many years of operations. Is it any wonder that it has come to be known as one of the most haunted hospitals in America?

16. ELECTRO-SHOCK PADDLES
ST. ALBANS SANATORIUM

America – like the rest of the world – has long battled with cures for mental illness. In centuries past, the mentally ill were chained to walls, locked in cages to contemplate sanity, wrapped into straitjackets, injected with massive amounts of insulin that would cause comas that lasted for weeks as a cure for schizophrenia, lobotomized, and drugged to the point of incoherence. And for the most part, none of it worked.

In the 1940s, "shock treatment" came into common use. By applying electrodes to the sides of the patient's head, an electric shock would be sent through their body, jolting them back into sanity – or so it was believed. The inhumane and most ineffective treatment, although discredited, remains in use today, and it was an especially popular treatment at a mental hospital in Radford, Virginia, which had seen more than its share of unusual history long before it became known for being haunted.

A History Dark and Bloody

Long before St. Albans Sanatorium stood outside of the town of Radford, the land was inhabited by the Shawnee Indians. In 1755, a small outpost that was located nearby was raided by a group of Shawnee warriors, who killed at least five people, including an infant child, and captured five more. The Indians took their hostages far away to a Shawnee village in Kentucky, but one of them, Mary Draper Ingles, later managed to escape and returned home through the wilderness. Although many elements of the story remain unknown, they are a bloody and stirring preface for what was to come for this land.

The original land tract where the sanatorium would be located was part of a 7,500-acre parcel known as Draper's Meadow. It was awarded around 1737 by Governor Robert Dinwiddie to Colonel James Patton, an Irish land speculator. At the time of the attack, the land had been settled by about 20 families, a mixture of folks from Pennsylvania with English and German origins.

Rising tensions between the natives and the settlers over encroachment on tribal hunting grounds were increased by fighting in the French and Indian War. Recent victories by the French over the British, although north of Virginia, had left much of the frontier unprotected. During the summer of 1755, several settlements had been raided by Indians. On July 9, British troops under the command of General Edward Braddock had been decisively defeated by French and Shawnee forces at the Battle of Monongahela, which encouraged further violence against settlers in the region.

On a day near the end of July (there is a disagreement about the dates), a group of Shawnee entered the sparsely populated camp and, with little resistance, killed five people, wounded another, and burned the settlement. Among the victims were Colonel James Patton, a neighbor, and two people in Mary Draper Ingles' family: her mother, Elenor Draper, and Bettie Robertson Draper, the infant daughter of her sister-in-law. The baby was killed after her head was beaten repeatedly against the wall of the cabin. Other children in the settlement were killed in the same way. Colonel William Preston, Colonel Patton's nephew, and John Draper, Bettie's husband and Mary's brother, were not at the settlement at the time of the attack. They were working in a nearby field and survived. Mary's husband, William Ingles, was attacked and nearly killed, but managed to flee into the woods.

One of the victims, the neighbor named Barger, was decapitated by the Indians and his head was delivered in a bag to a neighbor. Five of the settlers were captured in the wake of the battle and were taken back to Kentucky as captives to live among the tribe, including Mary Draper Ingles and her two sons, Thomas and George. Mary escaped without her children and made a journey of more than 800 miles

236

across the Appalachian Mountains back to Draper's Meadow. Mary's son, Thomas, and sister-in-law Bettie were eventually ransomed from the Indians, but others who were taken died in captivity.

In the aftermath of the massacre, Draper's Meadow was abandoned – as was much of the frontier for the duration of the French and Indian War. William Preston, who had been in Draper's Meadow on the morning of the attack, but left on an errand and so was saved, eventually obtained the property, which became Smithfield Plantation.

After her escape, Mary Draper Ingles reunited with her husband and in 1762 they established Ingles Ferry across the New River, along with a tavern and a blacksmith shop. Mary died there in 1815.

In time, the Civil War brought more bloodshed to the region. The battle of Cloyd's Mountain occurred on May 9, 1864, and was a bloody fight that allowed Union forced to destroy the last line connecting Tennessee to Virginia. During the battle, Union artillery bombarded the settlement of Central Depot (now the city of Radford) from the ridge where St. Albans would eventually be constructed.

The battle saw some of the most savage fighting of the war. Brigadier General George Crook commanded the Union Army of West Virginia, made up of three brigades from the Division of the Kanawha. When Ulysses S. Grant launched his spring offensive of 1864, two Union armies marched towards Richmond and a third moved into the Shenandoah Valley. Crook's troops were also involved in the offensive and began to march through the Appalachian Mountains into southwest Virginia. His objective was to destroy the Virginia & Tennessee Railroad. Brigadier General Albert G. Jenkins was in command of the few scattered Confederate units protecting the rail lines. Although he was an experienced soldier who had made a name for himself in Pennsylvanian during the Gettysburg campaign, he had assumed command of his troops in Virginia only the day before Crook's army began to approach the railroad.

Jenkins decided to make a stand at Cloyd's Mountain and he set up a strong defensive position. When Crook arrived, he decided against a frontal assault, concluding that the Confederate works were too strong and such an attack would decimate his army. The surrounding area was heavily forested and Crook used this as cover to swing his brigades around to the Confederate right flank.

Crook began the battle with an artillery barrage, then sent in his brigade of West Virginians under Colonel Carr B. White. Crook's remaining two brigades, under Colonel Horatio G. Sickel and future president Colonel Rutherford B. Hayes, were to launch a frontal assault as soon as the West Virginians had gotten under way. White's brigade, in its first fight, advanced to within 20 yards of the enemy line before heavy casualties forced it back. Crook, moving with Hayes' Ohio brigade, had to dismount and walk the slopes on foot because they were so steep.

Hayes' brigade spearheaded the main assault around 11:00 a.m. The troops fought their way to the Confederate works and deadly hand-to-hand fighting ensued. Sparks from the musket fire ignited a thick blanket of leaves on the ground, and many men from Sickels' and Hayes' brigades were pinned down and burned alive. The brigades had begun to fall back, when Crook sent two fresh regiments into Hayes' front. The West Virginians finally advanced against the artillery and overran its crew. The Ohio troops now began to overwhelm the Confederate center. Jenkins tried desperately to shift troops to the threatened areas, but he fell mortally wounded and was captured. His second-in-command, John McCausland, took command and conducted a rear-guard action as he withdrew his troops.

The battle of Cloyd's Mountain was short and involved few troops, but it contained some of the bloodiest fighting of the war. The engagement lasted a little over an hour, saw men engaged in hand-to-hand fighting and burned to death, and ended in a Union victory after Crook destroyed the railroad line at Dublin, severing the Confederacy's last vital lifelines and its only rail connection to East Tennessee.

It was another bloody incident that marred the history of the land where St. Albans Boys School came to be built in 1892.

St. Alban's School

The new school was envisioned by teacher George W. Miles, who wanted to create a preparatory school for boys that would form future southern gentlemen and put the town of Radford on the map. He named the new school St. Albans after the famous St. Albans School in England, which was founded as part of a monastery and was one of the oldest boy's schools in the world. Like its English counterpart, the site for the new school was on a steep hill overlooking the river and town.

On opening day in September 1892, 50 dormitory students from all over the south and 20 to 30 day students, who lived in Radford but came to classes, listened to the words of famous Virginia lawyer and writer, Thomas Nelson Page. He had a clear message for the new institution: a good education stressed physical condition first and scholarly endeavors second. In this, he was in complete agreement with Headmaster Miles, who had handpicked some of the best athletes from the south for his opening class. He was of the belief that a successful school must be built around championship football and baseball teams, and he had an eye for talent. St. Albans became one of the major athletic powerhouses in the state, so badly beating the other preparatory schools that they refused to play St. Albans anymore. The boy's school soon turned to playing college teams.

The focus on athletics left little room for scholarly excellence. The atmosphere at the school was rough and competitive. An article describing the school sums up some of the horror that plagued the intellectual students:

The atmosphere at the school was rough and competitive. It clearly favored the stronger boys (or bullies as we would say today) and made short work of the more cerebral types like one E. Blackburn Runyon, whose painful experience at the school was poignantly summed up by a yearbook editor in 1904 -- E. Blackburn Runyon did not return after Christmas, much to our sorrow, as it put a stop to the football games on the terrace in which he figured prominently as the football.

The initial success of the school had a major impact on Radford. The comparatively wealthy students provided a new source of income for the local economy. Entire families moved to town in order to send their sons to this elite institution. The successes at St. Albans made the city known all over the state.

Under the leadership of George W. Miles, the school prospered, even after the stock market collapse in 1893 that brought an abrupt end to Radford's first boom. The enterprising professor ran the *Radford Advance*, a local newspaper, and even took over the operation of the public utilities for some time. According to one source, he was even considered to serve as the first president of the University of Virginia, but didn't get the job. He supposedly then moved to Marion, where he was involved in the building of the Marion & Rye Valley Railroad. Other sources claim that he died of cancer in 1903. In any case, his departure or death dealt a serious blow to the school and student numbers began to dwindle. The St. Albans School for Boys closed down in 1911.

"A Place to Heal"
The next chapter in the history of St. Albans began in 1916 when Dr. John C. King, using $500 of his own money, formed a corporation and borrowed money to buy the empty school and the 56 acres of land that surrounded it. The young doctor – as enterprising as his predecessor in the building George Miles, had been – formerly served as the superintendent of the Southwestern Lunatic Asylum in Marion, Virginia, but unhappy with the state of things there, he sought a new place that could produce a higher rate of recovery for the mentally ill. St. Albans, he believed, would be that place. The old school was thoroughly renovated and, on January 15, 1916, the first four patients were admitted.

Like other havens for the insane, St. Albans began with wonderful intentions. Also like other facilities of the era, the St. Albans Sanatorium included a farm which, according to an old brochure, "affords ample space for out-of-door games, diversional exercises and employment, also vegetable and flower gardens, an adequate dairy herd and extensive poultry-raising, all of which are interesting and helpful to the patients."

St. Albans Sanatorium struggled initially with financial problems. However, Dr. King and his wife managed to keep the hospital open, and they gradually expanded its services and built a sterling reputation for the facility. After the building of an arsenal in Radford, the town grew rapidly. With St. Albans being the only hospital in the area, the asylum also began to provide general medical care as well. To accommodate all these patients, the staff worked six days a week while living in quarters provided by the hospital.

As the years passed, as with most mental hospitals of the era, the patient load continued to grow and care had to be provided with less and less money. Even though the treatment of mental disorders at St. Albans was far superior to the care given at other facilities, it fell victim to many of the trends that wreaked havoc at asylums starting in the 1940s – from lobotomies to various kinds of shock therapy -- all of which resulted in a significant number of fatalities.

Shock Therapy

The mid-twentieth century began a revolution in the types of treatments afforded to the mentally ill. The nightmarish conditions in the insane asylums of the nineteenth century gave way to scientific psychotherapy, based on theories of the mind proposed by Austrian physician Sigmund Freud, the founder of psychoanalysis. Its value was mainly observable in mild mental disturbances, particularly neuroses. But beginning in the 1930s, these methods began to be supplemented by physical approaches using drugs, electroconvulsive therapy, and surgery.

The idea of "shock therapy" to treat mental illness began with head trauma, convulsions, and high fever. In 1917, doctors began experimenting with using malaria-induced fevers to treat neurosyphillitic patients. Insulin-induced comas and convulsions, to treat schizophrenia, was first used in Berlin in 1927. Later, physicians began to be fascinated with the idea of treating mental illness by using electricity and the use of Electroconvulsive shock therapy was discovered in 1937.

The use of high injections of insulin to treat schizophrenia began as early as just six years after insulin was discovered in 1921. An internist named Manfred J. Sakel at the Lichterfelde Hospital for Mental Diseases in Berlin, Germany, discovered that by sending a morphine-addicted woman into an insulin coma, he obtained a remarkable recovery of her mental faculties.

He continued his experiments and discovered, accidentally, that by causing convulsions with an overdose of insulin that he saw improvement in patients afflicted with psychosis, particularly schizophrenia. In 1930, he began to put the treatment into practice and, in 1934, it made its way to the United States. Sakel believed that he had made one of the most important contributions ever to be made to psychiatry. According to his own findings, more than 70 percent of his patients improved after insulin shock therapy. Two large studies carried out in America in 1939 and 1942, brought him fame and helped his technique spread throughout the world.

Unfortunately, though, the treatment didn't last, and in some cases, caused dire results.

And it was not the only harmful treatment that was initially promoted as a "miracle cure." In 1933, the same year that Sakel officially announced his results with the insulin coma therapy, a Hungarian physician from Budapest named Ladislaus von Meduna started experimenting with a new approach, claiming that "pure" artificially induced epileptic convulsions would be able to cure schizophrenia.

He began testing several kinds of convulsive drugs on animals – then on his patients. He used many lethal drugs with insulin, but never alone. However, his goal was only achieved when he experimented with intravenous injections of Metrazol, a circulatory and respiratory stimulant that caused violent seizures in high doses. After a series of 110 cases, Meduna reported that half of his cases showed remarkable improvements and even "dramatic cures."

Meduna communicated his findings to the psychiatric establishment in a symposium convened in Switzerland in 1937 that was discussing the insulin shock therapy pioneered by Sakel. The findings of the two doctors created two separate camps – one in favor of insulin and one in favor of Metrazol, which was cheaper and more reliable. In the end, both turned out to do more harm than good.

Meduna was forced to immigrate to Chicago in 1939, and from there, he continued his experiments. Eventually, psychiatry recognized that his theory of biological incompatibility between epilepsy and schizophrenia was unfounded, but that artificially-induced convulsions were useful to reduce schizophrenia. However, in controlled trials, Metrazol turned out to be far less efficient than insulin in the treatment of schizophrenia, although worthwhile for treating affective psychoses like manic and psychotic depression.

Due to the appearance of many other methods to treat mental illness, though, both insulin and Metrazol were gradually discontinued in the late 1940s and eventually were stopped altogether. This form of shock therapy paved the way for a much more alarming method of treatment that came about in the 1930s.

In 1937, Italian neurologist Ugo Cerletti became convinced of the usefulness of Metrazol-induced convulsions to treat schizophrenia, but he felt that the treatment was far too dangerous and uncontrollable, since there was no antidote to stop the convulsions once they started. Cerletti knew that an electric shock to the head could also produce convulsions. He specialized in epilepsy and had done a number of experiments with animals. He soon began using an electroshock apparatus to provoke repeatable epileptic fits in dogs. The idea to use Electro Convulsive Therapy (ECT) in humans first came to him after watching pigs being jolted with electric shocks as a kind of anesthesia before being butchered. He convinced two colleagues – Lucio Bini and L.B. Kalinowski – to help him develop a method and apparatus that would deliver brief electric shocks to human beings.

They experimented with several kinds of devices with animals and then, believing they had established the correct parameters, began using the device on human test subjects that were suffering from acute-onset schizophrenia. After 10 to 20 shocks on alternate days, the improvement in most of the patients was startling. One of the unexpected benefits of the electroshock to the head was that it provoked short-term amnesia, or a loss of all memory of events immediately before being shocked, including any fear associated with the therapy. At best, at least it was safer than the convulsions being induced by drugs.

In 1939, Kalinowski began traveling to hospitals and asylums all over the world, including the United States, to advertise the uses of ECT. Researchers who adopted the methods of the doctor and his colleagues soon discovered that it seemed to have spectacular effects on affective disorders. Soon, it became the shock therapy of choice for mental hospitals all over the country, including St. Albans.

But just as it was with lobotomy procedures, the helpfulness of the therapy was soon outweighed by the damage that was done. Its use became highly troublesome when overcrowded and understaffed hospitals began using ECT to subdue and control patients. Inmates that caused problems often received several shocks each day, many times without proper restraint or sedation. It was far too often not used to cure, but to control patients for the benefit of the hospital staff.

In the 1970s, a backlash against ECT (along with lobotomies) began in Europe and spread to the United States. It was denounced by many, including most famously in the novel by Ken Kesey that was based on his personal experiences in an Oregon mental hospital. Titled *One Flew Over the Cuckoo's Nest*, it was later made into a highly successful film starring Jack Nicholson. Bad press turned into legal actions, all based on the abuses of shock therapy.

By the mid-1970s, ECT had fallen into disrepute. Psychiatrists increasingly made use of powerful new drugs, such as Thorazine and an array of other anti-depressives and anti-psychotics. However, this was not the end of the therapy. There have been many improvements made in the technique of ECT since then, including the use of muscle relaxants, seizure monitoring, and better devices. It had come back into use during the twenty-first century, making it the only psychiatric therapy from the 1930s that is still in use today.

End of Days

The hospital continued to grow and in the following decades. Unlike so many state hospitals, St. Albans never fell into the kind of condition that resulted in abuse and neglect. Things were not perfect, but weren't nearly as dark as other asylums of the era. But patients did die, and many of them perished by their own hand. A number of suicides were documented, including a number that were heartbreaking.

An obituary from the *Southwest Times* notes: "Mrs. Susan Jane Sayers, wife of W.B. Sayers, died Saturday night at the St. Albans Sanatorium, Radford, where she had been under treatment. Her condition had been extremis for some days and the end not unexpected, it being realized there was no hope."

In 1960, St. Albans became a fully recognized hospital and opened outpatient clinics in Roanoke, Blacksburg, and Beckley, West Virginia. In order to stay up-to-date with new technology, parts of St. Albans were relocated into a more modern facility, allowing the mental institution to become the only private, full-service, not-for-profit psychiatric hospital in the region.

The glory days of the old St. Albans were, however, almost over.

On June 28, 1980, a young woman named Gina Renee Hall mysteriously vanished from Radford and her blood-stained car was found only a short distance away from St. Albans on Hazel Hollow Road.

Gina, age 18, was described as a "very beautiful, well-dressed, pleasant, soft-spoken" young woman who was popular with her peers, respectful of her parents, and close to her older sister, Diana, with whom she was living in Radford during the summer of 1980. The two sisters were taking summer classes at Radford University, where Gina was a freshmen and her sister was in graduate school. Gina loved to dance and was quite athletic, friends and family recalled. She may have liked an occasional glass of wine, but she did not smoke or use drugs. In other words, Gina was "a very happy person," an ideal young woman of the era – and was certainly not the type to simply disappear on her own.

By late June, Gina had just finished summer mid-terms and was in a "great mood," Diana recalled. She wanted to go out dancing but her sister was too tired. Instead, Diana loaned Gina her brown Chevrolet and watched as her five-foot-tall sister adjusted the seat as far forward as it would go before she headed out to the Marriott in Blacksburg for a night of music, dancing, and fun. It was 10:00 p.m. on Saturday, June 28, 1980, and it was the last time that Diana ever saw her sister – alive or dead.

Two of the people that Gina met that night at the Marriott were Stephen Epperly and his friend, Bill King. The two young men had known each other since they were children, but neither of them had ever met Gina before. During the evening, Epperly and Gina seemed to get along well, dancing to several songs and sharing some drinks. At some point, Epperly came up with an idea. Bill King's mother and stepfather had a home on nearby Claytor Lake and the two men had stopped there earlier to check on things at the request of King's parents. So, Epperly asked King if he could borrow King's car and the keys to the lake house. He didn't say why he wanted them, but King assumed it was to take Gina there. However, King needed the car and wouldn't let his friend take it. Epperly was welcome to go to the house, but he'd have to find his own way there.

Because there had been a group of people dancing and drinking that night, Gina mistakenly assumed that when Epperly asked her if she wanted to go for a midnight swim, he meant that more than just the two of them would be going. King later told the police, "She seemed confused as to what car was going and exactly who was going. I think that when she came out she thought maybe there would be more people going."

Instead, Gina and Stephen Epperly left the Marriott alone together.

Several hours later, King and another woman decided to go out to the lake house for a swim. When the couple arrived, they saw Gina's borrowed Chevrolet in the driveway, but there were no lights on in the house. They didn't want to surprise anyone, so when they entered the house they slammed the doors and turned on the kitchen light, hopefully giving Epperly or Gina – if they needed it – time to get themselves together. King heard Epperly call out and ask, "Bill, is that you?"

King replied that it was and that he and his date were going swimming. Epperly answered, "She's got to be getting back," indicating that "they" were leaving. The woman with King saw Epperly standing without his shirt on, drying himself with a towel. However, neither King nor his date saw or heard Gina in the house that night.

Around 7:00 a.m. on Sunday morning, a patrol car spotted the dark brown Chevrolet parked near a railroad trestle on Hazel Hollow Road. The St. Albans Hospital was only a short distance away. The trunk of the car was open. Because this was a popular fishing site, the officer didn't initially suspect that anything was out of the ordinary, but when almost 18 hours later, the same deputy came by again and saw the car was still in the same spot with the trunk open, he stopped to investigate. After running the plates, he found that the car was registered to Diana Hall and it had not been reported stolen.

Meanwhile, as the deputy was investigating the abandoned car, Stephen Epperly was returning to the lake house, where he found Bill King outside playing with his son. He asked if he could go inside for a drink. King later told the authorities that he thought his friend remained inside for an unusually long time and when he asked about it, Epperly shrugged it off.

By this time, Diana was very worried about her sister. She called a few friends and they went out looking for Gina. After finding the car where the deputy had seen it, they called the police. One of the first things that the friends noticed was that the driver's seat was pushed back all the way – which would have made it nearly impossible to drive for a girl as short as Gina.

By the middle of the week, the media was widely reporting the story of the missing co-ed. Reporters tracked down King on Tuesday, July 1. King went to where Epperly was working and advised him to go to the police and report his encounter with Gina, "So they wouldn't think he had anything to hide." He asked King who he had talked to about the missing girl and was non-committal about going to talk to the police.

Later that day, Epperly talked to a friend whose brother was an attorney. He asked the man if his brother might be willing to represent him and then asked him to inquire, "If there was anything that they could do to him if they didn't find a body."

Uncomfortable about waiting any longer, Bill King went to the police the next day with his information. He brought investigators back to his family's lake house, and they found a broken ankle bracelet that had belonged to Gina.

After this discovery, Epperly was questioned by the police for the first time. He told them that he had driven Gina from the nightclub to the lake house, and he had heard her call her sister to tell her that she would be home in the morning. He said they went to the dock and that he went swimming, but Gina did not. They had "kissed some," he said, but Gina told him that she would have to know him very well before she would sleep with him.

The fact that Epperly was claiming this at all alerted her sister to the fact that he was lying. When Gina was very young, she was badly burned. The accident had left scares on her right side from her upper arm to her thigh. Although always friendly and outgoing, she was self-conscious about the scars and this kept her from getting to close to her boyfriends. Gina's sister later testified that she was very concerned about how a man might react to them and as a result, "she could not have handled the emotional stress of a physical relationship with somebody and never put herself in that situation." In addition, she had expressed concern to her sister about what might happen if she got pregnant and the skin grafts on her body failed to stretch.

According to Epperly's story, they left the lake house late that night and Gina dropped him off in Radford. He went to bed and he never saw her again. He had no idea what happened to her and no clue as to why her car ended up abandoned on Hazel Hollow Road.

As the days went by, Epperly and King talked more about Gina. At one point, King came out and point-blank asked Epperly if he had killed the missing girl. Epperly replied, "Bill, I don't know anything about it. We'll just have to wait and see."

But by this time, the Radford police had a warrant to examine the lake house. They discovered bloodstains on the driveway, on a walkway leading to the lake, and inside of the house. The interior of the house had been meticulously cleaned, but not enough to miss detection by the crime scene analysts who examined it. They found blood and hair on a golf shoe, blood on a dustpan, and blood and hair in the gasket on a refrigerator door. A large bloodstain, more than a foot across, was found inside of the living room and had been bleached to the point that it turned a faint pink. Testimony later showed that there had never been bloodstains in those locations before.

Searchers looking for Gina discovered a blue, blood-stained towel near where the Chevrolet had been left on the side of the road. It contained fibers that were consistent with those found in the carpet of the lake house. King's mother later identified the towel as one that was missing from the house. Nearby, a policeman found one of Gina's shoes at the opposite end of the trestle from where the car and towel were found. In the trunk of the Chevrolet, investigators found Type O blood and head hairs that were similar to those found in a hairbrush used by Gina. The blue towel also contained Type O blood and six hairs that seemed to match Gina's.

Two weeks later, other investigators found all of the clothes that Gina had worn on the night she vanished. The clothes were tied in a bundle and covered with blood. Forensic testing showed that this blood was also Type O, the same as Gina's. In the bundle of bloody clothes, forensic scientists found hair that matched Epperly, who had now officially become a suspect.

Some of the most compelling evidence collected against Epperly came not from forensics, but from a tracking dog that was brought to Radford by John Preston, a retired Pennsylvania State Trooper who was qualified as an expert animal handler in courts in 17 states. With his German Shepherd, he had worked more than 150 criminal cases across the country.

Preston and his dog arrived a week after Epperly had become the lead suspect in Gina's murder. However, he was not told that they had a suspect in mind and neither Preston nor the dog had ever been to the Radford area before.

The police secured a warrant for an article of Epperly's clothing. Preston was then taken to where Gina's car had been found and he allowed the dog to acquire the scent from the clothing. The dog then began what is known as a "casting search," passing back and forth in an ever-widening arc in an attempt to pick up the scent. The animal found it about 100 yards away from the Chevrolet's location. He left the road and headed up a hill toward the railroad trestle and started walking along the tracks. He led the officers on a tour of Radford, touching each location where searchers had found the items connected to the missing girl. Preston later testified that the dog indicated the scent had "paused" at three locations, as if the person had spent some time at each of those points. The pauses occurred at each spot where investigators had recovered evidence.

From the railroad tracks, the dog followed the trail through a box factory, a railroad switching yard, across the parking lot of the New River Valley Shopping Plaza, and past a car wash. Finally, the dog entered a subdivision, walked up to the front door of a house, and sat down.

The dog had stopped on the front porch of Stephen Epperly's house.

The next day, the dog was again given Epperly's scent and introduced to six different blue towels, including the one that had been found near Gina's car. The dog immediately sat down in front of the towel from the woods near the car. The towel contained blood of the same type as the missing girl and carpet fibers consistent with those found at the lake house. Apparently, it also contained something that carried the scent of Stephen Epperly.

The following day, while Epperly was being interviewed at the police station, Preston and the dog were called to the scene. While the suspect was inside, the dog was "scented" on the blue towel. The dog then poked around the parking lot, which contained several other cars, but stopped at the driver's side door of Epperly's car. The dog then picked up the trail from the car to the police station and came directly to the door of the interrogation room where the suspect was sitting. After the detectives told Epperly what the dog had done, he put his head down on his arms and said over and over, "That's a damn good dog."

Epperly was indicted by a grand jury and tried for first-degree murder. Gina's body was never recovered, which required the state to prove both that she was dead and that her death had resulted from a criminal act by Epperly. Furthermore, to sustain a conviction of first-degree murder, the state had to demonstrate that Epperly had the specific intent to kill.

The prosecution presented its case to the jury, revealing Gina's sudden disappearance, the evidence of a violent struggle found at the lake house, the efforts made by the killer to hide the evidence by disposing of her clothes and bloody towels, Epperly's discussions with his friends, and the unimpeachable evidence of the tracking dog. The prosecutor stated that all of this circumstantial evidence, when taken together, indicated that Gina Hall had been murdered and that Stephen Epperly had killed her.

The jury agreed and convicted him of first-degree murder. Although he filed an appeal, the verdict and the life sentence were upheld.

But what happened to Gina Hall? No one knows. It seems very likely that she is dead, murdered by the hand of Stephen Epperly, but what happened to her body? How did a man who left such clumsy evidence of the crime manage to hide a body so well that the police, scores of searchers, and an experienced police dog have never been able to find it? There have been some who have claimed that Gina's body was buried somewhere on the grounds of St. Albas, perhaps in an undeveloped area where it's never been found. Her car was found nearby and so it seems possible that Epperly might have disposed of her in the nearby woods since articles of clothing and blood evidence were found scattered about the area.

Could this be why some visitors to the hospital claim to have had contact with her in the basement of the now-decaying building? Many have reported that when Gina's name is mentioned in the building, a strange mist is often seen. Another witness stated that recordings he made in the basement picked up the plaintive cries of a woman who was calling for help and pleading for her life. Could it be the voice of Gina Hall, or at least an impression of her terrible last moments, somehow imprinted on the atmosphere of the place?

The answer to that question remains as mysterious as the location of her still missing remains.

Hauntings at St. Albans

St. Albans continued on for another decade and then in the early 1990s, it became part of a new health system, which moved ahead with plans to relocate it to another site, which would eventually be the "New River Medical Center." The old hospital was abandoned and left to the mercy of time, the elements, and vandals. In 2004, the buildings and the surrounding 78 acres became a gift from the hospital system to the Radford University Foundation. Plans were made to destroy the hospital and demolition on the 1890s structure was started in 2007 – only to be abruptly halted. A group of concerned citizens insisted on a proper historical review of the property, which had been mandated by the federal government. Today, the hospital has been opened again, now offering historic and paranormal tours of the property.

Thanks to the hundreds of people who have visited the property, hoping to preserve its history -- and perhaps experience the supernatural – there have been scores of witnesses to the hauntings that remain in the old hospital. There have been takes of lifelike apparitions that have been seen in the rooms, seemingly going about their business in another era, or crossing the corridors and vanishing into walls. Objects have been seen to move about on their own and in one reported incident, a heavy brick was seen to hover off the floor, remain in place for a few moments, and then drop back to the concrete. Visitors have been touched, pinched, pushed, had their hair pulled, and one woman stated that she was slapped across the face. Investigators tell stories of hearing disembodied voices – often threatening, angry ones – and recording those voices on various devices. If their accounts are accurate, then there may just be a multitude of spirits who have remained behind at St. Albans, perhaps unwilling to ever leave.

The building itself is in a state of disrepair today. Although structurally sound, times has not been kind to the place. Years of graffiti area sprayed across the walls, the walls are chipped and crumbling, and many of the windows are broken. And yes, the old asylum still stands, braving the elements and the vandals and providing a place for the myriad of ghosts who roam the halls.

In the basement of the hospital is an old two-lane bowling alley that is haunted by the ghost of a little girl. One room is apparently inhabited by a "whistling ghost" that will repeat the sounds that visitors make when they whistle to him. The room where so many of the patients withstood the cruelty of shock therapy is now alive with the sensations of spirits who are trapped there. The records of the asylum say that four suicides occurred in a single bathroom in the building and the presence of angry, confused entities have never left the cramped chamber.

St. Alban's Sanatorium is a building where time stands still. Beneath the layer of dirt, destruction, and grime is a shadowy place that exists just on the other side of our world. It's a place where the spirits of the past are doomed to endure their haunted lives over and over again. That shadowy place sometimes seeps out and makes it presence known in our own world – an experience that very few ever forget.

17. A STAIN ON A CONCRETE FLOOR
ATHENS LUNATIC ASYLUM

The story of the Ridges – originally known as the Athens Lunatic Asylum – will be a familiar one to the readers of this book. It was a place that was opened with the best of intentions and based on the philosophies of Thomas Kirkbride, the mental health advocate who believed in "healing through architecture" and that wide, open spaces filled with light would ease the troubles of a man or woman's corrupted mind. Many of the first patients at the asylum were Civil War veterans who suffered from horrific flashbacks of the battlefield and "lunatics" who had committed heinous crimes. Could such well-meaning treatments truly cure the mental illness of men who had seen more – and committed more – terrible acts than the human mind could withstand?

In time, as overcrowding and a lack of funding plagued the hospital, the staff turned to other methods to cure the suffering – lobotomies and other terrifying treatments that were meant to "shock" the illness from the brain.

Such horrors, as with so many other asylums, left a dark impression at the Ridges, and the spirits of yesterday have stayed close to their former home.

Building the Ridges

In the mid-nineteenth century, large public asylums for the insane had already been established throughout the state of Ohio, serving Cleveland, Cincinnati, Columbus, Toledo, Akron, and Dayton. Plans began to be made for a hospital in the southeastern part of the state in Athens, near the campus of Ohio University.

Originally known as the Athens Asylum for the Insane, the massive hospital opened its doors on January 9, 1874. The state and federal government had purchased more than 1,000 acres of land from the Coates family, who had farmed the property. Construction on the asylum took six years, using bricks that were fired on-site from local clay. For the design of the facility, the state had turned to Thomas Kirkbride, who believed in not only specific designs for the buildings, but that all of the asylums should be large, self-sufficient communities.

The four-story main building was designed to be symmetrical with two wings – one for men and one for women – and between the two wings was the administration section. The main building was massive, in the tradition of the Kirkbride buildings. His designs were centered around the idea that it was therapeutic for patients to be in a facility that resembled a home, not a prison. In a Kirkbride building, the less disturbed patients were housed closer to the center, where the administrative offices and employee housing were. This encouraged them to socialize and become more accustomed to human contact. Violent patients were kept at the far end of either of the stepped-back wings, which were farthest away from the center.

Herman Haerlin, a student of Frederick Law Olmstead (the designer of Central Park), was responsible for the design of the hospital and its grounds. By the turn of the twentieth century, orchards and farmland were maintained on the property, tended to by hospital inmates and employees. This made the hospital nearly self-sufficient. Nevertheless, at the time of its construction it was a major boon to the economy of the city of Athens, which was able to supply milk, eggs, linens, and other necessities. Local citizens made use of Haerlin's extensive grounds, which included landscaped hills and trees, a pond, a spring, and a creek with a falls.

The Athens asylum had 544 patient rooms. When it opened, it housed around 200 patients. The first patient is believed to have been Thomas Armstrong from Belmont County, followed by Daniel Fremau, who apparently believed that he was the second incarnation of Jesus Christ.

The original hospital was in operation from 1874 to 1993. The hospital was never totally self-sustaining, but it was close. For many years, the hospital had livestock, farm fields, gardens, orchards, greenhouses, dairy, a plant to generate steam heat, and even a carriage shop in the early years. As more patients arrived, the more sedate among them participated in recreational activities like boating, painting, dances, and picnics. They were offered church services and plays and largely allowed to roam about on the grounds. Some patients tended the farms and orchards. Nurses trained at the Athens State Hospital School of Nursing inside the asylum were able to live there while they cared for the inmates.

Over the years, more and more patients were admitted to the asylum. Soon, the numbers were double of what Kirkbride had recommended. And while this made for crowded conditions, it also benefited the asylum in that patients were put to work on the farm and at other facilities from which the asylum made revenue. Seven cottages were constructed to house even more patients. They could hold less capacity than the wards, but they grouped patients in dormitories. Eventually, the admissions got out of hand, and by the 1950s, the asylum was well over three times its capacity and was caring for close to 2,000 patients.

This was the downside of the progress accomplished by the Kirkbride plan. Thanks to the increasing popularity of asylums, in Athens and elsewhere, it was common for families to drop elderly relatives off at the hospital when they could no longer care for them. Parents committed teenagers merely because they were rebellious. The homeless used the hospital for temporary shelter. Overcrowding led to the sharing of patient rooms and a severe declined in the quality of treatment administered by the staff, which had barely increased in size since 1874.

The history of the asylum documents years of now-discredited theories as to the causes of mental illness, as well as the harmful treatments meant to combat it. Existing records tell a grim story about the background training of the employees. Some were fully-trained and some weren't trained at all. Some lived on the grounds, others did not. The most shocking information within the employee records are the evidence and documentation of hydrotherapy, electroshock, lobotomy, and psychotropic drugs, almost all of them discredited today as inhumane ways of treating patients. The leading cause of insanity among the male patients was masturbation, according to the annual report of 1876. The second-most common cause of insanity, as recorded in the first annual report, was alcoholism. In the hospital's first three years of operation, 81 men and one woman were diagnosed as having their insanity caused by masturbation and 56 men and one woman were diagnosed as insane due to drink. During those three years, the most common reasons for women to be admitted to the asylum were "puerperal condition" (now called postpartum depression), "change of life," and "menstrual derangements."

Epilepsy was also considered a major cause of insanity and reason for admission to the hospital in the early years. Early reports list 31 men and 19 women as having their insanity caused by epilepsy. General "ill health" accounted for the admission of 83 people during those early years. Overall, common ailments such as epilepsy, menopause, alcohol addiction, and tuberculosis were cause for enrollment in the hospital in those days.

As the population increased, staff members were at a loss as to how to deal with their patients. Attempts were made to treat everyone – no matter how cruel those treatments may seem now – but then there were those extra cruelties that were given out without the justification of therapy. Patients were often restrained and were forced to sleep in group bunks in rooms intended for one person. One nurse was sometimes responsible for as many as 50 patients. In these conditions some restricted patients would carve messages on the sandstone windowsills of their rooms, reaching through the ornate bars to leave an anonymous word or sentence. One poignant carving that has been recounted many times still exists today. It reads, "I was never crazy."

The "Water Treatment"

Staff members at the overcrowded hospitals of the early twentieth century devised novel methods with which to treat the insane. Despite how cruel they might seem and how much they might seem like torture, all of them have already been documented here as having been scientifically based. It was believed that the insanity could be "shocked" out of the patient and all sorts of horrific therapies were devised to do so. They included the already described electroshock therapies and the lobotomies that used an icepick-type tool to sever the frontal lobes from the brain. There was also the original lobotomy, which opened up the skull and separated their neural passages halfway through the brain. The difficult and arduous procedure killed many people, but those who survived forgot about their depressive and psychotic tendencies – along with how to feed themselves, walk, talk, and use the toilet.

An earlier type of "therapy" that was a holdover from the nineteenth century was the so-called "water cure." It offered a "cure" for insanity using natural means and was based on the use of pure, soft, mineral water in various forms of baths, wet wraps, and internal cleansings. The methods could vary. For instance, hyperactive patients got warm, tiring baths, while lethargic patients received stimulating sprays.

Some doctors, however, got a bit too zealous about the idea, prescribing therapies that sounded more like punishment than healing.

Patients were brought to the asylum's hydrotherapy rooms with certain items that were needed for treatment: two large wool blankets, three comforters, two coarse cotton sheets, one coarse linen sheet, six towels, and pieces of cotton for bandages. During the course of water treatments, a patient would be immersed naked into a tub of cool water and then placed into a tub of very hot water. She (since most who received the water cure were female, hoping to cure "unnatural occurrences" like menstruation problems and post-partum depression) might also receive a cold water douche and wet sheets that would be wrapped tightly around the body to restrict circulation. After that, the body would be vigorously rubbed to restore her circulation to normal. She would later be taken on a strenuous walk and then return to her room for a nap, where she would be wrapped with several blankets and comforters, leaving only her face exposed.

But not all of the water treatments were so restful. Some of the more extreme therapies involved mummifying the patient in very tightly wrapped towels that had been soaked in ice water. The loss of all feeling in the body was intended to "shock" the insanity from her mind. Another treatment required the patient to remain continuously submerged in a bath for hours, even days – which might not seem so bad, except that they were strapped in under a leather cover with only their heads showing and not allowed to leave the tub except to go to the bathroom.

Some doctors believed that only high water pressure would do. They used high-pressure jets to perform therapeutic douches on female inmates. Patients might be strapped to the wall and blasted with water from a fire hose.

Like many extreme treatments, hydrotherapy was eventually replaced with psychiatric drugs, which tended to be more effective and, usually, a little more pleasant.

As the years went by, the buildings and grounds of the asylum that would come to be known as the Athens Mental Health Center underwent many changes. In the 1920s, a fire destroyed the grand ballroom and in 1924, a building was erected on the grounds for the treatment of mentally-ill patients with tuberculosis. A dairy barn was added to the property in 1928, but it was near the end of the hospital's self-sufficiency.

For years, the hospital had been Athens' largest employer. A large percentage of the work that it took to maintain the facility, work the farmland, and tend to the livestock was carried out by the patients. Doctors believed that this was not only therapeutic for the patients, but it provided free labor for the hospital. By the late

1950s, though, treatments that had been used for years began to be discontinued and drugs began to be administered that made it difficult for the inmates to do their jobs.

The 1960s brought a new emphasis on the humanity of mental patients. They were no longer "slave labor" providing free work for the hospital. Lobotomies were condemned as barbaric, and psychotropic drugs like Thorazine replaced the old treatments. Although the massive drugs administered in hospitals at that time were far from perfect (the "Thorazine shuffle" was a term used to describe the zombie-like way people moved around when they were on it), the drugs seemed far more humane than electric shock or radical brain surgery, and they led to recovery for a greater number of people.

By the 1970s, asylums across the country were starting to wind down. An outcry had started about the conditions of many overcrowded, understaffed, filthy hospitals, and by the end of the decade, the Athens hospital housed fewer than 300 patients.

"The Minds of Billy Milligan"

Perhaps the most notorious patient at Athens was a man named Billy Milligan. He was a man that no one ever really knew – he was a criminal or a victim; a clever hoaxer or a man so disturbed that his mind fractured into at least 24 personalities. He kidnapped three women from the Ohio State University campus, raped them, and said that part of him did it for love. One of the women told a police officer that her rapist had a German accent, though Milligan was born in Florida and was raised in Ohio. Another said that her rapist had been so nice to her that, under different circumstances, she might have considered dating him.

Milligan's birth name was William – but he was also Ragen, Adalana, Christine and 19 others. He was the first person in American history to successfully use multiple-personality disorder as a defense for a violent crime. And the man who prompted the state of Ohio to change its laws to require a greater burden of proof for such a defense.

The first rape that Milligan committed was on October 14, 1977. He pointed a gun at an Ohio State University student and took her from a campus parking lot to a wooded area. When it was over, he made her write a check and cash it for him.

He raped a second student on October 22, and a third on October 26. Just one day later, one of the victim's picked Milligan's face out of a group of police mugshots. Milligan, age 22, had been convicted of rape before and had been in prison for a year on a robbery conviction. One of his fingerprints matched a print found on one of the victim's cars. Columbus and university police officers arrested him at his home in Reynoldsburg.

Elliot Boxerbaum, then the OSU police investigations supervisor, read Milligan his rights and rode with him to Columbus police headquarters. He later said, "I couldn't tell you what was going on, but it was like I was talking to different people at different times."

Doctors examined Milligan and even the skeptical ones saw what Officer Boxerbaum described. Milligan's defense attorneys, public defenders Judy Stevenson and Gary Schweickart, told the prosecution what they intended to argue in court. Terry Sherman, a Columbus lawyer who was one of the assistant Franklin County prosecutors on the case thought the entire thing was ludicrous.

Milligan was examined by more doctors and a subsequent psychiatric report spelled out their findings: A 23-year-old Yugoslavian named "Ragen" had taken over Milligan's consciousness and decided to rob some people. But before Ragen could rob anyone, a 19-year-old lesbian named "Adalana" took over Milligan's body and raped the women because she wanted to feel close to someone. The other personalities, including "Billy," had no memory of that.

Terry Sherman laughed out loud at the story – and then he sat in on an interview with Milligan and watched as he turned into different people right in front of his eyes. Bernard Yavitch, the other prosecutor, was also present. He later recalled, "I saw multiple personalities. His speech pattern was different, his accents were different. He sat different ways in the chair."

Dr. George Harding, the widely respected medical director of Harding Hospital in Worthington, spent months with Milligan and diagnosed multiple-personality disorder (now called dissociative identity disorder). With everyone in basic agreement --- the evidence showed that Milligan committed the crimes, but he wasn't responsible for them --- Franklin County Judge Jay Flowers found him not guilty by reason of insanity and sent him to the Athens Mental Health Center.

But the story of Billy Milligan didn't end there. In fact, it got even stranger, if that's possible.

Milligan had been born William Stanley Morrison in Miami, Florida, in 1955. He was the son of a singer, Dorothy Sands, and a comedian, John Morrison. The couple already had a son together and would later have a daughter, but Morrison remained married to another woman. Throughout his adult life, Morrison suffered from depression and alcoholism, and he committed suicide when Milligan was four-years-old. Milligan's mother moved to Circleville, Ohio, in 1960, where she married her ex-husband, then divorced him again.

In 1963, she married Chalmer Milligan and they moved to Lancaster. According to psychiatric reports that were based on Billy Milligan's recollections, his new stepfather repeatedly sodomized him and tortured him by burying him alive and hanging him by his fingers and toes. Chalmer Milligan denied all of those allegations and was never charged with any crimes.

The alleged abuse supposedly caused Milligan's personality to splinter and, from that point on, he was constantly in trouble. He was suspended from junior high school because he went into trances and began wandering around town. His parents committed him to a state mental hospital in Columbus, where hysterical neurosis was diagnosed. The hospital kicked him out three months later because his behavior was too disruptive. Lancaster High School expelled him in 1972, and he joined the Navy. The Navy discharged him a month later because he couldn't adapt to military life.

Later that same year, Milligan and a friend picked up some women and a few days later, the women accused them of rape. Milligan and his friend said the women were prostitutes and that when Milligan couldn't perform sexually, they weren't paid. A judge found Milligan and his friend guilty, and Milligan served six months in a Zanesville youth camp.

After Milligan's release, it has been claimed that his personalities began working as a security guard and also as a drug dealer. In late 1974, two cross-dressing men approached Milligan at a rest stop. He beat them up and took their purses. He helped plan a Lancaster drugstore robbery in early 1975. Not much later, Lancaster police arrested him, and he pleaded guilty to robbing the men and the store. He was sentenced to at least two years in prison and paroled in April 1977. Six months later, the Ohio State University rapes took place.

Dr. David Caul at the Athens Mental Health Center wanted to treat Milligan by "fusing" him --- combining all of his personalities into one. But it turned out Milligan was already fused in a personality called "The Teacher."

The Teacher helped the other personalities learn their special talents, but he didn't hold Milligan's consciousness. The others did. Caul learned of The Teacher in a conversation with Ragen, the personality who decided to commit the campus-area robberies. Dr. Caul played a recording of Ragen for "Billy," the core personality. Billy knew that he had other personalities, but that was the first time he had seen proof. In that way, Caul drew The Teacher into consciousness in December 1978. It was the first time Milligan had felt like one person since he was little.

The full story of Billy's strange life and perhaps even stranger treatment was recorded in the book *The Minds of Billy Milligan* by Daniel Keyes, the bestselling author of *Flowers for Algernon* and an Ohio University English professor at the time.

Keyes began interviewing Milligan around the same time The Teacher emerged and the book was published in 1981.

Not long after The Teacher emerged, Dr. Caul began giving Milligan unsupervised furloughs from the hospital – a fact that stirred a lot of criticism from state legislators and Athens residents when the newspaper broke the story. The Teacher receded during the stressful publicity that followed and Milligan's other personalities emerged. More news reports followed (which Keyes and others still described as biased and unfair) about Milligan faking an overdose, selling his artwork and buying a car, and of a party at the hospital. A local judge, after hearing testimony that Milligan was a security risk, transferred him to Lima State Hospital for the Criminally Insane.

Keyes wrote that Milligan found the hospital to be a "chamber of horrors." When it was transitioned into a prison in 1980, Milligan was transferred to the Dayton Forensic Center and then the Central Ohio Psychiatric Hospital; and, eventually, after more treatment and expert opinion that he was no longer a danger, he was transferred back to Athens – but not for long.

More trouble followed and he was returned to the stricter hospitals. He escaped from the Central Ohio Psychiatric Hospital in 1986, then left videotapes for local media outlets at the Columbus Greyhound Bus station complaining of his treatment at the hospital. At one point while he was on the run, he worked at a hot-tub business in Washington. He was arrested in Miami several months later.

In 1988, experts agreed that Milligan had fused, and he was released from Ohio mental hospitals after 11 years. He was released from all supervision three years later, in 1991. He began to fade from the public eye, but still popped up on occasion. He moved to California after being approached about making a movie about his life. As it often is with Hollywood projects, the film was never made. In 1996, it was learned that a California judge had ruled that Milligan was incapable of handling his own affairs. Ohio took him to court for royalties he had earned from the Keyes book and recovered $120,000 of the $450,000 spent on his treatment. He declared bankruptcy in San Diego and then he dropped off the map for years.

Then (during the writing of this book), news came that Milligan had died on December 12, 2014, in a nursing home in Columbus, Ohio. He was 59-years-old and his sister, Kathy, who had often spoken about her brother's poor treatment in state hospitals, confirmed that he had passed away. She told reporters, "He died last Friday of cancer. I believe he is finally at peace."

The Bell Tolls for the Ridges

As it turned out, Billy Milligan was among the last patients treated at the Athens Mental Health Center. The 1980s were the final days of the Ridges, as well as for many other mental hospitals all over America. The "de-institutionalizations" of the Reagan era redefined the official standards for mental illness, while shifting much of the burden to states that were unwilling or unable to keep centers like Ohio's state hospitals operating. The end result was that many thousands of mentally ill people were simply released. There were suddenly thousands more homeless people on the streets of America.

During the 1970s and 1980s, most of the land around the Athens hospital was donated to the university. The end was coming closer and it finally arrived in 1993, when the hospital closed down. The final patients left the Athens Center and were bused to a new, much smaller hospital across town. The building stood vacant for several years while Ohio University prepared to renovate it into museum, office, and classroom space. By that time, many of the original buildings had fallen into disrepair and were no longer used by the hospital and thus abandoned. The site of the original main building is now owned by Ohio University and is the one developed portion of a much larger parcel of land called, "The Ridges."

Most of the remaining buildings have since been renovated and turned into classrooms and office buildings. Ultimately, the former hospital administration building, of the grand Kirkbride tradition, was partially remodeled to house the Kennedy Museum of Art, as well as various offices and studios.

Now officially a part of Ohio University, the days of insanity, cruel treatments, overcrowding, and despair seem far in the distant past. But are they really? Not everyone thinks so, for the old buildings that make up the modern-day incarnation of the Ridges seem to hold more than a few spectral memories of the past.

Mysteries of the Ridges

Ghost stories at the former Athens Lunatic Asylum date back many years, almost to the day that the hospital closed its doors and the site was taken over by the university. One of the ghosts at the Ridges has managed to gain national fame - - not for what she did during life, but for the way she died and the bizarre way that she quite literally lingers behind to this day.

The Kirkbride building that made up the main structure for the hospital was renovated after it was taken over by Ohio University, and yet several wings and entire floors of it remain essentially untouched, even after all these years. In one of the abandoned rooms on the top floor, there remains the last vestige of Margaret

Schilling, the hospital's most infamous ghost. There is a stain on the floor of the room that is in the shape of a woman who died there in 1978.

Margaret's story is a mixture of truth and legend. Some say that she was a deaf and mute woman who hid from the staff when they were vacating the hospital and ended up locked into an upstairs section by mistake. Unable to call for help, she starved to death in a locked room that she was unable to escape from. But the truth of the story seems to be less dramatic, although just as terrible. Margaret Schilling was a patient at the hospital who had profound mental disabilities. She managed to lock herself into a ward that had once been used for infectious patients and had been abandoned during the years of declining population at the hospital. She disappeared on December 1, 1978, but her body was not discovered until weeks later, on January 12, 1979. She had died from heart failure -- likely as the result of exposure in the unheated ward. Oddly, though, as she lay dying, she took all of her clothes off, folded them neatly beside her, and laid down on the cold concrete floor.

Weeks later, her decomposing body, which had frozen and then thawed in the varying weather, was discovered on the floor next to a window. When the authorities attempted to move her body, they found that it had left a permanent stain in the shape of a woman on the floor. Apparently, the stain was caused by a combination of her body naturally decaying and the sunlight that was coming in from the large bay windows that were nearby. Despite vigorous scrubbing, staff members were unable to remove the stain. In fact, it remains there on the floor well over three decades later!

In addition, there are many who say that if you walk past the former asylum at night, Margaret's face can be seen staring down at passersby from the bay windows next to where her body was found. Her spirit, they say, still wanders the building where she lived and died.

But Margaret Schilling is not the only former patient that is said to be still haunting the Ridges. Other patients who died in the hospital over the years are also believed to be wandering the building and grounds.

For many years, one of the most haunted locations in the complex was a cottage that was added to the hospital in 1909 for mentally ill tuberculosis patients. Known as "Cottage B," it was sheltered on a hill, separated from the other buildings. One of the most notable aspects of the building was the large, screened-in porch that stretched across the front of the building. It was designed so that tuberculosis patients could take in fresh air, which, in 1909, was one of the only treatments known to ease their suffering. Ironically, since the building was designed to be fireproof, its walls were lined with asbestos. Since it was later discovered that asbestos was harmful and caused lung cancer, the patients exposed to the chemicals in the walls would have found breathing to be more difficult.

Cottage B became the frequent site of nighttime forays by college students, who broke into the building to explore and to track down the rumors of ghosts. For many years, trespassers told tales of eerie sounds, footsteps, disembodied voices, and numerous apparitions. Faces were often seen at the windows, peering out when the building was empty, or flickering across the old screened porch, where so many patients struggled for air before surrendering to the deadly disease that plagued them.

Finally, in early 2013, Ohio University demolished the former tuberculosis ward to prevent further break-ins and exposure to the asbestos inside.

Ghosts are also reported in the asylum's main cemetery, which occupies the downslope of the hill behind the former hospital. Only those patients who had families that could afford it were given professional stones that were identifiable by name. For the most part, the asylum cemetery is filled with simple, narrow stones that were marked by a number and provided by the state. Hospital records identified the patient that each stone belonged to, but many of the records were lost – along with the identities of those buried beneath the stones. There are at least 2,000 patients who were buried on the grounds, along with the cadavers that were once used by the medical classes at Ohio University – making for an unusual assortment of residents for the oldest cemetery on the grounds. There are also two newer cemeteries on the property, but it's the oldest one that is said to be infested with mournful spirits.

The cemetery itself is an oddity. Several of the gravestones on the hillside are arranged in a perfect circle – for no apparent reason and in no apparent order. It's been speculated that this was a prank that was carried out by university students in the 1920s, but no one can say for sure. Whatever the cause, the circle has allegedly become quite the draw to witches and practitioners of the dark arts, who hold séances at the site and believe it to be a powerful spot. Another oddity in the graveyard is the presence of a half dozen or so stones that are located on the other side of a creek that runs alongside the cemetery. They are buried in a clearing at the edge of the woods and legend has it that they are the graves of murderers and could not be interred in the same hallowed ground as the others. Their spirits are angry and vindictive, the stories say, and cannot cross the running waters of the creek. Truth or fiction? No one knows.

The dark tales of the Ridges are merely a small part of the many stories told about the town of Athens, Ohio, itself. It's a strange place, nestled into the

Appalachian Mountains, which for centuries has been considered a region of magic and ghostly folklore. There are many stories to Athens -- and many ghosts. From the mysteries of the Ridges to the tale of the headless train conductor near Lake Hope who tries to flag down passers-by with his lantern. The story dates back to a time when the citizens of local Moonville were quarantined because of a measles outbreak. The food and supplies in town were running low and this man went out to flag down a train that might bring help. Tragically, he was struck by the train and killed. He has haunted this stretch of tracks ever since.

Athens has also been plagued with tales of cults and strange rituals also. For many, these stories are simply a part of the Appalachian folklore of the area, but for others, these stories are terrifyingly real. During the 1970s, these stories became especially widespread, perhaps corresponding with what became known as the "Hocking Hill Murders." Over a span of about eight years, a number of animals in Hocking County were mutilated and then left to die in fields and farm lots. The crimes were never solved.

Athens' earliest weird tales involve the extraordinary "spirit room" of the Koons family. Jonathan Koons was a rough, self-educated farmer who became fascinated with the Spiritualist movement in the early 1850s. In 1852, he began receiving word from the spirits that he should build a spirit room, where ghosts manifested for more than six years – and were witnessed by hundreds of people. The reported events remain unexplained to this day.

There are also many haunted locations reported at Ohio University. One of them, Wilson Hall, is said to rest in the very center of one of Athens' most enduring legends. The building apparently falls in the middle of a huge pentagram that is made up by five of the area's cemeteries. The graveyards are located in the Peach Ridge area and, allegedly, when the positions of each are plotted on a map, they actually do form the shape of a pentagram, the occult symbol of magic and power. The stories say that an Ohio University student once computed the actual distances to create the pentagram and found that the distance of the side actually matched up to within less than one-quarter mile of each other. Could this be why the area seems to have attracted so many tales of the unknown?

Who can say? But can we be surprised by the fact that the old asylum located here boasts so many ghostly tales of its own?

18. A SCALPEL
TOPEKA STATE HOSPITAL

In yet another instance of "beginning with good intentions," the Topeka Insane Asylum (which was called the Topeka State Hospital by 1901) opened in 1879 as a haven for the mentally ill near the state capital of Kansas. At times in its history, the hospital was known for being a leader in the treatment of the insane and at other times, it was a "chamber of horrors." There were terrible stories told in the early 1900s about patients being abused, neglected, and even raped. Some said that having the inmates working in the large garden areas was therapeutic for them; others said they were used as slave labor to keep the hospital's food costs down.

But perhaps most notoriously was the reputation that the hospital gained when a 1913 law was passed that allowed the forced sterilization of "habitual criminals, idiots, epileptics, imbeciles, and insane." The Topeka State Hospital began carrying out such surgeries on a regular basis.

By the 1940s, the hospital was infamous in the state. The conditions had deteriorated to such a point that the place was unfit for occupancy. Many suffered and even died, and while the hospital is gone now, the horrors and tales of hauntings remain.

"A Quiet and Harmless Character"

After conditions became overcrowded at the Osawatomie State Hospital in 1875, the Kansas State Legislature appropriated $25,000 "for the purpose of building an asylum for the insane at some convenient and healthy spot within two miles of the state capitol building in the city of Topeka." The only condition of the appropriation was that the land on which the asylum rested had to be acquired at no cost to the state. The city of Topeka and surrounding Shawnee County each contributed $6,000 to purchase the original parcel of land on which the hospital was built.

Four years later, the first two ward buildings opened to accommodate 135 patients. The first superintendent at the Topeka asylum was Dr. Barnard Douglass Eastman, who had previously been the administrator of an asylum in Worcester, Massachusetts. Being of the Kirkbride philosophy, Eastman had grand designs for the hospital. During the initial call for funding, he told legislators that he planned to cure as many of his charges as possible, and patients who were released to make room for new inmates would be worthwhile members of society and "of a quiet and harmless character."

He described the treatment process this way: "Removal from the worriment, the overwork, the unsanitary conditions and the unsuitable food of many homes ... occupying body and mind in the new employment, cheering the drooping and melancholy and soothing the excited and irritable, are some of the elements of treatment of the greatest value, sometimes working rapid cures with but little medication."

Like most asylums of the era, patients worked around the asylum during the day. They built new buildings, cooked, tended the fields, worked with the livestock, worked in the laundry, cooked, and sewed. The tasks truly were meant to be therapeutic for the patients, giving them a purpose and a series of jobs to occupy their troubled minds. It also helped the hospital to be self-sufficient, which pleased both the administrators and state officials who oversaw the asylum's funding. Not surprisingly, though, the plan also had its critics, who only saw the "lunatics" being used for "slave labor" in the fields.

But Dr. Eastman was truly an advocate for those in his care. In those days, Kansas patients were admitted to the asylum only by court order. Eastman objected to such demeaning insanity trials, saying "The insane are sick, not criminal." But the policy didn't change until 1919, long after Dr. Eastman was gone. It was not until that time that the legislature allowed for shell-shocked veterans of World War I to be treated at the hospital without the indignity of an insanity trial.

Dr. Eastman remained at the hospital until 1896, when he left to go into private practice. He passed away in 1909, and sadly, was unable to help the patients he had left behind when conditions at the hospital became deplorable.

Rumors had started to spread that the hospital had turned into a "snake pit" in the wake of Dr. Eastman's departure. According to the stories, patients were being abused, beaten, chained to walls, strapped into straitjackets for days at a time, neglected, and even raped. The *Topeka State Journal* sent a reporter into the hospital who wrote a scathing article about what he found. He told of seeing patients sitting in rocking chairs in the hallways all day long with no opportunity for other activity, and most gruesome, a patient who had been confined in leather straps for so long that his skin was growing around the straps.

And things would soon get worse.

In 1913, the Kansas legislature passed the first sterilization law in the state. The law was directed at "habitual criminals, idiots, epileptics, imbeciles, and insane." Over the course of the next few years, at least 54 forced sterilizations took place in the state. Because there was still a great deal of doubt and uncertainty regarding the laws, sterilizations occurred at a relatively slow rate up until 1921. However, with the passage of new laws and a new widespread acceptance, sterilizations began to increase rapidly until 1950. The operations went on for the next decade, when they ceased altogether in 1961.

But in the early days, almost every single forced sterilization in Kansas took place at the Topeka State Hospital.

"Thinning the Herd"

It seems like something that could only happen in Nazi Germany, but that's not the case. In fact, forced sterilization was, before World War II, more popular in the United States than in any other country in the world. It's something that is rarely talked about today – a largely forgotten secret that most would rather have forgotten altogether – but a very harsh look at a very different time in our country.

The United States was the first country to concertedly undertake compulsory sterilization programs for the purpose of eugenics – the belief and practice aimed at improving the genetic quality of the human population. It was a social philosophy advocating the improvement of human genetic traits through the promotion of higher reproduction of people with desired traits and reduced reproduction of people with less-desired or undesired traits.

The idea of eugenics to produce better human beings had been around since ancient times but the idea of using it to decrease the birth of inferior people began in the nineteenth century, when some scientists began advocating the castration of the insane. Eugenics became an academic discipline at many colleges and universities, and received funding from many sources. It really didn't start to decline in popularity until the 1930s, a time when Nazi Germany began using eugenics as a justification for its racial policy of pursuing a pure "Nordic race" or "Aryan" genetic pool and the eventual elimination of "less fit" races. Adolf Hitler praised and incorporated eugenic ideas in his book, *Mein Kampf*, and emulated eugenic legislation for the sterilization of "defectives" that had been pioneered in the United States.

As a social movement, eugenics reached its greatest popularity in the early decades of the twentieth century. The principal targets of the American program were the intellectually disabled and the mentally ill, but also targeted under many state laws were the deaf, the blind, people with epilepsy, and the physically deformed. Some sterilizations took place in prisons, targeting criminals, but they were in the relative minority. Most of those who were forcibly sterilized where the mentally disabled and mentally ill, who, as wards of the state, had little say in what happened to them. In just that same way that scores of lobotomies would be ordered in mental hospitals in the 1940s, over 65,000 Americans were sterilized in 33 states under state compulsory sterilization programs.

The first state to introduce a compulsory sterilization bill was Michigan in 1897, but the proposed law failed to garner enough votes by legislators to be adopted. Eight years later, Pennsylvania's state legislators passed a sterilization bill that was vetoed by the governor. Indiana became the first state to enact sterilization legislation in 1907, followed by both California and Washington in 1909. As mentioned, Kansas adopted a sterilization law in 1913. However, sterilization rates across the country were relatively low until the 1927 Supreme Court case *Buck v. Bell*, which legitimized the forced sterilization of patients at a Virginia home for the intellectually disabled. In the wake of that later decision, over 62,000 people in the United States, most of them women, were sterilized in service of a nationwide eugenics movement. The number of sterilizations performed each year increased until another Supreme Court case, *Skinner v. Oklahoma*, took place in 1942. This case complicated the legal situation by ruling against sterilization of criminals if the equal protection clause of the constitution was violated. In other words, if you could castrate some criminals, then you could castrate them all – including white-collar criminals.

Most sterilization laws could be divided into three main categories of motivations: eugenic (concerned with heredity), therapeutic (based on the idea that sterilization could cure one of sexual traits such as masturbation or pedophilia), or punitive (as a punishment for criminals). The Oklahoma case ruled specifically

266

against punitive sterilization, which put all of it into question. Most sterilizations had not occurred in prisons, though. Most were performed under eugenic statutes in state-run psychiatric hospitals and homes for the mentally disabled. It was better, many people thought, that such people not be allowed to procreate.

After World War II, public opinion towards eugenics and sterilization programs became more negative as the genocidal policies of Nazi Germany finally became public. Even so, sterilizations continued in a few states and Puerto Rico into the 1970s. Some states continued to have sterilization laws on the books for much longer after that, though they were rarely, if ever, used. In recent years, the governors of many states have made public apologies for their past programs, beginning with Virginia and followed by Oregon and California. Few have offered to compensate those sterilized, however, citing that few are likely still living (and would of course have no affected offspring) and that inadequate records remain by which to verify them.

It seems a poor excuse for correcting a terrible policy that should have never been allowed to exist in the first place. The story of the Topeka State Hospital – and so many others just like it – remains a shameful part of our history that we are forced to remember so that nothing like it ever happens again.

From Bad to Worse

By the middle part of the twentieth century, mental hospitals across America were suffering. Budget cuts by both state and federal governments had created a shortage of psychiatrists, doctors, nurses, and support staff. With more and more patients being housed in states facilities, the institutions were becoming seriously overcrowded, and an alarm rose in 1948 about the deplorable conditions at Topeka State Hospital.

Legal commitment papers couldn't be found for some of the patients, and others couldn't even be accurately identified. Many patients still were being admitted as a result of the legal process and weren't having their actual mental conditions evaluated by hospital officials at all. There were simply not enough staff members to care for everyone. Patients were left in rocking chairs, endlessly moving back and forth, every single day. There were reports that inmates were sometimes kept chained and nude for months or even years.

In response, Governor Frank Carlson appointed a five-member panel to study the situation. After the committee released its report in October 1948, the legislature was so shocked that they doubled the appropriations for mental hospitals across the state. Changes were implemented, staff was hired, and Topeka State Hospital was turned into a training center for psychiatric personnel. More changes followed.

Incidents of patient mistreatment were investigated and the practice of placing patients in rocking chairs during the daytime was discontinued. Psychiatrists from the Menninger Foundation volunteered some of their own time to examine patients, and Menninger psychologists helped organize a department of psychology at the hospital.

It took almost 40 years, but things were finally starting to turn around at Topeka State Hospital. In 1949, the first social worker was hired. She began the first discharge plans for patients who were deemed ready for release. Social workers and volunteers often had to acquaint patients with clothing, household appliances, and everyday objects that didn't exist when they were admitted. Outpatient treatment began in 1951, and in subsequent years, the professional staff was increased, including physicians and dentists to treat physical ailments. In 1951, a fully equipped operating room was created.

But this "golden era" was short-lived. Conditions began to deteriorate again around 1958 after a series of state funding cutbacks. Salaries at Topeka State Hospital simply couldn't compete with salaries offered elsewhere, and experienced staff members began leaving. Of course, around this same time, tranquilizing drugs began to be offered that could keep patients in even overcrowded facilities under control.

By 1968, Topeka State Hospital was once again lauded for its place in the forefront of the mental health industry, at least in terms of how best to run a hospital. An organization plan that was developed there, called "The Kansas Plan," began to be used as a model for organizing other institutions around the country. It included treatment, research, training, and consultation to the communities it served.

But once again, this period did not last. In 1988, the hospital lost its accreditation to receive federal Medicare and Medicaid payments. The Health Care Financing Administration determined that the State had omitted two patients from its inspection of care review at the hospital. The institution appealed the case and lost.

Things looked bad for Topeka State Hospital, but they were about to get worse.

Murder at Topeka State Hospital
In 1992, a young woman named Stephanie Uhlrig worked as a music and activity therapist in the general hospital population at Topeka State. One of the patients at the hospital was Kenneth D. Waddell, who had been placed in the custody of state mental health authorities after having been found not guilty by reason of insanity on aggravated battery charges. Waddell was initially confined at the Larned State Security Hospital, but on April 1, 1987, he was transferred to the Topeka State Hospital. He was placed in the Adult Forensic Ward (called the "AWL

Unit"), which was a special segregation unit for higher risk patients, many of whom were violent. The unit was closed in 1992 and some of the inmates were sent to Larned, which was a more secure facility, but Waddell was put on another unit, where he sexually assaulted a female patient. He was then moved to a different unit and quickly earned full privileges, despite protests from the staff of the previous unit.

On February 23, 1992, Uhlrig and another therapist took Waddell and other patients off grounds to see *The Addams Family* at a local movie theater. After returning to the hospital and dropping off the other patients, Uhlrig was returning Waddell to his unit when he went into the building to go to the bathroom. After Waddell failed to come out, Uhlrig went in to check on him. Her body later was found leaning on a toilet in the men's bathroom, her shirt and bra lying on the floor next to her. She had been brutally strangled.

The Uhlrig family sued the state and lost their lawsuit. The state contended that Uhlrig had been told about Waddell's sexually violent tendencies, but her family said that she would never be able to say whether she had known or not. They appealed and lost again. The United States Court of Appeals, Tenth Circuit, decided on Aug. 30, 1995 that "While Uhlrig's murder was undeniably tragic, it was not the result of reckless and 'conscience shocking' conduct by the state mental health administrators."

The family's attorney, former state senator Wint Winter, Jr., stated that he did not believe Stephanie had any idea of just how dangerous Waddell was. He told reporters: "There were two failures. He probably should have been sent back to Larned based on his past, and there was no warning to patients and staff. They put a shark in the minnow tank, if you will. I'm not saying they should have stamped something on his forehead and put him in an orange jumpsuit, but they didn't even tag his file. Stephanie just didn't have a clue."

Many, including Winter, believed that the murder was not really a surprise. It occurred at a time when the hospital was under a tight budget and scrambling to deal with federal regulations and certification issues. Topeka State Hospital staff members said in court that supervisors had consistently told them not to talk to the accreditation officials about staffing shortages.

After the murder, the hospital hired additional temporary security staff, who worked for several months and then were dismissed. It was a temporary fix, much like the cosmetic fixes in the form of improved lighting and new locks. After the next legislative session, the hospital spent $116, 812.52 that politicians allocated for improved security. Some staff, however, later complained that only $149.75 was spent directly on staff safety, in the form of personal alarms, putting only four or five alarms on each unit. The rest was spent on gadgets for security guards -- two-way radios, body armor, nightstick rings, police-size Mace, sirens, spotlights, and baton carriers.

Most felt that the hospital should have learned a lesson from Stephanie's murder, but nothing really changed. In fact, if anything, things got worse.

Conditions at the hospital deteriorated even further in 1995 when, in response to staffing shortages, walls were torn down to combine four adolescent units (one male, one female, and two coed) into one large coed unit. After that, there were two full-scale patient riots, and Topeka police had to be called in with shields, tear gas, and police dogs. One patient punched a nurse and broke her nose, and another patient stabbed a nurse with a ballpoint pen, aiming for the jugular vein. Some nurses were afraid and would huddle near the nurses' station. The staff received special training in holds and verbal techniques to calm violent patients – but such training was useless against attacks. There was no question that things were becoming increasingly violent and there was little protection for the staff members. The end was definitely in sight.

The final days came in 1997. By that time, the mental health establishment was moving away from the hospital model and toward community-based programs. Partly because the community-based model appeared effective but mostly because it was cheaper, the Kansas Legislature decided to close one of its three mental hospitals. Topeka State Hospital was chosen for closing and was shuttered on May 17, 1997.

The buildings remained abandoned for a number of years and drew the attention of urban explorers and vandals. In 2010, the historic main building, along with several others, were torn down. A public park now stands at the site – although the stories remain.

Hauntings at Topeka State Hospital

During the years of abandonment, the hospital attracted more than its share of curiosity-seekers. Some came looking for thrills, others for history, some to cause trouble, and others to look for ghosts. The long and morbid history of the asylum seemed ripe for hauntings. Ghost hunters came seeking specters and they often found them.

Figures were seen looking out the windows. Lights were spotted behind the glass by security guards who found the forlorn structure to be free of living persons. Cries echoed in empty rooms and whispers were heard in crumbling corridors. Investigators who brought along equipment for tracking down evidence of the spirits recorded voices and strange sounds that could not be heard until the

270

recordings were played back. A few curiosity-seekers reported being so unnerved by the recordings that found their way onto their tapes that they never returned to the hospital again.

Even after the hospital buildings were torn down, weird stories have continued to be told. Visitors who come to the park today report seeing shadowy apparitions, experiencing cold chills that cannot be explained, and hearing the sound of an old, scratchy record playing at the same spot where the main building once stood.

Patient abuse, death, torture, rape, and even murder – these incidents alone would be enough to spark tales of ghosts and hauntings on the property, but the existence of almost three acres of unmarked graves in the cemetery on the grounds certainly added to the site's dark attraction.

The almost entirely unmarked cemetery occupies a plot on the northeast corner of the hospital's grounds and holds the bodies of patients that were buried there – unknown, alone, and abandoned – during 75 years of the asylum's operations. No signs, stonework, paths, or roads mark the area as a cemetery. Of the 1,157 graves there, only 16 have headstones. In 2000, the Kansas legislature authorized construction of a memorial for the people buried there, which included an inscription of the names of the dead who were known. Aside from that, there is no memory that remains of the broken souls interred at the site – except for the ghosts, of course.

The hospital cemetery remains a compelling draw for those with an interest in the asylum's hauntings. There have been many tales told of encounters in this sad and forbidding field – vanishing apparitions, blurry figures that fade away, cold spots, the sensation of chilly hands on skin, and more.

With only the old graveyard remaining from the hospital that once was, it seems that the dead are eager for the living to remember them in any way that they can.

19. A COLLECTION OF NAILS, PINS AND BUTTONS
STATE LUNATIC ASYLUM NO. 2

There is a glass case that is on display at the Glore Psychiatric Museum in St. Joseph, Missouri – once home to the State Lunatic Asylum No. 2 – that contains 1,446 objects that were removed from a patient's stomach at the hospital in 1929. No matter how closely watched by the staff, the woman swallowed nuts, bolts, screws, thimbles, safety pins, buttons, nails, and just about anything within reach. The objects didn't kill her -- but the operation to remove them did.

Her story is just one of the many tales that haunt the history of the former asylum that was designed to offer a place of safety and calm in the grand tradition of Thomas Kirkbride. But as we have discovered with so many of the other asylums within these pages, the road to Hell is often paved with good intentions. For many patients at the asylum, they found a different kind of hell than the abuse suffered in other places: an unending boredom. Patients were given nothing to do, nothing to stimulate their minds, and so they sat in rocking chairs all day, rocking and staring into the distance, their minds slipping away a little bit more with each passing day, month, and year.

Today, the psychiatric museum offers a glimpse into both the groundbreaking and the barbaric movements in America's history of treating mental illness. It is home to fascinating displays, historic relics, and chilling tales about the search for a cure for "minds diseased."

It is also home to a number of ghosts – the patients of yesterday who remain in the only home that they ever really knew.

State Lunatic Asylum No. 2

The lunatic asylum in St. Joseph, Missouri, opened its doors on November 9, 1874. The first superintendent, Dr. George Catlett, had been a medical purveyor for the Confederate military during the Civil War and had gained great experience in overseeing the treatment of soldiers, managing hospital staff, and maintaining supplies. He was well-qualified for his role – likely better than most superintendents in the still growing field of mental institutions – and stepped into it with the greatest of intentions. He wrote:

Taking it from a mere name, bare walls, untenanted and unfurnished halls into a systematically arranged operating institution prepared to take its position in the benign firmament with its sister associates, and to be consecrated for all time to the noble work of reviving hope in the human heart, and dispelling the portentous clouds that envelop and penetrate the intellects of minds diseased.

The asylum in St. Joseph was constructed and designed according to the Kirkbride Plan. It was built on large grounds to provide a safe haven for patients and designed in a grand, Victorian style, with staggered wings to allow sunlight into all areas of the building. It was a design, it was believed, which would offer a cure for mental illness.

The first Kirkbride hospital in Missouri was the State Lunatic Asylum in Fulton, which opened in 1851. It was the first asylum built west of the Mississippi River. The State Lunatic Asylum No. 2 in St. Joseph was the second. Although originally intended to hold 275 patients in 32 dormitories and 76 individual rooms, the new hospital was already overcrowded within its first two years. A new wing was soon needed to cope with the influx of the mentally ill, and in 1874 and 1875, the Missouri legislature appropriated funds for construction, as well as for furniture, tableware, water tanks, and surgical instruments.

Like other asylums of the day, the hospital was intended to be self-sufficient. Patients who were able worked in the fields, tended the livestock, cooked, sewed, did laundry work, and other menial tasks. When family members and state officials came to the asylum, they would see patients walking the grounds, playing board games, and even going to dances on Saturday nights. Swings, croquet sets, and gymnastic equipment offered both entertainment and ample opportunity for fresh air and sunshine.

But that was what everyone saw on the surface. While many of the patients were able to live fairly normal lives at the asylum, there were those who were simply too violent to co-exist with the others. They were locked away and restrained, far away from the eyes of officials. While Dr. Catlett did not approve of the cages and chains that had been used by many of his predecessors in the field, he had little choice but to protect society and the other patients from those that "moral treatment" was unable to heal.

On January 25, 1879, the east wing of the asylum caught fire. The staff worked furiously for more than an hour but when Dr. Catlett realized that the cause was lost, he instructed staff members to abandon their efforts and evacuate the patients. Some of them had already fled the burning building, while others, according to newspaper accounts, "were afflicted with the most violent type of insanity, and stubbornly refused to be removed." Regardless of the struggle, the staff managed to get everyone out of the building and no one was killed in the blaze.

Patients who could be managed were sent home, while others went to the Buchanan County Poor Farm. Violent patients, as well as those who needed continuous care by nursing staff, were housed at the Buchanan County Courthouse for a time.

Three months later, construction began on a new building that was just east of the burned shell of the original hospital. Soon, 65 male patients were being housed in the new structure and a house was rented on adjoining grounds for 55 female patients who had been displaced by the fire. In 1880, the new hospital was completed. It was much grander and could hold one-third more patients. It was also equipped with two 5,000 gallon water tanks to protect it from fire. It also included more amenities for entertainment, still keeping with the Kirkbride Plan of designing asylums to look like summer resorts for the wealthy. The new facilities included a gym, bowling alley, and a billiards room.

The farming operations at the asylum were expanded to increase the level of its self-sufficiency. The asylum grounds were extensive and field crops, like wheat and soybeans, as well as apples and walnuts, were grown and harvested by inmate labor. There were barns for horses and a prize-winning dairy herd. A slaughterhouse was constructed near the cattle and hog pens. A poultry house was also added, built from leftover construction supplies. There was little that had to be purchased from nearby St. Joseph, aside from salt, which was used primarily as a preservation agent until an icehouse was built on the grounds to store ice that was cut in the winter from the Missouri River. A greenhouse was added to the engine room, where steam kept it heated all year around and plants were grown for the wards and halls.

A constant source of frustration for hospital officials, though, remained overcrowding. Families who couldn't – or refused to – care for their mentally ill relatives, simply dropped them off on the doorstep of the asylum, and allowed them to become wards of the state. Dr. Catlett was constantly working to try and secure additional funds for the asylum and his efforts were rewarded in the mid-1880s after the patient population had doubled to over 550. Additions were added to the existing buildings just before Dr. Catlett's death on May 19, 1886.

The asylum's Board of Managers appointed Dr. R.E. Smith to succeed Catlett as superintendent. He served for four years. During that time, the first telephone lines were installed at the hospital. In 1887, a pathology lab was opened to better diagnose and treat the physical diseases that often afflicted the inmates.

In 1890, Dr. Charles Woodson was appointed as the new superintendent and brought a number of reforms to the asylum. Central to his philosophy was the new concept that patients with contagious diseases should be kept isolated from the rest of the hospital. As a result, he ordered the construction of a detached hospital building, which could hold 120 patients. Typhoid was a serious problem at the time and an outbreak in 1893 put the building into immediate use. He also dealt with issues with the local population. A ravine just west of the Administration Building contained raw sewage from the hospital, which was not only making patients sick, but was the source of protests from neighbors who complained about the stench and threatened to sue the asylum if the situation was not resolved. Gaining the right-of-way for a sewer system took months of paperwork and bureaucratic wrangling, but eventually the legislature approved the funds for a sewer that would carry waste from the hospital to the Missouri River.

In 1897, Dr. Woodson also ordered the construction of a power plant. Before that, the day halls were lit with gas fixtures and at night, nurses and orderlies had to carry kerosene lamps to complete their regular duties. Toilet rooms were not lit at all, requiring the use of chamber pots at night. Electricity became one of the most major changes in the asylum's history.

Therapy methods also changes during Dr. Woodson's tenure. One of the most commonly used treatments was hydrotherapy, where water was used to calm patients. When a new building was constructed to house female patients, a pipe with small holes was installed around the front porch. In warm weather, the staff ran water through the pipes, which produced the effect of gentle rain to soothe the inmates.

As methods of treating mental illness began to change in the early years of the twentieth century, more and more institutions began to move away from the use of confinement and restraint. Training programs for nurses improved and gave the staff a better understanding of how to handle patients. This training allowed for the removal of locks from the rooms, which gave the patients greater freedom.

The new philosophies also brought a change to the name of the institution. It shed the words "Lunatic Asylum" and simply became "State Hospital No. 2," a response to the negative connotations that had become associated with terms that were once commonly used.

In 1907, Dr. Woodson left the hospital to open his own sanitarium in South St. Joseph. The new superintendent, Dr. W.F. Kuhn, created a program that emphasized physical vitality, a popular movement of the early 1900s. All patients were required to walk at least one mile each day, while healthy men walked three miles each day. It was also under the administration of Dr. Kuhn that the new and "scandalous" practice of allowing female nurses and attendants to work in the male wards began. It was started on a trial basis, but was so successful that it quickly became permanent – male patients turned out to be cleaner and better behaved in the presence of women.

Dr. Kuhn also instituted a "non-restraint policy," where calming techniques were used rather than force. He also continued the idea of giving the patients work tasks as part of their therapy, which allowed the hospital to take even greater steps to become self-sufficient. A morgue was built, eliminating the need to take the dead into town. Other efforts involved massive expansions to the farm. More land was purchased and leased, and barns for the cattle and two more poultry houses were built. Dr. Kuhn's successors continued this policy of "work therapy" and patients were given consistent duties to support the hospital. Some patients even made products, including furniture and textiles, which were sold in the community. Money raised from these sales went to purchase materials and supplies and to raise money for operations.

And that money was desperately needed. As always, overcrowding was a major problem for the hospital. Superintendent Dr. George Thompson wrote in his 1914 report, "Every ward in the institution is filled to full capacity, and many beds are placed in hallways and day rooms throughout the institution."

By 1919, State Hospital No. 2 was the largest psychiatric hospital in Missouri. New buildings continued to be added and older ones were renovated in an attempt to keep up with demand. In the 1920s, a dental clinic was opened so that patients no longer had to be taken into town for treatment. A medical, surgical, and psychological reference library was added, making it possible for the hospital to open a school for nurses. In 1923, a surgical building was added, which is now used as the Glore Psychiatric Museum.

The hospital continued to expand during the Depression years with most of the work being carried out thanks to the Works Progress Administration (WPA). New streets and sidewalks were added throughout the hospital grounds and in 1934, the new Woodson Building, named for Dr. Charles Woodson, was opened as a clinic and receiving unit for the entire hospital. A new infirmary provided beds for 476 physically ill patients.

When the United States entered World War II in 1941, many of the staff, including Superintendent Dr. Orr Mullinax, joined the military. The resulting shortage of staff members proved difficult to handle, so the hospital enlisted the help of the Red Cross Gray Ladies, who provided invaluable assistance to the mental health field. These young women provided not only medical services, but were beloved by the patients. State Hospital No. 2 was the first psychiatric institution to use the Gray Ladies and while they were a great addition to the hospital, the staff shortage could not be entirely resolved by the use of volunteers. There was a high turnover rate for the regular staff, which made training new employees difficult. The hospital found itself forced to hire those who were "not eligible for the service or capable of working in one of the wartime industries." Needless to say, they were not the most desirable of employees and it was almost impossible to find male nurses who were physically fit enough to work with patients on the overcrowded wards.

And things got worse when the war ended. After World War II, the hospital began admitting an increasing number of soldiers in need of psychiatric treatment. It soon reached its peak population of 2,485 patients – 10 times the number of inmates the hospital was originally opened to serve.

In response to the overcrowding and the difficulty of handling so many disturbed patients, a new treatment was introduced at State Hospital No. 2 on July 8, 1949, by visiting physician Dr. Walter Freeman. Doctors from the state hospitals at Fulton, Nevada, and St. Joseph observed as Freeman performed his icepick lobotomy on 10 patients in just three hours. It was reported by the *St. Joseph Gazette* that "the effects of the operation would be followed closely by the staff. If successful, the institution would undertake a program of neurosurgery. Such a program would mean that many patients could be dismissed from the hospital to return to their communities and lead normal lives."

Dr. Mary France Robinson, a clinical psychologist who taught at St. Joseph Junior College from 1925 to 1958 and volunteered at State Hospital No. 2, took responsibility for monitoring the lobotomized patients after their surgeries. While

277

she initially hoped that lobotomies would be a new cure for some forms of mental illness, her research soon showed what other doctors would also discover in the years to come – that it was a treatment method that was doing more harm than good. After spending a year with Freeman in New York, observing patients before and after they were lobotomized, she determined that they were "unable to connect with their past, present, or future in a meaningful way." Lobotomies, she came to realize, were not the saving grace for the mentally ill.

With advancements in psychology in the 1940s, more advancements were added when Dr. Willis McCann became the first director of psychology in 1949. During his 35 years at the hospital, he put together a new form of group "round table" therapy, where patients worked together and were involved in the decision of whether another inmate would be discharged. Even more important was Dr. McCann's extensive study on the psychiatric aspects of delinquency and crime. He pushed for a more reliable method to determine responsibility for criminal actions and to provide a greater clarification of what it meant to be a psychopath, stating that those who were truly mentally ill needed hospitalization, not imprisonment.

By the 1950s, new regulations began to appear that ended the farm labor and work tasks that had been part of the hospital's patient regime for decades. With little to do, the patients were left on the grounds to wander about or in the wards, where televisions had been installed. The whitewashed version of the "advancement" was that it had a "calming effect" on the patients. Now, far too many of them simply sat in rocking chairs all day while the television droned on. There were some real advancements made during this era, however, like air conditioning, a new cafeteria, an eight-hour work day for staff to attract better and more qualified people, and an agreement with the University of Kansas City to allow graduate students to assist with psychotherapy at the hospital. Services continued to develop with the addition of music therapy and a chaplain, who attended to the patient's spiritual needs. The hospital also began developing new treatments in the form of tranquilizing drugs, many of which were now available for the first time. This enabled the almost complete removal of physical restraints from the hospital, but it had negative effects as well. Much like the television sets and rocking chairs, the new drugs numbed many of the patients into a semblance of what they once were. But for others, it had a stunning effect, allowing scores of them to be released to live in the community.

In 1952, the name of the institution was changed once again, this time to St. Joseph Hospital. It was around this time when a young professional came to work in the state's psychiatric program, and who would later become a director of the hospital. His name was Dr. George Glore and he would later open his collection of historical artifacts pertaining to the study of mental health to other professionals and the public.

The 1960s brought more changes. The hospital hosted its first open house to raise community awareness and this resulted in an influx of new volunteers. In 1966, Dr. Liam O'Brien was appointed as the new superintendent. During his tenure, he began the first steps in moving patients into home and family care environments. Patients were allowed to receive education and work at jobs outside of the hospital and take classes to learn social skills. The farming operation on the property officially ended in 1969, and the land was changed into recreational areas for the patients and staff.

The End of the Asylum and the Start of the Hauntings

After nearly 100 years, there were fewer and fewer long-term patients being treated at the hospital. The wards were starting to empty out and for the first time in the hospital's history, it was no longer overcrowded.

It was during this time when the hospital began to gain a reputation for being haunted. Staff members reported seeing images out of the corner of their eye -- flicking images that were there one moment and gone the next. Nurses spoke of feeling as though they were being watched. Orderlies told stories of humming and singing in empty rooms. Convinced that a patient had wandered away from their room, the staff members were stunned to find no one was present. One patient in particular was known for her interaction with the spirits. She would often write poems and songs and create artwork about the ghosts that she encountered in the building. Merely the trick of a damaged mind? Perhaps, or perhaps not.

By the early 1990s, the population of the hospital had declined to the point that the grand but aging old building was no longer needed. A decision was made to construct a new, downsized and modern facility across the street from the old hospital. Ground was broken that year, and formally opened in 1997 under the name of Northwest Missouri Psychiatric Rehabilitation Center.

A new use for the St. Joseph State Hospital came about due to a natural disaster. A major flood of the Missouri River in 1993 destroyed the Renz Correctional Farm near Jefferson City. Approximately 150 inmates from the farm were brought to the former hospital. It was supposed to be a temporary arrangement, but the correctional farm never reopened and so the former building, which housed the museum and Dr. Glore's museum, was taken over by the Missouri Department of Corrections and turned into the Western Reception Diagnostic and Correctional Center. Today, it holds slightly under 600 criminal offenders who are in treatment for substance abuse.

The Glore Psychiatric Museum was moved into another building at the site. Its current home was built in the 1960s and served as both an admitting building and health clinic for hospital patients. It was also where the hospital morgue and autopsy rooms were housed. For whatever reason, it appears as if the haunting activity associated with the original hospital followed the museum to its new location. The Missouri Department of Corrections reports no activity in their occupied space, but the museum, as well as the rest of the building, is a source of constant encounters with the supernatural.

Dr. Glore, who remained curator of the museum until his retirement in 1996 and remained involved until his death in 2010, claimed to witness a number of strange events during his time at the museum. He could never explain what it was that people were often witnessing inside the hospital's walls.

The museum is still open today and operates under the St. Joseph Museum, Inc. network. It's been called one of the "Top 50 Most Unique Museums" in the country and offers a variety of mental health treatments from over the years and – according to numerous witnesses – a number of ghosts.

Pages and pages have been devoted to the myriad of happenings that have been reported in the museum and the old medical-surgical building where it is housed. Visitors who come both in the daytime and at night have had brushes with the unknown. While the morgue area in the basement is rumored to be the most haunted spot, the rest of the building is active too. The apparition of a man has been reported near the elevators, running and screaming. A woman is heard whispering. Moaning sounds are common, as are feelings of not being alone and hearing your own name calling by a disembodied voice.

Perhaps the most frequently reported phenomenon is hearing footsteps following you down the otherwise silent hallways. I experienced this myself during one of my visits to the museum. I was visiting with a small group and was able to explore the museum at night. I had walked away from everyone else and started toward a section of the building that was devoted to medicine in the Civil War. As I walked down the dark corridor, I heard the sharp tap of what sounded like hard-soled shoes following me in the shadows. I glanced back over my shoulder to see who was there and the hall behind me was empty. As I stopped abruptly, the sound continued, passed me, and continued into the darkness in the direction that I had been walking.

I turned around and went back the other way.

During this same visit, my friend and company manager, Lisa Taylor Horton, and friends Becky Ray and Christina Anderson, heard the sound of someone talking behind one of the closed doors in the museum. Not wanting to interrupt anyone

280

who might be inside looking for ghostly activity, they walked a little further down the hall. A few minutes later, the voices stopped, but no one came out of the room. Curious, Lisa walked back and slowly opened the door to see who was inside. The room was empty.

Becky had experienced something similar during an earlier visit to the museum. She was on the third floor with some other visitors and heard a knocking sound. She explained, "While it may have been coincidence, the knocking corresponded with not only our requests for knocks, but how many knocks. We tracked the source of the sound down to a door that was locked. At this point we all took turns listening at the door and several of us heard what sounded like a child's voice coming from the other side."

Convinced that there had to be some logical explanation, she retrieved a museum staff member to open the room for her and she was stunned to find an empty office – and nothing that could have explained the knocking sounds.

The former St. Joseph Lunatic Asylum – and now the Glore Psychiatric Museum – remains one of the most fascinating and eerie locations in these pages. Unlike so many other asylums of the past where brutality, abuse, and horror were common, the St. Joseph hospital only suffered from the failures of misguided treatments, overcrowding, and a changing world. It managed, for the most part, to remain a place of hope for the inmates who found themselves within its walls.

And perhaps this is the reason why, after so many years, so many of them simply refuse to leave.

20. THE GRAVE OF "M. BOOKBINDER"
PEORIA STATE HOSPITAL

A few miles outside of the city of Peoria, Illinois, on a bluff that overlooks the Illinois River, are the crumbling remains of the Bowen Building, the administration building of the Peoria State Hospital. It was a place that was built with the best of intentions and part of an asylum filled with hope when the first patients arrived in 1902. By the time that it closed its doors in 1973, though, it had become a relic of the past and a sad reminder of the unrealized dreams of many of the people who had founded it more than 70 years before.

Before 1907, the people of the Peoria area took great pride in what was then called the "Illinois Asylum for the Incurable Insane at Bartonville." Their feelings did not changed when the name was altered to the "Illinois General Hospital for the Insane" or, finally, the "Peoria State Hospital" in 1909.

Early in its history, and throughout most of its years of operation, the hospital and adjacent grounds were almost park-like in appearance. This is a far different scene than what can be found there today. For many years, the few original buildings that remained after 1973 were decrepit and badly in need of repair. Those who visited the site were drawn to the large, looming structure, but always with a sense of unease. Today, the Bowen Building is almost all that remains of the Peoria State Hospital. There are a few others, but they are mostly unrecognizable from what they once were. The cottages and outbuildings have been destroyed and the grounds of the asylum on the hilltop have been filled with new buildings, industrial-type businesses, and garages.

For the most part, people don't come here today looking for the grand place that thousands of mentally ill men and women once called home – they come because of the ghosts. For well over a century, the Peoria State Hospital has almost become synonymous with ghost stories. It wouldn't be until the 1970s when the general public would start to hear stories of the abandoned building being haunted. Since that time, countless tales of encounters with the spirit world have swirled about the old asylum. Prior to that, dating back to the very early days of the institution, the Peoria State Hospital was known to be home to a very famous spirit.

He was called the "Bookbinder" when he was alive and after all of these years, his grave can be found in the oldest cemetery that is located on the hospital's former grounds. He only made one appearance, but it was a sensational one that was witnessed by several hundred people, including the superintendent of the hospital himself.

But there is much more to the story of the Peoria State Hospital than just ghosts – and more to the ghost story that haunts it than most people probably realize.

The Illinois Asylum for the Incurable Insane

The Peoria State Hospital (which was actually located in the small, nearby town of Bartonville but named for Peoria because it was the closest railroad station) got off to a rather inauspicious start. The original Kirkbride building that was built in 1896 had to be torn down just one year later after it was found to be collapsing into an abandoned coal mine. The asylum was started over from scratch and by that time, the Kirkbride Plan had started to fall out of favor and had been replaced by the "Cottage Plan," which involved a large administration building and a number of smaller buildings spread throughout the property. These cottages bore little resemblance to the harsh and foreboding look of the original building. When the first patients arrived in February 1902 (they would number 640 by April), they found a new, modern facility waiting for them – and a new way of thinking in regards to the treatment of mental health.

One doctor at the forefront of this new medicine was Dr. George A. Zeller, who was appointed as the first superintendent of the Peoria asylum in 1896, long before it had even been built. During the problems with construction, Dr. Zeller was serving with the military in the Philippines in the Spanish-American War. He did not return to Illinois until about eight months after the asylum opened, when he took over from Dr. H.B. Cariel, who had been acting superintendent in his absence. For Dr. Zeller, his arrival in Bartonville began his 36-year connection to the Peoria State Hospital.

Dr. Zeller's initial impression of the hospital was not a favorable one. He even expressed his dislike for the name, feeling that it hearkened back to mental illness treatment of the past. In time, he would see the name changed, but this was not what displeased him the most. He felt that this hospital had been created not to help the mentally ill people who were languishing in the poor houses across the state, as had been intended, but had been filled with problem inmates from other asylums. Of the 690 patients that he had when he started, Dr. Zeller found that not a single inmate had come from a poor house. He knew the horrors that were being experienced by those patients and wanted to do all that he could to help them. They would become the focus of some of his initial changes at the hospital.

Other changes were physical. While Dr. Zeller was away serving the military, the state had installed heavy iron gratings and bars on the windows and doors. He discovered this when he returned, along with the addition of rooms designed to be seclusion rooms, with heavy doors and peepholes so the staff could monitor those restrained inside. This had been common practice for many state hospitals of the era, but it was unacceptable to Dr. Zeller. He immediately started to implement drastic changes, starting with the removal of the bars and grates from the windows and doors of as many cottages as possible. At first, the bars were only removed from the dining rooms, and once success had been determined, then from doors and windows of other cottages. Dr. Zeller believed this would contribute to the bucolic, peaceful atmosphere that he was trying to maintain at the asylum, and he was right. By October 1905, the last of the bars and guards were removed from all of the buildings on the grounds.

Another of Dr. Zeller's programs involved the reduction and eventual banning of all forms of mechanical restraints. By June 1904, he wrote that all forms of straitjackets, chains, and shackles had fallen into disuse, except for rare cases with

284

the most violent inmates. He believed that such restraints were more for the convenience of the attendants, rather than for the good of the patient.

Dr. Zeller also instituted an eight-hour work day for the staff at the hospital, which was revolutionary at the time. He believed that employees who were forced to work longer than eight hours were, in many cases, too exhausted to properly care for their charges. He worked hard to get this into the hospital's budget and still make sure that all of the cottages were properly staffed. He solved that problem by having the hospital do a systematic reclassification of all of the patients. Once this was accomplished, Dr. Zeller was usually able to reduce the number of attendants needed in some cottages. The excess attendants were now able to not only supplement the cottages that contained violent and destructive patients, but to schedule more time off for all of the attendants.

Once the news of Dr. Zeller's innovations started to emerge, a great deal of attention was focused on him and the hospital – not all of it favorable. Many believed that he had gone too far. They could not fathom how he could manage a facility with 1,800 patients without any sort of restraints, no cells, and no places of seclusion and confinement. They were even more puzzled by the lack of bars and grates on the doors and windows. In fact, many of the wards and cottages were unlocked day and night. Some of Dr. Zeller's detractors were so alarmed that they voiced their concerns to his superiors in the state capital. According to Dr. Zeller, they had reported, "that a reign of terror existed in our neighborhood and that our paroled patients were committing all sorts of depredations."

As a result, and unknown to Dr. Zeller and the staff, an investigator was sent to the hospital by the State Board. After spending three days visiting various homes and interviewing people who lived in the area, the investigator found that there was no basis for the complaints. In fact, quite the opposite was found. He found that the community supported not only Dr. Zeller, but his new open-door policies as well. Due to the investigation, the board encouraged Dr. Zeller to not only continue what he had been doing, but to expand on it however he wanted.

But Dr. Zeller knew his days at the asylum were numbered. He had been appointed as the asylums superintendent in 1896 and his appointment, by his own admission, had been as the result of his political activities. In 1912, the general election saw the Republican Party's power and influence diminish both on a national and state level. As a result, Dr. Zeller was replaced as superintendent. He knew that no matter what he had accomplished at the hospital, politics would always get in the way. Dr. Zeller had been assured by many that his job was secure, but he knew otherwise, so he began lobbying for the position of state alienist. In those days, "alienist" was a term for a specialist in mental disease. He assumed the position on December 1, 1913, and was succeeded at Peoria State Hospital by Dr. Ralph T. Hinton.

The following year, Dr. Hinton began undoing many of the changes that Dr. Zeller had made over the last decade. His first order of business was to have the bars and restraints placed back on the wards and cottages. A zoo that Dr. Zeller had built for the patients using the metal bars that had once confined them in the buildings was shut down. Dr. Hinton remained as the superintendent until 1917, when he was replaced by Dr. Ralph Goodner.

It was during his tenure that the first staff member at the hospital died on the premises. She was a housekeeper named Anne M. Stuart, who had fallen ill while working. Soon after she was moved to her room, she slipped into a coma and died. Her death was never explained. And neither was the brutal beating of a patient in October 1903. Two attendants were accused of his murder, but they were never charged.

After his tenure as the state alienist, Dr. Zeller took over the position of superintendent at the state hospital in Alton, Illinois. He remained there for several years and then returned to Peoria State Hospital – although no one knew it right away. After hearing rumors of overall neglect and abuse at the asylum, he checked himself in as an inmate for three days, living on a different ward every night. He was so moved – and so sickened -- by his experience that he ordered all of the staff to serve an eight-hour shift as an inmate so they could see what the patients were forced to endure.

Once again, Dr. Zeller began implementing changes to the hospital. He reformed the nursing academy that had been allowed to fall apart during his absence, introduced new social services, and worked to bring the hospital back to its earlier standards. He was also active in social affairs in Peoria and bought the Jubilee College and grounds in 1933 and donated the grounds to the state of Illinois. His wife, Sophie, later donated the chapel. Dr. Zeller retired in 1935, and he and his wife continued to live in a home on the grounds of the Peoria State Hospital. He died on June 29, 1938, and his funeral was held at the hospital attended by friends, family, dignitaries, and former and current patients.

The End of an Era

After the death of Dr. Zeller, the hospital remained in use for many years, adding buildings, patients, and care facilities for children and tuberculosis patients. But not all of the advances that occurred in the modern era were positive ones, no matter how they might have seemed at the time. In October 1938, the hospital took a big step away from the hydrotherapy, color and music treatments that had been instituted by Dr. Zeller. It was in that month that the first Insulin Shock Therapies were introduced as "shock therapy." Lobotomies began being performed in the 1940s, and in September 1942, the first Electro Convulsive Therapy was introduced to treat epilepsy.

By the 1950s, the asylum's population had started to decline with the introduction of new drugs that could not only balance out the problems being experienced by many patients, but make them capable of leaving to live in the community again. In the 1960s, reform laws prevented patients from working at the institution, which led to increased budgets and patient idleness. The activities that had been given to these lost souls had given them a feeling of worth and usefulness, but that was now lost to them. They were left to wander about, likely wandering back and forth to the places where they had been working each day, only to be turned away from the tasks that made them feel useful.

By the 1960s, mental health treatment had changed from a pastoral community that cared for patients for decades to a quick turn-around, open-door treatment plan that fed the patients drugs and put them back out onto the street again. In 1965, the population of the Peoria State Hospital was at 2,300, and by the time it closed in 1973, there were only 280 remaining. Only five of the buildings were in use.

The final years of the hospital seem to have been a time of chaos and neglect. In 1967, a nurse was killed by one of the patients. He struck her in the head with a steel bar from a garbage can lid. In June 1972, patient Bernard Roe was struck in the head with a chair while standing in the line for lunch. He collapsed in the dining hall, did not receive treatment until the following day, and died a short time later. A few days later, another patient, Jerome Spence, was beaten to death by a fellow inmate. In August 1972, James Logan died from an untreated ear infection, which turned into spinal meningitis.

When the hospital finally closed down, it was in deplorable condition. A report from the Illinois Investigating Commission on December 18, 1973, told of the shocking condition of the buildings and the last remaining patients. The buildings were filthy and falling apart, crumbling into a state of decay and disrepair. The odor of urine and filth filled the air. Blood and excrement had been smeared on the walls. The patients wandered the halls, naked, or in torn and soiled clothing. Most of them were filthy and had open sores and untreated physical illnesses. The heavy use of narcotics kept them in a constant stupor – and, of course, under control. The last remaining patients were transferred to the Galesburg State Research Hospital.

The city of Bartonville acquired the hospital land, intending to turn it into an industrial park. All of the original buildings that formed the main part of the complex were left intact for a time, even though all of them were in various stages of decay, disrepair, and collapse. In time, most of them vanished altogether.

The end had come at last to what had once been one of the finest mental health facilities in the country.

The Tale of the "Bookbinder"

The first patients arrived by train to the Peoria State Hospital on February 10, 1902, and by June 30, of that same year, there had already been 22 deaths among them. Such numbers would not change much through the asylum's history, largely due to the poor health conditions often faced by the patients who came from terrible circumstances to find a new home at the hospital. They were quite literally killed by their pasts.

The Peoria State Hospital was in operation for a period of 72 years – 1902-1973. It was over this relatively short span of time that 4,132 patients died and were interred on the hospital grounds. This did not include those who died and then were taken to be buried elsewhere. The early reports gave numbers as to how many deaths occurred each year, but the later reports did not offer such detailed statistics. This makes it impossible to know just how many patients actually died during those 72 years.

Dr. Zeller was well aware of the fact that deaths would occur at the Peoria State Hospital and that not all of the deceased would be claimed by family and friends. He later wrote, "I recognized that along with the problem of the living, the disposal of the dead was one that must also have its share of attention. We buried the bodies of the friendless and unclaimed, as the remains of the well-to-do were shipped at the expense of friends and relatives to such points as they designated."

Dr. Zeller supervised the creation of cemeteries, where the bodies of unknown and forgotten patients could be buried. The burial grounds would eventually spread into four separate cemeteries. From the very beginning, every attempt was made by Dr. Zeller to show proper respect for those unfortunates that were interred at Peoria State Hospital. Dr. Zeller's sense of propriety when dealing with the deceased came about partially as a result of his military service, which left a lasting impression on him. He also believed any disrespect for the dead would inevitably lead to a disregard and unconcern for the living. With this in mind, Dr. Zeller instituted a short burial service for the staff to perform at the grave of the dead. For the first few years, he personally presided over the services.

It would be Dr. Zeller's close connection with the burial of the dead at the asylum that would lead to the telling of the very first ghost story associated with the hospital. And this was no mere rumor or folk story, but a documented account of a supernatural event – told by Dr. Zeller himself in his autobiography.

Shortly after organizing the cemeteries for the hospital, Dr. Zeller also put together a burial corps to deal with the disposal of the bodies of patients who died. The corps always consisted of a staff member and several of the patients. While these men were still disturbed, all of them were competent enough to take part in the digging of graves. Of all of the gravediggers, the most unusual man, according to Dr. Zeller, was a fellow that he dubbed in his writings as "A. Bookbinder."

This man had been sent to the hospital from a county poorhouse. He had suffered a mental breakdown while working in a printing house in Chicago and his illness had left him incapable of coherent speech. The officer who had taken him into custody had noted in his report that the man had been employed as "a bookbinder." A court clerk inadvertently listed this as the man's name and he was sent to the hospital as "A. Bookbinder."

Dr. Zeller described the man as being strong and healthy, although completely uncommunicative. He was attached to the burial corps, and soon, attendants realized that "Old Book," as he was affectionately called, was especially suited to the work. Ordinarily, as the coffin was lowered at the end of the funeral, the gravedigger would stand back out of the way until the service ended. Nearly every patient at the hospital was unknown to the staff so services were performed out of respect for the deceased and not because of some personal attachment. Because of this, everyone was surprised during the first internment attended by Old Book when he removed his cap and began to weep loudly for the dead man.

"The first few times he did this," Dr. Zeller wrote, "his emotion became contagious and there were many moist eyes at the graveside but when at each succeeding burial, his feelings overcame him, it was realized that Old Book possessed a mania that manifested itself in uncontrollable grief."

It was soon learned that Old Book had no favorites among the dead. He would do the same thing at each service and as his grief reached its peak, he would go and lean against an old elm tree that stood in the center of the cemetery and there, he would sob loudly.

Time passed and eventually Old Book also passed away. Word spread among the employees and as Book was well liked, everyone decided they would attend his funeral. Dr. Zeller wrote that more than 100 uniformed nurses attended, along with male staff members and several hundred patients.

Dr. Zeller officiated at the service. Old Book's casket was placed on two cross beams above his empty grave and four men stood by to lower it into the ground at the end of the service. As the last hymn was sung, the men grabbed hold of the ropes. "The men stooped forward," Dr. Zeller wrote, "and with a powerful, muscular effort, prepared to lift the coffin, in order to permit the removal of the crossbeams and allow it to gently descend into the grave. At a given signal, they heaved away the ropes and the next instant, all four lay on their backs. For the coffin, instead of offering resistance, bounded into the air like an eggshell, as if it were empty!"

Needless to say, the spectators were a little shocked at this turn of events and the nurses were reported to have shrieked, half of them running away and the other half coming closer to the grave to see what was happening.

"In the midst of the commotion," Dr. Zeller continued, "a wailing voice was heard and every eye turned toward the Graveyard Elm from whence it emanated. Every man and woman stood transfixed, for there, just as had always been the case, stood Old Book, weeping and moaning with an earnestness that outrivaled anything he had ever shown before." Dr. Zeller was amazed at what he observed, but had no doubt that he was actually seeing it. "I, along with the other bystanders, stood transfixed at the sight of this apparition... it was broad daylight and there could be no deception."

After a few moments, the doctor summoned some men to remove the lid of the coffin, convinced that it must be empty and that Old Book could not be inside of it. The lid was lifted and as soon as it was, the wailing sound came to an end. Inside of the casket lay the body of Old Book, unquestionably dead. It was said that every eye in the cemetery looked upon the still corpse and then over to the elm tree in the center of the burial ground. The specter had vanished!

"It was awful, but it was real," Dr. Zeller concluded. "I saw it, 100 nurses saw it and 300 spectators saw it." But if it was anything other than the ghost of Old Book, Dr. Zeller had no idea what it could have been.

A few days after the funeral, the Graveyard Elm began to wither and die. In spite of efforts to save it, the tree declined over the next year and then died. Later, after the dead limbs had dropped, workmen tried to remove the rest of the tree, but stopped after the first cut of the ax caused the tree to emanate what was said to be "an agonized, despairing cry of pain." After that, Dr. Zeller suggested that the tree be burned, however, as soon as the flames started around the tree's base, the workers quickly put them out. They later told Dr. Zeller they had heard a sobbing and crying sound coming from it. "In the clouds of smoke that curved upward," the workman said, "he could plainly outline the features of our departed mourner."

Eventually, the tree fell down in a storm, taking with it the lingering memories of a mournful man known as "Old Book."

The tale of the "Bookbinder" has been told so many times over the years that it has – and rightfully so – taken on the status of legend. For many, it seems hard to believe that Dr. Zeller would have confessed to witnessing a ghost in the cemetery that day. Surely the story was merely a tall tale, embellished by the superintendent to make his autobiography more interesting. Zeller also wrote fiction, it's been claimed, based on life at the asylum. He must have invented the character of "Old Book" for pure entertainment. Right?

We shouldn't be too quick to dismiss the story because as has been proven time and again, almost every legend contains at least a kernel of truth. In this case, records show that the "Bookbinder" really did exist.

In 1974, a newspaper reporter decided to track down the story of the Bookbinder and discovered that there really had been a patient at the asylum who had been dubbed "Manual Bookbinder," which would have been a description of his duties at the bookbindery where he worked. Dr. Zeller did slightly alter his name in the story. Bookbinder was a native of Austria who had been admitted to the asylum in 1904. According to additional records, he died during an outbreak of pellagra in 1910.

Pellagra was a vitamin deficiency disease most frequently caused by a chronic lack of niacin in the diet. It's classically described by "the three Ds": diarrhea, dermatitis, and dementia but makes its physical presence known by red skin lesions (often on the hands), hair loss, insomnia, mental confusion, and aggression. During the 1909-1910 outbreak, Dr. Zeller estimated that at least 500 patients were afflicted with the disease and this resulted in the death of 150 of them.

There is no direct reference to this man being "Old Book" and the character was never mentioned in any of the asylum's annual reports. However, in the statistical tables of the "Sixth Biennial Report of the Commissioner, Superintendent, and Treasurer of the Illinois Asylum for the Incurable Insane at Peoria," on page 32, listed under the "Nativity of All Patients Present June 30, 1906," there are six male patients from Austria. The "Eighth Biennial Report" contains a report dealing with the outbreak of pellagra, noting that there were 38 male deaths from the disease. One could say that this substantiates at least some of the findings of the newsletter reporter.

The most reliable evidence that "Old Book" really did exist was found in a 1905 Supervisor's Journal. This ledger contains the clothing accounts of the patients at the hospital and on pages 2 and 24, there are entries that state that "Bookbinder, M." received six handkerchiefs with a total value of 12-cents.

Does this mean that there really was a "Bookbinder" at the Peoria State Hospital? Yes, it does. But it's up to the reader to decide if the story of his ghost actually occurred or if one of the most respected doctors in the history of Illinois' treatment of mental illness simply made up the story because he wanted to concoct a spooky tale. We'll likely never know for sure, but there is no question that the legend of "Old Book" will make sure that the Peoria Asylum is never forgotten.

The Ghost of Rhoda Derry

While the legend of "Old Book" is the most famous tale of the Peoria State Hospital, if his ghost still walks the grounds, it does not do so alone. One of the most unusual of the thousands of patients who called the asylum home over the years was a woman named Rhoda Derry. Her story – albeit likely containing more than a little mythology – is a heartbreaking one and, truth or largely fiction, the end results of it were plainly visible on her ruined face and broken body. She was the perfect example of why Dr. Zeller wanted to rescue so many of the insane from the evils of the poor houses across the state.

Rhoda Derry arrived at the asylum in 1904. At that time, the population at the hospital was still growing rapidly with more than 200 new patients being admitted every month. One night, a train car arriving from Quincy, Illinois, was late and did not arrive at the Peoria station until after 1:00 a.m. The exhausted hospital staff had been admitting patients since early that morning and set off to meet the latest group of arrivals. As the group was led from the car, one of the railroad men handed down a clothes basket, which was taken along with the new patients to the hospital. It was believed that the large basket contained the effects of the newly arrived patients, so the staff was surprised when the basket began to move and a strange, guttural voice was heard babbling from inside of it. As the nurses uncovered the cloth from the top of the basket, they came face-to-face with Rhoda Derry.

The legend of Rhoda Derry states that she was born in Adams County, Illinois, and was the daughter of a wealthy farmer. She was a strikingly handsome girl, and while in her teens, was wooed by the son of a neighboring land owner. The young man's family, however, was opposed to the match. In order to prevent the couple from marrying, the boy's mother visited Rhoda and threatened to bewitch her if she did not release her son from the engagement. The mother scared the girl so badly that she went insane, exhibiting all of the signs of being possessed by an evil spirit. One night, Rhoda came home and jumped on her bed, standing on her head, and spinning like a top. She declared that the devil was after her and she was never the same again. For a time, she was taken care of by relatives, but was eventually sent to the Adams County poor house – and there she remained for the next 43 years.

After her time at the poor house, Rhoda lost the ability to walk upright. As a result, she moved about by using her arms and balled fists to drag herself across the floor. Her body was contorted in such a way that her knees naturally rested against her chest. She refused to wear clothing and was often tied to her bed to prevent her from wandering the halls naked. She slept each night in a Utica bed, a crib-like bed with a top that could be fastened down to hold a person in place. The bed was kept lined with straw that was changed periodically since Rhoda usually soiled the bed. She was often subject to violent episodes and would beat herself and others within her reach. During one such spell, she had scratched out her eyes and was now blind. She ate with her hands and would shove into her mouth anything that she came into contact with. She was in such pitiable condition that her handlers at the poor house bundled her into a basket and placed her on the train to the Bartonville asylum, likely happy to be rid of her.

She was 66-years-old when she arrived at the hospital and she quickly became the object of sympathetic interest to the nursing staff, and they treated her with love and compassion. For the first time, she slept in a clean bed at night, was given edible food, and was cleaned and cared for. When the weather was nice, the nurses would place her on a mattress and place her on one of the open porches where she could get fresh air and feel the sunshine.

Rhoda only lived two more years but her last days were peaceful and filled with affection. Although likely so demented that she could barely understand what had happened to her, it seems likely that she could comprehend that her circumstances had changed and perhaps she felt at peace for the first time in more than four decades.

And perhaps this is why her spirit allegedly never left her last home. Soon after her death, there were stories that claimed Rhoda's spirit had remained behind at the beloved institution. The nurses would frequently claim to see her sitting on the sun porch, just as she had done during the last years of her life.

Asylum Hauntings at Bartonville

After the hospital closed down and the site was sold at auction in 1980, the doors were seemingly thrown open for every kind of trespasser, vandal, urban explorer, and ghost hunter imaginable. Many of these curiosity-seekers, drawn to the building because of its legends and ghosts, claimed to encounter some pretty frightening things in the old Bowen Building, which was added to the asylum campus in 1929 for administration offices and dormitory rooms.

So, is what's left of the old hospital really haunted? Scores of people who have visited the place certainly think so. The reader must agree that the place certainly has the potential for a haunting, even without the story of the Bookbinder and Rhoda Derry. The atmosphere of the place alone is more than enough to justify the reports of apparitions and strange energy. The impressions of the past would certainly be strong in a building where mentally ill people were housed and where "psychic disturbances" would be common. And then, of course, there are the spirits who simply don't want to leave. The hospital was the only home that many of the patients knew and, even after death, there was no reason for them to leave.

Even before the hospital closed its doors for the final time, rumors spread about disturbing sights and sounds inside of the asylum buildings. There were reports of strange lights, footsteps, eerie sounds, disembodied voices, and doors that opened and closed on their own. The stories continued after the hospital was abandoned and curiosity-seekers began their journeys into the crumbling building. Some reported seeing shadows that flickered past doorways and darted around corners. They would walk into freezing blasts of cold air that seemed to come from nowhere, without explanation, and then fade away.

The first floor of the building was once used for administration offices, and there is said to be the ghost of a young woman in a white hospital gown who often appears at the north end of the hallway. She wears her hair in two long braids and she is believed to be the spirit of a former patient.

On the second floor was patient rooms, nurses' dormitory rooms, and communal areas. At the north end, more than 120 women lived and worked within the hospital. Sadly, many of these women had been sent to the hospital while pregnant, or became pregnant as a result of what was then termed a "hospital romance." At that time, insanity was considered to be a hereditary disease and few were willing to risk adopting the child of a woman who had been pronounced to be insane. The women were allowed to keep their child with them at the asylum until the age of four, at which time they became wards of the state. Many of the nurses who cared for their women later adopted the children and raised them on hospital grounds. This may explain accounts of the presence of children in the building. A number of accounts tell of hearing the sounds of small feet running through the hallways, often accompanied by singing or children's laughter. The asylum was home to many children over the years and it seems possible that some of their spirits simply never left.

The second floor also contained classrooms and work areas at the south end. In one of these classrooms, the apparition of a nurse is said to sometimes be spotted. She wears a long gown, crisp apron, and has her hair pulled back into a bun. The figure, dressed all in white, had been seen in the classroom and also peering out of the second-story windows at the south end of the building.

The nurses' ward was at the opposite end of the hallway. The small, dormitory-style rooms were each shared by two nurses at the school that had been established in Dr. Zeller's time. The sounds of doors opening and closing, as well as the giggling of young women, have often been reported in this area.

The third floor – which I found to be the most menacing while shooting with a documentary film crew at the Bowen Building in 2008 – was once the men's living quarters. There was a large metal gate installed in the 1960s to separate part of the hallway from a communal area. It has been reported that this gate can often be heard going up and down on its own, but the gate itself is never actually disturbed.

There were also medical treatment rooms on the third floor, some of which were used as late as the 1960s. It was in these rooms where many of the "treatments" took place, including shock therapy and, most disturbing to me personally, lobotomies. There have been many reports of people being touched and feeling hands gripping their arms and shoulders while in the treatment rooms. While I have visited the Bowen Building a number of times over the years, I have only been in the old treatment rooms one time – I've never gone back.

Even the attic of the building is alleged to be haunted. The massive room, with its high, exposed-beam ceiling, is in much the same shape as it was in Dr. Zeller's day. It was mainly used for storage of hospital supplies. The center part of the attic contains the original elevator that would have been in use during Dr. Zeller's tenure. Toward the end of his life, Dr. Zeller maintained an interest in every aspect of the hospital's operation and often went to the attic to inventory supplies and equipment. There are stories that say that the figure of Dr. Zeller can still be seen exiting the elevator and walking across the attic floor to a large dormer window, which looked out over the asylum grounds.

Whether the figure is actually Dr. Zeller's ghost or a residual impression of this piece of history, it is not the only presence in the attic. Another is said to be an orderly who worked at the hospital in the 1960s and who became despondent over the poor treatment of the patients during that declining period of the facility. One night, he took the elevator to the attic and ascended a metal staircase that led to the storage loft. He tied a rope to the overhead rafters and hanged himself. His body was not discovered until two days later. The stories say that his ghost remains behind, manifesting in the sounds of heavy boots that thud up the metal staircase. There are also claims that on moonlit nights, passersby can peer into the attic windows and see the body of the orderly hanging there, swaying on the end of the rope that strangled him.

At the far north end of the attic is another woman in white that lingers at the asylum. In life, her name was Anne Stuart and she was a housekeeper at the hospital until she died in 1933. There are many stories surrounding her death, including that she died after contracting an illness during her rounds. Another more lurid account claims that she was in love with a married doctor and following his rejection of her affection for him, she jumped from an attic window to the ground below. Since then, she has been seen looking out of the attic window and has been heard moving about and singing – apparently as she still goes about her cleaning duties after all these years. Several visitors to the hospital today have asked about the source of the singing that they have heard echoing on the upper floor and are chilled to discover they have heard the voice of a dead woman.

Beneath the building is the old hospital basement, which once marked the entry way to the tunnels that ran between many of the cottages on the property. Those who have spent any time in this area report the eerie feeling of being constantly watched and often don't stay underground for long. It's not uncommon for visitors to hear knocking sounds, footsteps, and men's voices in the darkness. Legend has it that in the 1970s, after the hospital was closed, two homeless men were trapped inside one of the tunnels beneath the building and died there. The stories say their spirits never left, which causes many visitors to walk quickly toward the stairs leading out of the basement when they hear the slightest strange noise.

When the hospital closed in 1973, there were 4, 132 patients buried in the asylum's four cemeteries, most of them in unmarked graves in the two oldest burial grounds. Dr. Zeller developed a numbering system for the cemeteries and that system – as well as all of the names that went with each number – have never been publicly disclosed. For many years, the cemeteries have been a great source of controversy, mostly relating to the lack of care and maintenance that they have received. Gravestones have fallen and been lost, the grounds are often overgrown, and in the 1980s, a large portion of one cemetery began sliding down into a ravine. A huge section of it has been lost in the years since then.

There have been many sightings of mysterious figures in the cemeteries, which still remain on the hilltop, hidden among the trees and behind the buildings that have been constructed there over the years. One of the most-reported ghosts is that of "Old Book." It is said that if one goes to the cemetery where he was buried on a peaceful summer day (he can be found in Cemetery II and grave #713 is the grave site of Manual Bookbinder) his spirit will appear, crying and wailing and mourning the loss of the patients who died, appearing just as he did before Dr. Zeller, the staff, and patients on that day many years ago.

Pollak Hospital

During its time in operation, the Peoria State Hospital not only treated mental illness, but a wide variety of physical maladies and ailments as well. Pollak Hospital was built on the grounds of the Peoria State Hospital in Bartonville in 1949 to serve

296

the needs of patients at the state asylum that were suffering from tuberculosis, even though tuberculosis deaths on the grounds dates back to the earliest days of the asylum.

By 1906, it was the leading cause of death at the hospital, and during a single year, 64 patients succumbed to the disease. The high number of deaths convinced Dr. Zeller to try and control the spread of the illness by segregating the sick in tent colonies.

The first colony at the hospital was a large porch on one of the cottages that was enclosed by heavy canvas. The canvas could be rolled up during fair weather to allow patients to take in fresh air, one of the earliest treatments for consumption. The experiment was largely successful, so more tent colonies were added to the grounds. The tent colonies remained in use until Dr. Zeller left the hospital in 1913.

Tuberculosis, though, continued to be a problem. In 1937, patients and employees of the asylum were tested by Dr. Maxim Pollak, director of the Peoria County Tuberculosis Sanatorium, and it was discovered that more than half of all of them tested positive for tuberculosis.

In 1949, the Pollak Hospital and Infirmary Building was built to care for patients with tuberculosis. The northern wing was for female patients and the southern wing was for male patients. It was named in honor of Dr. Pollak, who carried out the exhaustive research at the asylum in the late 1930s. As medicines finally came along to treat the illness, fewer patients died but many still contracted the disease. By 1973, the Pollak Hospital was one of the last buildings on the grounds of the asylum that was still in use.

During the hospital's years of operation, hundreds died within its walls, and according to stories and eyewitness accounts, scores of their spirits stayed behind to walk the wards and hallways of the crumbling building. A number of the ghosts believed to linger at Pollak Hospital are children. Many witnesses have heard their voices and the patter of small feet as they pass by them in hallways and on staircases. As one guide who worked in the building in recent years pointed out, "Just because you heard a child laughing doesn't mean that there's actually anyone there."

Pollak Hospital took in not only the mentally ill from the asylum, but also tuberculosis patients from the surrounding area. For this reason, many of the tuberculosis victims who were treated – and died – at Pollak were children. For whatever reason, their pain and suffering kept them lingering behind. They seem to be especially attracted to visitors to the hospital who have children of their own. One of the guides suggested that perhaps "they are looking for their mommy and daddy."

I spent most of the night at the Pollak Hospital in April 2014 with a group of American Hauntings guests and my company manager, Lisa Taylor Horton. We were able to spend a lot of time exploring the old building, and aside from a few odd noises that weren't easy to explain, we hadn't experienced anything that we would call supernatural. After walking around for a while, exploring the historic old structure, we sat down in one of the rooms with some electronic equipment to see if we could pick up anything unusual with it. It was when we stopped looking for anything weird that the weird finally found us.

Lisa was unpacking some equipment from a case and suddenly looked up at me. Before I could ask her what was wrong, she said she was making sure of where I was sitting. There was no way, she realized, that I could have reached her from where I was. She explained that when she looked down, she felt a small hand pat her on top of the head. It was very gentle – as though a child had done it. I didn't have time to say anything before I realized that the hair on her head was moving, as if someone was stroking it. That was when Lisa called out that it had happened again! Startled, she looked all around but there was no one behind her. Except for the two of us, the room was empty.

Had she made contact with one of the young ghosts at Pollak Hospital? Perhaps so, for the guides had assured us that they tend to seek out parents. Perhaps this would be a good place to mention that Lisa's daughter, Lux, was just about six months old at the time. Maybe one of the lost spirits had found some little girl's mommy that night at Pollak Hospital.

BIBLIOGRAPHY

American Correctional Association – *The American Prison*; 1983

Berton, Mark – *Dixmont State Hospital*; 2006

Bourdain, Anthony – *Typhoid Mary: An Urban Historical*; 2001

Brake, Sherri – *Haunted History of the Ohio State Reformatory*; 2010

------------------ – *Haunted History of the West Virginia Penitentiary*; 2011

Bruce, J. Campbell - *Escape from Alcatraz*; 1976

Churchill, Allen – *Pictorial History of American Crime*; 1964

Davis, Jamie with Samuel Queen – *Haunted Asylums, Prisons & Sanatoriums*; 2013

Dobson, Mary – *Disease*; 2007

Eghigian, Mars, Jr. – *After Capone*; 2006

Erickson, Gladys – *Warden Ragen of Joliet*; 1957

Esslinger, Michael - *The Rigid Silence: A Brief History of Alcatraz*; 2001

Helmer, William J. and Rick Mattix – *The Complete Public Enemy Almanac*; 2007

Jeffries, Benjamin – *Lost in the Darkness*; 2013

Kahan, Paul – *Eastern State Penitentiary: A History*; 2008

Keene, Michael T. – *Mad House*; 2013

Kennedy, Richard A. – *Essex Mountain Sanatorium*; 2013

King, Jeffrey – *The Rise and Fall of the Dillinger Gang*; 2005

Leavitt, Judith Walzer -- *Typhoid Mary*; 1996

Lisman, Gary L. – *Bittersweet Memories*; 2005

Lyle, Katie Letcher - *The Man who Wanted Seven Wives*; 1986

McCarthy, Stephanie E. – *Haunted Peoria*; 2009

Moran, Mark, Mark Sceurman, Troy Taylor, Chris Gethard – *Weird U.S.*; 2004

Odier, Pierre – *Alcatraz: The Rock: A History of the Fort & Prison*; 1982

Payne, Christopher – *Asylum*; 2009

Phillips, Ben - *Eastern State Penitentiary: 140 Years of Reform*; 1996

Rosenberg, Jennifer – *Typhoid Mary*, 2011

Sifakis, Carl - *Encyclopedia of American Crime*; 1982

Shults, Sylvia – *Fractured Spirits*; 2012

St. Joseph Museums, Inc – *A Home for Minds Diseased*; 2012

Symphonette Press – *Crimes & Punishment: Pictorial Encyclopedia of Aberrant Behavior*; 1973

Taylor, Troy – *Bloody Illinois*; 2008

------------------ - *Dead Men Do Tell Tales*; 2008
------------------ - *Haunted St. Louis*; 2000
------------------ - *Haunting of America*; 2010
------------------ & Rene Kruse – *A Pale Horse was Death*; 2012
Vernor, E.R. – *Haunted Asylums*; 2012
White, Thomas – *Ghosts of Southwestern Pennsylvania*; 2010
Yanni, Carla – *Architecture of Madness: Insane Asylums in the United States*; 2007

Personal Interviews and Correspondence

Special Thanks To:
April Slaughter – Cover Design and Artwork | Story Submissions
Lois Taylor – Editing and Proofreading
Rene Kruse – Story Submission
Lisa Taylor Horton & Lux
Hannah Grey
Ben Jeffries
Sylvia Shults
Rachael Horath
Elyse & Thomas Reihner
Bethany & Jim McKenzie
Orrin Taylor
Haven & Helayna Taylor

ABOUT THE AUTHOR

Troy Taylor is a crime buss, supernatural historian and the author of more than 100 books on ghosts, hauntings, crime and the unexplained in America. He is also the founder of American Hauntings, which holds events and tours across the country. When not traveling to the far-flung reaches of America in search of the unusual, Troy resides somewhere among the cornfields of Illinois.